T0291302

Sustaining Workforce Engagement

How to Ensure Your Employees Are
Healthy, Happy, and Productive

Sustaining Workforce Engagement

How to Ensure Your Employees Are Healthy, Happy, and Productive

By

Lonnie Wilson

A PRODUCTIVITY PRESS BOOK

First edition published in 2019
by Routledge/Productivity Press
711 Third Avenue New York, NY 10017, USA
2 Park Square, Milton Park, Abingdon, Oxon OX14 4RN, UK

International Standard Book Number-13: 978-1-138-31603-4 (Hardback)
International Standard Book Number-13: 978-0-429-44234-6 (eBook)

Library of Congress Cataloging-in-Publication Data

Names: Wilson, Lonnie, 1947- author.
Title: Sustaining workforce engagement : how to ensure your employees are
healthy, happy, and productive / Lonnie Wilson.
Description: Boca Raton : Taylor & Francis, 2019. | Includes bibliographical
references.
Identifiers: LCCN 2018038234 (print) | LCCN 2018051302 (ebook) | ISBN
9780429442346 (e-Book) | ISBN 9781138316034 (hardback : alk . paper)
Subjects: LCSH: Employee motivation. | Employees--Attitudes. | Organizational
behavior.
Classification: LCC HF5549.5.M63 (ebook) | LCC HF5549.5.M63 W58 2019 (print)
| DDC 658.3/12--dc23
LC record available at https://lccn.loc.gov/2018038234

Visit the Taylor & Francis Web site at
http://www.taylorandfrancis.com

Contents

PART III THE SIX ECLECTIC MANAGEMENT SKILLS

PART IV   THE ROLE OF MOTIVATION IN ENGAGEMENT

Acknowledgments

Many thanks

This is the fourth book I have written, and it was the most rewarding to write for one simple reason. In my consultancy where I wish to assist firms as we work to implement a lean manufacturing system, I find that, almost without exception, the ability to **create an engaged workforce** is the limiting condition to success. So, I wish to share that concept so more firms can be successful. Also, I have worked 49 years to crystalize these thoughts and numerous people have helped me along the way. I wish to pay homage to them as best I can. As I recount the many who assisted me in one form or another, it is truly humbling. No matter what I say, nor how I say it, it will be insufficient in many ways as the assistance I have gotten is literally incalculable. So, in some manner, I will slight this effort, and I apologize up front. Nonetheless, I will give it my best.

The many thanks I wish to express are further amplified as some things come easily to me, however, writing is not one of them. To me, writing is very effortful, so those who have assisted me, hold a special place. I owe a great deal to the people on my technical review team who read and assisted me with every chapter of this book. They include Brandon Hughes, Jason Farley, Jose Alejandro Tatay, Randy Kooiman, Thom Longcore, Fred Kaschak and Shirley Folmar. Special thanks to Michael Wiseman who read the transcript with exceptional rigor and through his comments we were able to make the text flow better with improved grammar. In addition, Robert Simonis, Kelly Moore, and Greg Williams, who in addition to being on the team; challenged the text and made significant contributions to the content. These people, with all their activities including both work and family obligations, took the time to pour over each chapter and supply me with assistance. They did not do this for the pay, as their remuneration is a free copy of the book; they did this for other reasons. Thank you for being the model of what we wish this book to speak to, intrinsically motivated behavior.

Those who have taught me the most are, not surprisingly, my family. I owe a never-ending debt of gratitude to my father who passed away in 1988 but still guides me as he hangs around and whispers in my ear from time to time. And my mother who at 96 is still providing me with moral support and is an incredible model of positivity, strength and courage, for me – and many others. My three sisters, all accomplished writers, have assisted me on this journey as well. However, the largest practical and sustaining input has come from our four children (actually, they are all adults now) Eric, Kirk, Brianne and Kevin. From them, I have learned about many relationship and management topics that directly led to improved content of this book. I have learned more from them than from any of the many books I have written; any of the books I have studied; or any of the classes I have taken or taught.

There is a long list of people from my work with Chevron who had coached, guided and mentored me. The list is too long but four special people assisted me greatly and they include Paul Pendergrass, Wendell Larson, Jesse Crider and Chuck Schumann. Following my retirement from Chevron I was blessed to cross paths and be assisted by some very influential people including Lynn Torbeck, Dr. W. Edwards Deming and Joseph Juran. With these three, I had limited personal contact, mostly due to distance issues; yet on many occasions we spoke. In addition, I tirelessly read and studied their books. The discussions, the reading and the study taken together created a lasting and significant impact on me. Others include Donald Wheeler, David Chambers, Robert "Doc" Hall, Dr. Edward L. Deci, Brian Joiner, Peter Scholtes and my most recent mentor and a man I hold in the highest regard, Toshi Amino.

In addition, I have learned a great deal from literally hundreds of authors, peers, and colleagues as well. And I cannot forget my clients who have worked to increase engagement in their facilities. Some have been successful, others not so much. Although in each case I was their advisor and teacher, each of them taught me a great deal. From each client I have gained a treasure trove of both new understandings and reinforced understandings of engagement and human relations in general. Thanks to each of them, they taught me endlessly.

This book would not have been a reality without the guidance from Michael Sinocchi and his team at Productivity Press and Deanta Global. I trust we can do more together in the future. Thank you, Michael, for sticking with me and helping me as you have.

Finally, and most importantly I owe deep appreciation and gratitude to my wife Roxana. We frequently discussed many of the concepts presented in this book, and it turns out that a quality which is often overlooked but is necessary to create an engaged workforce, is empathy. Roxana is the most impressive model of empathy I know. Through her behavior, she has taught me endlessly. Not only is she concerned about others, unlike many who only express concerns, she acts on hers. In the last couple of weeks, she not only was gathering jackets for the Honduran immigrants huddling in the cold, awaiting their turn to seek asylum at the port of entry but she was sending money to the Mexican Telethon which supports the building of children's hospitals. She was doing this while she was counseling a mother having trouble with her mentally challenged son. Her work with others is impressive indeed and she has provided me with wonderful insights for this book. But more importantly, she is a constant reminder by her real-life role modelling that one act of kindness is more important than even the best of intentions. She often refers to this as our book and mock seriously she chides me that in addition to my name, her name is not on the cover; it probably should be. But most importantly, she is the center of, and the love of my life and none of this would be possible without her guidance, her support and her patience. I love you.

Author

Lonnie Wilson

His background includes 20 years in manufacturing management with Chevron Oil Company. In 1990 he started Quality Consultants whose clients include firms in manufacturing as well as the fields of education, healthcare and other service sectors. Quality Consultants serves small firms as well as Fortune 500 firms in North, South, Central America and China.

Mr. Wilson is an expert in Lean Manufacturing techniques and applications. He not only instructs management professionals in the applications of these lean techniques; he is an on-the-floor and in-the-boardroom implementation professional. Mr. Wilson's focus is to assist firms who are now struggling in their cultural transformations plus those who have struggled and failed to transform their company into a lean enterprise – and wish to try again.

His prior books include both the first and second editions of *How to Implement Lean Manufacturing* (McGraw Hill, 2015), as well as *Lean Refining – How to Improve Performance in the Oil Industry*, (Industrial Press, 2017). His bestselling book *How to Implement Lean Manufacturing* has been used as a textbook in 13 colleges and universities and is currently being used at Beijing University, which facilitated the translation of this book into Mandarin Chinese.

In addition to his consulting practice, Mr. Wilson has taught statistics and small group problem solving at the University of Texas at El Paso. And for the last several years he has been a guest lecturer in their MBA and Executive MBA programs. On a volunteer basis, Mr. Wilson uses these same skills to assist churches and non-profits in meeting their goals. In addition, Mr. Wilson is a USSF licensed soccer coach and recently retired from coaching after 33 years in the field.

Lonnie lives in El Paso with his wife Roxana and the youngest of their four children, Kevin. He loves to talk about lean, employee engagement, management principles, leadership, the teachings of Dr. Deming and all those peripheral topics related to lean manufacturing. If you wish to discuss any of these, don't hesitate to call him or email him at law@qc-ep.com. And by the way, the consultant is always in, when the topic is soccer.

Preface

Aim of this preface ... to introduce you to the book and both my motivation for writing the book and my hopes for the book. Finally, I will give you the key questions answered in this book, along with an outline of the book's contents so you might see the overall structure of the subject matter.

To pay forward

I have been working for over 48 years now, and although I am having too much fun to retire, I begrudgingly accept that it must be somewhere on the horizon; not the near horizon, but the horizon nonetheless. For the last 20 years, at least, I have dedicated a certain amount of my time to pay forward the many things I have learned and experienced; so hopefully I may help others, as others have greatly assisted me as I traveled along my way. To that end, I have

THE GODFATHER CONTRACT

For firms that are genuinely and actively pursuing lean but do not have the resources to afford an external consultant, I offer them my Godfather Contract. It consists of 3 days of consulting where I come to the facility and we jointly explore their approach to lean. On the third day, I provide an oral report and am available for Q&A and training for the rest of the day. I only charge for my expenses; the consulting comes at no charge.

I call it the Godfather Contract because if you want some help on lean, I like to think, "it is an offer you just can't refuse".

Note: I would like to say this was my own idea and take credit for it, but I heard it from someone else many years ago, and have since forgotten to whom I should give credit.

chosen three activities that I do above and beyond my normal work; these include:

- pro bono consulting;
- mentoring; and
- writing.

The pro bono consulting includes providing help to anyone asking for it; this is often initiated by a random phone call or an email. In addition, I provide a more structured option with my Godfather Contract (see sidebar).

As part of my consulting practice, I also provide mentoring as a normal service. Specifically, there are four young engineers/managers/consultants with whom I have a mentor–mentee relationship. In addition, it is not uncommon to get a call from a prior client for "mentoring-like" support. Not to mention, my mentor is Toshi Amino, so I have an excellent role model to continue to teach me how to not only deliver but improve in this area.

The third area is writing. I have written scores of articles that have been published, and this will be my fourth book. With it, I hope to pass forward the things I have learned so others might be able to avoid some pitfalls and traps as they work on the improvement projects for their employers, as well as work on self-development.

The genesis of engagement as the topic for this book

There are two reasons I chose this topic. One is technical and very logical; the other is ... well, the great psychologist Carl Jung would call it a result of "tapping into the unconscious".

The technical reason

As you may be aware, Quality Consultants specializes in assisting firms that have tried to implement a lean transformation, failed and want to try again, as well as firms that are really struggling in these efforts. As such we have a lot of information on "what not to do". There are the "10 Lean Killers" and the "6 Roll Out Errors", which we cataloged and documented in *How To Implement Lean Manufacturing*, 2nd Edition (McGraw Hill, 2015, available at www.qc-ep.com).

However, when it comes to the natural question of, "OK, then, if that's what we are supposed to 'not do', what is it that we need to do to make a lean transformation?" To answer that we start with the following definition. Lean is the creation of a culture of continuous improvement and respect for people. Furthermore, the "Means to Lean" is to:

■ Problem solve your way to the Ideal State,
■ Through the total elimination of waste,
■ Using a fully engaged workforce.

As we work with these firms wishing to become lean producers, we almost universally find that they normally have some skills in problem solving. Also, they normally have some sense of their Ideal State or at least their annual goals; that is, they have some destination in mind. As they work to improve, they are normally getting rid of some kind of waste, although they seldom think of "it" in those terms; rather, they wish "to improve" something. However, when we get to "using a fully engaged workforce", virtually all the firms are woefully deficient. Problem solving and improvement activities are left for a select group of engineers, supervisors and managers … and the rest of the organization, although highly capable, just watches and laments what could really be done if everyone "were allowed to fix some things".

So the technical reason to embark on this book is to more fully explore the topic of "a fully engaged workforce" and how you can attain this. This lack of having a fully engaged workforce is normally the limiting condition preventing the transformation of becoming a lean producer. Make no mistake, this deficiency in engagement which is normally and erroneously attributed only to the rank and file workforce is equally applicable to the management team as well. Typically, they also have serious engagement issues.

The "other" reason

I was brainstorming for my book on management

I did not start to write a book on engagement; rather, inspired by some reflection on my mentor, Toshi Amino, I wanted to write a book on the "The Unique Management Skills and Traits That Facilitate a Culture Changing Transformation, such as a Lean Transformation". I am sure the real title would have been different – but you get the idea. So, as I often do, I got out a couple sheets of 22" and 28" tagboard and started writing down ideas and creating my version of an affinity diagram. I would brainstorm and document for maybe 2 hours a day, and then I would reflect on these thoughts ... mostly just let the ideas sit and I would think about them. I call this "mulling them over". After about 2 weeks of this, I had three sheets completely filled and decided to do a word recap. I found there were six words that were very popular. They were: leadership; control; awareness; teamwork; competency; and initiative.

CHANGE AGENTS AND WEIRDNESS

If you wish to be a change agent, you need to be "just a little weird". Weird people, in a business, are those folks who "act a little differently". So if you want improvement, this means you need to change, and to change things people need to act differently. So if you want to improve, you need to be – at least a little – weird. There is a danger ... if you are "too weird", you lose credibility. If you are not weird enough, there is no change. Such is the nature of change agents ... they must be weird – just not too weird.

To read more about this concept, go to www.qc-ep.com and under "White Papers" read "So You Want to be a Change Agent" and "Walking the Weirdness Tightrope". You can get copies if you wish.

When I get interrupted by a world class sociologist

I was then interrupted by an email from Dr. Edward Deci. I had been studying the concept of self-determination theory (SDT), a topic he and Dr. Richard Ryan created, and I had some questions so I called Dr. Deci. In this process, we exchanged several emails. This email – which interrupted my work on the affinity diagram – went into detail on what Drs. Deci and Ryan believe are the intrinsic needs as part of their SDT. What Dr. Deci calls "needs" most laypeople would call intrinsic motivators. They are autonomy, competence and relatedness.

I then got "clarity" from out of the blue

In a flash, I could see that three of my terms from the affinity diagram: control; competency; and teamwork were very similar if not synonyms with Dr. Deci's terms of: autonomy; competency; and relatedness, respectively. And this struck me like a thunderbolt – and I mean a thunderbolt.

I cannot explain clearly enough, nor strongly enough, the impact this had on me. Although my head was swimming in concepts and connections as well as data from my files, there was a distinct and impressive clarity to it all. It was as if I had on a new pair of glasses that allowed me to "really and clearly see" these concepts of intrinsic motivation, needs fulfillment, and worker satisfaction. In addition, I could also "see" in a profoundly clearer perspective the positive effect of these concepts on the individual, the group and the business as a whole. I was able to see with a distinct clarity and sharpness how these concepts – which were scattered all over my brainstorming and so succinctly described by Dr. Deci – were the key to making cultural change transformations a reality.

Soon enough I was able to connect these concepts and make the link to what I now call the Intrinsic Motivational Loop (IML):

■ that when workers execute tasks, such that the three intrinsic needs of autonomy, competence and relatedness are satisfied,
■ workers remain intrinsically motivated and not only work harder but
■ actually find joy and fulfillment in their work; and consequently
■ they are more highly motivated and want to do more, thus completing the loop

In a phrase, these people then become "fully engaged".

And I get redirected

I cannot explain this dynamic that happened to me, except to say that these concepts must have been rattling around in the back of my brain and were buried in my subconscious. And then something caused them to leap into my consciousness and not only leap but leap with a strength and clarity that not only amazed me but shocked me as well. I now knew, with clarity and conviction, that engagement was the subject I must write about; my book on leadership and management would just have to wait.

This book is all about making changes and improving your workplace

I have published this book for one reason only, to precipitate improvement actions. There are some who will read it as an intellectual pursuit, and to you, I say, "Congrats; hopefully the information contained herein is interesting". And quite frankly I would be proud to write an interesting book that broadens your awareness, but that is not my purpose here.

I seek your assistance

However, my passion for this book is not to be interesting **...** it is to be relevant. And to be relevant, you must help me by putting the strategy, tactics and skills discussed in this book to use. You must precipitate action or this book will not be relevant. To that end – action – I solicit your help.

My three friends who will assist you on your journey

As you embark on the journey to make yours a fully engaged workforce, I would like to introduce you to my three friends. They are: awareness; initiative; and introspection.

- ■ Awareness is the gateway quality to: understanding your present situation; creating and assessing your available options; more fully understanding your own paradigms and values; assisting in the choices you will make; to enhanced learning.
- ■ Initiative is the gateway quality to improvement; for if we do not act, nothing changes and, hence, nothing improves.
- ■ Introspection is the gateway quality for personal change. For I find that before any business changes, as a part of it, "I", the manager, must change.

If you are a manager reading this book, all the improvements in your business are contingent upon how you yourself change. There is no larger litmus test to changing a workplace than if the management does or does not change. My three friends are explained by quotes from three famous people:

- ■ "Men stumble over the truth from time to time, but most pick themselves up and hurry off as if nothing happened" Sir Winston Churchill.
- ■ "Opportunity is missed by most people because it is dressed in overalls and looks like work" Thomas Edison.

■ "In the choice between changing one's mind and proving there's no reason to do so, most people get busy on the proof" John Kenneth Galbraith.

Reader beware ... likewise, be alert

Seldom are ideas original. This book is no exception. In Chapter 2, you will learn that the concept of employee engagement has been around for quite some time, certainly before the industrial revolution. However, sometimes people are not able to understand how these ideas apply to their environment. My hope is that I present these ideas in a manner that will connect with you and your experiences; and assist you to a higher level of understanding. If that happens, don't be lulled into a sense of complacency that "Now I know enough" or worse yet be sucked into the hubris of "Now I am an expert in this thing". No sooner than that thought creeps into your ego than the world will bring you back to reality – which is, we never know all there is to know. The truth is that no book can tell you all there is nor will

PARADIGMS

A paradigm is a standard, a commonly held belief, a perspective or even a set of ideas. Paradigms are underlying assumptions that color and subtly dictate both our thinking and the subsequent actions. For example, if you hold the belief that people only come to work for a paycheck, you will treat them accordingly, and then your efforts to improve motivation will focus almost solely on pay, benefits and other perks.

There are two major concerns with paradigms: sometimes our paradigms are wrong; but worse yet, most paradigms are unconscious and we are not really aware of them.

In this book, I will give you a number of "paradigm shifts" businesses likely must undergo. That means three very basic things ... as a minimum. First, we must challenge our beliefs and underlying assumptions to make them conscious. Next, we must critically, dispassionately and introspectively decide what paradigms we should keep and which paradigms we must change. Finally, we need to change our behaviors to be in harmony with our new found beliefs, values and assumptions.

This is not easy ... all three steps are very challenging technically, but even more so, they are emotionally challenging.

Changing paradigms is an ego-challenging effort and hence requires great courage. A list of key paradigms is included as Appendix D it answer all of your questions. This book is no exception.

However, I am equally sure it will answer many of your questions and hopefully broaden your understanding of these concepts. As quickly as you have those answers and that understanding, my hope is that those answers and understanding will spawn additional questions you did not have earlier. My prayer is that these new thoughts will then catalyze new actions so you can put them to use for the betterment of your customers, your employees, your stockholders – and yourself. For as surely as you practice these techniques, you, too, will grow and benefit.

To shake your brain

Earlier I mentioned that my purpose was to be relevant. Well, I have another purpose; I wish to be provocative. You will find in this book a number of concepts you may not agree with. To me, that is good. From my perspective as a teacher and a mentor, if I can shake up your brain a bit or even a whole lot ... I will

> ### ON BEING CRITICAL AND DIRECT ... IS IT WORTH IT??
>
> For each book I have written, I use a Technical Review Team to assist me. Almost without exception, at some point, they have cautioned me about being too critical or too direct, particularly in my comments on management. Typically, they say we are not trying to alienate there people; we are trying to get converts. More often than not, I soften my comments. However, I have come to a decision. I am not trying to make friends, although I would like more friends. However, I am on a mission to find converts. That is managers who are willing to not only be aware enough to see the need to change their businesses but also humble and wise enough to know that before the business will change, as individuals, they must first change. And if I cause the hair on the back of your neck to stand up a little, so be it.
>
> On the other hand, if you feel my advice is not true or even not well balanced, or worse yet, if you think I am "goofier than a loon", give me a call and we can discuss it. I'm always willing to listen and learn.

be very pleased. If I challenge your paradigms, your beliefs and even your entire belief system, and create a discomfort that leads to reflection, I will be pleased. To be provocative is one of the roles of a change agent, and I am hopeful that this book will be a productive and vicarious effort by me to assist you as you become a change agent in your company ... and in your life. (see sidebar.)

15 Questions you will get answered in this book

1. Why is "hard-working" not a synonym for engaged?
2. What is a practical, easily understood definition of engagement?
3. How can I measure engagement?
4. How can I improve engagement?
5. What gains can I expect with a fully engaged workforce?
6. What is the role of intrinsic and extrinsic motivation in engagement?
7. What are the "basics" to achieving engagement?
8. Why must I go "beyond the basics" to sustain engagement?
9. Why is losing engagement four times easier than attaining engagement?
10. What are the very important roles of management?
11. What is the role of the employee in attaining and sustaining engagement?
12. Why is "creating a fully engaged workforce" another phrase for "good management"?
13. Why is engagement a "system"?
14. What are the high leverage points to the "system of engagement"?
15. What are some very popular things we "must not do" if we want engagement?

The contents of the book ...

This book is divided into Acknowledgements, a Preface and six parts.

- Part One is dedicated to the history of our understanding of engagement and the many benefits that follow from an engaged workforce. We will discuss the theory of the social scientists and how engagement is viewed by those who wish to use it as a weapon to improve their businesses.
- Parts Two and Three are all about management. You will learn about Management 1.0, 2.0 and 3.0. We will discuss many of the basic management skills needed to achieve engagement. We will also introduce you to the Six eclectic management skills needed to attain a Management 3.0 system.
- Part Four is all about the role of motivation and motivation theory in the attainment of engagement. We will explore the basics of motivation and show how many popular "motivational techniques" are actually

counterproductive. Finally, in this part, we will address the topic of intrinsic motivation and its crucial role in achieving a fully engaged workforce.

■ Part Five is all about treating engagement as a system and both defining and quantifying the various causal loops we can build and manage so engagement is attained.

■ Part Six is about how to analyze and improve your levels of engagement.

It's all about the management ... and paradigm-busting

We will study engagement from top to bottom and explain how it is achieved and why people try so hard to create a fully engaged workforce with both the best of intentions and a true passion to achieve it ... yet fall short, often very short.

There is a simple reason and that is, achieving engagement is all about management and the many changes that must be made. And herein lies the rub. Is the management team both willing and able to recognize, accept and execute the needed paradigm shifts? The stark reality is that the changes which need to occur are in the thoughts, beliefs and actions ... of the management team, themselves. In this book, we will give you a path to follow that may achieve just that. And the remaining question for the senior management is ... **What are you prepared to do?**

The mystery of achieving engagement is known. The science is known; the answers are not technically complicated, and now it comes down to a simple choice. Are you or are you not willing to change? And with that choice ... there are resultant consequences; it is no more complicated than that.

Just what will this journey look like?

You are about to embark on the most demanding of business challenges. You are about to embark on a large and enlightening and uplifting cultural change in your business. Not only is it a large change but once underway you will see benefits to your customers, your stockholders, your employees and even to you yourself that will exceed your wildest expectations. You will not only see your present leaders, at all levels, take a stronger role in improving the business. But you will also see those who formerly were very quiet and subdued step up, take charge and make changes that will improve not only their work environment but improve the competitive position of the company. You will see initiative explode. You will see creative and imaginative ideas come from people you hardly even noticed before. With this revelation, your list of future team leaders, future supervisors and future managers will grow exponentially. You will literally see the potential of each and every person expanded and you will be able to bask in both the improved productivity and the improved work satisfaction that is a natural result of unleashing the potential of each worker from the newest hired floor worker to the CEO. All will benefit. And this will all follow the effort you and your team put forth when you are truly capable of fully exploiting the Intrinsic Motivational Loop and strengthening the Engagement Loop.

This is all accomplished by making the huge cultural change that will end in a fully engaged workforce. Recall that culture is the combined thoughts, beliefs, actions, artifacts and language of a group of people; or, more simply "just how we do things around here". And that is what we are going to do; we are going to embark on an effort to change not so much **what we do** but more specifically "**how we do things around here**". We are going to change how we train, how we write, teach and deploy job instructions. We are going to change how we plan, how we problem solve ... and especially who does the problem solving and precisely when they do it. We are going to change how we supervise and how we develop employees. We are going to change how we communicate. But most of all, we are going to change how we both manage and lead.

Chapter Summary ... I have shared with you my reasons for writing this book and my hopes and expectations for it. We also introduced you to the limiting factor in achieving a fully engaged workforce: the ability of the management team to recognize and undergo the needed paradigm shifts. Before you dive headlong into reading this and hopefully both learn from and enjoy it, let me give you one last challenge. I told you I hoped to be provocative and "shake your brains". I challenge you to "shake mine". As you read, if you want clarification, wish to share a thought or just think I am "plum full of canal water", let me know. If email is your preferred form of dialogue, email me at law@qc-ep.com, but if you prefer to talk, give me a call; my cell is 915-203-4141.

What's next ... In Chapter 1, we explore some background information necessary to our understanding of employee engagement. Some of these items include a bit of history on human resources efforts, the business benefits of employee engagement and a lot more.

ENGAGEMENT BACKGROUND AND THEORY

1

In this section, we discuss the basics of engagement and other human resource programs designed to activate the workforce and why these have failed to be successful cultural changing initiatives. We will discuss what the current state of engagement is overall and in manufacturing in particular. Next, we delve deeply into the psychology and sociology of engagement, from both a scholarly and a practical perspective. We explore, in depth, the weaknesses of these models and what must be added to make these models effective in the world of business. Finally, we end this section with a simple, practical definition of engagement.

Part I contains five chapters:

Chapter 1

Background Information

Aim of this Chapter ... is to discuss some background concepts necessary to our study of engagement. First, we will discuss the history of some human resource programs and why they were not effective. Next, we will briefly discuss the concept of business cultures and their relationship to employee engagement as well as the relationship between employee engagement to Toyota's concept of respect for people. We'll then explore how you should go about making the change and why you don't want to have an "engagement program, project or initiative" but rather a cultural change. Finally, we will wrap up the chapter with three technical topics: a quantification of the business benefits of a fully engaged workforce; three common business strategies that must be avoided if you wish to attain a fully engaged workforce; and the data used in this book.

Some history of human resource improvement programs

There have been many efforts by businesses to achieve more with their available human capital. Numerous well-intended efforts have been started. They include:

- empowerment efforts
- improving the quality of work life activities
- teams – with many adjectives added such as: self-directed; logical-work-group; and even matrix teams
- the motivation and discipline movement

- the "I don't care about the method, just get me the results" approach
- the effort to incentivize them
- the accountability movement
- the need to reengineer and reinvent ...
- and numerous others

Yet these came, and for the most part ... they went.

Some created an initial positive effect; others had no effect. But a surprisingly large number of these initiatives, when officially placed in their casket, left the workplace worse off than if they had never shown up on the scene in the first place. They all sounded good. Most start very well with lots of folderol and initial energy, raised expectations and often some early gains. But finally, in the normal flow of doing business, and normally very quickly, those initial high hopes and desires get crushed by the reality of just doing business. Those hoping to get motivated, incentivized or teamed up, were left back at the starting line – but now with the bitter taste of disappointment and unmet promises still fresh in their mouth. Like Tom Sawyer said, "I had to sneak up to the attic and cuss for ten minutes just to get the taste back in my mouth", and they do too.

Why did these efforts die??

Many of these initiatives died of their own weight as they were a bad idea to begin with. This includes the "incentivizing" and the "I don't care about the method, just get me the results" approach; those were two really bad ideas. First, people do not need incentivizing; they come to work all ready to go. As for the "anything goes" or what I call the "Al Davis approach", "Just win, baby", which was his mantra with the Oakland Raiders of old, will work for any short-term gain, but the long-term issues are another story altogether. Some died because they were a decent idea but were poorly executed. All team efforts, along with quality circles, fall into this category. Others died because, even though they were basically good ideas, they did not mesh well with the existing and frequently dysfunctional culture. The empowerment and quality of work life initiatives were examples of this failure mode.

The bottom line to the failures

Either quickly or in the fullness of time, the vast majority of these hoped-for "silver bullets" failed. The good and the bad ideas alike failed – for two common reasons. First, they were almost universally treated as if one could "just bolt them on" to their existing way of doing things. Second, and more importantly, these initiatives were treated as "employee" efforts and as such the management made little or no change in the way they, themselves, behaved.

The "bolt on" fallacy

Implicit in using the "bolt this thing on" approach are two underlying assumptions, which were:

- they could start these efforts and they would not have an impact on any other part of the operating system, and
- that the existing management system was fundamentally sound.

This penchant for managers to try to "bolt on" these changes to their existing systems failed because these assumptions were not only incorrect, they were often grossly incorrect.

The changes were "independent" and did not affect anything else

First, any change

LEADERSHIP AND MANAGEMENT

Clearly, the subject of this book is engagement. But soon enough you will learn of the absolutely critical nature of "the actions of the top few", the management team. In Part II, we will discuss this in depth, but while discussing engagement we will speak of leading and managing, so let me briefly define them here. Managers fulfill two roles. They must provide both leadership and management skills to make the business a success. The key distinction is this. Managers use **management skills** when they are dealing with the P&L statement or the plant metrics; managers exhibit **leadership skills** when they get the people to follow them as they jointly develop and execute plans.

I have heard it summarized two ways:

- We manage things, but we lead people, or ...
- Leaders are people who do the right thing; managers are people who do things the right way

Both are accurate, if not complete, but they can be used to clarify your thoughts until we cover this absolutely critical topic in Part II

to a complicated business culture will have multiple effects. Any change to one element will have an effect on many other elements, and the effects can be both synergistic and antagonistic. Furthermore, except in the very short term, these effects are very hard to predict. For example, change the pay structure or the reporting structure and other things such as motivation and morale change; in addition, you may have an unexpected spike in attrition. So if you try to just "bolt on this new thing" you are ignoring the concept of interactions, which is a reality in all systems as well as a reality in all cultures.

The soundness of the underlying system   Second, if you are going to bolt on something, like a new hasp to your garden door, you will not do that if the wood in the garden door is rotten or decaying. However, managers by the droves are more than willing to attempt to "bolt on" this teamwork effort (e.g.), or this engagement effort (e.g.) to their existing business and management systems without so much as a review of what is currently in place. Quite frankly, the management norm is to presume the existing system is perfect and needs no change … which is NEVER the case. What normally happens is that when you make the changes to implement employee engagement (e.g.), which is a large cultural change, it will highlight weaknesses in other elements of the existing system. For example, in trying to bolt on something like employee engagement, it is very common to find that you need to make substantial changes to your systems of training, planning and supervision.

The big reason … They are not "just employee" change efforts

The more important reason these initiatives failed was that they were treated as "employee" efforts and as such the management made little or no change in the way they themselves behaved. Somehow, the management felt that the only people who needed to change were the rank and file. I have run across a variety of "reasons" given by senior managers that they don't need to change … and all are wrong in the most fundamental way (see www.qc-ep.com, White Papers, "Lean Leader or Cheerleader" and "No Change Occurs Until Management Changes…Really!!!").

I have found it to be axiomatic that the degree to which the rest of an organization is willing to change is dependent upon the willingness of the management to change. When there is no change in the behaviors of the management team, there will be no planned change in the day-to-day routines of the business. It is a litmus test.

Why are these problems so common??   The impacts of trying "to bolt this effort onto" your existing system with little or no change by the management team are so powerful that if they are not properly addressed they will render the rest of the transformation useless. You will find that as we address how to improve engagement, these two issues are addressed repeatedly in this text. Do not underestimate them. As Dr. Deming taught us, a full 94% of the problems in a business – and employee engagement is no different – are system related; and hence lie squarely at the feet of management (Deming, 1982).

But why?? The common thread to these failures is that the management team proceeded as if these large human resource efforts were some construction project or as if they were installing "a new thing" like a new piece of planning software. However, these broad-reaching human resource efforts have large intellectual and especially emotional impacts on the entire workforce. The management is not installing "a new thing"; rather, they are literally changing the way they do a broad range of activities, and when we change "the way we do things around here", we change the culture. The common problem was that the management team grossly underestimated the size of the cultural change that is required and ignored the impact of these large human resource efforts on the existing culture.

The root cause of this problem is that the management team, top to bottom, was sufficiently unaware of their existing culture – and even sometimes sufficiently unaware of the concepts of culture itself – to proceed without any cultural review whatsoever. In so doing – while this approach may be convenient, and it certainly is easy – they ignored the large emotional and intellectual impacts that these human resource efforts have on the entire workforce. They ignored the cultural implications and forged ahead as if they were doing some minor tweaks around the edges … when in reality, they were changing "just about everyone and just about everything we do around here".

To ignore the culture, to ignore everyone and everything they do – when put in those terms, it seems incomprehensible. Except that is what often happens and it explains the repeated and consistent failures of these human resource efforts, despite the input of significant effort.

So we are going to avoid those pitfalls; we are **not** going to treat the conversion to "a fully engaged workforce" like a "thing". Not at all; rather, you will learn how to implement employee engagement and treat it as it truly is … a large cultural change affecting everyone and everything we do. As part of the cultural change, we will not only teach you:

- how to weave the new features into your existing culture, but also
- we will show how to find and fix the weaknesses in your existing culture, and

■ finally, we will explain how to get the management team to adopt the principle that they must not only lead the cultural change, but they must lead the actual change effort – by being the first to change.

A word about "culture"

Defining, analyzing and changing business cultures is the primary product of Quality Consultants. And recently, business culture has been a very hot topic on blogs, and many articles have been published in e-zines. However, as you read these blogs and articles, it is often difficult to discern precisely what the author means by "culture". I want no such ambiguity in this book, so I will give you the definition I have used for nearly 40 years:

THE TOYOTA WAY, 2001

"The Toyota Way, 2001", is a 13-page pamphlet published by Toyota Motor Corporation in 2001. This is a document Toyota published when they declared that they wanted to be the world's largest automobile producer. Since they would be expanding a great deal into new and different cultures, they thought it would be prudent to define their own culture. In the introduction, Chairman Cho says, "In this booklet we have identified the company's fundamental DNA, which summarizes the unique and outstanding elements of our company culture and success. These are the managerial values and business methods that are collectively known as the Toyota Way" (see Appendix C for more details.).

Note: Do not confuse "The Toyota Way, 2001" with any other book with a similar name; there are a couple.

"Culture is the combined actions, thoughts, values, beliefs, artifacts, and language of any group of people".

(www.qc-ep.com)

In simple terms, culture is "just how we do things around here". For example, when some new member of the organization might ask, "Why is it that people normally arrive 15 minutes early here? It was not like that at my prior employer's". The answer is "It's just how it is". And he goes on to clarify, "It was that way when I got here. Maybe some people like to make sure they don't miss the AM briefing, some people want to get a good parking spot and yet others want to socialize for a few minutes before shift start". And he summarizes, "Not really sure … it just is". Then you know that arriving early and probably being on time for meetings is a cultural norm. It is: "just how we do things around here".

Cultural design

There is a lot of chatter on blogs and in e-zines on the topic of culture. Most of the talk is about the power of culture as a weapon in the

> ### MORE ON "THE TOYOTA WAY, 2001"
>
> "The Toyota Way, 2001" describes the culture within the entire Toyota Corporation. Do not confuse "The Toyota Way, 2001" with the vaunted Toyota Production System (TPS). Rather, the "The Toyota Way, 2001" describes the overarching beliefs, thoughts, actions, artifacts and language for the entire corporation, including the TPS. Consequently, throughout this book, I will frequently refer to beliefs, thoughts and actions in the TPS and refer to their overarching cultural design as described by "The Toyota Way, 2001". Said another way, the TPS is subsumed within, but the TPS is only part of, "The Toyota Way, 2001".

battle to survive and achieve business success. All this chatter notwithstanding, I find very few, I mean **very few** firms, that directly, consciously and consistently give the topic of culture much management attention.

I can find few who have qualified their culture and even fewer who have quantified their culture. They cannot discuss the cultural elements nor can they measure their cultural strength, their cultural flexibility and most do not question the appropriateness of their culture. Hence, most cultures have not been designed; they have grown organically into what they are today. The development of their culture has been largely an unconscious event. In this book, we will work very hard to help you redesign a part of your culture, the part that is needed to achieve engagement. If we use the terms of the "Toyota Way, 2001", we will help guide you in creating a culture of respect for people.

What it the key cultural change leading indicator??

There is no secret here. **The key factor is the behavior of the top few managers**. If the management wants to change "just how we do things around here", they first must model the change. If they want you to improve problem solving and start using the Six Questions of Continuous Improvement, management itself must become proficient in and use these

Six Questions. If they want you to make meetings more focused and efficient, they first must make their meetings more focused and efficient. It surprised me how many managers are unaware of this basic dynamic. To expect others to change when you yourself are unwilling is hardly being a good role model. It tells them loud and clear that "you must do as I say, not do as I do", and that metaphor, born out of command and control management style, will no longer work. (For a funny but true and insightful story on cultural change and the need for management to lead the way, go to my website, www.qc-ep.com and under "White Papers" read, The Loyalists, The Lurkers, The Laggards … and The Lemmings".)

This strong control of the culture exerted by management is a key factor in the ability of the facility to create engagement – or not. This impact by management really cannot be understated. That is a key underpinning of this book.

Cultural characteristics

Cultures should be strong, flexible and appropriate. When cultures are strong, there is a strong agreement on what are the appropriate actions, the important values and beliefs, as well as the proper jargon and phraseology to be used. Another word for strong is – predictable. This allows people to proceed to action with some sense of confidence that they are operating within the cultural norms, improving their chances of success and acceptance. While strong cultures do not guarantee business success, a weak culture will usually doom a business to failure. Cultures need to be flexible so they can change when the external environment changes. Most importantly, they need to be appropriate so it serves the needs of a business. A culture in a fire department, for example, is going to be very different from the culture at Disney.

I have written a great deal more on culture, so I refer you to "How To Implement Lean Manufacturing", 2nd Edition (Wilson, 2015). Here you will get all the information you need to understand the heart and soul of cultural understanding and management. You can learn about the 5 Leading Indicators of Cultural Change as well as a great deal more on cultures, business cultures in particular. You may also want to check out our website at www.qc-ep.com for even more information. There you will find a litany of White Papers and evaluations of several books on culture in "Lonnie's Technical Library".

Culture and engagement

As you read this book and seek to create a fully engaged workforce, you will find that some of the values and beliefs you now hold will be challenged, and some will need to change. You will start to use a new language. This is the jargon of engagement, including terms like intrinsic needs, motivation and hygiene factors. Other words, like vigor, dedication and absorption, will have a completely new, different and more precise meaning. Finally and most importantly, you will need to change the behaviors, the specific actions, of many people. In fact, you will find the behavioral changes will permeate the entire enterprise from the board of directors to the C-suite, through all levels of management supervision and finally to the value-add workers on the floor. All will change.

So, in a phrase, as you work to "create a fully engaged workforce" you are simultaneously and systematically changing your culture. And changing it so your enterprise can become:

- a better money-making machine,
- which is a more secure workplace and is
- the supplier of choice to your customers.

Yes, as you are creating a fully engaged workforce, you are changing your culture and simultaneously improving your business in an integrated, systemic manner. Make no mistake, creating a fully engaged workforce is a large cultural change and a dynamic weapon in the battle for survival and growth.

Engagement and the connection to lean manufacturing and "respect for people"

From the data near the end of this chapter, you will see a matrix containing the "Top Seven" and the "Bottom Seven". The "Top Seven" have high engagement scores. As a group, they average 67% engaged which places them in the top 10% of the Gallup survey data. They also, without exception, have a lean culture and are lean producers, and by lean, I mean TPS Lean. I do not wish to diverge into the many definitions and variations of lean production. Since the days of its definition in 1990 as a total copy of the Toyota Production System, many people, some quite influential, have caused the definition to morph, and in my opinion, they have weakened the concept. It is my contention that they have done this because to get to the TPS Lean system is very hard indeed. (If you wish to read more on this, there is a comprehensive treatment in my book, "Lean Refining" (Wilson, 2017) available at www.qc-ep.com. (When I refer to the TPS Lean system, I refer to the system as defined by Ohno in his landmark book, "Toyota Production System, Beyond Large Scale Production" (Ohno, 1988), and, equally important, for these firms to be TPS Lean, they must also follow the cultural guidance given in Toyota's own document, "The Toyota Way, 2001", (Toyota, 2001). (See the sidebar in this Chapter and Appendix C.)

Finally, the TPS is a culture of continuous improvement and respect for people. As I embarked on this effort into understanding how to create a fully engaged workforce, I was not aware that, a fully engaged workforce, is, as close as I can measure, synonymous with the Toyota "respect for people" concept. Now I equate those two concepts. Consequently, when you are working to create a fully engaged workforce, you are showing what Toyota defines as "respect for people" as articulated in "The Toyota Way, 2001" (Toyota, 2001).

It's not an initiative, it's not a project – It is cultural change

What is my advice about making your efforts to become a fully engaged workforce into an engagement initiative, an engagement project or even an engagement program?

Don't.

These have a beginning and an end, yet your work to improve engagement has already started and will have no end. Do none of that; rather, just do what you are doing, but do it better. As you read this book you will see there is not much that is really new. At some level and to some degree you are likely doing most of what we will describe in this book. However, as you progress through the book you will also find that your practices may be OK – in concept – but your execution of these actions will normally need to be improved and in many cases, such as the management of motivation, vastly improved.

As a typical management practice, you don't create a project, program or an initiative when you want to improve profitability, quality or customer delivery. You just focus differently. The effort and system are supposed to be "there". You simply need to get better at it. Employee engagement is one of those issues. For years, you have been working at it; now you need to "knock off the edges and clean it up" so you can unleash the true power of a fully engaged workforce.

Change, it's more like evolution than revolution

There certainly will be changes made and people will need to change. But since most businesses are already surviving, we won't propose many "right-hand turns"; rather, we will generally make a whole series of small course corrections so the culture can systematically and gradually change to assimilate these improvements. At times it may not seem that way, but we are not looking for a revolution; it is more like an evolution we seek. An evolution of your culture into one that typifies a fully engaged workforce.

I am reminded by a quote from Takeo Fujisawa, the co-founder of Honda Motor Company, who said:

"Japanese and American management is 95% the same – and differs in all important respects".

(Pascale and Athos, 1981)

But don't treat it lightly

This book is about that 5%. It is a book intently focused on management and the need for management to change. And don't be fooled, "knocking off the edges and cleaning it up" may in some cases be easy; yet in other areas, it will be a great deal of hard work. That last 5% oftentimes is the toughest 5% to get.

It is a journey into increased management awareness, new management learning and extensive management change. For these reasons, do not be surprised if it is both effortful and frequently uncomfortable as your paradigms get challenged and often are required to change. The gist of this effort is to unlearn some wrong concepts and to learn some new ones so they can be integrated into your existing culture.

Russell Ackoff would say we are attacking "A Mess"

If it's not an initiative, program or project, just what is it we are doing? Russell Ackoff, one of the great thinkers of our time, would say we are trying to clean up "a mess". Specifically, he says:

"Problems seldom (if ever) exist in isolation. Problems are extracted from reality by analysis. Almost any problem exists as part of a set of interacting problems called by some a mess. A mess, then, is a system of problems. The characteristics of a mess derive from the interaction of the problems and their solutions, and not from the problems and their solutions taken separately. As is the case with systems, the solution to one part can make the mess worse if its interactions are not taken into account. A problem is a situation that presents a choice, where what a decision maker does can make a difference in the value of the outcome to him or her, and the decision maker is in doubt as to which choice to make. The problem, then, is which choice yields the best outcome. The hitch is that the solution to a problem that is part of a mess may make the mess worse. On the other hand, the best choice relative to a mess may not require the best solution to any part of it".

(Ackoff, 2010)

Ackoff points out several of the concerns that must be considered when working to improve engagement – which is the same as working to change the culture.

■ First, "almost any problem exists as part of a set of interacting problems called a mess";
■ Second, "the characteristics of a mess derive from the interaction of the problems and their solutions, and not from the problems and their solutions taken separately"; and
■ Third, "The hitch is that the solution to a problem that is only a part of a mess may make the mess worse. On the other hand, the best choice relative to a mess may not require the best solution to any part of it".

In a phrase, Ackoff is saying that "messes" are systems that are fouled up. This is precisely the case with engagement; it is a system. And with engagement in the 25% range in the manufacturing sector, it is pretty hard to say it is not "messed up". Yes, it is a system, a very complicated system; a topic we will more fully explore when we discuss systems and the system of engagement in Chapters 13 and 14.

The irony, and the power, of improving employee engagement through cultural change

As we embark on this undertaking, we need to keep some thoughts in mind. First, we need to recognize this is a cultural change we are embarking upon and it is all about the "combined actions, thoughts, values, beliefs, artifacts and language …" of our people. It is all about the people; it is not about a "thing". Being all about people means we will need to focus on and sharpen our people skills, often what consultants call the "soft side" of the business. Second, we must recognize that we are working to improve employee engagement. We are not working on the hard metrics of profits … quality … safety … and on-time delivery. Yet as we work on engagement, achieving higher levels of employee engagement, not only will our profits, quality and on-time delivery improve, but safety performance, morale and customer support will reach new heights as well.

The irony is that by working on the "soft side" of the business, we improve all the metrics. As a direct result of paying attention to and acting on the soft side metrics, they will improve. Predictably, with little or no additional effort, the hard metrics will dramatically improve as well.

Employee engagement, its impact on business performance

In the scientific literature published by psychologists and sociologists, there is a great deal written on the benefits of engagement. Most of it is not quantitative in nature and avoids citing bottom-line business gains such as cash flow, return on investment or profits. Rather, most of the benefits of improving engagement cite marked improvement in morale, customer satisfaction, absenteeism and employee retention, for example. In addition, there are often general comments like, "engaged employees also generate greater returns on profitability, assets and shareholder value compared to disengaged employees" (Macey et al., 2009), yet scarce few have much, if any, data to back up their claims.

However, Gallup has a huge database of information on *__their version__* of engagement. Their database includes thousands of firms across a wide range of industries, and it is studied worldwide based on their proprietary survey. In addition, they have stratified the data, including stratifications by country, by industry, by company size and by almost any classification of interest at the time. For example, in their last survey, they had a whole section dedicated to engagement amongst the Millennials. In their 2012 survey (Gallup, 2013), they state that since the late 1990s they have administered their survey to over 25 million people, 1110 clients in 195 countries and 16 major industries. It is extensive.

The Gallup data

The real benefit of the Gallup data is that they have used the same survey for almost 20 years. This makes year-to-year comparisons significant. Consistency of questions, consistency of analysis and consistency of the overall methodology is a significant strong point to the Gallup data. I do know of other engagement surveys that have been evaluated consistently over time, yet none has as broad a database as the Gallup data. There are, however, some weaknesses in the Gallup survey, which we will discuss later.

My interest and my focus here is on engagement in manufacturing, and, luckily, Gallup has data on that as well. However, the bulk of their information is not stratified by the manufacturing industry. Since engagement is a human topic, the data across industries should not vary greatly and Gallup's data support that.

I have included a wealth of data supporting the basis that improving engagement is a powerful strategy to affect the bottom-line and key business metrics. They, Gallup, say rather succinctly and directly:

> "Despite massive changes in the economy and technology, the results of the most recent meta-analysis are consistent with the results of previous versions. Simply put, engaged employees produce better business outcomes than other employees – across industry, company size, and in good economic times and bad. Business or work units that score in the top quartile of their organizations in employee engagement have nearly double the odds of success (based on a composite of financial, customer, retention, safety, quality, shrinkage and absenteeism metrics) when compared to those in the bottom quartile".

(Gallup, 2017)

The business opportunities of improved engagement

The graphic below is the Gallup data for the 2012 survey, showing key business metrics. Note that their comparison is the median values for the top quartile of engagement as compared to the median values for the bottom quartile (Gallup 2013) (Figure 1.1).

These numbers are impressive and statistically indistinguishable from the 2017 data. (Here, like other places, I used the 2012 information, instead of the 2017 data only because Gallup made a much better graphic

ENGAGEMENT'S EFFECT ON KEY PERFORMANCE INDICATORS

Median outcomes between top- and bottom-quartile teams

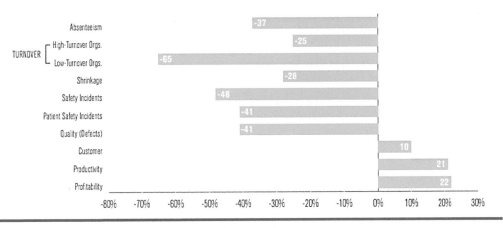

Figure 1.1 **Engagement impact on business outcomes.**

presentation.) Of note to those interested in the bottom-line effects is the 22% improvement in profitability and the 21% improvement in productivity for higher levels of engagement. Many of the other numbers are even more impressive in terms of magnitude but might have a lesser bottom-line impact, depending on the company's particular business situation.

Overall, this makes a compelling business case to improve engagement. And it will become even more compelling when we make the case that you get it for free – especially when you enact the correct management practices.

Business behaviors that are engagement "killers"

There is a growing interest among businessmen to use "improved employee engagement" as a strategy for success. It is critical for them to recognize that improving engagement is a broad-based, fully integrated, human-centric, long-term strategy and as such is inconsistent with a number of strategies present in many businesses today. Three strategies that preclude engagement are:

- A focus on bottom-line profits only; as contrasted to a balanced scoreboard and/or
- A focus on results only; as contrasted to focusing on the results as well as the means and/or
- A focus on short-term results only; as compared to a balance of long and short-term results

The Bottom Seven in my database were all firms rated as weak on engagement; average engagement levels were 14%. All seven had serious problems with all three items above.

Is this conscious behavior or not??

Interestingly enough, all seven had balanced scoreboards and some had posted their metrics in an "Information Center" which might indicate some sense of balance. Furthermore, several had Vision and Mission Statements that said they were "driven by a long-term vision", "striving for long-term excellence" as well as "striving to achieve excellence not only for customers but stockholders and employees as well". One even stated that "Our purpose is to provide meaningful and challenging work for our employees".

However, among this Bottom Seven with an average engagement level of only 14%, when the actions of the management were observed, and when the actual behavior was compared to the words in the Vision and Mission Statements, the monthly balance sheet was all that mattered. Their actions showed no "long-term vision", no "striving for long-term excellence" and no "striving to achieve excellence not only for customers but stockholders and employees as well". However, it is not what they publish about themselves, and most of it is not what they would like others to believe about them. All seven firms, like many other firms, seem to exist in an alternate reality where "they wish they could be", but in reality – are not.

At one time, the individual in these firms probably paid attention to all of the facility metrics and all the constituencies. However, the senior management very clearly defined, through their actions, that short-term financials were the only meaningful measure of success. Soon enough, this became learned behavior and was a cultural norm. Then, through repeated "practice", this behavior became almost automatic and **is now largely unconscious and extremely consistent behavior**; it is now "just how we do things around here".

How does the dysfunctional culture play out at the behavioral level?

Of course, there is nothing wrong with focusing on the bottom-line monthly results. The problem is the extreme and singular focus given to this concept, which poisons the entire culture in three very distinct and measurable ways.

▪ Rather than focusing with a sense of balance on the three key entities of customers, employees, as well as the stockholders (or owners in some cases), the focus was alone and intent on the stockholders. This meant focusing on the short-term profits only. When customer issues came up, regardless of their merit, the customer was treated as a nuisance at best and an enemy at the worst. And in each case for this "Bottom Seven", the employees were not engaged in a joint effort to problem solve their way to the ideal state. Rather, the ***employees were just another variable expense to be minimized***; even if that is not what the management team advertised, that is how they behaved. The focus was solely on the need to show short-term bottom-line results to the stockholders, and if that meant "corrections" had to be made, they were made. Nothing was sacred when compared to the bottom-line financials. Trainings were canceled, vacations were canceled, overtime was canceled, capital work and maintenance was deferred or canceled and people were let go. In some cases, I have seen senior people, whose performance was just fine, released to hire people with less seniority at a lower pay rate. That reality, to sacrifice anything and everything in the name of short-term profits was clearly understood by everyone. It was not even a secret and was probably discussed in the informal discussions over a cup of coffee between friends. However, it was just not openly discussed in business meetings with senior management present. It was what Chris Argyris referred to as one of the "undiscussables"(Argyris, 1993) or, metaphorically, as the "elephant in the middle of the room" which no one could discuss. These "undiscussables" are nothing more than complex defense mechanisms to avoid facing reality. (See sidebar.)

■ Rather than focusing on a balanced scorecard that includes quality, safety, delivery, productivity, morale, engagement and financial metrics, only financials were attended to. Other metrics may or may not have been recorded but received no significant attention. A common response to bad financials was to create a "recovery" plan. It was not even called a "financial recovery plan" simply a "recovery plan" and everyone was familiar with the term. However, if quality problems or delivery problems persisted, that never, not even once, precipitated a "quality recovery plan" or a "delivery recovery plan". Recovery plans were always financial and everyone knew it. They did not even need to have the adjective "financial" attached; that was understood.

■ Rather than focusing on the means to achieving the results as well as focusing on the results, the entire focus was on results. There was no serious process focus whatsoever. For example, when the quality metric "slipped" and the results were subpar, then the common response was to "game the numbers" at the very best and sometimes either hide or ignore them at the worst. These firms made "pencil-whipping the data" a new art form. Frequently, defects were not recorded and new ways to count the data and calculate the process metrics were "invented". There was seldom any effort to "review the process" and improve defect clarification or employee training, for example. And the most common casualty of any improvement efforts uniformly started with a reflexive effort at blaming the floor workers involved. By the way, when it came to "gaming" the numbers or inventing new ways to interpret and calculate the metrics, for these dysfunctional cultures, this was often the only manner in which the team would express any creativity or imagination at all; all seven firms had this skill set: **"creativity through blaming and gaming"**.

THE UNDISCUSSABLES

Or "the elephant in the room ..."

Regarding "the undiscussables", Chris Argyris writes, "All these actions require that human beings communicate inconsistent messages but act as if they are not doing so, and they must be covered up while being enacted. In many cases, the cover-ups must also be covered up. To do this, individuals learn to communicate inconsistent messages, act as if the messages are not inconsistent, make the previous actions undiscussable, and make the undiscussability – undiscussable. Individuals on the receiving end of these actions must collude. If they recognize the cover-up, they learn to act as if they do not recognize it. They also expect the deceiver, distorter, or manipulator to recognize the collusion. *These actions are organizational defensive routines*. They overprotect individuals or groups and inhibit them from learning new actions. They are routines because they occur continually and are independent of individual actors' personalities. Defensive actions are highly skilled. Skillful actions are executed immediately and automatically. Skillful actions "work". Most of the time they are executed without the actors' conscious attention. This behavior yields patterns of skilled unawareness and skilled incompetence that result in the inability to learn and grow" (adapted from Argyris, 1993).

The largest and most glaring dysfunction is ***NOT*** that the company says one thing ... such as "Our purpose is to provide meaningful work for our employees", then in the fullness of time, the management treats them worse than a forklift, which at least gets some maintenance. The largest problem is that the company pretends this is not the case. They conjure up excuses and explanations that defy logic and reason and they take denial and other defense mechanisms to a new level of sophistication. They are unwilling to admit to the dysfunction … although it is blatantly obvious when you compare their words to their actions. Clearly, the management does not walk the talk. This denial of any problem, in the face of overwhelming and compelling evidence, while it is convenient and easy, absolutely precludes any correction.

If your company has even the hint of an issue with any of these three "killers", I suggest your organization, led by your senior leadership, address that issue directly before you undertake any sort of effort to focus on engagement. These three issues of imbalance are so important they will preclude ANY effort from achieving even mediocre levels of engagement.

The science and the data used in this book

This book contains data from two sources. One is the literature that is generally available in books or on the internet, including psychological studies, individual case studies, practitioner information and even full-length books. A surprisingly large amount of very meaningful data has come from books that were written long before the topic of engagement was defined as a concern to business management. What I have found is that management scientists, including Drucker, Maslow, Deming, Juran, Ishikawa, Pascale, Athos, Shein, Argyris and a passel of others, who wrote decades ago about how to improve businesses often speak of creating behaviors which today we would call employee engagement. Terms like vigor, dedication, fulfillment, being absorbed in the work, focus, passion, intellectual and emotional commitment were commonplace in their writings. They knew what it was; they just did not yet have a name for it. So, engagement, at the behavioral level, has been discussed before as a key element of business success by the wise and aged.

The second source of data is contained in a database I have kept for more than 30 years. It is a large matrix which contains various measures that are important to any business. It has some data on over 100 businesses, and it has significant data on 36 businesses where I have categorized leadership, motivation, engagement, teaching/learning/experimenting and a variety of other qualities. Of this group of 36, I have evaluated the top and bottom 20% on engagement and the precursors to engagement. I have included those here in a partial matrix for your information. (Each subset of seven is listed in random order.) I will refer to these in the narrative frequently (Table 1.1).

Table 1.1 Database on Engagement

| | | My Database of Engagement | | | | All Companies | | | |
	Company	Country of Owner	Country of Operation	Product	Supply Chain Position	Country of Owner	Number in Database	Industry	Number in Database
Strong Engagement	A	Germany	Mexico, USA	Electronics	Tier 1 and 2 to Auto Ind	USA	12	Manuf'g	28
	B	Japan	USA, Canada	Ind Equip	Direct sales	Mexico	7	Healthcare	4
	C	Japan	USA, Mex	Auto parts	Tier 1 and 2 to Auto Ind	Japan	6	Education	3
	D	Japan	Mexico	Electrical components	Tier 1,2 & 3	Canada	4	Logistics	1
	E	USA	USA	Plastic inj molding	Tier 2 and 3	Germany	3		
	F	USA	USA	Electrical wire	Tier 1 and 2	Netherlands	2		
	G	Neth	Mex	Electronics	Direct sales and tier 1	England	1		
						Sweden	1		
Weak Engagement	AD	USA	USA	Health care	Direct				
	AE	USA	USA	Plastic inj molding	Tier 2 and 3				
	AF	USA	USA	Petroleum products	Tier 1 and 2				
	AG	England	Mex	Electrical components	Direct sales				
	AH	USA	USA	Plastic inj molding	Tier 2 and 3				
	AI	Can	Can	Steel industry	Tier 1				
	AJ	Can	USA, Can	Auto interior parts	Tier 1,2 & 3				

In the spirit of transparency, let me be clear. Many concepts and evaluations require the use of information and data. Yet I find a great deal of inconsistency in the data of the scholars (more on that later) who are the only ones to really test the theory of engagement. I also have significant reservations about the material published by the practitioners as I know it is not a representative cross-section of data. Rather than publish all the data, they selectively publish only their successes and even some of that data is questionable. To do otherwise is normally not good for their business. So, for those reasons, where there is a discrepancy in the published information and my personal data, I will first let you know, but I will typically defer to my data. I know its origin, I know its context and I trust it.

Chapter Summary ... Most human resource change initiatives failed because they were bad ideas; others failed as a direct result of the implementation methodology. Nearly all failed because they unable to grasp that these were culture-changing events. Culture is a powerful, overriding concept which is not widely understood, and, hence, it is often left "to manage itself". Improving employee engagement is a large culture-changing event and has to be managed as such, just as you would design and manage a lean transformation. As a culture-changing event, it can produce wonderful benefits. However, there are three very common pitfalls that must be avoided if you wish to be successful by any measure. Finally, we discussed some of the problems we have in the quantification of engagement.

What's next?? Now we will dive headlong into the history of employee engagement, how we lost most of it, what we still have left and what that all means.

Chapter 2

History and Current State

Aim of this Chapter ... is to explore the history of worker engagement. We will show that, much earlier, engagement in the workforce was the norm. But since the days of the cottage industries, engagement levels in the workplace have significantly diminished. We will explore this dynamic. Finally, we will then look at the actual levels of engagement in the workplace and focus on engagement levels in the world of manufacturing.

Engagement, are you aware of it?

The concept of engagement

This is a book about engagement. It is interesting that the concept of engagement, as commonly expressed, has been around for quite some time, as far back as the 15th century in England. From my Merriam Webster dictionary, I find ...

> *"Engagé* is the past participle of the French verb *engager,* meaning "to engage." The French have used "engagé" since the 15th century to describe socially or politically active people. ... By 1946, English speakers had adopted the word for their own politically relevant writing or art, and within a short time "engagé" was being used generally for any passionate commitment to a cause."

And the psychological/behavioral reality of what we call an "engaged person", even if different adverbs and adjectives were used to explain those traits, has been around since recorded history. You immediately think of involvement, commitment, passion, enthusiasm, absorption, focused effort, zeal, dedication and energy. You can read about people that acted with those traits in the *Iliad*, the *Odyssey*, the Bible and in all recorded history that describes the behaviors of people.

However, unlike the wheel, the steam engine, the telephone and the computer, engagement was not a concoction of man. Literally, it was a characteristic that existed in mankind since history has recorded how people have behaved. There is nothing new about the phenomenon of engagement … and this is very important. The concept of a "passionate commitment to a cause" is not new.

Just what is this common (mis)understanding??

In my work, I will often discuss engagement with managers and floor workers alike, and there is a very common thread to their understanding. I hear a lot of metaphors, including engaged workers are the "head down ass up" people here, or they are the "hard-working, nose-to-the-grindstone" folks on the payroll. A common definition I hear from some, especially supervisors, is: "when you ask for overtime work, they don't ask a bunch of questions, they just say OK".

This exclusive focus on physical contribution is hardly synonymous with "a passionate commitment to a cause", so likely there is something missing from this type of common understanding. Yet others will say, "they are the folks who will go the extra mile" somewhat better capturing the "passionate commitment" but still falling short. Many cannot describe engagement with a clear practical definition, but it is very common for them to say, "yet I know it when I see it". One salty, old manager once told me, "it's like falling in love; I can't define it, but I surely know it when it happens".

Yeah, there probably is a common understanding of "what engagement is"; unfortunately, it falls short of "a passionate commitment", and as such, it falls short of what businesses really need to survive and prosper. In the ensuing chapters, we will develop this definition of engagement, but suffice it to say here that it goes beyond just a physical component and goes well beyond the common understanding we have today.

However, there are some metaphors we can explore to show "a passionate commitment"

Two examples of "a passionate commitment" that most people can relate to, which often look very much like work, but are not, include: hobbies and

volunteer activities. I often find
that those people who have
hobbies and those who do
volunteer work expend substantial time and energy, with
no financial remuneration. Yet
they do so with "a passionate
commitment". How is it that
these two activities motivate people to such levels?

JUSTICE HOLMES ON "SIMPLICITY"

"I don't give a fig for the simplicity on this side of complexity, but I would die for the
simplicity on the other side".
Justice Oliver Wendell Holmes

As we go through this book, keep those two concepts in mind. Almost
surely, the behavior exhibited in these two activities meets the definition of
"engaged behavior".

The danger of "too many details"

Yet as we "get into the details", there is yet another danger. It is the danger of seeming to know "too many details" at the risk of losing sight of
the bigger picture. Metaphorically, "we cannot see the forest for the trees".
Unfortunately, this is a common problem I find amongst the scholars and I
see it in my research on engagement. This is one of the criticisms the practitioners have of the scholars.

In so doing, we are in the danger zone of losing sight of what the overall concept is as we get intensely involved in all the details, intricacies and
subtleties, and almost unwittingly lose sight of the larger issues. If we are not
careful, employee engagement can be one of those. As we do a deep dive
into the topic of employee engagement, we will study what the scholars say,
and quite frankly I think they have it nailed. Yet employee engagement can
be a very complicated subject with many twists and turns as well as details
and subtleties. In Chapter 4, we will explore some of these "wrong paths
taken" as we review some of the "detours" our understanding of engagement
has passed through. Understanding
engagement is a little like understanding how we develop a relationship
based on trust. Extensive books have
been written on the subject, but most
of it can be reduced to a simple formula which is "be honest and honor
your commitments"; that nicely covers
99% of what it takes to develop trust.

ON ENGAGEMENT

Kahn (1990) said "the harness-
ing of organizational member's
selves to their work role. In
engagement, people employ and
express themselves physically,
cognitively and emotionally".

Unfortunately, although many scholars cannot express engagement in a simple, practical way, there is a way and we do have a simple, practical definition as we work our way toward "the far side of complexity" (see sidebar). It will, however, take us a few chapters, as we work through the details and intricacies, making sure to touch all the bases, as we find this simple, practical definition of engagement.

History of engagement

It has been a valued trait forever – even if we did not know what to call it

The concept we now call engagement has been around forever, even if not by that name. Employers have been looking for hard-working, dedicated and motivated workers since time immemorial. It does not matter if it is the kings of medieval times looking for workers to farm the fields, repair the wagons, tend to the livestock and guard the castles or if it is the managers of today trying to provide the wide range of the functions required in the technologically advanced factories of today: these qualities are always being sought after – and found far less often. And in these factories, it does not matter if these employees are the entry-level hourly workers or the top of the management pyramid; people with these traits have been sought after. My suspicion is that King Henry VIII could easily have found these qualities in his workers; however, the managers of today find it far more difficult to find these qualities, at least in the quantities they would like to have. But things have changed since the time of King Henry VIII.

What's different

Two things have changed dramatically that have literally driven the sense of engagement out of most of the workforce. These two changes are directly related to the Industrial Revolution which: caused businesses to become much larger; this was later exacerbated by the concept of Taylorism

Before the Industrial Revolution … craft production

Up until the early 1800s, there was no "industry" in the United States. It was the era of craft production. Almost all goods were produced one at a time by tradespeople who also sold their wares. There were no distinct business functions of design, manufacturing, marketing and sales. It was a shop of one, or very few tradesmen, making specialty products, one piece at a time, often to the exact and differing specifications of their individual customers. Some businesses expanded and took on other tradespeople and apprentices, but they were still very small. A small businessman, a store owner perhaps, may have one or two other employees, and more likely than not they were family members. At this time, the workers in these businesses were almost surely engaged. Not being there, I could only surmise, but their very life depended on their businesses so I would expect they were hard-working, dedicated and motivated. They had a laser-like focus on their customers; many products were made exactly to the needs of the customer and the tradesman dealt directly with the customer. Whether it was the village blacksmith making a wheel for the owner's carriage or the tailor making pants, the customer could very often get exactly what he wanted. The very livelihood of the tradesman depended on that dynamic. This created an emotional (they cared), intellectual (they knew the work) as well as a physical attachment (they worked hard) to the work from all the workers. Furthermore, there was yet another emotional incentive. The merchant, who was part of a small tight-knit community, did not want his name disparaged.

This smallness of the business, direct connection to the customer and direct connection to both his livelihood and reputation all created not only a physical need but an emotional as well as intellectual need for the merchant. To fail to pay attention to these three aspects of his work, the physical, the intellectual and the emotional, would almost guarantee failure. This was soon to change.

The emotional attachment is affected by mass production

In the Industrial Revolution, with the use of oil and coal power along with the advent of the railroad came the opportunity for mass production and its inherent cost advantages. Both product manufacturing and product sales changed, and much larger industries were born. These naturally employed many more employees. From a "jobs" standpoint, that was wonderful as many new jobs were created; however, it had a huge deleterious impact on the emotional attachment of the employee: to the product; to the customer; and to the owner. Now the business was no longer just the family; there was hired help as well. And soon enough, as these businesses grew, the workers no longer knew the owner, they no longer knew the customer, and with mass production, products were no longer made to the exact needs of the individual customers. The workers no longer had a large emotional stake in the business. At this time, the "contract to work", whether oral or written, was created. It basically said, "I will sweat for you and you will pay me", while the emotional attachment of the worker, to the business, was virtually severed.

Taylorism becomes an industrial norm – Worker thinking is discouraged

By the late 1800s, businesses had become much larger and mass production was clearly the norm. Since labor was a significant cost, there was a large incentive to reduce it. There were significant efforts employed to improve labor efficiency and effectiveness. One of the first to embark on the task to improve labor efficiency was Frederick Taylor. His work was a large part of what later become known as Scientific Management, and his contribution is often called "Taylorism". Taylor observed that floor workers were largely left on their own to "get the job done". He further noted that the measures of labor efficiency varied largely among floor workers doing the same task. To improve upon this, his approach was to create "best methods".

To create the best methods, engineers and managers would study the work. Then, using principles such as division of labor plus time and motion studies, they created what today we might call standard work. People were trained in these work methods and piece rate pay was arranged to create the proper motivation. And, quite frankly, labor efficiencies improved for several decades. However, the method of creating the best methods sent a clear message to the worker. That message was, "managers will do the thinking, you do the work" – and this message was intentional. At this point, whatever intellectual attachment floor workers had was clearly lost. Their job was no longer to "get the job done"; instead, their job had become, "follow the best methods … or else". However, at that time, this transition was not much of an intellectual or emotional problem. In the late 1800s, educational levels were very low and only a very small percentage of the workforce even had a high school education. They were not well equipped to find the best methods.

The problem is that this method of managers specifying the work and floor workers doing just what they are told – persists even today. Today's workforce is capable of doing much more and in many cases would be far better equipped to create the "best methods" than the engineers and managers who are still doing that today. Furthermore, when the floor workers are prevented from creating their own "best methods", this goes a long way toward creating a demotivating work environment.

More on Taylorism, which has been given a bad name

In its day, Taylorism was a large boon to both worker and owner during this time of Scientific Management. Although the name, "Scientific Management" largely become obsolete in the 1930s, many of its themes are still in work today, largely in the field of industrial engineering. These include: time studies; work flow; work flow synthesis; work rationalization; division of labor; elimination of waste; standard work and knowledge transfer – to name a few.

The net result of engagement due to the Industrial Revolution and Taylorism

Engagement involves the expression of physical (hard-working), cognitive (intellectual) and emotional (caring) contributions. Since the days of craft production, not much is left. The Industrial Revolution with its larger mass production facilities have effectively stripped the worker of his cognitive and emotional contribution, and all that is left is his physical "expression". In other words, he is just a pair of hands … nothing more. It is no wonder we frequently hear the expression "they check their minds at the time clock".

They do that because that is precisely and intentionally what management has trained them to do.

Today, it would be nice to change that.

LEVELS OF ENGAGEMENT TERMINOLOGY

The most widely used terms for engagement are those coined by the Gallup organization. They have three stratifications:

- engaged,
- not-engaged and
- actively disengaged.

Engagement – Current levels

The Gallup data

In this next section, we will show the levels of engagement prevalent in the US today as measured by the Gallup organization. They have the largest repository of this information in the world. I find these levels to be very low and quite disturbing. However, they are not surprising as they mirror what I have seen in many of my clients (Figure 2.1).

EMPLOYEE ENGAGEMENT AMONG THE U.S. WORKING POPULATION

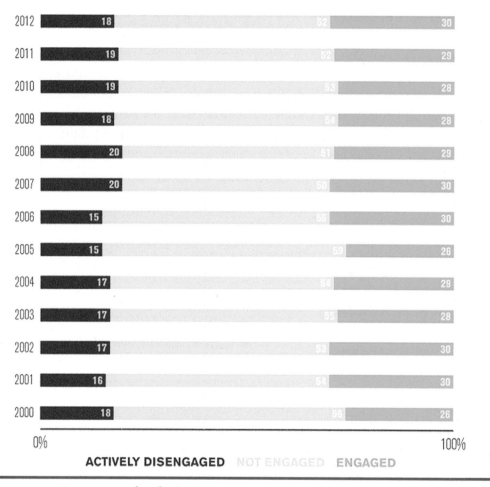

Figure 2.1 **Engagement levels since 2000.**

For Gallup, they stratify the levels of engagement into three categories: engaged; not-engaged; and actively disengaged. By these terms, they state that:

■ "Engaged employees work with a passion and feel a profound connection to the company. They drive innovation and move the organization forward.

■ Not Engaged employees are essentially "checked out". They're sleep-walking through their workday, putting time—but not energy or passion—into their work.

■ Actively Disengaged employees aren't just unhappy at work; they're busy acting out their unhappiness. Every day, these workers undermine what their engaged coworkers accomplish" (Gallup, 2013).

The Gallup data show engagement levels in the high 20s and low 30s since they started using their new survey in the late 90s **with manufacturing seldom rising above 25%.** When managers first see these data, in general, they are quite skeptical. Most believe the engagement levels in their manufacturing plants are much higher than 25%. Most of the skepticism is due to a lack of understanding of the true meaning of engagement. Once they get a true understanding of engagement and its elements, much of this skepticism disappears. Even after that, there are some who just don't want to believe these low numbers and so shrink into denial. I have done many surveys and find these numbers, prior to any cultural improvement efforts, to be representative if not optimistic; especially in manufacturing.

Engagement by company size

Of particular interest, to this author and to my hypotheses regarding engagement, is the Gallup data relating to company size. You can see that for companies of any size, engagement is in the 30% range with one exception … those with ten or fewer employees. Store this fact away; it is very important to keep in mind as we develop the correct concept of engagement: very small firms have much higher engagement than larger firms (Figure 2.2).

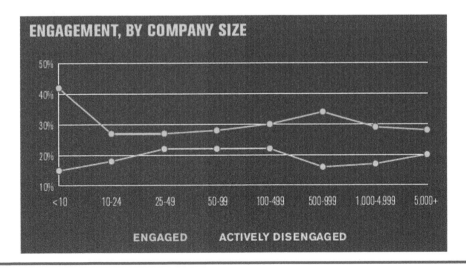

Figure 2.2 **Engagement by company size.**

Engagement levels in manufacturing

In the literature and on the internet, for the field of manufacturing, there is very little available data on engagement. It seems that those involved in engagement research are doing so in industries outside of manufacturing.

Data from the scientists and scholars

The fact is, we know very little about engagement levels in manufacturing because most of the research has been in non-manufacturing fields. For example, in a comprehensive literature search, it was listed that Kahn's seminal work was based on summer camp counselors and employees from an architectural firm. Rothbard's work was based on 790 respondents from a public university. The work of Schaufeli et al was based on 314 university students and 619 university employees. Harter et al had 198,514 respondents from multiple business units (some may have been from manufacturing; he did not say). The work of Robinson et al, in the UK, had data from 10,024 respondents within the National Health Service. A Canadian study was done by Saks using 102 employees selected from various jobs. Czarnowsky's work was based on a study of 776 responses from HR professional and learning executives. Witemeyer, et al. used responses from 2342 employees from private education organizations/USA. Not one of these studies focuses on manufacturing, and it is questionable if there is any data at all from manufacturing (Ababneh and Macky, 2015).

Data from others, most notably Gallup

First, Gallup has very little to say about manufacturing. Their focus is on the workforce in general, and since manufacturing is a small fraction overall, it gets little ink.

In their 2013 report on the "State of the American Workplace", a 68-page document, a word search for "manufact?" yielded only three hits. All three hits were related to the table below, plus two bits of commentary on the table. Their commentary was limited to the following statements, which are largely redundant:

> "Employees in manufacturing or production are the least engaged, possibly because the traditional management mentality in these industries tends to put process ahead of people. Still, engagement

	ENGAGED 2009	ENGAGED 2012	NOT ENGAGED 2012	ACTIVELY DISENGAGED 2012
Managers, executives, and officials	26%	36%	51%	13%
Professional workers: physicians	*	34%	57%	9%
Professional workers: nurses	*	33%	52%	15%
Professional workers: teachers	*	31%	56%	13%
Professional workers: other categories except physicians, nurses, and teachers	*	30%	55%	15%
Clerical or office workers	27%	30%	51%	19%
Construction or mining workers	29%	30%	52%	18%
Government worker	28%	29%	53%	18%
Sales workers	24%	29%	51%	20%
Installation or repair workers	25%	29%	51%	20%
Service workers	32%	29%	50%	22%
Transportation workers	21%	25%	47%	28%
Manufacturing or production workers	18%	24%	50%	26%

*Sample sizes too small in 2009 for comparison.

Figure 2.3   **Engagement by occupation, 2012 survey.**

among employees in this industry increased by six points since 2009."

"Employees in manufacturing and production are among the least engaged, perhaps owing to the fact that the management culture in these companies tends to focus on process ahead of people. An investment in managers' engagement in all industries, but these in particular, could go a long way in boosting employee engagement. Gallup finds that managers continue to be the most powerful influence on workers' engagement levels" (Figure 2.3).

(Gallup, 2013)

The data from this 2012 survey show only 24% engagement among manufacturing workers – with 26% of the workforce being actively disengaged – a very disturbing set of data. While there was more information available in their 2015/16 survey, the numbers did not change much, with only 25% engaged (Figure 2.4).

In their 2015/16 survey, they compiled these data:

In their 2015/16 survey they go on to say:

"Employees in manufacturing jobs are the least engaged. Equally discouraging is the alarming number of actively disengaged employee in manufacturing roles. The manufacturing industry has as many actively disengaged workers as it does engaged workers.

Occupation	% Engaged 2016	Change from 2012 (% Points)
Managers and Executives	38	+2
Professional workers	34	+3
Construction or mining workers	34	+4
Clerical or office workers	33	+3
Sales workers	33	+4
Farming, fishing or forestry workers	33	+1
Installation or repair workers	32	+3
Transportation workers	30	+5
Service workers	31	+2
Manufacturing workers	25	+1

Figure 2.4   Engagement by occupation, taken from the 2015/16 survey (Gallup, 2017).

The traditional management mentality in this industry tends to put process ahead of people, possibly accounting for some of the engagement obstacles".

(Gallup, 2017)

The Gallup results on engagement in manufacturing – Summarizing their hard data

In the 2012 survey "State of the American Workplace", engagement levels for manufacturing in the US were 24%. However, the 2013 Survey was entitled "State of the Global Workplace" and the evaluation was done by regions of the world. Canada and the US were combined as one region, with a reported 23% engagement level. This region, in their report, had the highest level of engagement among manufacturing workers worldwide. Finally, in the 2015/16 survey, in Figure 2.4, they quote 25% engagement for manufacturing workers.

It is pretty safe to say that, using the Gallup methodology, engagement among US manufacturing workers is a paltry 25%. Worse yet, there is a very similar percentage that are actively disengaged. That is disturbing ... but not surprising.

Chapter Summary ... from the early 1700s, during the time of the cottage industries, engagement was very high. Then, in a systematic and programmed fashion, management "designed out" the emotional and intellectual aspects of engagement until all that was left was the physical component. Rather than whole human beings at the workplace, floor workers were little more than a pair of hands. What many find surprising is the low levels of engagement, disturbingly low: 30% overall, 25% in manufacturing.

What's next?? The external environment has now changed; once again the managers want the worker to change again, only this time to become more engaged. So let's take a look at the history of engagement, starting with the work of the scientists.

Chapter 3

Engagement Theory – A Top-Down Perspective

Aim of this Chapter … to review what catalyzed the recent (since 1990) and intense interest in engagement as a sought-after business advantage. We will explore and learn the commonly accepted definition(s) of engagement, which actually converge to one concept. In addition, we will show the strong relationship of high levels of engagement to not only workplace health but to worker's physical and emotional well-being. Finally, we will look at some "wrong paths taken" on the way to defining engagement, and how these wrong paths actually strengthened our definition and understanding of engagement.

This engagement stuff … Where did it all start?

Up until 1990 there were few, if any, scholarly articles written on engagement. In 2000, there were less than five with the word engagement or employee engagement in the title. By 2005, around 60 were published, and by 2010, there were over 300, leading to over 350 such articles by 2012 (adapted from Truss, Deldridge et al., 2015). The almost exponential growth of these publications makes it clear that engagement is an emerging topic of great interest.

The single most important article, to spur this huge flurry of publications on engagement, was an article published by William Kahn, "Psychological Conditions of Personal Engagement and Disengagement at Work", published in the *Academy of Management Journal*, December 1990.

An effort to make psychology more balanced ... was initiated

Yet another topic that has accelerated the publication of articles on engagement is the creation of the positive psychology movement. Since so much had been written about the mental and emotional problems of individuals and society, psychology had become a study of dysfunctions.

Then, in 1954, Abraham Maslow wrote:

> "... science of psychology has been far more successful on the negative than on the positive side. It has revealed to us much about man's shortcomings, his illness, his sins, but little about his potentialities, his virtues, his achievable aspirations, or his full psychological height".

> (Snyder and Lopez, 2009)

This, however, even with substantial efforts by others, got little traction in pushing psychology away from pure dysfunction toward a more balanced human perspective. Then, around the turn of the century, brought to the forefront by Martin Seligman and others, there became an emphasis on positive psychology (Frederickson, 1998).

> "With a message for managers who wanted to boost their bottom line, Drucker (1993) simply stated that executives should build on strengths not weaknesses. In 1998, Seligman picked up the mantle of those who came before him, Maslow, Menninger, Drucker, and many others ... and paired scientific zeal with good timing to make positive psychology come alive and round out psychology". And....

> "Positive psychology is the 'scientific study' of what makes life most worth living. It is a call for psychological science and practice to be as concerned with strength as with weakness; as interested in building the best things in life as in repairing the worst; and as concerned with making the lives of normal people fulfilling as with healing pathology".

> (Snyder and Lopez, 2009)

The positive psychology movement catalyzed a great deal of interest in engagement, beyond Kahn's article, and also spurred interest in a similar topic, "flow", which shares some of the same fundamental strengths as engagement. We will discuss "flow" in Chapter 12 on intrinsic motivation.

Kahn's work catalyzed the "top-down" interest in engagement

Since Kahn's article in 1990, this "top-down" approach has created a number of theories and constructs which have been studied. By "top-down" we mean starting from the general, that is, the theory, and moving to the specific, that is, the outcomes. We will look at the two most common theories that have survived the scrutiny of both time and academia. They are the work of William Kahn and the work of Schaufeli, Salanova, Gonzalez-Roma and Bakker (Schaufeli et al., 2002). We will use and refer to these two in this book. Most other theoretical constructs have added to, deleted from, modified or otherwise used these two in some substantive way.

Kahn's Work

Prior to the publication of Kahn's theory in 1990, although many people sought this seemingly unique set of behavioral traits, it did not have a common name. He classified engaged employees as those who:

> "…express and employ their personal selves, and disengage or withdraw and defend their personal selves".

> (Kahn, 1990)

He further goes on to define three psychological conditions whose presence influenced people to engage and whose absence influenced them to disengage. They were meaningfulness, safety and availability. He further said:

> "…members seemed to unconsciously ask themselves three questions in each situation and to personally engage or disengage depending on the answers. The questions were:
>
>   1. How meaningful is it for me to bring myself into this performance?
>   2. How safe is it to do so? and
>   3. How available am I to do so?"

> (Kahn, 1990)

In his article, he defined:

> "…psychological meaningfulness as a feeling that one is receiving a return on investment … as though they felt worthwhile, useful and valuable – as though they made a difference and were not taken for granted. Psychological safety was experienced as feeling able to show and employ one's self without fear of negative consequences to self-image, status, or career. People felt safe in situations in which they trusted and they would not suffer for their personal engagement. Psychological availability is the sense of having the physical, emotional or psychological resources to personally engage at a particular moment. It measures how ready people are to engage given the distractions they experience as members of a social system".

(Kahn, 1990)

His overriding concept is that in doing their work or play, people in social situations are engaged when they express themselves physically, cognitively and emotionally. In lay terms, he means that engaged people are more than just hard-working, nose-to-the-grindstone types as this would only represent the physical expression. Engagement goes much deeper into their "personal selves"; it goes well beyond just the physical commitment but also being engaged with your mind as well as being emotionally engaged in one's work. Kahn's research suggested that engagement is the personal expression of "self-in-role"; someone is engaged when they are able to express their "authentic self" and to invest themselves personally into their job. Kahn makes it very obvious that engagement goes well beyond "just working harder" and requires deeper involvement by the person. "Self-in-role" and "authentic self" are terms that explain a deeper, more personal and intrinsic involvement in the work.

Kahn's conclusions in simple terms

A practical, non-academic way of saying they "employ their personal selves" might be "they do it with their heart and soul" or "they put it all on the line". A Texas Hold-Em poker metaphor is that they are "all in"; yes, engaged people have their body (physically), heart (emotionally) and mind (cognitively) invested in the activity.

In lay terms, he means that engaged people are more than just hard-working, nose-to-the-grindstone people. They all of that but they are more.

They are not only engaged with their body, working hard. But they have head and heart engagement as well. They are actively thinking about the task at hand and they genuinely care about the work.

Kahn and C. G. Jung …

In his writing on engagement, Kahn uses the very specific word "self". C.G. Jung, the famous psychologist, also used the term "self" with a very specific meaning. Jung meant the word self to be that inner part of who you truly are. When you uncover your "true self", you act with authenticity. You no longer put on airs, but more importantly, you have a clear understanding of your skills, your abilities and your place and purpose on this planet. Furthermore, Jung felt we were all on a life-long path known as "individuation", which was a search for our authentic self. Then, when and if we find our true self, we are more than satisfied with our life experiences, we are joyous and fulfilled beyond measure. However, we often used a less authentic tactic when we interact with society; he called this our persona. It is the mask we wear to "fit in". Jung's process of individuation is much like Maslow's concept of the fifth level of the motivational pyramid, self-actualization (which we will discuss in Chapter 7).

I could find no references to Jung in Kahn's work, but I do not think his choice of words was random. The concept of Jung's self is a widely studied topic in psychology, and Kahn and all of Kahn's academic colleagues would have resonated with this term. Consequently, I believe that Kahn is saying that "true engagement can't be faked", it must come from your inner being where you get all the benefits of that authenticity, including satisfaction, joy, happiness and fulfillment. You can, however, put on your persona and fake engagement, and others may give you rewards associated with your outward behavior. Nonetheless, the real benefits of engagement at the personal level, including inner satisfaction, real joy, deep personal happiness and true fulfillment, will only flow if you are intrinsically engaged, engaged by your inner self. Or, more simply put … you can't fake it and really make it.

That is the very reason that real engagement always leads to better emotional and physical health for the individual.

Schaufeli, Salanova, Gonzalez-Roma and Bakker's work…

This group created yet another definition of engagement. They said:

> "Engagement is defined as a positive, fulfilling, work-related
> state of mind, **that is characterized by vigor, dedication and**

absorption. Vigor is characterized by high levels of energy and mental resilience while working, the willingness to invest effort in one's work, and the persistence even in the face of difficulties. Dedication is characterized by a sense of significance, enthusiasm, inspiration, pride and challenge. Absorption is characterized by being fully concentrated and deeply engrossed in one's work".

(Schaufeli et al., 2002)

In addition, this group later created the Utrecht Work Engagement Survey (UWES). This survey has, by far, the greatest volume of collected engagement data – among the scholars. The largest volume of overall data comes from the Gallup organization using the Q[12] survey, however, with the Gallup data, as we mentioned earlier, it is arguable that what they are measuring is the engagement construct.

I like this definition because it is very tangible. It describes the concept of engagement and does so in words that are more easily understood by those outside the field of psychology. The terms "vigor", "dedication" and "absorption", are more easily grasped by lay folks than Kahn's wording, which may resonate better with the scholars.

My opinions on these two theories as "helpful tools" to drive to a fully engaged workforce

Intellectually, I like Kahn's construct better because he stresses the intellectual and emotional elements of his theory better than the construct of Schaufeli, driving that point home nicely. Although, Schaufeli says that "engagement is a … work-related *state of mind*", clearly interjecting the intellectual and emotional elements as well. Others prefer the construct of Schaufeli. First, it emphasizes the positive and fulfilling nature of engagement. Second, it is much easier to measure directly. This reason alone may be why so many people are using the UWES to measure engagement.

Although the constructs are different, and they have a different emphasis, the similarities and overlap in these two definitions are very large indeed. Both academic conceptualizations agree that engagement entails a physical-energetic (vigor) component, an emotional (dedication) component and a cognitive (absorption) component, resulting in a "whole person" engagement.

Using either of these constructs as guidance in an industrial setting will work nicely as you work to improve the workplace environment and attempt to achieve a fully engaged workforce.

Schaufeli on "positive, fulfilling, work-related state of mind"

The significant part that Schaufeli et al. have in their construct is the opening line, which says, "Engagement is defined as a positive, fulfilling, work-related state of mind …". I cannot mention often enough nor can I say it loud enough: when a person is engaged in their work they are not only engrossed in it but they are fulfilled, healthy and happy employees. This benefit supersedes all else and is not only the key precursor to improving the well-being of the worker but also a key element in improving many human-dependent business metrics that follow directly from a fully engaged workforce.

Although Kahn does not say it specifically in his discussion of engagement, he implies it. The work done by Kahn and follow-up work done on his construct shows that engagement leads to many positive outcomes including personal well-being, job fulfillment and general overall better health at both work and away from work.

I have found this is the very critical thought which management needs to keep in mind as they work to get the engagement they so ardently seek. That is, when they create engagement, they not only get employees a greater passion for the work but they are promoting worker health and well-being.

Engagement – Worker and workplace health

While managers are rabidly seeking some panacea to their woes, off they go on their search for the holy grail of business success: a fully engaged workforce. While a fully engaged workforce is a powerful weapon in the battle for customers and profits, a much under-stressed value of engagement is the benefits of health and well-being to the worker himself.

In both the writings of Kahn and Schaufeli, they stress the positive outcomes of worker engagement. They both state very clearly that engagement leads to a more fulfilling work experience. In addition, they both cite in their research that it leads to not only better emotional health but better physical health as well.

Gallup repeats this often in their writings, specifically:

"ENGAGED WORKERS LEAD HEALTHIER LIVES
One of the more intriguing findings Gallup discovered while studying engagement outcomes is a correlation between employees'
engagement levels and their physical health. Gallup found that
employees who are engaged in their jobs are generally in better health and have healthier habits than employees who are not
engaged or are actively disengaged. Engaged employees have lower
incidences of chronic health problems such as high blood pressure,
high cholesterol, diabetes, obesity, diagnosed depression, and heart
attacks than actively disengaged employees".

(Gallup, 2013)

Prior work on positive effects experienced by engaged workers

Finally, to see how engaged employees can expect to experience positive
emotions, such as excitement, enthusiasm and happiness, read below what
Schaufeli said. He created this graphic based on prior work done by J. A.
Russell. Russel's work was entitled, "A Circumplex Model of Affect", published
in the *Journal of Personality and Social Psychology*, 1980. Schaufeli wrote:

"By way of summary, Figure 3.1 depicts a classification of work-
related well-being. Various types of well-being, including burnout,
boredom, satisfaction and engagement can be mapped using the circumplex model of emotions (Russell, 1980). This model assumes that
all human emotions may be plotted on the surface of a circle that is
defined by two orthogonal dimensions that run from pleasure to dis-
pleasure and from activation to deactivation. For instance, employees
who experience mainly negative emotions may suffer from burnout, boredom or workaholism, whereas employees who experience
mainly positive emotions may feel satisfied or engaged. In addition,
employees may either feel activated, as in workaholism and engagement, or deactivated as in burnout, boredom and satisfaction".

(Schaufeli, 2015)

From it, you can clearly see the large positive effects that are the direct
result of engagement.

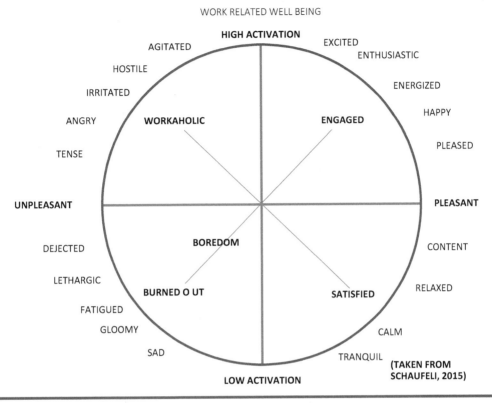

WORK RELATED WELL BEING

Figure 3.1   **A taxonomy of work-related well-being.**

Issues amongst the scholars

It turns out that, within the academic community, there are many issues with the theories of engagement. I am not referring specifically to the theories of Kahn and Schaufeli et al. No, I mean all the theories, and not the least of which is that they are all hard to define and even more difficult to measure. Problems in defining and measuring have led psychologists off on some "detours" as they try to better understand this importance.

They can't reach a common understanding on the definition of engagement

A word about constructs

To discuss definitions like engagement, scientists create constructs. Constructs try to define a concept by describing its characteristics. If a concept is unique, it should have a unique "construct", which is a unique set of characteristics. The characteristics referred to are not causes … a more appropriate lay term would be "symptoms".

Let me use a medical metaphor and discuss two problems nearly everyone is familiar with: allergies and the common cold. Your son comes to you complaining of fatigue, a cough, a runny nose and a sore throat. You immediately think of a cold, since you yourself had one just 2 weeks earlier. However, your son had allergies a while back and you recall these are the same symptoms. Recalling your doctor's advice, you ask your son if he has an achy feeling; in addition, you check for a fever. You find both and conclude he has a cold, and you are now able to treat him appropriately. While the "construct" of a cold had many of the symptoms of the "construct" of allergies, they were different. Once you got past the commonalities and found out that his symptoms included aches and fever, usually not present with an allergy, you knew it was likely the "construct" of a cold. Both the construct of a cold and the construct of an allergy have several common symptoms. When you understand that both colds and allergies are an over-stimulation of the immune system, it makes sense they might share many symptoms. In the case of a cold, the overstimulation is due to a virus, where with an allergy the overstimulation is caused by particulate matter, likely pollen or even dust.

So if your employees have the "condition of engagement", as described by the construct of Schaufeli et al., you would find them exhibiting the symptoms of vigor, absorption and dedication. I suspect you would say that is a nice "condition" to have.

Trait or state or ???

There is some work done that focuses on whether engagement is a trait or a state. Traits are characteristics of the person as opposed to a state, which is more of a fleeting situation where the characteristics come and go and fluctuate with the environment. I have found that there is a very high correlation between people who seem to get engaged more easily and who possess the three personality traits of curiosity, initiative and a positive outlook on life. So I believe that, to some extent, engagement is a personality trait, not just a fleeting condition that comes and goes with environmental changes. Clearly, the jury is still out on this one.

However, although I consider this to be interesting, to me it is largely irrelevant. What I have found, which is far more important and practical, **is**

that virtually everyone (in excess of 90% of the population) will be engaged in business if the culture, and hence the behavior of management, creates and sustains the elements necessary for engagement. That is the real issue; just how do we define and create these positive management behaviors. As much as anything, that is the unique contribution this book makes to the field of employee engagement.

Other engagement stratifications

There are other stratifications and sub-categories of engagement that scientists have struggled with. Is it personal engagement? Is it behavioral engagement? Is it work engagement? Is it organizational engagement? In the literature, I have even seen the term "strategic engagement". I am not sure of the practical importance in these stratifications and have not gotten bogged down in them. Getting engagement, by any name, is beneficial.

The theories seem to take some intellectual "detours"

While studying engagement, many academics and scholars went on tangential studies, sometimes to find the boundaries of engagement qualities and sometimes to find out what it was not. As you read these comprehensive and detailed treatments, you almost get the impression that the authors believed there "had to be more to it", as if engagement, as a concept, was too good to be true. They believed there just had to be a catch. These studies all smacked of the concept that there had to be a downside to engagement, there had to be some unintended consequences.

I have included the prominent "detours" here.

The detour into "leading to burnout"

Schaufeli writes:

> "As a matter of fact, two schools of thought exist on this issue. According to Maslach and Leiter (1997), engagement and burnout are the positive and negative endpoints of a single continuum. More specifically, engagement is characterized by energy, involvement, and efficacy, which are considered the direct opposites of the three burnout dimensions exhaustion, cynicism and lack of accomplishment, respectively".

However, since their findings on engagement studies differ from that of Maslach and Leiter, they expand further by saying:

> "The second, alternative view considers work engagement as a distinct concept that is negatively related to burnout. Work engagement, in this view, is defined as a concept in its own right: 'a positive, fulfilling, work-related state of mind that is characterized by vigor, dedication, and absorption'".

(Schaufeli, 2015)

This detour did not go far nor did it last long. The missing point in the definition by Maslach and Leiter was the deep involvement of the "self" as described by Kahn. This involvement of the "self" will naturally lead to positive outcomes. Without exception, outcomes of employee engagement include improved wellness, both physical and mental.

The detour into "workaholism"

This may be the acid test to the true distinction between working hard and being engaged. On the surface, based on all outward behaviors, workaholics "appear" to be engaged. As Schaufeli would say, they are showing vigor, dedication and absorption. And this detour, although it was studied a great deal, like the other detours was also short-lived. Again, Schaufeli discusses this nicely and says:

> "Not surprisingly, for engaged employees work is fun, which is precisely the reason why they work so hard, as was shown in a qualitative interview study (Schaufeli, LeBlanc, Peeters et al., 2001). However, the reverse is not true; not all employees who work hard are engaged. Although there are various reasons to work hard, such as financial needs, promotion prospects, or perhaps a poor marriage, some do so because they are driven by an obsession to work. These so-called workaholics are not pulled towards their work because they like it, but they are pushed by a strong inner drive they cannot resist. Following this lead, Schaufeli, Taris and Bakker (2006) define workaholism as the compulsive tendency to work excessively".

He summarizes, explaining the heart of the matter which is a key determinant of "engaged work" and simultaneously explains how it differs from "workaholism":

> "The underlying work motivation of engaged and addicted employees differs fundamentally. **Engaged workers are primarily intrinsically motivated**, they work for the fun of it, whereas workaholics are primary driven by external standards of self-worth and social approval that they have internalized (Van Beek, Hu, Schaufeli et al., 2012). They work because their self-esteem depends on it and because they do not want to fail in the eyes of others".

Workaholics exhibit all the correct outward behaviors. They work long hard hours, showing dedication. They will frequently work very hard to overcome obstacles, exhibiting absorption. And they will also exhibit great energy while they are working, likewise meeting the vigor requirement. I have found at least three types of workaholics in my experience. The most common one is the person seeking power and prestige by working very hard to get promoted and achieve preferential salary treatment. The second one is the person who is seeking peer recognition as "being a very dedicated and hard-working guy". The third is the saddest of all. I have seen more than a few who work long hard hours because work is a retreat from the rest of life, often from family obligations or a failing marriage. In each case, the driver to the absorption, dedication and vigor is some extrinsic motivator. The problem with workaholics is not that they do not work hard enough or are not conscientious enough; rather, it is that the motivating force is external and, hence, fleeting. Soon enough, the external situation will change and the worker is left isolated. Second, to remain extrinsically motivated takes a lot of personal energy; it is very effortful. For example, if you are driven by a need for promotions and raises, you will make sure to dress "correctly", behave in the "right" way, say all the "politically correct" things and, most of all, treat the boss "properly". This takes a tremendous amount of not only physical but psychic energy. Like I said earlier … it is very effortful; or, as Jung might say, you are working hard to maintain a strong persona … which is not your true self. And this expended effort, while it may improve the "appearances", does not lead, in actuality, to a greater contribution or improved performance. In the fullness of time, this expenditure of effort to "appear to be …" will take its toll and will detract from the employee's health and well-being.

The bottom line is this … the engaged worker is intrinsically motivated, and this leads to better performance, as well as better employee health and well-being.

You can see this explained by the definition of Kahn where he says, "express and employ their personal selves". Schaufeli et al. are not quite so clear on this topic but say, "Engagement is defined as a positive, fulfilling, work-related state of mind". Both make it clear that engagement comes from your very inner being, and as such it is fulfilling, it makes the work enjoyable and it always leads to both physical and mental wellness. Workaholics are not "well".

The detour into "discretionary work"

The unfortunate detour into discretionary effort and equating it to engagement is not only incorrect but it also has a certain appeal to management that made it popular for a little while. First, this definition misses the point as the adjective "discretionary" is focused only on physical work. Engaged employees go "above and beyond", but they do so cognitively and emotionally as well as physically. Their "discretionary" contribution is to all three elements of engagement. Second, this definition appeals to management, and in that it allows them to evaluate engagement as "time spent on discretionary work", again an error. Finally, management has and will come to expect this discretionary effort and redefine this as the "new normal".

To that point specifically, in "Employee Engagement in Theory and Practice" (Truss, Eldridge et al., 2015), regarding the definition of engagement, Keenoy states;

> "Engagement is not about driving employees to work harder but about providing the conditions under which they will work more effectively – it is about releasing employees' discretionary behaviour. This is more likely to result from a healthy work life balance than *from working long hours* [emphasis added]".

And then he states the logical conclusion, and confusion, of equating engagement with dedication.

"Not surprisingly, there are fears that 'engagement can drive work intensification, with employers coming to expect employees to "go the extra mile" as a matter of course [with] overtime becoming normalized [and probably unpaid]'".

(all quotes from Keenoy, 2015)

The detour into "an old wine in a new bottle"

Several authors hypothesized that engagement was not a new concept but, rather, an old concept simply with a new name. One of the often quoted articles had the catchy title of, "Been There, Bottled That: Are State and Behavioral Work Engagement New and Useful Construct 'Wines'" (Newman and Harrison, 2008). Some of the "old wines" include job satisfaction, organizational commitment, psychological empowerment, job involvement, job enrichment and organizational citizen behavior, to name a few.

This detour was short lived as well. For example:

" … what is more, engagement shows different patterns of correlations with other variables as compared with satisfaction, involvement and commitment. For instance, Christian et al. (2011), also using a meta-analysis, showed that engagement predicted in-role as well as extra-role performance, after controlling for job satisfaction, job involvement, and organizational commitment. … This means that the explanatory power of engagement goes beyond that of the three attitudes …".

(Schaufeli, 2015)

"Engagement is above and beyond simple satisfaction with the employment arrangement or basic loyalty to the employer—characteristics that most companies have measured for many years. Engagement, in contrast, is about passion and commitment—the willingness to invest oneself and expend one's discretionary effort to help the employer succeed".

(Macey and Schneider, 2008)

"So, in conclusion, although engagement is positively related to work-related attitudes such a job satisfaction, job involvement, and organizational commitment, it nevertheless seems to be a distinct concept that is more strongly related to job performance".

(Catherine Truss, Rick Delbridge, Kerstin Alfes, Amanda Shantz and Emma Soane, 2015)

Why the "detours" to the basic theory are just that, detours

While studying engagement, many academics and scholars went on these tangential studies mostly because engagement, as a concept, sounded too good to be true. They believed that "you cannot have your cake and eat it too". They hypothesized that if you wanted engagement you would also have to accept a certain amount of burnout and learn to deal with the problem of workaholism.

Others were even more skeptical and thought it was not really a new construct and it was really just another way to describe discretionary work or even the same old thing with just a new name.

What they found out was that:

■ you could have engagement without burnout, and, rather than burnout, engagement re-energizes people
■ you could have engagement and not create workaholics. Engaged workers are working very hard since they are intrinsically motivated, they become "enjoyaholics" of the work
■ engagement is more than just discretionary work and
■ engagement was a new construct that leads to not only improved employee and business performance but also improved levels of employee health and well-being.

What they found out was that "you can have your cake and eat it too". All these detours, while looking for weaknesses in the basic construct of engagement, in the end just strengthened it and showed the present definitions of Kahn and Schaufeli to be very robust.

Chapter Summary ... Kahn and his writings catalyzed the fairly recent interest in engagement, and this was further supported by the positive psychology movement. These two issues, in turn, seem to have created a renewed interest in engagement in the business community. Now it seems these ephemeral qualities they sought as they worked to improve their bottom line now had a name and a means to evaluate and even possibly improve them. Partially due to the new positive psychology movement, the sociologists and the psychologists have an intense effort to relate engagement to worker health, both physical and emotional; while the business managers are content to seek engagement as a bottom-line enhancement. Finally, the scholars keep looking at aspects of engagement thinking it might be "this thing or that thing" and keep returning to the definitions of Kahn and Schaufeli … and reaffirming the natural robustness of these constructs.

What's next?? Having looked at engagement from the scientists' view, we will now look at what the practitioners have to say … and the issues missed by both of them, and more.

Chapter 4

Issues with The Theory

Aim of this Chapter … In Chapter 3, we looked at engagement from a "top-down" perspective; now, we will look at it from the "bottom-up" and see how the practitioners view engagement. As you might expect, these are two dramatically different viewpoints. We will then look at the common ground they share; but more importantly, we will enumerate the six major points both groups miss. One major issue causing problems for both the scholars and the practitioners is the data and the "crazymaking" that flows from these data. A special set of widely used data is supplied by Gallup, and it has broad application; we will discuss it at length. Finally, we will address the business conundrum; that is, if we know what it is and know how to improve it and want to improve it … why don't we just get busy and do it??

The scholars and the practitioners …
Two different perspectives

As you read the literature from the scientists and scholars and compare it to the literature from the practitioners, it is hard to tell they are talking about the same topic.

Scholars and their "top-down" look

The scientists and scholars with their "top-down" approach look at the theory to find the proper construct to define engagement and seem to stop there. They seem more than satisfied when their intellectual curiosity is satisfied by proving the theory.

The business practitioners and their "bottom-up" look

On the other hand, the practitioners are looking at the desired business results and looking seemingly from the "bottom-up" and trying to find the "high leverage points" so they can better manage these issues. And their overriding belief is "If only we can control these high leverage points, then we can capture this thing called engagement and we will be able to cure the ills in our business". The entire issue of employee engagement, to the majority of managers, is that engagement is simply another tool to augment the bottom line. This is just another futile search for the silver bullet for those managers.

The businessmen want "it"… regardless of what "it" is, as long as "it" helps

Quite frankly, for the typical practitioner, whether it is a business looking for "it" or the consultants selling "it", the business manager does not really care what "it" is. If "it" improves his business, he wants "it". If more of "it" will help further, he will push harder to get more of "it". It makes no difference if that "it" is better machinery, more customers, Six Sigma, quality circles, improved processes or things like engagement. If "it" improves his business, he wants "it" almost by any means necessary. He's not interested in its construct, its nuances or even the theory behind "it". If "it" augments his bottom line, he wants "it" and he wants "it" – right now.

However, there are some introspective businessmen who are digging deeper into the theory so they may further implement the concept. They are pursuing increased engagement because they sincerely want to create a more fulfilling work experience for their people. I firmly take my hat off to these lean leaders. Unfortunately, they are the in the minority.

The short-term thinkers will narrowly and shallowly grasp at "it" like "it" is a lifeline, almost reflexively and without much thought. They are lazily, hopefully and frantically looking for the proverbial silver bullet, and to many, that is this thing called engagement.

The disconnect

So, between the theorists and the practitioners, there is a disconnect in this concept. The scholars seem to stop when the construct is proven and the theory is validated. Yet the majority of the practitioners really don't care about the theory; they are focusing solely on the practical applications and the resultant benefits. Schaufeli referred to this as "talking past one another".

" ... we became aware that these various groups (scholars and practitioners) are largely talking past one another, lacking a shared vocabulary, and understanding of engagement. This has been exacerbated by the fact that, until very recently, engagement has not been featured in university or business school generalist or specialist programmes at any level, and so many practitioners are unfamiliar with its academic foundations. Scholars therefore debate the meaning and status of engagement without reference, in many cases, to the needs and concerns of practitioners, and practitioners often do not have access to the thinking and insights that are being developed in the academic world".

(Schaufeli, 2015)

I am sure the scholars would like the practitioners to become more involved in understanding the theoretical constructs; however, the business practitioners

DEMING ON MELDING THEORY WITH PRACTICE

Dr. Deming had a lot to say about theory. First, he lowers the boom on those who think common sense and experience are the manager's best friends, "Experience without theory teaches nothing".

After saying that: "management is prediction".

He basically punctuates the need for management to have theory to gain knowledge. "Knowledge is built on theory. The theory of knowledge teaches us that a statement, if it conveys knowledge, predicts future outcome, with risk of being wrong, and that it fits without failure observations of the past".

Next, he reminds not only the managers but also the scholars that they must refine their theories by using the Plan, Do, Check and Act (PDCA) cycle. "Rational prediction requires theory and builds knowledge through systematic revision and extension of theory based on comparison of prediction with observation".

Finally, he makes it clear that to do this they need to work together. "Meetings of scientists and other professional people, at which speakers and participants contribute to other members' new theory and methods, with exchange of theory and experience" (Deming, 1994).

normally don't see the merit in that. What they want are results, not intellectual understanding. Yet the scholars are trying to understand "engagement" more from the standpoint of what it is rather than how it can augment a company's bottom line.

Once again Dr. Deming hit the nail on the head … (see sidebar)

I think they are both short shrifting this issue … to the detriment of both groups. Each group has a wealth of both information and opportunity, and, quite frankly, to have a seemingly clear and full understanding of a concept without understanding its utility and application is – in reality – to not fully understand the concept. Yet to have a seemingly clear understanding of the applications and utility of a concept without understanding the basic theory is likewise to not understand the concept.

I wish there were a greater meeting of the minds, and for the reasons stated both by the scholars and the practitioners, but also for reasons that have not been discussed. That is, no matter how good some laboratory experiments are, there is no laboratory any better than the factory floor. With its strict focus on meeting business metrics of quality, delivery, costs and profitability and its naturally competitive nature, it will be a far better testing ground than the

WHO'S THE WORKER??

The critical concepts of engagement, intellectual, emotional and physical commitment to the work, apply to all workers.

So who's a worker? Everyone in the workplace is a worker. We casually speak of managers and workers. However, managers and supervisors are workers as well; they work.

In this book, when I use the term "workers" I refer to all workers; to floor workers, to supervisors, to middle managers, to denizens of the C-Suite and the board as well – all workers.

To distinguish the workers who are on the floor touching the parts, stocking cells or driving forklifts, I add the adjective, "floor". Specifically for the floor workers who are making the assemblies, I refer to them as "value-add" workers.

You will come to understand, later in the book, that all these distinctions really don't matter when it comes to engagement, the principles are universal.

government-influenced healthcare industry and the world of education with its obvious flaws. So, if we could get more scholars working on engagement, on the factory floor, especially in the world of manufacturing, they would be in the most demanding laboratory environment and they would not only gain useful knowledge but would also begin the coupling of the knowledge of the scholars with the practical applications so desired by the practitioners.

In Chapter 5, we will discuss a much more intuitive model to describe engagement, by way of a metaphor. I presume this metaphor may help create a better connection between the scholars and the practitioners.

What the scholars know that the practitioners should know – Engagement is the natural state

The one overriding concept that keeps rearing its head is that being engaged at the workplace is the natural state for most workers. They come to work to seek it out. They come to work wanting to be engaged, they come to work so they can be engaged, and when they are **allowed to be engaged**, workplace health is improved.

People enjoy the benefits of being engaged:

■ They enjoy the feeling that they can affect the environment in which they reside. They like to have choice so they can exhibit some volition in what they do and how they do it;
■ they enjoy the feeling of being competent and being recognized for being competent;
■ they enjoy the feeling of being challenged and the satisfaction that comes from overcoming challenges;
■ they enjoy working together in harmony with others toward a common goal; and
■ they enjoy contributing and knowing they are making a difference.

These are the things people seek out to have a more fulfilling, happier life. They are not only natural, they are universal … they are intrinsic to the human condition.

And the vast majority of management have forgotten that concept.

Just why has management forgotten that??

I am sure there are some who never knew that concept; however, for a variety of reasons, I believe they are a distinct minority. Rather, I think there are three problems, common to many firms, that manifest themselves as if these managers had "forgotten" this message.

First, the most common problem I find is that many companies, contrary to their protestations, treat employees as an expense to be minimized, rather than as an asset to be utilized. This is not only the most common problem it is also the most devastating, with consequences that permeate the entire engagement concept. They have forgotten, or failed to recognize, that no matter how accurate and sophisticated the plans might be, the key people who are necessary to execute those plans are the rank and file on the factory floor. They are typically the lowest paid workers, yet are the only ones adding value. If they stop, the cash flow stops. The CEO can go on a 2-month, around the world cruise and products are delivered and money continues to flow. If the worker on the floor stops producing … everything stops, right now. Many managers are blind to this reality.

Second, many companies do not have a balanced scoreboard and also do not make decisions based on a balance of long-term and short-term benefits. Rather, they are laser-focused on short-term profits, and all other aspects of the business, including employee development, are subjugated to secondary importance … at best.

Third, they have spent too much time thinking like robotic MBAs (don't worry, I don't think all MBAs are this way), disjointed from the asset that is really providing the value-added service, the factory floor employees. They have learned many bad habits that need to be unlearned. They have spent lots of time working on the profit and loss statement, the stock values, their own bonuses and their own promotability. Quite frankly, there is nothing wrong with paying attention to those things; each has its own merit. The problem is that they have forgotten that the profit and loss statement, the stock values and the executive bonuses are all largely dependent upon how the individual factory floor worker actually performs … and they must be taken care of first. Anything else will create both a short-term loss as well as a long-term loss.

Peter Drucker captured all three of these issues very nicely in one of his quotes:

> "So much of what we call management consists in making it difficult for people to work".

And why is that??

I have worked with hundreds, actually thousands, of managers and find them, for the most part, to be highly motivated and well-intended. Most of the companies I have worked for, even those in the Bottom Seven, were reasonably well managed. For those in the Bottom Seven, even if monthly turnover was in double digits while engagement was in single digits, they still employed hundreds of people and kept customers happy enough to stay in business. So the managers were not inept; they just lacked some skills that their workers, the customers and board of directors wished they had. At the risk of being hypercritical, I would say they lack certain personal skills and traits, and my list is short, containing three items:

- First, I found them insular, if not insecure. They did not want outside input; rather, they wanted to hear that what they were doing was the "best that could be done under the circumstances". They did not "look" beyond the spreadsheets and feedback at meetings to assess how the business was performing. Being insular and isolated, they spent scarce little time interacting with the people, products and processes at the gemba. They wanted to read the "maps" and stay as far from the "terrain" as possible.
- Second, they had a warped sense of responsibility. If things were not going well, and they usually weren't, they wanted those around them to confirm that the problem was "out there". By being "out there", it was beyond their control and they were no longer responsible for it. Hence, they could be reassured that they were doing all they could.
- Third, I found them to be less than humble. Consistent with ignoring outside input, and failing to question and explore, is the concept that you must believe that you know all that is needed. And it is pretty hard to "know it all" and be humble at the same time.

Regardless ... they share some commonalities

Regardless of the lack of cooperation and interaction on the development and use of the concept of engagement, the academic community and the practitioners share some common beliefs. It is interesting to note that both groups share these thoughts and do so with a significant passion. The scholars seem to be driven by a desire to understand, whereas the practitioners are driven by a desire to improve businesses. There are at least four areas of agreement:

- There is a concept called engagement that goes beyond what we call commitment, it goes beyond what we call job satisfaction and it brings a unique type of job performance.

- This concept is very powerful
- It includes elements that come from within the worker. There are also elements that come from the worker's environment.
- It is worth exploiting for the benefit of not only science but the individual and the business unit as well

What is everyone missing??

When it comes to the theory and the application of engagement, there are several extremely important points that are missed by both the scholars and the practitioners. Most of these points have been superficially discussed by both groups. Unfortunately, the discussion is so superficial, or the crux of the matter has been minimized to the point such that it is rendered inconsequential. All these points will be discussed in much greater detail later. I mention them here to introduce you to them, so the subsequent chapters will have that context. Those points are:

1. The role of management in creating and sustaining engagement, especially their role as supervisors, is largely misunderstood, and when discussed, it's importance is grossly understated. The role of management is not just misunderstood and understated by both the scholars and the practitioners, it is misunderstood and **understated to the point that it is the number one reason that engagement levels are so low.** My hypothesis throughout this book is that most workers (95%+) – were engaged when they were first hired. Then, systematically and consistently they became disengaged because of the way they were supervised and managed, until we now have a workforce that is only 25% engaged. Furthermore, much of that management activity that created disengagement was actually designed to create engagement. The need for good management is not completely missed by the scholars or the practitioners. But both groups have largely ignored this critical need, and when it is discussed, it is being downplayed and marginalized to the point of being an "oh-by-the-way" thing. As you read about the role of management, you will find superficial and condescending statements, such as "and of course management follow-up is a key issue" and "training in supervisory skills is important", without discussing the presence or absence of these qualities; without even once defining how these qualities affect engagement, nor how to achieve these management and

supervisory skills. The critical role played by management at every step cannot be overstated. Without good management, there is no engagement … pure and simple. You might think the topic of management is not more properly addressed because some very new management skills are needed and this is too large a topic to cover simultaneously with the topic of engagement. The surprising aspect is that this type of "good management" is nothing more than management as described by Deming, Maslow, Juran, Ishikawa, Drucker and McGregor some 50 years ago. **The only logical conclusion is that neither the scholars nor the practitioners understand the critical role of management.** This error, while egregious is explainable, not justified, but explainable.

a. First, the scholars, mostly sociologists and psychologists from academia; although these academics have a strong and growing understanding of the technical topic of engagement, like many other academics, they have a very shallow understanding of management. We will discuss that topic more in Chapters 6 and 7.

b. Second, among the managers who are trying to achieve engagement of their workforce, they have a weak understanding of the technical topics of engagement. There are those who have studied and understand it, but many of them have misunderstandings of their role, a topic we will fully explore in Chapter 6.

c. Finally, among the group of consultants who understand engagement theory and practice, if they truly grasp the critical role of management they are often compromised. You see, they must tell the people who are hiring them that they, the management, is the group that must change the most. For any consultant that is a tough sell, so consultants minimize this issue, to improve their chances for a sale.

Virtually every chapter has references that stress the impact of management actions and the need for management's total physical, emotional and intellectual commitment so that creating a fully engaged workforce is a reality. In addition, Chapters 6–10 are dedicated exclusively to the role management plays in creating and sustaining a fully engaged workforce.

2. Almost all discussions of engagement, and especially the studies done by the scholars, focus on floor worker engagement – as if managers are fully engaged. While my experience tells me that managers, as a group, are more engaged than floor workers – they are far from 100% engaged. While the average level of engagement among manufacturing workers is around 25%, my data suggest that management engagement of

manufacturing managers and supervisors is around 45%; you have seen that Gallup in 2013 quoted the number of 38%, for all managers and professionals, not just manufacturing managers. While this appears to be a substantial improvement over 25%, it is far from world class and far from what is needed to attain any type of competitive advantage. In the effort to attain a fully engaged workforce, engagement of management is a given short shrift by both the scientists and the managers. As with item one above, virtually all chapters focus on this point.

3. Both scholars and practitioners alike speak of "engaged workers". That is how the dynamic is manifest, by the behavior of the individual, and many then conclude it is an individual thing, dependent and controlled by the individual himself. It is not an individual dynamic, not at all. It is a group dynamic. It is dependent on at least four entities to make engagement a reality. These four entities are: the individual, his peers, his supervisor and his management ... to the very top, including those on the board of directors. Again, this topic is covered in virtually every chapter but is carefully detailed in Chapters 10 through 15.

4. Both communities think of engagement as a linear construct with: (1) antecedents; (2) a process; and (3) outcomes – it is not. Rather, it is a dynamic system where the outcomes often become feedback and act like antecedents in a complicated set of interactions. In fact, with no feedback, the entire concept of engagement implodes and is destroyed. In addition, there are antagonistic elements within the model that are working, 100% of the time, to reduce engagement, so digression is an ever-present reality. Finally, all three of these issues: dynamics; interactions; and feedback can be either synergistic and create a more positive response or they can act in an antagonistic manner, creating an exaggerated loss of engagement. This concept is treated in Chapters 13 through 16, with examples in Chapters 17 and 18.

5. The concept of the feedback system is largely missed, and to make this worse, the feedbacks are often the elements with the greatest power to perpetuate the system of engagement. These concepts are explained in Chapters 13 through 16, again with examples in Chapters 17 and 18.

6. Both communities miss – either completely or in part – the connection to and the overwhelming power of intrinsic motivation in the system dynamics of creating and sustaining engagement. This topic is introduced in the Preface, discussed in Chapter 11 and fully explained along with the Intrinsic Motivational Loop in Chapter 12. Finally, using examples in Chapters 17 and 18, its impact is quantified.

The special case of the Gallup survey and data

The Gallup Q^{12} is an issue among the scholars, not so among the practitioners. The scholars are skeptical because they believe that Gallup's construct of engagement is theoretically weak. The practitioners seem to like it because it is intuitive, simple to use and, if administered properly, can deliver bottom-line business results.

There is a concern that the Gallup data is not even engagement data …

This is a controversial and technical topic. In the literature, you see comments such as:

> "… study undertaken by Gallup uses the Q^{12}, which instead of the experience of engagement assessed its antecedents in terms of perceived job resources. So, in fact, the results of the meta-analyses of Harter et al. (2002) indicate that resourceful jobs are positively associated with business success. However, despite the usefulness of the Gallup Survey, an analysis of the items shows that it measures the work environment rather than employee engagement".

And later they say:

> "Although it has been used extensively in many organizations around the world and has been shown to predict various business-unit performance indicators (Harter, Schmidt and Hayes, 2002), there have been many criticisms levelled at the measure (Schaufeli and Bakker, 2010; Briner, 2012; Macey and Schneider, 2008). Specifically, rather than measuring 'engagement', the Gallup Q12 may instead be assessing the extent to which a range of positive and motivational working conditions are present (Little and Little, 2006) (e.g. clear expectations – 'Do I know what is expected of me at work?', supportive supervisor/ coworkers – 'Does my supervisor, or someone at work, seem to care about me as a person?', and personal development – 'This last year, have I had opportunities at work to learn and grow?')".

(Truss and Delbridge, 2015)

Most of the concerns and criticism of the Gallup survey, as a means to assess engagement levels, are stated by the scholars and the scientists. Among the business owners and the consultants and in the blogs and e-zines, no one seems concerned with this issue. In most cases, the business concern is "how can I promote engagement and improve my business", and those who use the Gallup methodology and data cite no such concerns with these theoretical issues.

The Gallup Q^{12} does not directly measure the engagement construct

Take a look at the first six (of 17 total) questions from the Utrecht Work Engagement Survey (UWES), a recognized engagement survey (Ababneh and Macky, 2015), and compare them to the first six (of 12 total) questions from the Gallup Q^{12} (Gallup, 2012).

You can see immediately that the UWES questions stand out as diving deeper into the engagement of the individual; the UWES survey questions, compared to the Gallup questions, focus directly on the engagement construct. Terms like "bursting with energy", "time flies" and "full of meaning and purpose" dig deeply into the inner psyche of the individual and focus directly on the critical emotional element of engagement. The Gallup questions elicit no such responses directly. Although, without too much effort you can infer some of the same emotions. For example, if you get a strong positive answer to: "At work, I have the opportunity to do what I do best every day", you might infer the worker is both dedicated and absorbed. Nonetheless, the Q^{12} does not directly measure engagement.

Rather, Gallup believes that their study measures practical conditions that, in sum, predict the states such as absorption, dedication, etc. Hence, although their study does not directly measure the construct, "the symptoms" of engagement, they claim it predicts engagement. Furthermore, Gallup believes their measurements are superior as they are "actionable" while concepts such as absorption, dedication and vigor are not directly actionable. Today, and for the most part, I find that concern to be irrelevant, and in a minute I will tell you why.

However, having used the survey I can say two things. It is easy to use their analyses to find and focus on improvement items; hence, I agree it is highly actionable. Second, if you take action and make improvements, the follow-up survey data will find the improvements when they occur.

Table 4.1 Comparison of Questions, Q¹² to UWES

Gallup Questions	UWES Questions
1. I know what is expected of me at work	1. At work, I feel I am bursting with energy. (vigor)
2. I have the materials and equipment I need to do my work right.	2. I find the work that I do full of meaning and purpose. (dedication)
3. At work, I have the opportunity to do what I do best every day.	3. Time flies when I am working. (absorption)
4. In the last 7 days, I have received recognition or praise for doing good work.	4. At my job, I feel strong and vigorous. (vigor)
5. My supervisor, or someone at work, seems to care about me as a person.	5. I am enthusiastic about my job. (dedication)
6. There is someone at work who encourages my development.	6. When I am working, I forget everything else around me. (absorption)

I asked Gallup "Why don't you measure engagement directly?"

Gallup's survey does not measure the engagement construct directly, and Gallup scientists do not dispute this. However, they maintain that engagement can be "inferred with high confidence" (their words not mine). I have spoken with the Gallup people on this, and Gallup's Senior Scientist for Q¹² wrote in one of many emails we exchanged:

> "… Gallup's measure is a 'formative' measure of engagement— it measures practical conditions that, in sum, predict the states. The correlations of Q12 to the states, at the workgroup-level, are extremely high (.80-.90). Theoretically, yes, the two approaches are different but empirically the Q12 items capture a very high percentage of the variance in the states, have the added bonus of being actionable, and each item is predictive of multiple performance outcomes. **Most businesses want to use an employee survey to create meaningful change…the Q12 is a practical measure that organizations have used to create change".**

(emphasis mine, June 6, 2017 email, Gallup to Wilson)

Regarding these statements, although I have not even attempted to validate the high correlations cited, I can support that "the Q12 is a practical measure that organizations have used to create change" because I have used it to improve engagement levels. You will find some of that data is in Chapter 16 when we discuss two case studies. Furthermore, I can say that the Q^{12} is easy to administer and when analyzed statistically will give you excellent guidance on opportunities for improvement. My experience in using the Gallup Q^{12} has been very positive. But, the Q^{12} survey, while I have found it useful, is not the only one. There are others such as the UWES, which measures engagement directly. If you are a purist, this may be more to your liking.

Some more background on the Gallup Q^{12}

In the book *First, Break All the Rules* (Buckingham and Coffman, 1999), which discusses the history of the Gallup survey, they say,

> "This book is the product of two mammoth research studies undertaken by the Gallup Organization over the last twenty-five years. This first concentrated on employees, asking, "What do the most talented employees need from their workplace?" Gallup surveyed over a million employees from a broad range of companies, industries, and countries. We asked them questions on all aspects of their working life, then dug deep into their answers to discover the most important needs demanded by the most productive employees".
>
> "When the dust finally settled, we made a discovery: Measuring the strength of a workplace can be simplified to twelve questions. These twelve questions don't capture everything you may want to know about your workplace, but they do capture the most information and the most important information. They measure the core elements needed to attract, focus, and keep the most talented employees".
> "Armed with all this data, we were set to go. We knew the productivity, the profitability, the retention levels, and the customer ratings of these different business units. And we knew how the employees of the business units had answered the twelve questions. We could now see, finally, whether or not engaged employees did indeed drive positive business outcomes, across 2,500 business units and 24 companies".

These excerpts imply the purpose of their survey was initially focused on employee retention and workplace performance and not on engagement. In the third reference, they say, "we have the business results and we have the people's self-reported surveys". Somehow, they infer that those employees that score high are engaged. Nowhere is there a discussion of what engagement is nor any serious discussion of the characteristics of engaged employees. They simply hoped to conclude that "engaged employees" correlated well with good business performance.

And what did they find:

> "This is what we found. First, we saw that those employees who responded more positively to the twelve questions also worked in business units with higher levels of productivity, profit, retention, and customer satisfaction".

Hence, their major findings were to focus on high scores on the survey and its positive correlation to business unit measures and not any connection to employee engagement.

Then the Q^{12} Meta-Analysis

In the spirit of balance, Gallup published a document, "Q^{12} Meta-Analysis", in which they make the case that their survey actually measures engagement and is a predictor of business outcomes. Specifically:

> "The authors conclude from this study, as with prior Gallup studies, that employee engagement, as measured by the Q12 items, relates to meaningful business outcomes, and that these relationships can be generalized across companies".

> (Gallup, 2006)

The document is a scholarly article, is available on the internet, and makes a case that their Q^{12} document measures employee engagement. I leave it to you to evaluate and decide.

Another possible explanation to the engagement connection

Lucky timing. At the time Gallup was doing its work and before the book *First, Break All the Rules* (Buckingham, Coffman, 1999) and the Meta-Analysis (1993) came out, the engagement movement was in full swing. Recall that Kahn got it started in 1990. Maybe, just maybe, Gallup, whose original purpose in creating the Q^{12} was to " … measure the core elements needed to attract, focus, and keep the most talented employees", found their data correlated well with the engagement construct and "voila" they decided to ride this very attractive wave called engagement. Who knows? Better yet … who cares? More on that later.

The "bottom line" to the Q^{12} survey and its data

General data … *Its value to me as a consultant*

My interest is workers, from the floor worker to the C-suite and all jobs in between, specifically in manufacturing. I am not interested in the Gallup data on call center workers, on workers doing sales or even data on teachers in educational settings. My interest in my work and particularly my interest in this book is focused on understanding and improving engagement in manufacturing and particularly amongst the "hand-on-parts" workers. I am particularly interested in them because they are the people who provide the value-added work which is the focus of real productivity. Soon enough you will learn that to get the "hands-on-parts" workers engaged we need to get the management team and especially all supervisors engaged, so in the end, it includes ALL workers.

Overall value judgments from bulk data

For example, in Gallup's publication "Q^{12} Meta-Analysis" (Harter, 2006) they discuss their methods and use a database of 681,799 respondents of which only 48,953 are from manufacturing. While almost 49,000 is an extremely large sample, it still is only 7% of the respondents and hence can easily get lost in averages and other generalizations. The largest groups are: "retail" with over 364,000 respondents; "service" with over 114,000 respondents; and "health" with almost 81,000 respondents. The work requirements, support and type of work for these other large groups are so divergent from manufacturing, I have no idea how reflective their overall results and overall conclusions are of manufacturing in general.

More stratified data are helpful

However, as you will recall from Chapter 2, (Figure 2.3) (repeated here), the level of engagement among manufacturing workers is at the lowest level

	ENGAGED 2009	ENGAGED 2012	NOT ENGAGED 2012	ACTIVELY DISENGAGED 2012
Managers, executives, and officials	26%	36%	51%	13%
Professional workers: physicians	*	34%	57%	9%
Professional workers: nurses	*	33%	52%	15%
Professional workers: teachers	*	31%	56%	13%
Professional workers: other categories except physicians, nurses, and teachers	*	30%	55%	15%
Clerical or office workers	27%	30%	51%	19%
Construction or mining workers	29%	30%	52%	18%
Government worker	28%	29%	53%	18%
Sales workers	24%	29%	51%	20%
Installation or repair workers	25%	29%	51%	20%
Service workers	32%	29%	50%	22%
Transportation workers	21%	25%	47%	28%
Manufacturing or production workers	18%	24%	50%	26%

*Sample sizes too small in 2009 for comparison.

Figure 2.3   Engagement by occupation, 2012 survey.

among the occupations they studied in their 2012 Study of the American Workplace (Gallup, 2012).

Using the Gallup Q¹² to make meaningful business comparisons in a plant

I have used the Q^{12} survey and, despite the criticisms by the scholars, in my opinion it stands on its own merits … even if it does not directly or even accurately measure engagement. If it does not accurately measure engagement, it is measuring something very close to engagement, and for today's business purposes, close is more than good enough. However, if you are an academic, that answer may not be adequate, but not being one, that is not my worry.

Good enough for what??

Meaningful business comparisons, that is what it is good enough for. Those are almost exclusively limited to evaluating a given business in a given location and comparing the engagement levels over time as you work to drive engagement up and improve business metrics. By difference, I find it NOT meaningful to:

■ compare engagement of one plant to another, no matter how similar they appear on the surface;
■ compare engagement from one company to another even if they are in the same industry; and
■ certainly, no comparison that crosses an international border makes any sense.

Those concerns are not unique to the Gallup survey. It is common practice for managers to attempt to make these comparisons, and for reasons we will discuss later, comparisons of this nature, are simply not valid, and it makes no difference if the Gallup or any other survey is used; that is a specious use of the data.

Quite frankly, if you wish to compare one company or one location to another, the mathematical comparisons can be made, but there are two problems. First, generally the motivation of those wanting the comparisons will almost always drive behavior that is counterproductive. Second, although you can compare the math and the math is sound, the comparison has a no real meaning. For example, if you have ten grapes in your right hand and four apples in your left, the average is 7 … but seven whats??. The math is sound, but what about the logic? Plants have significant differences that preclude making valid plant-to-plant comparisons.

Why is it good enough??

First, most plants are plagued with very low levels of engagement. For example, in manufacturing, average engagement levels are 25%. Using the Gallup jargon that means that 75% are "not engaged" or are "actively disengaged". Under these circumstances, almost anything you do, including promising to do something, will yield a positive outcome. Simply pay attention to the workers and you will get a positive response; this is the essence of the famous Hawthorne studies. The Gallup survey, as long as it is administered properly, with management follow-up and improvement actions, will do that also. I don't need to read any peer-reviewed articles to conclude that you can make substantial improvements using this survey; I have done it.

Second, even though many people have been critical of the Gallup survey as a mean to assess engagement, I have not seen any criticisms of it as a business improvement tool. Furthermore, besides engagement, there are a number of measures of workplace health, such as job satisfaction, job involvement, organizational commitment, organizational citizenship behavior and job demands-resources model. Each measure shares some characteristics with the others … there is a lot of overlap. At the current level of engagement, a good case could be made that if you implemented any of these programs previously mentioned, employee engagement would rise.

Third, the window of opportunity is very large. We are at 25% engagement in manufacturing and seek to be in the 75% range; that's a 50% target to hit. On the other hand, if we were at 95% engagement and wanted to get to 99%, we would need a tool that focused much more sharply on engagement. Unfortunately, we are not there … so close is good enough for today.

The bottom line

The bottom line is this. I have used the Gallup survey and data and have evaluated workplace engagement. In every case, we have then gone on to make workplace improvements. It works even though the scholars may not like it due to its lack of "purity" in measuring engagement. At the levels of engagement for most businesses, the Gallup Q^{12}, or others, will likely serve your purpose to:

- quantify engagement levels;
- find opportunity areas to address so you can improve engagement; and
- be able to make comparisons, over time, as you work to improve these engagement levels.

That is if – and only if – you do not violate any of the three caveats listed below. (See "Your way out of the crazymaking … Managers beware!!".)

Two big problems – The data and crazymaking

Data quality … No standards, variation gone wild

The data on engagement is just about as un-lean as you can get and still have data – and this leads to what I call crazymaking. First, there is no standardized definition of "engaged", although the scientists seem to have settled on one or two constructs (Kahn's definition and Schaufeli et al. (Delbridge and Soane, 2015)). Here lies a huge problem; while the scholars seem to have settled on one or two constructs, practitioners have dozens if not hundreds of constructs being used. Second, there is no standardized way to quantify engagement. Third, even though some constructs have standard surveys to use, there is no standard to check accuracy. When the survey results show that you are 35% engaged, does it mean 35% or is it REALLY 25% or 45%? Without a standard, without a calibration technique … you simply don't know. Fourth, if all this is not bad enough, the way data is gathered in both surveys is by self-report, which is inextricably connected to feelings with all the attendant fluctuations and temporal variations. The data can change a great deal based on what is happening in the business at any time. To make it even worse, frequently the data is self-reported – via phone. Fifth, survey data is quantified by a number of measurement scales. The Likert 5-point and 7-point scales are the most commonly used. Furthermore, often the answers, rather than being reported numerically, are qualitative reports using scales such as "Never, Sometimes, Most of the time, Always". The result is that, as you work to quantify and improve engagement, these data are not the type you like to have so you can say, "well at least I have a good set of data to start with" – no, not at all.

Strangely enough, it might still be "good enough"

Being a lean geek and weaned in my early years with Chevron on process management, you would think I would be a data purist. Well, I am. However, my larger interest is in teaching others to improve. Normally good data is required for that … however, exactly how good does the data need to be? None of these engagement data would be good enough to use to analyze and improve most processes; not even close. And yet that is exactly what we are doing when we measure engagement. And as I mentioned earlier, the window of opportunity is rather large, so less than perfect data, will certainly work.

Now for the real crazymaking … Comparisons

Knowing they are:

- different constructs;
- measured by different surveys;
- using different data collection methods;
- of self-reported data;
- analyzed using different methods;
- evaluated against divergent criteria,

scientists and manufacturing managers alike still try to compare these engagement results, one against the other. I often see companies compare their levels of engagement to some benchmark, possibly national averages. Comparisons are made to evaluate one facility against another in a given industry and even within a given corporation.

What I have found is that these "comparisons" are fundamentally and seriously flawed … all of them. At the best, they are simply bad evaluations. At the worst they become counterproductive. They promote competition and gaming rather than cooperation and dealing with reality.

Yet people, even the scholars whom I would expect to be a bit more circumspect, are simply dying to make comparisons. For example, I recently read a peer-reviewed article – peer-reviewed, no less – that had these statements:

> "However there is great disagreement surrounding how to define engagement … unless employee engagement can be universally defined and measured, it cannot be managed, nor can it be known if efforts to improve it are working … "

Following this introduction to the ambiguity and the uncertainty cited, the author goes on to say:

> "Evidence from the USA indicates roughly half of all Americans in the workforce are ***not fully engaged*** or they are ***disengaged.*** Another survey found that only 14% of all employees worldwide were ***highly engaged*** in their jobs. The survey also indicated that … the percentages of ***highly engaged***, ***moderately engaged*** and ***actively disengaged*** employees varied considerably.

So, for this concept that the author believes has "great disagreement" on the definition, and then implies they cannot measure it, he came up with at least five sub-categories to further define this thing he can't define in the first place. His original ambiguity of engagement is now ***clarified and classified*** into: not fully engaged; disengaged; highly engaged; moderately engaged; and actively disengaged … and among all this ***clarification and classification***, no one seems to be just engaged with no other modifiers attached. Strange. Now, if this is not crazymaking at its very best, I am afraid to ask what might be worse. It might make a person a bit skeptical … if I weren't such an optimist.

Your way out of the crazymaking … Managers beware!!

As horrible as this sounds, this situation with the engagement data is manageable – if only a little common sense is applied. The point is, how do you reduce the variation such that these data can be used? The answer is this:

■ Carefully determine which survey you wish to use … then stick with it; use just one survey design. This will reduce any survey to survey variation and any within-survey variation. With this caveat, it is possible to do time-based comparisons.

- Second, administer the survey using a standardized method and use a standardized method to analyze and report the results. This will reduce these sources of variation
- Third, when evaluations are made, **only compare a given location to itself over time … this is absolutely critical.** Virtually all managers want to make comparisons across locations and even across business units. You can look at the numbers, but they are meaningless to compare because you are looking at different cultures. Virtually all managers who manage multiple locations desperately want to make these comparisons and they are completely WRONG-HEADED in trying to do so. It is like trying to compare the crime rate in Saudi Arabia to the crime rate in Iceland or the high school graduation rates in Los Angeles to the high school graduation rates in Barcelona or the divorce rate in Antarctica to the divorce rates in New Jersey. You can compare the numbers all you want … but what meaning do they hold?; and what logical conclusions can you draw? Not many that make any sense at all. There is only one valid comparison to make … and that is one facility compared to itself, over time. It will tell you all you need to know. The question you want answered is, "has my culture improved, or not, over time". No comparisons to other facilities, no matter how similar they appear on the surface, are valid. Worse than that, these comparisons, when made, are useless as the very best and counterproductive at the worst.

Gallup supports this position

Gallup, in their 2015/16 "Survey of the American Workplace", state:

> "Employee engagement can vary substantially from organization to organization and team to team. Most of the variation in engagement can be attributed to the way performance is managed locally".

> (Gallup, 2017)

The conundrum

This takes us to the conundrum I see in the field of engagement. That is, "what it is", as a theoretical construct has been widely understood and accepted since 1990. When I speak with managers about employee engagement, they literally salivate at the possibilities, "if only they could cultivate this powerful technique". Furthermore, after almost 30 years of discussions with managers, we are not making much, if any, progress. Based on my interaction with dozens if not hundreds of managers, I can tell you my clients spend more time talking about it – than doing it. It would appear from the Gallup data, that my information is a representative sample, as nationwide improvement is not occurring. This conundrum among the managers wanting this and the consultants selling it seems to be: "If we know what it is and we really want it, then why can't we seem to exploit it?"

First, given the six points above, even though the construct is well understood, the understanding of how to create engagement is missing these six elements in sufficient quantity so as to explain why there is so little progress.

Second, I want to remind you of "my three friends" from the Preface, who seem to be grossly underutilized as we embark on improving engagement.

> "They are: **awareness; initiative; and introspection**.
> Awareness is the gateway quality to enhanced learning, and we all need to learn. Initiative is the gateway quality to improvement, for if we do not act, nothing changes and hence nothing improves. And introspection is the gateway quality for personal change. I find that before any business changes, as a part of it, 'I' first must change. If you are a manager reading this book, all the improvements in your business are contingent upon how you yourself change. There is no larger litmus test to changing a workplace than if the management does or does not change. My three friends are explained by quotes from three famous people:

> - 'Men stumble over the truth from time to time, but most pick themselves up and hurry off as if nothing happened' Sir Winston Churchill.
> - 'Opportunity is missed by most people because it is dressed in overalls and looks like work' Thomas Edison.
> - 'In the choice between changing one's mind and proving there's no reason to do so, most people get busy on the proof' John Kenneth Galbraith".

So how do we break the conundrum?

Or, more specifically, "are we going to change?" There are three basic rules I follow with change management. For the clear majority of us, we first need to wrap our heads around the need for change, which means we need to get an intellectual understanding; I call this head engagement. Second, we need to get people to want to change. Since this deals with acceptance at the motivational level, I call this heart engagement. For people to embark on a change, they need both a head and a heart engagement.

Regarding head engagement, we have discussed the concept and construct of engagement as well as the current levels and the list of benefits to be obtained for not only the company and its stockholders but the customers and employees as well. We will discuss the concept of engagement even more, but by now you should have a grasp on both what it is and what we have done to destroy it from the days of the cottage industries. Even though this may not yet completely satisfy your understanding of engagement at the intellectual level, it surely should whet your appetite. However, when it comes to creating a fully engaged workforce, the head engagement is the lesser of the issues. As is the case with virtually all cultural change issues, the limiting factor is the heart engagement. So, whether you are a supervisor, manager or C-suite resident, it is a now a simple question, "do you want to create a fully engaged workforce?" It is a simple, up or down choice … a yes or no answer.

■ If your answer is "yes", then read on and we will guide you to the third rule of creating change; we will give you the path to follow. If you are the leader of this initiative, you will recall that the first – and the defining – aspect of leadership is that they have a vision and can articulate it into a plan which you can understand. We will take you on an intellectual and behavioral journey that will allow you to not only achieve improved plant performance, improved customer satisfaction but also improve employee morale, health and well-being. The science of creating a fully engaged workforce, as well as the path there, are known and will be explained. Achieving a fully engaged workforce is no longer a technological mystery. The rest of this book provides that plan.

■ If your answer is "no", then put this book down and address a different element so you can improve your group, plant or corporation.

A simple choice ...

It is now a simple choice ... do you want to? – or not? It is the simplest of questions, "exactly what are you prepared to do?"

Chapter Summary ... As we looked at engagement from a bottom-up perspective, we see that the scholars and the practitioners have different perspectives. However, the commonalities they share are all major and important points. Unfortunately, when both positions are integrated, we find that there are six major points missed. A great portion of this book addresses these six points. Of interest to those working to improve engagement at their facility is the question of how to measure engagement. Although there are methods, they lack the normal qualities we like to have in measurement systems, such as accuracy. However, if we use the same survey over time and just compare one facility to itself, the issues of measurement variation largely disappear. The use of facility-to-facility comparisons are not valid and should not be used even though managers continually wish to do this, which we rightly call "crazymaking". The Gallup data, although it is very controversial among the scholars, has broad application and has proven itself to be very useful when used properly. Finally, we discussed the business conundrum; that is, if we know what it is and know how to improve it and want to improve it, we are left with one obvious question, "why don't we just get busy and do it?? It is then reduced to a simple choice, "do you or do you not wish to improve engagement?".

What's next?? The perspectives of the scientists and the practitioners, while very useful, seem complicated. Maybe we can find a simple, explanatory metaphor to guide us? It is to that we now turn.

Chapter 5

Toward a Practical Definition

Aim of this Chapter ... is to explain the concept of an "engaged worker" in correct yet more easily understood terms than those used by the scientific community. We will examine the concept of engagement using several examples. Finally, we will develop a practical metaphor so the concept of engagement can be more easily understood, remembered and managed.

A simple working definition

As I discuss the theory and practice of worker engagement with managers, their reaction is odd. They seemingly have a clear concept of what engagement is; at least, they claim they can find it when they see it. However, rarely can they give a practical definition. I get descriptions like: hard-working; nose-to the-grindstone; will do what is needed; puts in lots of extra time. Most descriptions pay close attention to the time and effort people put in, and often their model of engagement is nothing more than "hard-working" or "dedicated". Although that is part of the definition of engagement, it misses key points.

When I discuss the definition given by Kahn, most don't resonate with it at all. On the other hand, engagement as defined by Schaufeli et al. seems to click with them, but only a little.

> **ON MANAGEMENT**
>
> "Most of what we call management consists of making it difficult for people to get their work done".
>
> (Peter Drucker)

To discuss engagement with others, especially managers, I needed a simpler working definition. It is to that we now turn, but first, an example of engagement in action.

An example of "engagement in action"

Policies, rules, procedures and approvals galore tend to reduce engagement; unnecessary ones, kill engagement

In my time with Chevron, I found I worked with a company that had a rule, a procedure or a policy, replete with numerous approvals, for everything. Initially, as a young engineer, I found this very comforting. It made it easy to design a foundation for a vessel or for sizing the wiring, the starting circuitry and switchgear for a 500 hp motor installation, for example. "Follow the rules and procedures" was the advice, and even if there were flaws in the design, at least it was not your fault; and you would not get in trouble.

Unfortunately, once you got beyond design engineer and became a supervisor or a manager, dealing with people ... all of a sudden there were no longer so many specific rules and procedures but rather we had policies to guide us. The problem was, these policies were written for the middle-of-the-road occurrences and did not cover many real-life human circumstances you often encountered. Unfortunately, the application of many of these policies was expected to be by-the-letter, with no deviations. So, this put virtually every supervisor or manager in a bind. You could follow the procedure and be safe, which frequently would force you to do something that was less than optimal from an HR standpoint and sometimes even cruel, thereby irritating even the most reasonable of employees. Alternatively, you could step out and try to do right by the employee; however, this ran the risk of catching the wrath of your boss and HR as well. Most supervisors, out of self-preservation, chose the low road of safety and comfort. On the other hand, I got in trouble a lot; that is, when I got caught.

A case study – Policies, rules and procedures ... Or engagement

In my first supervisory assignment with Chevron, I was asked to be the head draftsman. I took over a large group of poorly managed and poorly supervised, yet highly talented, workers. They had been emotionally beaten down by others in the refinery, even their own management. As part of our work, I fully intended to upgrade the drafting room facilities. Quite frankly, I wanted to move fast as I saw this as a key element in changing the culture. I did not want to be slowed down by some of the bureaucracy I knew we would have to face just to get the work done. To upgrade the drafting room, we would be faced with complying with *The Office Manual*. This was an antiquated manual that described in excruciating detail all the criteria for all offices. And I decided I did not want to deal with it. Down the hall was an engineering technician we had recently hired. He was French Canadian and his prior job was as a locksmith. Henri would frequently look me up for advice as his boss was too busy checking his stock portfolio while preparing for retirement; hence, Henri and I had a great relationship. One evening, when we were both working late, I asked Henri if he would help me. He was totally non-plussed when I asked him to pick the office door locks and the cabi-

HOW MANY RULES??

I find that too many companies have too many policies, way too many. I have no idea how many rules, procedures and policies are the right numbers to have. But when you have a *"**not engaged**"* workforce as we had, it **appeared** that we needed lots of rules, procedures and policies.

Although it appeared that the low levels of engagement created the need for the proliferation of rules, procedures and policies, this was not the case. Rather, people came to work engaged and then the bureaucracy embodied in the rules, policies and procedures, literally squelched this intrinsic engagement.

I have come to learn that there is a strong and inverse relationship between bureaucracy and engagement. More bureaucracy creates less engagement – period.

net locks to the library and my boss's office, where the only two office manuals were kept. I picked up the manuals, stored them in my office until we were done and we never had to worry about them at all. When it came time to get the drawings and the contracts approved, I made sure I got the approvals on Friday afternoon when my boss was preparing to go to his mountain cabin. You could always get fast signatures on Friday afternoon. He asked about *The Office Manual* and I told him (it was not a lie; well, maybe a small fracturing of the truth) that the only two copies I knew of were supposed to be in his office and the library. We could not find them, but I assured him that the draftsman who prepared these drawings did not violate any of the rules in *The Office Manual*. Pressed for time, he signed everything.

We got the renovations done, and the chief engineer came by to view the remodeling. Immediately he took me to task when he saw the carpet runners we had installed to cut down on the noise. He chastised me and told me to take up the carpeting; he said it was not allowed for areas other than management offices. I told him this was not carpeting but rather more like a throw rug, which was allowed for certain locations. In fact, it was allowed, but mostly just for the women's bathrooms; but it was allowed (again, not a lie; I was just exercising a certain moral flexibility with the truth). Regardless, I went on and told him that we have a unique problem with all the traffic and the resultant noise hindering concentration and productivity. He wasn't buying it until we showed him that the runners were rubber backed and each night the janitor vacuumed them and once a month the cleaning service rolled them up and sent them out for cleaning.

No sooner had we sold him on this than the refinery manager showed up. This guy had a giant stick up his ___ and acted like there was no rule, no procedure nor any policy he did not like. And the more restrictive and the more prescriptive – the better he liked it. He said the carpeting would have to go. At which time, the chief engineer chimed in, saying very eloquently, "No Thron, I checked it out myself and there is an exception to the rule of carpeting as long as the carpeting is in high-traffic areas and is removable for ease of cleaning. They followed *The Office Manual* to the letter". Of course, he was lying through his teeth, but he delivered it in a way to make any high-pressure salesman proud. The refinery manager just grunted "OK" and left. My mentor then looked at me, winked and told me to watch my step as he followed the refinery manager out the door. I listened carefully but continued to fracture the rules … and do the right things. Which is what he really wanted.

Now, the upshot of this was that my job was to change the culture in the drafting room and to see if we had the talent to supply both maintenance and construction supervisors to the refinery. In the last 15 years, only one draftsman had been promoted to positions outside the drafting room. And the remodeling was a key factor in changing the culture, and change the culture we did. Soon enough, the maintenance manager and the manager of major projects were interviewing our draftsmen, and in the next 2 years, six draftsmen were promoted to supervisory positions.

Make no mistake about it, those promotions were made possible by the way we did this project to remodel the drafting room and the way we ran the drafting support function. We modeled the right behaviors in that we were high energy; we focused on the critical needs; we imaginatively solved many problems and most importantly we got the job done … even if we did not follow all the rules. You might say we were "eclectically compliant". I used to tell them, "there is no rule you cannot break for the right reasons, and I'll have your back", and fracture a few rules we did, but soon enough we got known for "getting it done". Both of my lead draftsmen, myself and all the draftsmen were highly engaged and we completed a project that was estimated to take 12 months at a budgeted cost of $200,000 in less than 4 months for under $80,000. Now, if that were my money and my time … that is what I would have wanted. And guess what? We treated it as if it were our money and our time – and they certainly were our people. (An editorial comment. I would be remiss if I did not put a qualifier here. This "fracturing" of the rules was not cavalier, not at all. However, had we been questioned carefully on many things, I would have gotten in trouble, at some level. I don't want to recommend you do this lightly. I was also single at the time.)

Which takes me to a simpler … yet more descriptive definition of engagement

Engaged people do the right things, in the right way, at the right time and for the right reasons

Does that sound like the drafting room revamp; doing the right things, in the right way, at the right time and for the right reasons?? If it doesn't, it should. We needed to change the culture and we could not wait 3 weeks for drawing review, followed by 5 weeks for the appropriation request approval, and we certainly could not go through the typical tortures of the archaic bidding process, often taking 12 weeks, just to get bids and then another 2 weeks for quotation review and approval and then waiting another 2 weeks to start work. We found a logical, safe and business-like way around these time obstacles and completed all the requirements – plus got the actual construction done – in 16 weeks. And all we did was completely ignore the redundant bureaucracy. Rather, we got the job done properly, following all legal, safety, engineering and accounting practices.

And, quite frankly, my boss was a stickler for the details, as was my boss's boss. However, three layers up the organization, my boss's boss's boss, was not. He was a "get-the-job-done" type of guy, and that is exactly why he winked at me and told me to "watch my step". He knew we were "engaged" and what he meant with his wink was, "keep doing the right things and don't get caught", and we did. For sure we were doing it "at the right time" and for the "right reasons", as we wanted to change the culture and do it right now! However, when you get to the "***how*** we were doing it", probably the entire hierarchy at the refinery would have scolded me. We followed all legal standards and did nothing unsafe or of low quality. Unfortunately … exactly ***"how"*** you are supposed to do things in a business like Chevron's is "to follow the bureaucracy", no matter how inefficient and ineffective the rules, practices, procedures and policies might be. Quite frankly, if you are more interested in promoting your career over "getting the work done", marching in step with the bureauracracy is the only safe way to protect yourself.

All too often, it is this bureaucracy that literally steals the very heart and soul from workers and causes disengagement.

So what's wrong with that definition? … Sounds pretty good to me

Doing the right things, in the right way, at the right time and for the right reasons is a good definition – except for one thing. How do you define "right" in each case? That is a little too iffy for me and begs for a more explicit definition, and that is precisely what we will address next.

A better metaphor for engagement

To create and put this better metaphor in context, let me first give you two vignettes.

First, the refinery manager and my discussion with a colleague

Before writing my last book, *Lean Refining* (Wilson, 2015), I interviewed dozens of people in the oil industry. One particularly helpful interview was with a refining consultant who I had known for over 30 years. During the interview, he asked me, "First thing in the morning, do you know what is on the mind of the typical refinery manager in a major oil company?" Not knowing where he was going with this, I said "No" and waited. He went on, "They have three major concerns. First, 'Has there been an accident, environmental release or major upset?' Or, as my colleague put it, "should I expect a call from a federal agency, the union or the home office?", Second is, 'What meetings do I have to attend today?' and third, 'How is my bonus calculation doing?' What he is not doing is treating the stockholder's money as if it were his own".

I thought about this, and I can safely say that I have seen many plant and divisional managers with precisely the same priorities. It is a long way from: "doing the right things, in the right way, at the right time for the right reasons" and the best you can say about this example is that the manager was engaged in his own personal interest, and not engaged in his role as a plant manager.

Second, leading with intent

We teach a concept called "leading with intent". We find many people and businesses suffer from being "initiative challenged" and routinely place themselves in "wait until told" mode. Unfortunately, the majority of these times, they really know what to do as a next step but either they lack the confidence or maybe they have been scolded just once too often. Hence, they hesitate. **Leading with intent** consists of following the four work rules, which are:

1. **No one can wait until told**; all must be working or seeking assistance from their supervisor.
2. **No one can ask what to do**; after all, they are the experts in their work
3. **The worker must state what he intends to do**; being experts in their area, who might have a better idea
4. **The intent must be accompanied with sufficient detail** so the supervisory can respond with a pithy statement such as, "Well done, sounds like you have covered all the bases", or "I agree".

During supervisory training, when we teach the supervisors the four work rules so they may teach their direct reports, we also teach them how to "coach through questioning". As part of this, normally in a role-playing format, we teach them some of the good questions to ask. Good questions are open-ended questions which will "guide" the worker to think toward the desired behaviors. When the worker gets stuck at work rule three, the most powerful question is: "If this were your company, what would you do?". We want them to think, "If this were my money, how would I spend it". And "If our owner or our customer came by and asked me 'Why?' would I feel comfortable explaining my actions?" By pursuing answers to questions like that, they will be guided to act in consort with our Mission, Vision and our Values. An alternate question might be, "What would you expect me to recommend?"

Do you think those questions might get the worker to do the right thing, in the right way, at the right time for the right reasons? To be blunt, it is surprisingly effective in a variety of ways.

The metaphor … An engaged worker will act like she owns the business

Does that sound like any small business entrepreneurs you might know?? I know many and they are giving of themselves, not only physically but also intellectually and emotionally, to their business, 100% of the time. Those people, who act like they own the business, are the best metaphor of engaged workers I can find. That's my opinion, but just how good a metaphor is this? To be a good metaphor, first, it must be accurate, and second, it must be useful.

Regarding the accuracy of this metaphor

Do those people who own their own business exhibit the qualities described by Kahn and Schaufeli et al.? Recall Kahn's definition of engaged workers:

> "… they employ their personal selves". By "employing their personal selves" he goes on to say that they express themselves physically, cognitively and emotionally. Kahn's research suggested that engagement is the personal expression of "self-in-role"; someone is engaged when they can express their "authentic self" and to invest themselves personally into their job.
>
> (Kahn, 1990)

And Schaufeli et al. said:

> "Engagement is defined as a positive, fulfilling, work-related state of mind, that is characterized by vigor, dedication and absorption. Vigor is characterized by high levels of energy and mental resilience while working, the willingness to invest effort in one's work, and the persistence even in the face of difficulties. Dedication is characterized by a sense of significance, enthusiasm, inspiration,

pride, and challenge. Absorption is characterized by being fully concentrated and deeply engrossed in one's work".

(Schaufeli et al., 2002)

Do the small business owners you know take their business very person-ally and are they viewed as dedicated, invigorated and totally absorbed in their work? I can give this description of small business owners a resound-ing positive reply and say yes, that describes them well. Of all the categories of workers, next to volunteers, I do not know a harder working, dedicated and involved set of people than small business owners. However, do we have any data to support my effusive statement?

What data do we have to support this metaphor??

In very small companies, I find engagement much more prevalent amongst **all** workers; guess what? So did Gallup!! (Figure 5.1)

This may not be proof, but it sure is compelling evidence. Not only does the percentage of engaged employees of small businesses show an increase, there is also a drop in the percentage of disengaged employees, just as you would think. Finally, both the increase in engagement and the decrease in disengagement are dramatic in magnitude. What we see is not a subtle but

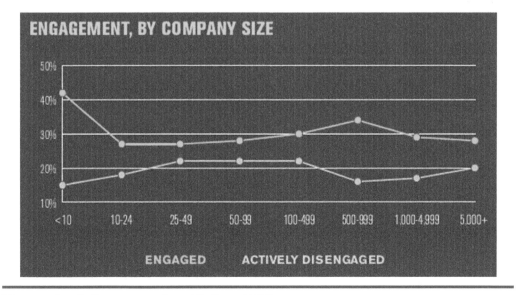

Figure 5.1   **Gallup survey data (Gallup, 2012).**

a pronounced change in engagement when we compare the small businesses to the large one. That is totally consistent with our metaphor.

Just how useful is this metaphor??

To be useful, it needs to make sense to almost anyone. In small firms, everyone's job is bigger and they typically "wear more hats". As a direct result of this, they know more about the business and are more intellectually engaged. Again, as a direct result of being smaller they can "see" and "feel" what is happening in the business in terms of sales, profits and customer

> **PARADIGM SHIFT NO. 2**
> Management must rid themselves of the mental model that engagement is synonymous with hard-working and has only a physical component. It is more than that. It involves a physical, emotional and intellectual commitment. Engaged workers behave as if they owned the business.
> (A complete list of paradigms in order of importance, is listed in Appendix D, this is no. 2.)

response; hence, they logically are more emotionally engaged. Finally, because they are more connected to the product, more connected to the customer and more connected to each other, there is a final dynamic, that of feeling like a "family", further enhancing engagement. In fact, this category of businesses is often referred to as "small family businesses", even if they are not staffed entirely by a single family.

It passes nicely the two tests of accuracy and usefulness. It is a metaphor we frequently use in our teaching and consulting and as such has passed the test of practical functionality. In fact, you will recall we use this metaphor as we teach managers the concept of "leading with intent". (You may want to reread that a few pages back.) I have always liked this metaphor, and I suspect it will help you as you work toward getting a fully engaged workforce at your facility.

The simplicity of the metaphor; the complexity of achieving it

However, there is a deeper and more personal topic I'd like to discuss as we wrap up this chapter. Specifically, if it is such a simple concept, why do we need to work so hard to get employee engagement? Why is it such a struggle to get them to act like it's their own business? Recall that my hypothesis is that employees came to work ready to be engaged … but soon enough they are not engaged. This lack of engagement is neither desirable nor intended, but make no mistake about it, their disengagement is a natural response of the workforce that is caused by a certain style of management behaviors. The rest of this book is dedicated to just those topics.

Chapter Summary … One of the benefits of a good metaphor is that you can use it to explain a concept and people can immediately grasp what you are talking about. It simplifies the discussion and takes it from the conceptual level and puts it in simple everyday language that people can relate to. So doing the right things, in the right way, at the right time for the right reasons takes you a step closer to explaining the behavior of the engaged worker. However, the word "right" has many meanings depending upon your values. On the other hand, *acting like they own the business*, takes the metaphor to a new level of use as almost everyone can relate to this. Personally, I have found this to be a very useful metaphor in discussing the topic of engagement with others as it not only clarifies what we need but furthers that understanding as well.

What's next?? The foundation of engagement is management. Want to learn about Management 1.0, 2.0 and 3.0? Go to Chapter 6

MANAGEMENT BASICS

In this section, we discuss the absolutely critical role the management team plays in creating and sustaining a fully engaged workforce. In Chapter 6, we will discuss the evolution, or lack thereof, from Management 1.0, through Management 2.0 to elite Management 3.0. In Chapter 7, we first explore why most of management's efforts to create engagement are counterproductive and create disengagement instead. This is largely due to lack of understanding of the concept of engagement, lack of understanding of management's role and the lack of understanding of key motivational concepts. Further, we enumerate the two skill sets that all managers must learn, the skills of leading and the skills of managing, and show that the Six Skills of Lean Leadership are a practical solution to that issue. Finally, we discuss the critical skill of becoming a good supervisor, so you can be a better manager, and acquiring the skill set of the situational leader.

Part II contains two chapters:

Chapter 6

Management 1.0, 2.0 and 3.0

Aim of this Chapter ... to explain the role that mental models have in shaping management behavior and, hence, in shaping the culture. Also, if you wish to become a world class supplier, the role the manager must play has changed dramatically over the last 30 or 40 years. We will discuss the evolution of management styles and what has caused those changes. Finally, we will explain Management 3.0 and why it contains the key elements that are needed to create a fully engaged workforce.

The importance of the manager

As we discuss the topics of business success and the engagement of the workforce, it is hardly possible to understate the importance of the manager. Disregarding certain non-competitive situations such as holding a monopoly or some protection provided by either patents or fortuitous geography, good management will turn a plant into a more profitable venture, while bad management will do just the opposite. It is as close to a litmus test as you can get. In a competitive environment, good management leads to success, bad management leads to failure. **It is an underpinning of this entire book that the key factor to success or failure and the key factor to achieving engagement – or not – is based on the quality of the management.**

The largest problem I see with management attempts to improve engagement is "what" they try to work on. They spend way too much time on adding "frou-frou" items. Things like the "employee of the month", which is normally a popularity contest which defies statistical justification. Or painting the lunch room, letting employees pick their own uniforms or even having a daycare for single parents. Some of these may be good efforts to improve employee retention and in that regard may have merit. However, when it comes to achieving engagement, they completely miss the mark. At work, as other places, people want to: demonstrate competence; experience autonomy; development community; and provide a meaningful service to their employer. They want to satisfy their intrinsic needs and that is the key to achieving engagement.

The popularity of many of these "frou-frou" items is that they have two qualities that appeal to immature management teams.

■ First, they are easily done, uniformly liked and sound good. It is like giving a 6-year-old candy, with the same adult involvement … and the same short-term results

CULTURES … THE STARTING POINT

Mental models, paradigms and stereotypes are all generalizations we use in everyday life. They guide our information gathering and our decision making. They are a form of thinking and talking shorthand. When broadly understood and accepted, they provide psychic economy. For example, when I speak of an "open culture", my mental model is one where: data is readily available to everyone; discussions are open, frank and honest; and information is widely shared. It is much easier to use the use the term "open culture" than to redefine that term each time it is used. However, it only works if we have the same mental model for "open culture".

When we have a shared set of mental models, discussion, problem solving and decision making is much easier; this is psychic economy. However, mental models, paradigms and stereotypes have two problems; at least.

■ First, as generalizations they are not always correct. Tall guys make better basketball players; that's generally but not always true.
■ Second, they are largely unconscious. As such, they can guide our behavior, and we may not even be aware of it.

Hence, they can control us and we will make unconscious errors. We will gather biased data and make incorrect decisions. And just where do our mental models begin?? … in our beliefs, that's where. As such, our beliefs then dictate "just how we do things around here", which is the operational definition of our culture.

■ Second, the management team themselves have very little to do except supplying some resources, and, even better, while supplying these "things", they themselves do not need to change. This is a little like buying your teenager a car so you might have a better relationship with him or her.

Strong, effective management; where does it start?

The essence of strong, effective – or weak, ineffective – management largely flows from the belief systems the managers hold. And by no small margin, the managers at the top of the management pyramid are far and away the most influential. It is their belief system that literally drives the entire management system. Their belief systems are reflected in the paradigms, often called mental models, they both use and expect others to use. For example, a common mental model we need

WORD HAVE MEANINGS; MEANINGS MATTER

Many people believe that honesty is a synonym for integrity. It is not. Integrity has come to mean honesty because so many people misunderstand the word "integrity" and misuse it. Words will often change meaning due to misuse. Unfortunately, this is quite common, at least in American English. Integrity, integrate and the word integer all have the common root in the Latin word *integrare*, which means "to make whole". For example, in math, the integers are not fractions, they are whole numbers. The word integrity means "state or quality of being complete; undivided; unbroken" (Webster's New Collegiate Dictionary). Likewise, a management system that is integrated is one that is whole. All that is needed is included; the parts are properly connected into an effective and efficient system that has a specific purpose. In the specific case of a management system, its purpose is the execution of the company's Mission, Vision and Value System.

to overcome is the definition of what we call "a problem". In many businesses – most actually – problems are viewed as something undesirable and should be avoided. Consequently, and unfortunately, all too often, problems are intentionally hidden. If that is your mental model, you will never be able to implement lean, because lean is all about finding and fixing problems.

The strength of mental models, of how they end up determining not only actions but destinies for people and businesses alike, is reflected in the following logic attributed to Mahatma Gandhi:

"Your beliefs become your thoughts,
Your thoughts become your words,
Your words become your actions,
Your actions become your habits,
Your habits become your values,
Your values become your destiny".

This is true not only in business but in virtually all aspects of life as well. While you may not have total control over all the variables in your life, you can have a very large impact on them. It is as my mentor, Toshi Amino, once told me, "Lonnie, you can believe that you can or you can believe that you can't; and you will probably be right". Your success – or failures – be it in business or another aspect of your life is greatly affected by your initial beliefs; that is where it all starts.

THE LITMUS TEST

"It's all about management ... the rest is just details".
(Author Unknown)

Management evolution

There were harbingers, wise ones

A variety of national and world-wide factors have created a need for changes in American management. Back in the '50s and the '60s, academics like Abraham Maslow, Peter Drucker and Douglas McGregor were writing about the need for American businesses to improve and especially the need for a new, improved style of management. Later, in the '70s and '80s, others were writing and they too were focused on the needed changes in American management. Some of those authors included Edgar Schein, John Kotter, Chris Argyris, Anthony Athos, Richard Pascale, and there were even more books and articles published by Peter Drucker during this period. Additionally, many new practitioners joined the list of those stating a need for management change. These practitioners include Dr. W. Edwards Deming, Taiichi Ohno, Shigeo Shingo, Kaoru Ishikawa, Robert "Doc" Hall, Richard Schonberger and a litany of others.

The most direct harbingers

Among all these authors, while writing about the behaviors of the management team, most could best be described as polite. Most of these authors were also consultants. Considering that consulting pays much better than selling books for most of us and "telling it like it is" is often not conducive to getting consulting contracts, it is common to see that many of the management weaknesses which were seen were not written about in a direct, matter-of-fact style, but often soft-pedaled by the time the book hit the market. If that was not enough, I am sure editors would say things like, "Maybe we should not be so critical of the very people who we hope will buy this book". The net effect was a watering down of the facts. Yet some authors were more direct, and although their information may not be as well received by the audience of their book, it was nonetheless more sincere – and more accurate. These include the writings of Deming as well as Athos and Pascale.

Dr. W. Edwards Deming

Dr. Deming was very clear on this point when he wrote *Out of the Crisis* and published his 14 Obligations of Management. Point No. 2 is:

> "Adopt the new philosophy. We are in a new economic age.
> Western management must awaken to the challenge, must learn
> their responsibilities, and take on leadership for change".

When you parse these sentences, the words sound harsh. "Western management must awaken", he implies they are asleep or otherwise unaware. Further, they must "awaken to the challenge". He could have said to "get their head out of the sand, look around; the world has changed", and if Dr. Deming had been speaking with you, one-on-one, he just might have. The next phrase is my favorite, "learn their responsibilities"; the implication is that not only are they being irresponsible they are unaware that they are being irresponsible. That is one short step from calling them dense and uninformed. He ends with "take on leadership for change", implying they are neither leading nor changing. It is no wonder Dr. Deming was frequently unpopular among American managers. On the other hand, based on my experiences, I would characterize his writings as "telling it like it is". I took seminars from Dr. Deming and spoke to him on many occasions. I found him to be direct and borderline rude but to the point and seldom wrong.

His books continue to sell and every year his writings are quoted more often. I fully expect his writings will become stronger and more prophetic as time passes.

Richard Pascale and Anthony Athos

The second very direct harbinger was the book *The Art of Japanese Management* (1981) by Pascale and Athos. They did extensive research on Japanese methods and compared them to American methods, not only looking at results but managerial processes and managerial styles as well. From this research, they were able to focus on key differences in not only results but methods. They came to several conclusions, but their overriding observation was a compelling and penetrating statement, which was:

> "Japan is doing more than a little right. And our hypothesis is that a big part of that 'something' has only a little to do with such techniques as its quality circles and lifetime employment. In this book, we will argue that ***a major reason for the superiority of the Japanese is their managerial skill***".
>
> (emphasis mine, Athos, 1981)

Pascale and Athos get right to the point. Good management will yield superior results; no beating around the bush. I call this the litmus test and it is a major underpinning of this book. Although their book was written almost 40 years ago, I find the discussion topics and recommendations to be the very prescription that many businesses still need today. The "major reason" as stated by Athos and Pascale, is not music to the ears of managers, but it still is a tune they desperately need to hear.

My position on these harbingers

Based on my 20 years in business management, my 29 years consulting, working with large and small firms, I find the wisdom of the words of Athos and Pascale and especially those of Dr. Deming to paint a compelling picture. First, if a business is succeeding or a business is failing there is no better place to look than the quality of its management. Second, the better Japanese firms have prospered largely because they have a superior management system. Third, we can make huge strides in business performance, especially in creating a fully engaged workforce, by stealing the best methods of Japanese management. It is a key premise of this book, and will be stated many times, that the litmus test to create an engaged workforce is to ratchet up our style of management and create a true cultural transformation; and we can creatively steal many wonderful ideas from the Japanese.

Then there was management lethargy, indifference and resistance to change until …

Most of this advice went unheeded and only later, much later, was it acted upon; if at all. This advice was not acted upon because residents of the C-suite took heed to what those people said; rather, they paid heed because others, most notably the Japanese, started intruding on their markets and stealing their sales and shrinking their profits. Competition had hit these complacent US managers squarely between the eyes. However, before there were able to summon up the courage to change, they first exhibited denial in a variety of forms. Rather than accept reality, they first tried to ignore these new competitors. When this failed to work, they vigorously tried trade embargos and other legislative tools to retain sales and margins. However, because their new Japanese competitors were supplying better quality products at a lower price, this effort to legislate away competition – was a losing battle. Finally, there was no ignoring the fact of this Japanese presence and their power as they chewed away at the margins and profits of their American competitors. From a consumer standpoint, the first major industries affected were in the field of electronics; soon enough, RCA and Sylvania were replaced by Sony, Toshiba and others. That really did not spur many US businesses from their lethargic, business-as-usual management style. However, when the biggest and the most sacred of the world of business, US automobile manufacturing and sales, was relegated to second-rate status on quality and price, the Western managers, finally, stood up and took notice. In addition, the management advice they had so militantly ignored and denied now came back to roost. It started to dawn on American management that they would need to change if they wanted to survive. The amazing part of the Japanese intrusion into American markets is ironic. The irony of all of this was that the Japanese were using management and production methods they had been taught by Americans; the same advice that American managers had ignored. The simple fact is that the Japanese listened to the aforementioned harbingers and changed – the American managers did neither. Up to this point in time, the mid-'80s, the predominant Western management style was Management 1.0.

What is Management 1.0?

I call Management 1.0, Results Management. The predominant belief is that the only thing that matters, is the results, the bottom line results. The talk is centered on the pronoun "I" and the common noun used is "results". The most common phrases were "I want results" and "How do your numbers look?". The management style bristles with directness as senior management will say, "I don't care how you get it, but I want results". Others are even colder, will say, "I don't care if you coddle them or you kick ass; I want to see improvements in the bottom line". The relationships in a Management 1.0 system are characterized by dependence. A few people create and enforce a loosey-goosey

> ### WHAT IS KAIZEN?
>
> Kaizen in simple jargon means an improvement effort. The basic principle in kaizen is to make an improvement over a standard. For example, a production line's rate has deteriorated over time from 100 pcs/hr and demand can no longer be met. Hence, people are then assigned to improve the rate. This is NOT kaizen, this is maintenance, which is restoring things to original condition. If, however, the standard rate was 100 pcs/hr and by removing a bottleneck the line can now produce to 125 pcs/hr, the effort expended to improve over the old standard was kaizen.
>
> If there is no standard, there can be no kaizen

rules system that can change on a whim and everyone else is supposed to hop-to. Everyone is dependent upon this select small group for directions which are extremely short-term and frequently inconsistent in nature. They are doing whatever is necessary to make short-term augmentation of the bottom line. In this system based on dependence, long-term planning, and even hope, are merely far-flung fantasies. Consistent with this system of beliefs, the talk in Management 1.0 is all about dollars and cents. Everything is reduced to bottom-line impact; sometimes even quality, safety and morale are analyzed on a cost to benefits ratio. The entire value system is based on bottom-line performance. Customers at the very best don't count and at the worst are the enemy. Employees are a cost to be minimized. Suppliers are only a necessary nuisance and are routinely browbeaten and threatened to get costs down. Every value-driven decision is made with an intense and laser-like focus on the bottom line. In addition, the financials are almost always short-term in nature. Long-term thinking is often viewed as pie-in-the-sky. Management talk is all about financials, and as a manager, regardless of your level in the pyramidal power structure, you need to know the financial impact of everything you do. If you want to implement some training, you will need to show an immediate bottom-line impact or likely it will not be permitted. It's all about money and it's all about "right now". Successful managers are those who can routinely meet or beat their monthly budget. If you meet the budget, all is well, everything is good, life is wonderful. If you don't meet the budget, even if there is a sound rational explanation, nothing is right, absolutely nothing. Worse yet, if you don't meet the budget not only is the budget fouled up, but you, as an individual, are fouled up. You can hear the top management say, "Maybe we don't have the right guy in there". And make no mistake, when the sacred budget is not met, they will change out the manager, sometimes several times, never recognizing the obvious logical flaw in simply replacing the managers. Consequently, to save face, if not their career, managers become very "creative" in accounting practices and are good

THE PROCESS ZEALOTS

Since Management 1.0 was deficient in many ways, and directly connected to Drucker's Management by Objectives (MBOs), many people were prone to discard all of MBO and create a system they called Management by Means – which focused intently on the Means, the process. Many process zealots believed so strongly in process management, that is, "the right process will create the right results", that they resisted even checking on the results. However, if you create Management by Means – only – without taking care to evaluate the results, you are in real trouble. First, businesses make money because of the results; this fact cannot be ignored nor minimized. Second, the only way to tell if the process is working well is the "Check" process in the Plan, Do, Check and Act (PDCA) process cycle; and this is the check on the **results**. So, logically there is no best process, unless it creates the best results. Consequently, those professing this "Management by Means-Only" philosophy are in danger of throwing the baby out with the bathwater.

at pencil-whipping the data. Sometimes the correlation of budget analyses to reality is purely coincidental at best, often "unicornish". Meeting the budget is clearly the litmus test of success for Management 1.0. The management style is usually hard-driving, my-way-or-the-highway, very directive, myopic management with little delegation. Predictably, there is a definite destiny for businesses employing Management 1.0; they will do OK until the competition gets better or the environment changes. Unfortunately, both are certainties. Predictably, when the competition gets better and when other changes occur, this type of inflexible, top-down management style is ineffective in navigating the changing waters. Faced with these two eventualities, those employing Management 1.0 styles predictably make changes that transfer money quickly to the bottom line but damage the business irreparably for the long term. Their primary weapons are three-fold; first, delay any work that does not have an immediate bottom-line impact, for example, maintenance and training; second, implement manpower layoffs; and third, reorganize, which is just manpower reductions by another name. Both layoffs and reorganizations are euphemistically and energetically renamed rationalizations or right-sizing. Using these three techniques, they are making the management moves that require the skills of a 6th-grade math student. Although this Management 1.0 has long outlived its usefulness, it is still present in many businesses; none of which are high performing and certainly none that are world class. They predictably have engagement levels in the 10–25% range, seldom reaching industry averages. However, for those wishing to mature in the world of management, Management 2.0 is there for the asking.

What is Management 2.0?

I call Management 2.0, Process Management. The predominant belief in Management 2.0 is that the right process will create the right result. The talk has changed, and the pronoun of importance is "we". The most important nouns are now, "process, process capability, quality, teams, problem solving and delivery". Best of all, the basis for the relationships among the people has changed; efforts are focused on becoming independent. There are now meaningful goals and objectives that are deployed and delegated with a sense of local ownership. Metrics are measured and acted upon, and a rewards and recognition system based on performance is employed. The belief system and the language has changed; there is a completely new language used, with new terms galore. The talk and the resultant behaviors in Management 2.0 are all about: customers; suppliers; flow charts; standardized work processes; the Six Questions of Continuous Improvement; Yamazumi charts to codify wastes; muda; 5S; three-part inventories;

heijunka; kaizen events; Six Sigma problem solving; visual management and production-by-hour boards; metrics; planning; statistical process control; measurement system analysis; designed experimentation; Cps and Cpks. It is also about problem solving, quality circles and the concept of continually improving the processes to improve competitive position. A guiding concept is that everything is part of a PDCA cycle. All this jargon is, in one way or another, used to define and improve processes. There is no ignoring the fact that the addition of process management to Management 1.0 is what makes Management 2.0 much more effective and efficient. In addition, with the process management, there are clearer goals and objectives, direction is much clearer and there is a dramatic increase in training. Working together is emphasized and group problem solving becomes a way of life. Management 2.0 is a lot more personal, adds several human elements and predictably the engagement levels increase dramatically over Management 1.0. Now engagement levels are 30–45%, well above the all-manufacturing average of 25%. The destiny of those using Management 2.0 is to create a much-improved business position.

ENGAGEMENT, RESPECT FOR PEOPLE AND A LEAN MANAGEMENT SYSTEM

A quick look at the discussion topics of Management 2.0 might lead you to conclude this was the management system for a lean manufacturing business. It is filled with many of the lean tools and is rife with Japanese terms. However, that would be a bad conclusion. Actually, that conclusion is half correct – but woefully inadequate. If you refer to the cultural document of Toyota, "The Toyota Way, 2001" in Appendix C, you will see that the discussion topics in Management 2.0 are largely the topics that Toyota uses to describe their continuous improvement pillar; precisely half of their culture. However, you will note the other half, the respect for people pillar, is missing from 2.0. The respect for people pillar is best described by the added elements of Management 3.0. Toyota's respect for people pillar, if fully realized, will lead directly to the creation of a fully engaged workforce.

So, while respect for people may not sound to many like the creation of a fully engaged workforce, it is a distinction without a difference.

What is Management 3.0?

Many firms made significant progress as they incorporated process management into their management system. For quite a while this gave them an advantage over their American competitors, although the better Japanese firms such as Honda and Toyota still were clearly superior in business and management performance. Management 2.0 was a radical change and improvement over Management 1.0, so why are these Japanese firms still superior?

INTEGRATED ... ANOTHER WORD

Management 1.0 and 2.0 are largely transactional management systems. They are "you do this for me and I'll do that for you" systems. An integrated system is transformational. That is, "we will work together to reach these common goals so everyone benefits". Furthermore, we will make these changes using a fully engaged workforce such that they are not only successful but sustainable, and finally, they will become part of the culture. We will jointly transform this business.

Problems with Management 2.0

Management 2.0 was a large step beyond Management 1.0, but it still had three major weaknesses when compared to the best Japanese lean firms, notably Toyota.

- First, there was no real mechanism to sustain the gains once they were initially achieved.
- Second, the improvements were largely events and as such were not continuous in nature.
- Third, the improvements were largely done by a small group of engineers, supervisors and managers in what are called kaizen events. The largest part of the workforce, the line workers, were not encouraged, not trained and not supported to be able to make process and product improvements. This asset of using the mind and heart of the worker was not exploited to any degree. Simply stated, Management 2.0 did not have a fully engaged workforce.

That leads us to the management system that is needed for a lean transformation, much more like the vaunted Toyota Production System; it is Management 3.0.

Management 3.0

I call Management 3.0, Integrated Management. When you hear Management 3.0 managers talk, you hear that they talk about and are focused on results. As you listen *and watch their behavior*, it is also clear they have a strong understanding of, and investment in, all the processes that create the improvements toward those much-improved results. But now you hear and see much more. The talk *and the behaviors* (see sidebar on Pseudo-Management 3.0) have advanced beyond the production processes; the discussion now includes talk about

PSEUDO-MANAGEMENT 3.0

Be wary when you hear managers talk about their management systems. Managers are bright and practical people and they have learned that the world does not operate so much on reality but on *the perception of reality*. They have also learned that for each cultural change one leading element is the language of the culture. Many managers, some consciously, others unconsciously, combine these concepts and have learned the new language but do not go so far as to exhibit, teach and deploy the strategies, tactics and skills; *they are creating the perception* that they have a Management 3.0 system, when the real management system is Management 1.0 – or less. I call these systems *based on all talk with no action,* pseudo-management. Pseudo-Management 3.0 is a disease of galactic proportion in the US – be aware.

Listen to the management talk; it may be important. It is a necessary but not sufficient condition to create culture-changing habits. *But pay attention to the management behaviors; these are important* and when repeated they create a habit, which develops values, which lead to a destiny. And the right behaviors will create an excellent destiny.

systems. The training system, the planning system, the system of motivation and the entire management system are open and frequent topics of discussion. The pronouns are now "we"-based but not just on you and I; rather, it is a "collective we". Management 3.0 is a system of inclusivity, not exclusivity. The basis of the working relationships has also changed. We now have evolved from the dependence of Management 1.0, transcended the independence of Management 2.0 and, consistent with the inclusivity of Management 3.0, we are now interdependent. Working relationships, rather than being transactional, are transformational. For example, the engineer is the customer of production as he receives a problem to solve and then is the supplier as he returns with a solution for production. It is an integrated system where we synergistically count on one another to perform as an integrated whole. We realize that all the parts must function well for the entire system to perform well. Now you hear things like: sustaining the gains; operator-led kaizens; transformational improvements; kaizen events as well as operator kaizens; leadership for change; layered management audits; The Process Improvement Mantra; the Initiative Mantra; leading by intent; leading from the front; management modeling; Training Within Industry (TWI); leader standard work; Hoshin Kanri planning using catchball; visual management and the visual factory; the five supervisory tools; working on trust; extrinsic motivation, intrinsic motivation and other motivational concepts such as motivators versus hygiene factors; Theory X and Theory Y applications; Genchi Genbutsu; and more than anything, you hear about the Six Skills of Lean Leadership. There is still a strong focus on results, but now the focus is on balancing the long-term results with the short-term results. The focus on process has been intensified, but rather than process management and process improvements being the sole province of engineers and managers, everyone from the CEO to the floor worker is engaged in kaizen activity. The overriding issue is that the management system is designed to teach and support so that it voluntarily extracts the best from each individual and not only allows but encourages the complete commitment of the individual.

In Management 1.0 and Management 2.0, all too often the worker is simply a strong body to be exploited. He is encouraged to work hard but will check his intellect and emotions at the time clock. More often than not, the worker is a cost to be minimized rather than an asset to be fully utilized. However, in Management 3.0, while the physical commitment is still expected, now the worker is not only encouraged but trained, supported and expected to apply his intellectual strengths along with a caring attitude so he can apply his total self to the task at hand. ***In Management 3.0 the worker is trained, supported and expected to join the management team in a joint effort to continuously improve the business.*** The purpose of the management team is to utilize the full potential of every worker whether they are hourly workers on the floor, staff support personnel, middle management or senior management. Like we said, it is a system of inclusivity. Predictably, engagement levels in Management 3.0 now approach world class, in the 60–80% range.

IS ALL JAPANESE MANAGEMENT GOOD MANAGEMENT??

The answer to that is no. Based on my experience with over 30 Japanese firms, I can say the answer is no; however, in my case, it is not a resounding loud and clear NO … just no. I have had Japanese clients which had mediocre management systems, but I can give you no personal examples of really poor Japanese companies, although I am certain they exist; colleagues whom I trust have told me of them. You will find in my writings that I almost speak of Japanese management and good management as synonymous terms … they are not. However, we cannot overlook the huge transformation they accomplished as a nation following World War II. That transformation was largely a result of a strong system of management which has been documented by Deming, Juran, Hall, Athos, Schonberger and others. Yet don't miss two points.

- First, a very large part of their success was because they listened to a broad range of American teachers.
- Second, they worked hard to understand the basics and apply them to their systems.

I urge you to do the same as you work to learn from their efforts. Learn the basics and then apply them to your environment. And remember, just as they did in 1945, technology and techniques travel well. There is nothing uniquely Japanese about lean manufacturing.

There is a lot of discussion of Japanese management methods especially as it refers to engagement and what Toyota calls respect for people in "The Toyota Way, 2001". These concepts are highly Japanese and not uniquely Toyota. For example in a document published by the Japanese Union of Scientists and Engineers (JUSE) while discussing quality circles they say:

"The Basics Idea Behind QC Circle Activities … is as follows:

1. Contribute to the improvement and development of the enterprise,
2. Respect humanity and build a worthwhile to in and happy bright workshop
3. Display human capabilities fully and eventually draw out infinite possibilities".

(JUSE, 1980)

This resonates very well with Toyota's respect for people concept and contains many of the key factors to create and sustain an engaged workplace.

A transformational management system and the "The Critical List of Six"

Management 3.0 is the only management system that can be counted upon for sustained long-term business gains. It is transformative rather than transactional and by its very nature creates a long-term cultural transformation. Many of the elements of Management 2.0 are also culture-changing. Unfortunately, these culture changes are only temporary in nature. They will persist only as long as the change agent, who initiated these changes in beliefs and behaviors, is resident. To persist and make these changes habit-forming, the change agent will need to continue to monitor, support and model those changes. Once he leaves, very often the culture regresses and the gains are lost. In an Integrated Management system (3.0) the changes are sustained because rather than having individuals advocate for change, these changes are integrated into the corporate culture. Management 3.0, by its nature, contains the six elements that are needed, beyond those in Management 2.0. They are the "The Critical List of Six" and are:

1. Management technical competence in the strategies, tactics and skills is required at very high levels. This is a must for six very solid reasons. First, how can a manager plan anything if he is unaware of the details? Second, how can he make the decisions he needs to make? Third, as my mentor, Toshi, asks, "How can he possibly help his people?" Fourth, how can he go to the gemba and observe if he is not clear on what he is observing? And fifth, without having a grasp on the concrete details, how can he ask the questions to lead? Managers do not need to have intimate technical skills, but rather they need to be competent, at their level. Many seem to think that even knowing these details is demeaning and good managers don't need those skills. They often, and illogically, equate knowing the details with micromanaging. Knowing the concrete details of that work, and that fact leading directly to micromanaging, is no more logical than the idea that knowing how to drive a car will lead directly to vehicular homicide. Knowing the concrete details of the work is simply a skill which can be used or abused. I hear many, I mean many American managers, use the excuse that they actually avoid getting involved in the concrete details because they are afraid it will lead to micromanagement. Quite frankly I find their comments, while a convenient excuse to free them from a key responsibility, lack merit … of any kind. It is an excuse, a rationalization, a form of denial, that not

only lacks merit but is putting American firms in an increasingly non-competitive situation. Finally, if you wish to take advice from your boss, it is imperative you and he have a trusting relationship. It is pretty hard to trust someone who does not know the business and who you might view as technically incompetent.

2. Managers who are also strong supervisors who are good at delegation and are strong situational leaders. They train all their subordinates in the needed skills and create an environment based on trust, openness and honesty, so all may prosper and grow. This is especially true of the higher-level managers. Somehow, in Management 1.0 and even 2.0, senior managers think that the managers reporting to them, often with 10, 15 or even 20 years of experience are not in need of attention, direction and support. This is a huge mistake. The lack of good supervisory skills among these top managers is a disease of galactic proportions needing immediate correction. In contrast, Management 3.0 managers are always good supervisors.

3. Managers who impeccably model the behaviors they wish to see in others, including both personal traits and technical abilities. As they will expect their subordinates to create development plans for their reports, they too will have developmental plans for those reporting to them. When they introduce the Six Questions of Continuous Improvement to their staff, they, too, will use this technique in their problem solving as they try to unravel the problems at their level, such as customer acceptance, compliance with the annual plan or hiring issues. They are good role models and via their actions say, "do as I do" and can lead from competence and integrity as well as from position power.

4. Managers who practice and foster a teaching, learning, experimenting culture. Managers who not only provide a continuing challenge to their workers but also provide the guidance and support to nurture the benefits of that challenge. This is especially true of the need to teach lean leadership at all levels in the organization. It is not enough to know what lean leadership is and be able to describe it; it also must be practiced at all levels. Not only must it be practiced but it should be actively and aggressively taught.

5. Managers who support a system of mentoring, in addition to the normal employee growth processes of:
   a. Leader standard work and subordinate performance feedback
   b. Performance planning and
   c. Five-year growth and development planning

6. Managers who integrate the new changes – on an evolutionary, ongoing basis – into the existing system for continuous improvement. The most common tool to do this is the use of Hoshin Kanri planning. When someone else, besides top management, is implementing change in the management system, soon enough there will be a conflict. This is precisely why staff-led changes have no staying power. This integration process begins with the top manager, and he then teaches all those reporting to him the needed skills to facilitate and sustain the needed changes.

Management 3.0, Japanese management and the List of Six

When I visit plants, I often find management systems that look a lot like 3.0 systems. All the physical things are in place. There is an information center, the cells have good 5S markings, the heijunka boards are in place and all looks well. Furthermore, the talk is replete with the correct language and the Japanese terms flow from lips like it was their original language. However, when we get beyond this superficial perspective and perform a cold, dispassionate, introspective analysis of their system, we often find it fails to measure up to the TPS. It reminds me of the quote from Takeo Fujisawa, the co-founder of Honda Motor Company who said:

> "Japanese and American management is 95% the same – and differs in all important respects".

> (Pascale and Athos, 1981)

Upon a breakdown of how this plant I just reviewed is falling short, it is amazing the number of physical similarities I find when compared to Toyota, for example; yet they are not even remotely performing as Toyota performs. Upon dispassionate scrutiny, I find the most common issues preventing them from approaching Toyota's level of manufacturing excellence is in the six areas mentioned in the preceding paragraphs. I find managers who are technically weak on the concrete details of their business and failing to effectively integrate change. I find them, as a group, to be rather superficial supervisors, and in terms of what they expect of their subordinates, they are bad role models. Finally, I find them to be weak in some, often many, of the six elements of lean leadership. It is these weaknesses, in these areas, that are specifically what Fujikawa was talking about. **That is the 5% that is different and important**.

I have seen a lot of American management systems that look a lot like Japanese systems. They have a visual factory with heijunka schedulers, production-by-hour boards, neat plants with great floor markings. They have a TWI training system, employed layered management audits replete with a kamishibai system all over the place and with an impressive record of employee-led kaizens. You also see counter-clockwise, U-shaped production cells supported by a water strider with andons galore. You see all this and more, and not only that but the cells, and all the support systems, including the materials delivery systems, are all well designed … yeah, a full 95% of what they have done looks just like it came from the best of the Japanese systems … yet these firms still cannot provide the level of excellence we see at Toyota and Honda facilities.

WHY CULTURAL CHANGE HAS LITTLE STICKINESS

Cultural change occurs when someone has the power to, and takes the initiative to, create change; these are the change agents. As so often happens, a strong dynamic leader is sent to some poor-performing business unit and his job is to improve the bottom line. Soon enough, he has the business in the black and our knight in shining armor (KISA) has also initiated many culture-changing initiatives. The business improvements are quickly noticed and soon enough our KISA is sent to a new location to "fix that place". Well, shortly after he departs, slowly and predictably that business will regress to its prior state, both economically and culturally. The problem is simple. If the time it takes to improve the financial position of the business is X, the time it takes to make those same cultural changes permanent is 5–10 X. (Unless a different manager takes on a determined effort to change it once again.)

But most senior managers are impatient, focused on the short-term and encumbered by a recognition and rewards system that is driven by short-term economics. Hence, they feel a need to move this guy to keep him. It is a system that is guaranteed to give you short-term gains … only. The KISA who can make the changes is also needed to monitor and support those changes, and when he leaves, the cultural changes do not stick. It is a pattern that is repeated and repeated … we don't seem to learn. Senior management brings in the KISA to *initiate* change. Rather, they should adopt Management 3.0 and *institutionalize* cultural change; you'll then have stickiness for cultural change.

The difference is that 5%, and it is largely the six critical items listed previously. And guess what? They are all management issues. If others wish to compete with the best of the Japanese, they need to get to a true Management 3.0 system and make sure they have addressed and implemented the Critical List of Six.

With a destiny

The destiny of a Management 3.0 is a dramatically improved competitive position and world class levels of engagement. Recall that world-wide engagement levels in manufacturing are at 25% and world class is >70%. I have worked with companies with engagement levels exceeding 70% and they are not only world class in virtually all measures they are also a joy to work with. As a direct result of creating a fully engaged and integrated workforce using Management 3.0, not only do engagement levels rise but margins improve; both internal and external quality levels improve; non-expedited, full-load, on-time delivery improves; safety incidences fall; employee retention is improved; and morale predictably skyrockets to new levels. It is a win-win-win-win-win-win-win management system.

Next, as an example, we will discuss the Theta cell transformation here, and then in Chapters 17 and 18, we will review two other case studies so you might see how the transformation to Management 3.0 affects the quantitative business metrics.

The story of the Theta cell

Let's look at an example of a company mired in Management 1.0 which makes a quick journey into Management 2.0 and was well on their way to implementing Management 3.0. It is the story of the Theta cell.

The Theta cell was one of several value streams in this plant in Mississippi making products for the auto industry. The Theta cell made headrests for Toyota. The production cell was an inside, counter-clockwise u-cell. Labor was poorly balanced, flow was erratic, standard work did not exist, 5S was a mere dream, scrap rates were modest and the process had been operating for over 2 years at very low levels of productivity. The economics of the cell were highly dependent upon labor productivity. At start of production (SOP), the cell productivity was 65 headrests/person/day (hpppd); profitability was based on 100 hpppd minimum. After over 2 years of hard work including projects, Six Sigma approaches and numerous visits from the home office staff, productivity lingered at 80 hpppd. We were asked to intercede to make the cell profitable, that is, improve labor productivity to greater than 100 hpppd.

We put together a team, mostly managers and one supervisor, and met to begin a kaizen event. After gathering floor data, including doing time studies and spaghetti diagrams on each work station and performing "paper kaizen" to eliminate some waste, we met to redesign the cell. After working most of the night, we had redefined the work at each station, reduced some waste and effectively rebalanced the work. In addition, we clarified several work rules. Late that night we made minor modifications to the physical layout, implemented some visual controls, rewrote the work procedures and set up for the day shift. Upon their arrival we gave them an overview of what we had changed, completed some minor training and started production with the new layout and new work rules; this went smoothly. When the second shift arrived, we trained them, and by the end of the day we were producing 158 hpppd. The impact was immediate. Although we made some minor changes, we focused the rest of the week by training the senior plant management so they could train the rest of the plant on worker-led kaizens. By the end of the week, we had several worker-led kaizens completed and were producing 188 hpppd. An interesting thing happened. Since we had simply crushed our goal of 100 hpppd and improved another 80% beyond that after only 3 days, the whole team, including the management, was no longer focused on the goal of 100 hpppd; they wanted to set new records, every day. They wanted to continuously improve … in spite of our original objective.

Over the next months, we visited the plant for 1 week each month. In addition to this cell, we also worked on other value streams. On each visit we would focus on teaching the plant management new skills. The management team, in turn, trained their subordinates and this system cascaded down until everyone was trained. In November, when the model year ended, this value stream had improved to 304 hpppd and the cell was now wildly profitable, experiencing >30% margins.

From Management 1.0 to Management 3.0 and the results

When we started with the plant, the manager Dirk was a seasoned and salty veteran well versed in the process. Dirk's management style, like most of those in the corporation, was a clear command and control style. Training for cell workers was done by the buddy system, with no procedures or standards. Supervisory and management training was non-existent and help from the home office was virtually non-existent. However, when there was a major problem, the home office staffers would show up; but they were universally viewed as a hindrance. I saw this several times and calling them a hindrance was a kind characterization. When the plant met delivery and quality standards, they were largely ignored; if they failed in this, or failed to meet their monthly budget, all hell broke loose. Their management, especially their most senior management support systems, were not even the Management 1.0 model; Management 0.25 would be more appropriate. They had no industrial engineers and almost no industrial engineering skills. They could not even do a decent time study. The only statistical analysis they did was a Pareto diagram of defects they prepared each month. They had no statistical process control skills at all and were not capable of calculating Cp or Cpk. When a customer requested a measurement system analysis or capability study, someone from the home office was dispatched. I saw that work done by the home office personnel and it was hardly professional. They were capable of fill-in-the-blanks information with little thought or considerations for theory or practice. The plant did not have the skills, nor the management guidance and support, to improve, and it was easy to see why they had struggled so mightily for over 2 years with very little progress. They were stuck somewhere shy of Management 1.0 with little hope of progressing.

Recognizing this, we immediately started an aggressive management training focused on learning-by-doing. We used this first kaizen event as a kick-off to that process. As they were learning the typical Management 2.0 skills, we also taught them in a transformational manner, so they began acquiring Management 3.0 skills directly. The cell productivity results, in graphic format, are shown in Figure 6.1.

About 4 months into this project, they hired an industrial engineer. He provided a great deal of support and technical muscle that had been missing. When we left the plant, 15 months after the first kaizen event, they were proficient in a variety of skills. They had many of the skills of 2.0 and were well on their way to implementing Management 3.0. Most importantly, these included TWI training, OEE (overall equipment effectiveness) calculations, standard work, the Six Questions of Continuous Improvement, takt calculations, line balancing and time studies. In these tactics and skills, they not only were skilled but were capable of teaching others. For other tools, such as the three-part inventory system, SPC (statistical process control), leader standard work, and Hoshin Kanri planning using catchball, they were

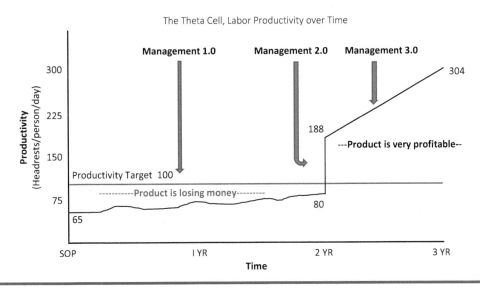

Figure 6.1 **Theta cell productivity.**

applying and rapidly learning. Yet with other skills, such as Kepner-Tregoe problem solving, statistical problem solving, job succession planning and the 5-year facility staffing plans, they were just getting started. Still, Dirk and his team were well on the way to learning both how to apply these tools and how to integrate them into a system that mimics the Toyota Production System. But best of all, the training mode has changed from the buddy system to management-led training. First, we taught Dirk the skills and then taught his functional managers who in turn taught their supervisors who then taught the lead hands and finally the floor workers were taught the appropriate skills. The management team, coupled with the new industrial engineer, were technically competent and were capable of teaching all their subordinates. But the area of greatest progress was in teaching all people, supervisors and above, the Six Skills of Lean Leadership. On each plant visit we would address one of the six elements. Like other training, we taught Dirk first, using hands-on training, at the gemba, as he learned by doing. When we would leave for 3 weeks, prior to our next visit, they would then deploy these skills to their subordinates until all had been trained.

What else happened in the plant, in addition to the huge productivity improvements?

Recall that this was just one value stream in the plant. Well, not all value streams got the same level of attention in year one. The Theta cell was the beta test site for this plant, but they did not wait long and implemented many of these skills on other value streams as well. The results after the first year were:

- The plant had its best safety year ever.
- Morale was visibly improved and confirmed in the Annual Engagement Survey.
- On-time delivery was practically 100% with a 30% reduction of inventory.
- All quality metrics, both internal measures and external measures, had improved. They had their best quality year in the plant's history.
- Most telling of all is that the gross profit of the plant had risen from 5% at the beginning of the year to 14% at year's end as they set new records for profit margins, and they did this as overall demand in the plant had dropped.

Theta cell – Summary

The story of the Theta cell is a great metaphor explaining just how to begin a culture-changing event in a plant so that you can not only achieve great bottom-line benefits but also create a fully engaged workforce. Here, like other transformations, there are two large and common elements. First, is the total engagement of the management team from top to bottom. You will note that they did very little that was new, rather, they just did everything in a different manner. Especially in the areas of training, guidance and support. Second, no lean transition occurs, and very little engagement is gained until you are able to have the entire organization engaged in volunteer kaizen activities. Although most of the activities in the plant were focused on the Theta cell, there was a tremendous effort at yokoten, or best practice sharing, that allowed the entire plant to prosper.

Chapter Summary ... The theme of this chapter is the overriding importance of management in not only plant performance but in attaining a fully engaged workforce. The starting place for good management lies in the belief systems held by the management, and this then guides all behaviors and finally will dictate the very destiny of the business. We discussed Management 1.0, which is based on a results-only belief system. Few can use this system today – and survive. Management 2.0, based on the belief that good process management will yield good business results, is the prevalent system used in the US today. It is a system that is easily copied; and it has been. The bottom line is that since it is much easier to duplicate, rather than innovate, US businesses have copied. Soon enough, everyone is the same and no one rises to world class performance. In the '90s with the advent of management-driven kaizen events pushed by either the Six Sigma concept or the Japanese concept, Management 2.0 was improved. However, all of this is still easily duplicated and hence does not have the power to distinguish one company from the other. On the other hand, the real power to create the world class performers is available to those who adopt Management 3.0. The key distinguishing factors are twofold. First, in Management 3.0, everyone is engaged, and the true manifestation is that not only are large management-driven kaizen events executed but also everyone is involved in individual kaizen activity; most importantly, the floor-level workers are engaged in kaizens. Second, a new style of management is involved. Managers, as well as knowing the classic skills required in a Management 2.0 system, are also proficient in The Critical List of Six. Finally, we studied the Theta cell, which was an example of working toward a fully engaged workforce. With this example, we were able to show in graphic format, and with quantification, the financial and business benefits that are available to those willing to undertake a transformation to a fully engaged workforce.

What's next?? Managers must do more than just managing … they need to lead and supervise as well. We'll cover that in detail in Chapter 7.

Chapter 7

Management and Leadership – The Basics

Aim of this Chapter ... We will explore why managers want engagement. At the same time, we will examine why they are not acting in their own best interests, as their actions, contrary to their intentions, often cause disengagement. To that end, we will distinguish the skills of leadership from the skills of management and understand their individual importance as managers work toward creating a fully engaged workforce. We will also delve into one critical management trait that is a direct result of good leadership, risk tolerance. Next, we will explore what the management team must do to create a fully engaged workforce and introduce the two management realities they must understand as well as discuss the critical role of the supervisor. Finally, we will look at a much-needed management trait, the ability to create an environment in which people can perform well and how the subject of situational leadership adequately meets that need.

Managers, in the worst way, want engagement

Most businesses, at least those who sell tangible goods, have three major efforts. They must create products the marketplace wishes; hence, they need a design function. Second, they must find, develop and satisfy a customer

PARADIGM SHIFT NO. 1A

The system of engagement is owned and controlled by management. To create engagement takes a cooperative effort that must be led by the management team.

base; hence, they need sales. Finally, they need to produce these products to the quality standards the customer wants and at a price they are willing to pay; hence, they need manufacturing.

These three aspects of design, sales and manufacturing are widely used in many businesses; even those you may not think of their activities in these simple terms. Take a restaurant, for example. Not only do they usually have a food-type or ethnic specialty but they are continually trying to introduce new "products or services". Their specialty may be in the type of food they provide, it may be in the type of service they provide or it may be in the quality of the service. It may be a simple restaurant specializing in home-style Italian food with red and white table clothes and empty Chianti bottles all over the place. Or it could be an Italian American restaurant specializing in takeout. Or finally, it may be an upscale, Italian bistro with an extensive wine list, waiters in white shirts and bow ties and accompanied by the high-priced menu they feel their service and ambiance deserve.

Whether it is a tier one auto supplier, a restaurant or a law firm, they still must design, sell and then provide the products and services to the customer.

What is the common denominator to supplying all these needs and doing it well?

The common denominator in these three aspects of a business is that they all use people. Furthermore, if the people exhibit certain common charac-teristics, all three of these aspects will prosper and very likely the business with prosper. The one common characteristic most business leaders want is for their people to be engaged – fully engaged. Engaged with 100% of what they have to give 100% of the time in 100% of the activities. They want them engaged not just with their bodies (hard working) but engaged with their hearts (emotionally), so when they see opportunities to improve they care enough to take action, and engaged with their minds (intellectually) so they can apply their unique expertise to turn these opportunities into process and product improvements.

No secret here.

So just what is the problem??

In my 49 years in industry, managers have told me time and again that they are looking for hard-working, devoted, smart, creative and caring people. Unfortunately, just as quickly they lament that they do not have these characteristics in their employees and they have reams of data to support their assertions. With both a high degree of passion and conviction, they point to problems with the union, low morale, attendance and retention issues, serious safety problems and, the data of all data, the engagement surveys that show numbers in the range of 25%. All of this supports their position … or so they believe. Let me be very clear … I do not doubt the sincerity of their beliefs. But do not confuse sincerity of beliefs and even conviction of beliefs … with correctness.

I think they are wrong … very wrong

Again, let me clarify. When they say that they have engagement levels of 25%, I don't doubt that at all; rather, I agree. What I disagree with is the belief that "they do not have these characteristics in their employees". I believe they do have these qualities of hard-working, devoted, smart, creative and caring people. Time and again we have proven this to be the case.

This error in logic has become so commonplace that at Quality Consultants we have incorporated three beliefs into our value statement:

- "The vast majority of the talent needed to vault your enterprise into becoming a lean enterprise are already inherent within your organization
- The key to success is largely an issue of unleashing these abilities
- The major and very critical tool needed to unleash these abilities, and hence to become a Lean Enterprise, is to learn and employ the skills of Lean Leadership at all levels of the organization" (www.qc-ep.com).

The reality

Rather, my experience is that, almost without exception, employees, when first hired, are highly motivated and want to be engaged. However, the very way they are managed and led creates an environment that does not cultivate – rather it often discourages – the very qualities the management team is looking for. So even if these workers came to work with these qualities, at day one, soon enough these qualities are driven out by the existing management culture, and then you get what managers see today, low levels of engagement. That, however, is not what the management team had started with.

Please reread that last paragraph; it is a summary of this entire book.

Just why does management work to discourage engagement??

Certainly not because they are trying to do that … far from it. In my discussion with senior managers, for those wishing to improve engagement levels, they usually believe they are working hard to cultivate engagement – yet equally frustrated by their inability to achieve it. Most of the management problems stem from a lack of understanding of engagement basics; a lack of understanding of motivational principles; and a lack of understanding of the role of management in creating – or destroying – engagement. This is further exacerbated, as too many consultants have taught a model of engagement that is far more salable than it is functional.

At any rate, the key issue that causes management to act in a manner that all-too-often is discouraging, rather than encouraging, engagement is a lack of understanding of many practical issues discussed in Chapter 4 (What is everyone missing).

> **ACHIEVING ENGAGEMENT AND SUPERVISION; THE READER'S DIGEST VERSION**
>
> "Achieving engagement" is a topic we will cover in detail beginning in Chapter 12. Although the topic of achieving engagement is a many-faceted construct, it is largely achieved when the supervisor does a good job of directing, training, resourcing, supporting and following up on his employees. All of these tasks are basic supervisory tasks, pointing out the absolutely critical role played by the supervisor in achieving engagement. (See Appendix B.)

Misunderstanding of the concept of engagement

This is the genesis of most of the misunderstandings by management, so it is worth restating here. This incorrect management paradigm is that engagement is:

- equated to "hard-working";
- something for the floor worker but not the management team; and
- totally worker controlled; that is, if the workers want to be engaged, they would be.

So far, to show the incorrectness of this paradigm, we have fully discussed the first bullet point in Part One and found it to be incorrect. Soon we will discuss the second and third bullet points. We will address the desire of individuals to become engaged in Chapters 8 and 9 when we discuss motivation, especially intrinsic motivation. We will find out that all three bullet points are erroneous management paradigms.

Misunderstanding of "the need for the engagement of managers"

First, read the sidebar, "Achieving engagement and supervision; The Reader's Digest version". The "symptoms" of engagement include a cognitive (intellectual), physical (hard-working) and emotional (caring) commitment by the individual. I am not sure why anyone would think this is a construct reserved for floor workers alone … but most managers do, especially top-level managers, including those in the C-suite. Somehow, they believe that, first, they themselves, their peers and their direct reports are engaged, despite the Gallup data quoting 38% engagement among managers. Second, while they may (the majority do not) understand those duties of the first line supervisor which are required to activate and sustain engagement of their floor workers, they believe that, somehow, the rest of the management team is magically released from those same responsibilities.

Well, news flash!! Managers are almost always supervisors. Don't they have people reporting to them? Don't they need to give work direction, supply resources, provide support and follow up with these people?? Aren't they accountable for the quality and quantity of the work output of those people? If it walks like a supervisor, talks like a supervisor and works likes a supervisor, it's probably a supervisor. Most of these people (those called managers) don't like to be called supervisors, so we call them managers. Make no mistake, they have supervisory duties they must execute, that is, if they wish to be successful. The bottom line is while a first line supervisor may supervise floor workers, a manager will supervise those supervisors, a general manager will supervise those managers, a VP will supervise those general managers and the C-suite will supervise those VPs. In fact, the board needs to direct, resource, support and follow up, and, in a word, supervise the C-suite. Seems like everyone at the facility who is a manager is also a supervisor … and that is true.

Failing to understand the need for managers to practice engagement leads to two very large and very negative impacts. First, in their roles as supervisors to their subordinates, they will fail to supply all or some of the elements that create and sustain engagement. This fosters lower levels of engagement among their subordinates, and, due to the leveraging effect which managers naturally have, this telescopes down the organization with a multiplicative effect. Second, only when the managers model the correct behavior can they become good role models. They must plan, resource, support, follow up as well as supply all the elements of engagement. It is no longer acceptable for managers to say, "Do as I say, don't do as I do". Skills that are common to multiple organizational levels absolutely must be modeled at the higher levels, or they will soon enough fall into disuse.

Creating a fully engaged workforce is not something management can talk about, they must practice it in their everyday activities. They too must be engaged, and in their role as supervisors, they need to supervise those people so they too can become engaged.

Misunderstanding of the concepts of motivation

This is a serious problem with management in particular, but this misunderstanding is not reserved just for management; it is pervasive. Unfortunately, management's misunderstanding of motivation and their role in motivation – or lack thereof - has a strong effect on employee engagement. In Chapters 11 and 12 we will discuss the key theories of motivation in the workplace and the special place for, and the power of, satisfying the intrinsic needs. We will also explain why some of the best intentions of the management team to motivate the workforce – in the fullness of time – work to demotivate them. The topic of worker motivation has been a mystery to many managers for quite some time and continues to be a problem in many aspects of the workplace, including attaining a fully engaged workforce. In Chapters 14, 15 and 16 we will discuss the elements of engagement and management's role in supplying all workers (yeah, managers included) with the elements to create and sustain engagement.

Management's role: What are we talking about?

In this book, the word management is used in two forms. First, it is the part of the job title for those people who are exercising specific skills to run a business. They are often referred to as the senior management, the senior leadership, the top management or just the management. It is also a skill set that allows these "senior or top" people to run the business.

Management (the skill set) is distinguished from leadership, which is a separate skill set. To further complicate the issue, the people who are doing the managing are also the people who are doing the leading. And for mostly historical reasons we call them the manager of production and the manager of engineering, for example. Seldom are they called the leader of production or the leader of engineering.

So, the **management** team is exercising the skills of **management** as well as exercising the skills of **leadership**. It can be confusing as we write about and discuss these topics. To distinguish the management, as a group of people, in practice, is easy. However, to distinguish the skills of management from the skills of leadership is a bit more delicate. To distinguish the two skill sets, I refer to John Kotter, who very nicely defined this distinction, as outlined in Figure 7.1.

Needs	Management Skills	Leadership Skills
Desired outcomes	Producing a predictable, orderly outcome of key results expected by key stakeholders.e.g: on time; on budget; high quality	Produce change, particularly change that is needed to respond to the changing environment of the business
Creating an Agenda	Planning and budgeting	Establishing a vision for the future and the strategies to producing the changes needed
Developing a human network to accomplish the agenda	Organizing and staffing	Aligning people by communication and deeds
Execution of the agenda	Controlling and problem solving	Motivating and inspiring

Figure 7.1   Management-leadership comparison matrix. (Adapted from *A Force for Change*, Kotter, 1990.)

There is an increasing need for leadership skills

The past decades have emphasized management over leadership as the key skill set

For the longest time, certainly until the 1990s, most American businesses had a growth strategy for profitability improvements, and many still do. Although there were some firms that embraced a change strategy, they were and probably still are the minority. If your business strategy for profitability improvement is based on "more of the same", you are looking for "a predictable, orderly outcome". Well, more precisely, you are looking for "**more** of that predictable, orderly outcome". In that case, your business will value and reward the skills of management; often at the expense of developing leadership skill. This is precisely what has happened in the US, certainly since the end of World War II. Consequently, if you shake a tree filled with people who have the word "management" in their job title, for every 30 good managers who fall to the ground, you might find one with the skill set to be a good leader as well. So, just as the skills of leadership are required more and more, we find we are not well prepared to meet this need; unfortunately, this story gets worse.

Times are changing rather dramatically

There is a new dynamic hitting American business like a Gulf Coast hurricane. Even if businesses are not interested in changing to get better, the external environment is changing, and it is changing so fast that change is no longer a profit improvement strategy ... it is a survival strategy. To make things even worse, the rate of change is accelerating. All the evidence says tomorrow we will change more and faster than we did yesterday, with no end in sight. With all this change, the need for improved leadership skills is growing at an exponential rate. Earlier, a management team with good management skills, but weak in leadership skills, was able to guide a business to success and even prosperity. That is no longer a reality. Good leadership, the ability to negotiate the minefield of a changing business culture, has become a skill set that is needed for business survival.

Good management, by its very nature, is: somewhat conservative; methodically incremental; filled with bureaucracy, reports and follow-ups; risk-averse; and focused on the short-term. As a result, the very best management simply cannot produce major change. Only with the leadership does one get the boldness, the courage, the long-term vision and the energy needed to activate the workforce and create changes.

Is more leadership all we need?

While seeking to get "a fully engaged workforce" you will need to make many changes. To properly navigate these changes, your management team will need to be proficient in the skills of lean leadership (described later in this chapter). Yet, change is not all you have to deal with. Your day to day activities will still need to be well managed. You still need to execute the skills of management as you: staff and budget; plan and organize; as well as control and problem solve. Make no mistake, the management team must have a strong complement of management skills as well as a strong complement of leadership skills as you work your way to "a fully engaged workforce".

One of the unique – and absolutely necessary – contributions of leadership

Good managers are looking for predictable outcomes; they are risk-averse. Their mantra is "we need to win all the time". Good leaders recognize that with change, there is risk. Although leaders do not like failure, smart failures and some risk is acceptable to them. Their mantra is "we need to win most of the time". Hence, good leaders will tolerate risk and even failures, especially if a great deal was learned from the failure. Good leaders will even insist that we learn from our failures. The relatively few companies that do this very well (truly learn from failures) have a significant competitive advantage over those who just talk about it but don't effectively learn from their failures.

The problem becomes very large when the management team recognizes there are risks but really do not want to admit that things may not work out as desired. Too often they effectively delegate the task but attach the rider "but don't screw up" as if you had total control over all the variables. It is like the baseball manager who walks to the mound and in all seriousness tells his pitcher, "This guy is a great hitter, don't give him anything to hit … but don't walk him". The pitcher is placed in a double bind and the only one who comes out unscathed, no matter what the results happen to be – is the manager.

ON BEING CRITICAL AND DIRECT … WORTH IT??

For each book I have written, I use a Technical Review Team to assist me. Almost without exception, at some point, they have cautioned me about being too critical or too direct, particularly in my comments on management. More often than not, I soften my comments. However, I have come to a decision. I am not trying to make friends, although I would like more friends. However, I am on a mission to find converts. That is managers who are willing to not only be aware enough to see the need to change their businesses but also humble and wise enough to know that before the business will change they, as individuals, must first change. And if I cause the hair on the back of your neck to stand up a little, so be it. Furthermore, if you think I am "plum full of canal water", give me a call and we can discuss it; I'm always willing to listen and learn.

However, in business, unlike baseball, the worker who is placed in this double bind has an out … he can make no changes. In most cases, the benefits of making changes are small and often go unnoticed; however, the risks are large and the failures **never** go unnoticed. This imbalance in the risk-to-reward ratio normally forces the rational worker or manager into **concerted, thoughtful and conscious inaction** … precisely what we do not want.

Management, even good management, is risk-averse and too conservative to support any types of failure. Leadership alone is the effective antidote to this paradigm of "change but don't make any mistakes" and consequently does not paralyze the worker into inaction with the resultant lack of progress. Leadership alone effectively promotes change, because it tolerates an acceptable risk such that "we win most of the time". Only with this paradigm shift is it possible for the employees to become engaged and for the business to improve.

The Six Skills of Lean Leadership

For the managers in a plant, be they the facility manager, a mid-level manager or the first line supervisor, they will simultaneously, every day, be using the skill set of both leadership and manager, as outlined previously. Kotter's matrix does a good job defining the structural differences between management and leadership, but it does not go very far to answer the "how?" question. As a manager, just "how do I exhibit the skill set of leadership and management in my daily activities?" To that end, we created the Six Skills of Lean Leadership that apply to all management and supervisory roles, independent of the business or the function within that business as well as being applicable to all levels within the business … they are largely a universal skill needed in today's businesses, and we have tried to relay them in easily understood terms and metaphors.

The Six Skills of Lean Leadership

1. **Leaders as superior observers:** They go to the action – they call it the gemba – to observe not only the machines and the products but also to spend significant time with the employees. They strive to be aware of not only the products and the processes but more importantly the people. They also are in contact with their customers. A much-overlooked leadership skill they have in abundance is the ability to be an empathetic listener.

2. **Leaders as learners:** They do not assume they know it all. Rather, they go to the floor to learn. They are in "lifelong" learning mode. They are masters of the scientific method. They learn by observing and doing, but most importantly they are superior at asking questions; they learn by questioning.

3. **Leaders as change agents:** They plan, they articulate and sell their plans, and they act on their plans. They are not risk-averse, yet they are not cavalier. They do not like to, but are not afraid to, make mistakes.

4. **Leaders as teachers:** They are "lifelong" teachers. When something goes wrong, their first thought is not "Who fouled up?" but "Why did it fail?" and "How can I use this as a teaching opportunity?" They teach through the use of questioning rather than just instructing.

5. **Leaders as role models:** They walk the talk. They are lean competent. They know what to do and they know how to do all of lean that is job-specific to their current function in the organization. There is no substitute for this. NONE.

6. **Leaders as supporters:** They recognize they mainly get work done through others, so they have mastered the skills of "servant leadership" (Adapted from *How To Implement Lean Manufacturing*, 2nd Edition, (Wilson, 2015)).

We have found that over the years these terms like "leaders as superior observers, teachers and role models" resonate well enough that they are easily understood by both the management and the rank and file workers. In addition, we find that few firms teach leadership and this gives them a simple, yet comprehensive, model that is easily taught.

The importance of the management team's behavior

If you hear this once from me, you will hear it dozens of time … there is nothing more important in "creating a fully engaged workforce" than the specific behaviors of the management team. They will need to manage and lead in a manner that likely is very different from how they have managed and led in the past. There is no more clear litmus test to success or failure of any culture-changing effort than the need for management to change. They need to change the very system they have created, and, in many cases, will have to change what they themselves: think; believe; say; and routinely do.

A plant that has a management team that embodies the Six Skills of Lean Leadership has a fighting – actually a very good – chance to create a fully engaged workforce. Conversely, a plant management team that is weak in the Six Skills of Lean Leadership has no chance to create an engaged workforce.

Just what must the management team do??

Getting work done through others

The overall task of the management team in a production plant is to properly manage and lead in a manner to utilize all the available resources to safely supply their customers with high-quality products and services on time and on budget. Many say that management is getting these things done by working with and through others. Although simply stated, this is a formidable task and frequently requires an awesome skill set for it to be accomplished day in and day out.

However, that really does not capture the essence of the management task. For many this "getting things done through others" conjures up visions of some manager sitting in his second-story office overlooking the floor like a slave owner watching his minions produce. Well, 50 years ago that may have been a decent description of how some managers performed, even if they should not have. But that model does not have a fighting chance in today's world … not at all.

Two realities managers need to deal with

If you doubt that, think about these two things.

- In most manufacturing plants, the plant manager can take a 4-week vacation, and the plant hardly misses a beat. On the other hand, if you are not able to staff the position of the shipping clerk for even one shift … all shipments stop – you have no production. This leads me to:

   Management Reality No. 1. The manager needs his people, more than they need him.

- Second, the manager is only successful if his people do their job well and the plant succeeds. The best strategic plans, in the end, rely on the value-add workers properly executing their tasks … independent of what management wants or does. This leads me to:

Management Reality No. 2. Managers do not get paid for what they do, they get paid for what their subordinates do.

It's all about being successful

Hence, the job of management is to do everything possible to make their subordinates as successful as possible. The manager only succeeds when the plant succeeds, and the plant only succeeds when the workers succeed. This leads me to revise the role of management from:

IS YOUR MESSAGE GETTING ACROSS??

As a manager, how do you assure your "message" has been properly received?

My friend Robert Simonis reminds me of a principle he learned in the army: the "two levels down" principle. In which, I communicate what I want to my subordinates, but I check what their people are doing: If the correct message was both sent and received, then the actions of the subordinates two levels down matches the intent of what I told my subordinates. A nice management technique for all.

"getting work done through others" to "doing all that is necessary to make your subordinates as successful as possible".

Supervision … The most basic task of management

The most basic task of management is a supervisory task. If your overall task as a manager is "to do all that is necessary to make your subordinates as successful as possible" you need to make sure they know what is necessary and they know how to define success.

To that end, the supervisor needs to make sure his people:

- Know what to do
- Know how to do it
- Have the resources to do it.

Although this is not only a basic but also a seemingly simple set of requirements, ***I find it to be a major problem in virtually every client I now have or have had.***

- *Knowing what to do* is often compromised by having work processes that are poorly defined. Any time there are processes which are statistically unstable or have inadequate process capability, it is clear someone or something does not know what to do. This a common industrial problem.
- *Knowing how to do it* is often compromised by having poor work quality standards, and few companies have 100% yield.
- *Having the resources* to accomplish the task at hand, likewise, is a common problem. Often, the resources were reasonably well supplied at day one, but are often poorly maintained or not updated as process demands change.

The litmus test to any facility that fully, and I mean fully, satisfies these three requirements is an accident-free facility that has 100% quality yield, 100% full load non-expedited on time delivery. I don't know of many such plants and that is precisely why I refer to this seemingly simple set of requirements as a major problem; it often is.

The umbrella task of all supervisors ... to create an environment where it is conducive to produce

In my first supervisory assignment, my mentor took me aside and gave me some advice. After going through the Five Roles of Supervision,

- work assignment and instruction;
- worker training and development;
- worker support;
- work quality control; and
- providing a communication line to and from the management team,

he went on to say that, although those Five Roles were critically important, he felt they were secondary to yet another concept. He said to be an effective supervisor, to be an effective manager and to be an effective leader, I needed to "create an environment where it is conducive to produce" and he went on to say, "and it is the job of the people who are working for you, to produce". We had several discussions on this topic, and as I supervised and later managed groups, I wanted to explain this more fully to my subordinates. Consequently, I combined the teachings of my mentor with my personal experiences and distilled this concept into seven rules. As a manager, I then taught these seven rules to all the supervisors in my organization.

They were:

1. Challenge your people continually. With no challenge, there is no growth.
2. Don't treat everyone the same; treat everyone in a manner so they can succeed.
3. Know your stuff technically. You will need to give people good line ups, you will need to evaluate the quality of their work and you will need to intercede to make sure they don't fail and have a decent chance to win.
4. However, for them to learn, they must be afforded the opportunity to fail along the way; don't hover over them, but provide support and be a safety net to contain the failure. In the end, if they succeed you succeed, if they fail – you have failed. It is best to not make that a habit. To never fail means you have not been challenged. To balance failure with challenge, you have to know your stuff; remember – you must be technically competent. Work to create a trusting relationship based on competency, integrity and success.
5. Know your people and know both their strengths and their weaknesses; technically and personally. Follow up at appropriate times but don't be a mother hen. Stay in touch with them. Work to create a trusting relationship based on caring about them personally, their growth and their success.
6. Train people in an incremental step-wise fashion so the work does not overwhelm them. To keep them confident, you must make sure they are competent at each step. People will only grow when they are confident, and they are only confident when they succeed and they only succeed when they are competent.
7. And don't forget … challenge them.

I never forgot that lesson from my mentor, and I later taught it to all my subordinates. It was a lasting piece of management training, and it has served me well to this very day, and it will serve you as well. Not only did I use this model in my work roles, I used it very successfully in my role as a soccer coach and in my volunteer activities as well.

Situational leadership

While with Chevron, and after I had been a supervisor for maybe 2 years, I attended a seminar which taught these same concepts, but they were delivered in a dramatically different format. The seminar was "Situational Leadership" taught by Dr. Paul Hersey. Later, Dr. Hersey wrote a book entitled *The Situational Leader*, and I recommend it to all. To those of you who don't like to read, take heart; this 112-page book, with lots of "white space", can be read on a flight from Los Angeles to San Francisco.

The underlying premise of situational leadership

His underlying premise is that to be an effective leader of others, you must:

> "assess the performance of others and take the responsibility for making things happen".
>
> (Hersey, 1984)

This is simple in concept – on the surface.
He goes on to say that leaders:

> " … know what ought to happen, plan a way to make it happen, and takes steps to see that it does!".
>
> (Hersey, 1984)

Now, that is first and foremost a great sentence describing leadership, but it also lets you know it is no longer so simple. The leader needs to "know his stuff" technically; he needs to structure a way to get it done, and then he needs to follow up, intervene and support as necessary to assure success.

In this simple definition, can you now see all the Six Skills of Lean Leadership in action?? Is it now obvious why leaders need to be "lean competent"? Is it now obvious why they need to be "change agents" as well as "supporters"? This seemingly simple concept of "assessing the performance of others and taking the responsibility for making things happen" takes on a dramatically different approach than what I see happening on shop floors and in the offices of many firms (Figure 7.2).

On Hersey's matrix, the two axes are "Task Behavior" and "Relationship Behavior", and each is very important and draws heavily on the skill inventory of the supervisor.

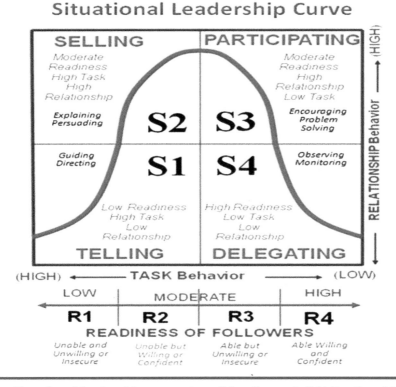

Figure 7.2   **Situational leadership curve. (en.wikipedia.org/wiki/situational leadership theory)**

Task behavior – The X-axis

This is mostly one-way communication from the supervisor to the subordinate that focuses on giving the subordinate the information he needs to execute the task at hand. It normally involves explaining what to do, when to do it, how to do it and why to do it, if that is relevant. It is largely a one-way communication; we used to call it a "job lineup". At the one extreme it is "telling", that is, being very directive, which is appropriate for the new person in their job. Often, those new in their jobs are not extremely secure and need additional direction, support and follow-up. On the other end of the spectrum, rather than the directive nature of "telling", the situational supervisor is more likely to "delegate" the task with less follow-up, and for the confident and competent worker, he provides little follow-up and gives the greatest freedom to act independently. The administration of "task behavior" is not only "job-specific" but this "telling/delegating" continuum is ***very*** worker-specific, considering both the complexity of the task and the relative skill inventory, willingness and confidence of the worker.

Relationship behavior – The Y-axis

Supervisory relationship behavior, unlike supervisory task behavior, is mostly two-way communications and involves listening, encouraging, facilitating, clarifying and providing necessary support, including training and supportive follow-up. This is very worker-specific but may also be job-specific as well.

> ## SITUATIONAL LEADERSHIP, IT'S NOT MANDATORY
>
> Situational leadership is not mandatory. There are two options. First, you can pretend that all people are the same – or, you can recognize that people are different but ignore their needs. Either way, you will not " … **take the responsibility for making things happen"**.

Situational leadership styles

Using these two dimensions and dividing each dimension into two levels, Hersey creates a 2×2 matrix and codifies leadership into four styles: Telling; Selling; Participating; and Delegating.

Once the leader has assessed the situation and assessed the individual, he then supervises the person accordingly; he leads and supervises situationally. It is not the workers adapting to the supervisor, it is the supervisor adapting his skills and his style to the needs of each individual for the expressed purpose of "making things happen". Many supervisors think this is beneath them; they want to mass-produce supervision when they are dealing with individuals even if these individuals have variant skill and confidence levels. Certainly, this is easier; it, however, is neither humane nor is it productive. Even for the senior-level manager whose subordinates are normally very talented people … they too need to use situational leadership.

The leader, the supervisor, needs to carefully determine the subordinate's ability, willingness and confidence in approaching the task at hand. It is then up to the supervisor, using the Five Roles of the Supervisor, to "fill in the gaps" so he can … "take the responsibility to make things happen".

The issue of supervisory responsibility – to Hersey

The essence of responsibility is inherent in the word itself. Break down the word and it is, "response – ability": the ability to respond. It is based on action. Hersey makes it clear who is responsible; the leader, the supervisor, must "… make things happen". So, if things do not get done or do not get done well, it is the worker's supervisor who is the first person to contact and ask the "why?" question … not the worker. Now this concept applies to anyone doing any task. He need not be a line worker; he could just as easily be a support person such as an engineer. Likewise, it could be a mid- or high-level manager. We all have supervisors who have the task to "… take the responsibility to make things happen". Unfortunately, when a business misses a shipment or produces scrap material, I see the managers and supervisors almost reflexively and with laser-like precision look to the value-add worker to find the weaknesses in the system. Well, seldom is the problem there. More often than not, it is with his supervisor, or the mid-level manager who is his supervisor, or yet another higher-level manager who is the mid-level manager's supervisor.

Consequently, I can tell you with certainty that if the company has quality or delivery problems … the CEO has a problem.

Toshi on supervision

In one of my early discussions with Toshi, my mentor, I asked him, "What was the first large problem you encountered while working in the US". Quickly, he replied, "I had a very difficult time getting the supervisors to understand, that if their workers were not performing, that they (the supervisors) had a problem they first must address. It was a long uphill battle to institute this norm". When I asked Toshi this question, I thought he would say that the language or the unions were a key part of the problem. But Toshi answered quickly, and it was neither the unions, the language nor anything else – it was the quality of the supervision. Specifically, getting the supervisors to take responsibility for the skills and outcomes of their workers. I found that very revealing.

The essence of situational leadership

I am a huge fan of situational leadership for three reasons. First, it is the same model my mentor taught me over 40 years ago and it worked nicely for me. Second, it has proven itself to be an excellent model to use when teaching supervision. Third, it systematically and directly addresses two management issues I see as an increasingly larger problem in Western management:

- Managers knowing the work; and
- Managers knowing the people.

I see these as two problems so prevalent amongst Western management that I believe them to be at the heart of the quotation by Athos we discussed in Chapter 6:

> "Japan is doing more than a little right. And our hypothesis is that a big part of that "something" has only a little to do with such techniques as its quality circles and lifetime employment. In this book, we will argue that ***a major reason for the superiority of the Japanese is their managerial skill".***
>
> (emphasis mine, Athos, 1981)

Knowing the people

Practicing and teaching situational leadership addresses nicely the people issue. To be a situational leader, you must be able to assess not only the technical abilities of your people but their willingness and confidence in doing any task. Then, as a supervisor, adjust your approach and train, direct, support and follow up as needed to "make things happen".

This is in stark contrast to how many firms treat their people, that is, **like an easily replaced and fungible commodity, which they are actively working to minimize.** In these firms, there is little recognition of workers as an asset and even less about workers as individuals. These crass and inhumane management practices can only lead to a complete collapse of the "respect for people" concept, and it also has a large negative impact on bottom-line financials. There is little doubt that practicing situational leadership helps people be as successful as possible and vastly improves your likelihood of being successful at the financial level.

Knowing the work

In my earlier book, *How To Implement Lean Manufacturing*, 2nd Edition (Wilson, 2015), I wrote extensively on the concept of "the MBA gone awry". In this extremely popular mode of Western managers, they "become so enamored of the map, they ignore the territory". Rather than go to the gemba and observe and learn from the products, processes and especially the people, these poorly prepared managers review the spreadsheets and monthly business reports, focusing primarily on financials. They believe they can run the business from the quietude and serenity of their offices using the business meeting and emails as their primary form of communication. This is so prevalent, as an acceptable management practice, it has caused entire businesses to lose their competitive edge, and I believe it was exactly what Takeo Fujisawa was talking about when he said:

> "Japanese and American management is 95% the same – and differs in all important respects".

> (Pascale and Athos, 1981)

That 5% difference is focused largely on the management's ability to:

- know the work and
- know the people

Chapter Summary ... We explored why managers want engagement and found they are not acting in their own best interests, as their actions, unfortunately, often cause disengagement as a direct result of not properly understanding the concrete details of engagement and motivation, as well as their role in the creation of both of them. We examined the differences and the similarities of the management and the leadership skill set. Leadership is focused on causing and facilitating change while management is focused on creating and maintaining predictability. In the environment businesses operate in today, there is a growing need for leadership skills, which too often are in short supply. One very critical difference is that while in leadership mode, the manager must create an environment where appropriate risk is not only tolerated but encouraged. This is a critical issue when progress and change are addressed. Starting with the "Two Realities of Management" we enumerated the three elements that managers must supply so their people can produce. They are: to know what to do; to know how to do it; and to have the necessary resources. We also outlined the five supervisory tasks for all supervisors and managers. Finally, we looked at a much-needed management trait, the ability to create an environment in which people can perform well. A review of situational leadership shows that it too is a model that, when followed, will create a productive environment. The key message of situational leadership is that the supervisor/manager must not only know the work to be accomplished but he must also know the strengths and weaknesses of his people. He then must assess the work to be done and the people doing it and intercede in a way to make sure that both the project and the people are successful. The key measure of good supervision is ... are our people set up for success??

What's next?? Over the years, managers have lost two critical skills; that is what we will next discuss.

THE SIX ECLECTIC MANAGEMENT SKILLS

In this section, we discuss some rather unique and needed management skills. These deserve some explanation.

As I was preparing to write this book, I prepared several "thought documents" including: mind maps; affinity diagrams; brainstorming lists; and copious notes enumerating, evaluating and quantifying dozens of traits and skills managers must possess. However, I found six eclectic traits that would be particularly powerful if you wish to attain and sustain a fully engaged workforce. These traits applied equally well to the first line supervisor and the members of the C-suite ... and all managers in between.

This list of eclectic skills can be nicely divided into two categories. There are the two "Lost Skills"; that is, 30, 40 and 50 years ago, these were commonly used, strongly emphasized and even taught. They are:

- managerial competence in the technical details of the work; and
- the ability to delegate well

And a second set of four "New Skills", which almost everyone has heard about but far fewer execute with excellence.

- creating a teaching, learning, experimenting culture;
- management modeling;
- managers as mentors; and
- inquisitiveness and integration

These four "New Skills", coupled with the two "Lost Skills", are generally the core skills, above the basics, that are needed if you wish to attain a Management 3.0 system.

Part III contains three chapters:

Chapter 8

Management and Leadership – The Two Lost Skills

Aim of this Chapter … We will discuss the two crucial skills that management once had in abundance but are no longer commonplace. They are the lost skills of management's technical competence and the ability to delegate. The issue of management's technical competence had been undermined by the concept of the MBA gone awry and further diminished as technology had made distance management easier and more prevalent. These two lost skills, together, create a third dynamic which is the kryptonite to engagement: micromanagement. We will explore these dynamics and explain how they are so impactful when trying to create a fully engaged workforce

The first lost skill – Technical competency among management

The case of the MBA gone awry

In my earlier book, *How To Implement Lean Manufacturing*, 2nd Edition (Wilson, 2015), I state very clearly that "lack of understanding by top management" is cultural change Killer No. 1. That is, if you wish to stifle or even prevent cultural change, make sure your management team does not possess a strong understanding of the concrete details of the business.

There is simply no substitute for this. It is what I call "the case of the MBA gone awry" discussed in much greater detail in *How To Implement Lean Manufacturing*, 2nd Edition (Wilson, 2015). Yet today I see many manufacturing businesses run by MBAs with little floor experience. Rather than understand the people, the products and the processes, they bury themselves in spreadsheets and management reports. Unfortunately, they believe that "the map is the territory" as described by Locke and Spencer's provocative and revealing book, *Confronting Managerialism: How the Business Elite and Their Schools Threw Our Lives Out of Balance*. They attack this Western norm directly when they said:

> "Americans conscious in the 1980s of the need to reform US manufacturing to meet the Japanese challenge cursed the "New Look" in US busi-

DR. DEMING ON MANAGEMENT BY NUMBERS ALONE

As part of his obligations of management, Dr. Deming enumerated seven deadly diseases, and the fifth deadly disease was: "Running a company on visible figures alone (counting the money). One cannot be successful on visible figures alone. Now, of course, visible figures are important. There is payroll to meet, vendors to pay, taxes to pay; amortization, pension funds, and contingency funds to meet. But he that would run his company on visible figures alone will, in time, have neither company nor figures". (Deming, 1982)

ness school curricula. Johnson complained about it in "Relevance Regained"... He observed: Successful [US] managers believed they could make decisions without knowing the company's products, technologies, or customers. They had only to understand the intricacies of financial reporting … By the 1970s managers came primarily from the ranks of accountants and controllers, rather than from the ranks of engineers, designers, and marketers. This new managerial class moved frequently among companies without regard to the industry or markets they served … A synergistic relationship developed between the management accounting taught in MBA programs and the practices emanating from corporate controllers' offices, imparting to management accounting a life of its own and shaping the way managers ran businesses … At first the abstract information compiled and transmitted by these computer systems merely supplemented the perspectives of managers who were already familiar with concrete details of the operations they managed, no matter how complicated and confused those operations became. Such individuals, prevalent in top management ranks before 1970, had a clear sense of the difference between "the map" created by abstract computer calculations and "the territory" that people inhabited in the workplace. Increasingly after 1970, however, managers lacking in shop floor experience or in engineering training, often trained in graduate business schools, came to dominate American and European manufacturing establishments. In their hands the "map was the territory". In other words, they considered reality to be the abstract quantitative models, the management accounting reports, and the computer scheduling algorithms".

(Locke and Spenser, 2011)

WHAT IS YOUR MANAGERIAL STYLE?

Are you a "map" or a "territory" manager? Do you practice distance management? Or can you be found frequently at the gemba?

Keep in mind that all spreadsheets, P&L statements and monthly business summaries (maps) are just theoretical models trying to reflect business reality (the territory). Regarding this, the great statistician Stuart Hunter said,

"All models are wrong, some are useful".

Dr. Deming said,

"Every theory is correct in its own world, but the problem is that the theory may not make contact with this world".

In fact, I would suggest an alternate title to Locke and Spencer's book:

"Managerialism: How the Business Elite and Their Schools **Weakened Western Management Techniques and Allowed the Japanese To Become a World Manufacturing Power**".

Where can we find managerial teams with high levels of technical competency?

I see this problem of low technical competency in many places, yet most companies, even if they happen to see it, don't view it as a problem. Not at all. Rather it has become – at the very least – an accepted norm and – at the worst – a desirable management attribute. However, as I work with the elite firms, I do not find this problem. Rather, the management team, even the senior management, are well versed on the concrete details of the operation. Coincident with a management team that is well versed in the concrete details of the business, I find two other commonalities:

■ First, most of the management team came up through the ranks, rather than being hired in at the supervisory, managerial or even executive level. Before being the COO, they were a plant manager and before that a materials manager, e.g. … in this firm.
■ Second, they normally have high levels of company seniority, and consequently, they are familiar with the business, they are familiar with the people and they are familiar with the company culture.

Who, in my database, has high levels of technical competence in the management ranks?

Here I find a distinction held by my Japanese (and some German) clients. On this topic – technical competence – I find my Japanese clients, whether they were a top performer or more middle of the road, all shine very brightly on the topic of management's technical competence. The entire management team, up to and including the C-suite members had a good understanding of the concrete details of the business. After 49 years in business, I cannot give you one example to the contrary among my Japanese clients (although I am sure someone can). There is no doubt this is a huge strength in their favor.

What are the issues?

The obvious questions that arise when the senior management is not versed in concrete details of the operation are, "Just how do they make the decisions they must make, with a truncated knowledge base? How do they make the investment decisions and a litany of other technical issues, missing key information?"

There is yet another whole class of problems that is sprung upon the manager who has only a superficial understanding of the details of his business. How does the manager exhibit the Six Skills of Lean Leadership if he is not technically competent? Specifically, "How does he teach and how does he support his people?" Without being competent on the concrete details of the product, the process and the business itself, it is practically impossible to be people-centric and provide the help your people need and so dearly want.

Yet another issue is a lack of systems thinking. Decisions tend to be sub-optimized because the executive does not have a good grasp of the entire system.

Toshi's perspective on the importance of managerial competency – The needs of the people

The fact that company after company continues to perpetuate this wrong-headed belief that the details just don't matter is as much as anything fostering the outsourcing and transfer of manufacturing overseas. Like I said earlier, it is so commonplace as to be a cultural norm in the majority of Western businesses. It both irritates and frustrates me, and I wish I could make a greater impact.

To punctuate this point, let me share a little vignette. Several years ago, I was discussing this topic with my mentor, Toshi Amino. Specifically, I asked him why this disinterest in the concrete details was so prevalent in Western managers? I recall with great clarity his response. Specifically, I recall his facial expression and his entire body language as he conveyed this thought to me. It is as if I am sitting there – right now. He developed a little frown; the skin on his forehead wrinkled; and his head leaned a little to the right and then he humbly and introspectively said, "I just don't understand how those managers who do not know their production systems and are not familiar with its details can really help their people". He did not think about it; he did not pause and ruminate. He responded almost reflexively and instinctively, and his singular focus was on "helping their people". He did not even question such related business topics as "How do they budget?" or "How do they make the tough decisions?". Rather, with laser-like focus, he worried that they could not assist their people. That simple, one-sentence reply, more than any amount of studies I have seen or books I have read, clarified to me why the Japanese have been so successful. Managers focused on and helping their people – think about it.

The typical "shift" a manager makes as he becomes gemba focused

Based on my experience, when senior leaders begin to go to the gemba, at first they almost reflexively tend to focus their conversations on how the workers can help to solve problems of interest to the senior leader. If they are coached properly, then they focus on solving the workers' problems. This doesn't come naturally for most leaders at first, but it's powerful when they make that shift – from self-focus to worker-focus – in the purpose of their gemba visits.

The effect of distance management

A contributing factor to the continual deterioration of management technical competence is a term I call "distance management". If your paradigm is that you can manage a business by paying attention to spreadsheets, P&L statements, monthly summaries and at the same time feel comfortable with most of your communications being from emails, webinars and Skype calls, you can become a "distance manager". You need not be present at the facility … or even on the same continent … and this paradigm of management will allow you to feel comfortable that you can lead and manage. Such is the essence of "distance management". There is, however, one rather large problem … it does not work. Much like "distance parenting", "distance coaching" or "distance doctoring", it is a concept you can believe in and even be passionate about, but the reality is it simply does not work in manufacturing management.

Accepting and believing in "distance management" is simple and it is convenient. For mostly these reasons, simplicity and convenience, it is surprisingly popular. But it is not something that is practiced by the elite or even the good firms. What is practiced by the elite firms is "Situational Leadership" and going to the gemba – distance management is totally antithetical to the concepts of situational leadership. Situational leadership requires you to assess both the task at hand and the readiness of your people and then intercede as appropriate. It's hard, if not impossible, to make these assessments and then intercede if you are three states over. In addition, situational leadership requires you have a working relationship with your subordinates, which is on-and-beyond hard to do – from a distance.

Rather than discussing the myriad dysfunctions of this managing, or parenting, or coaching, or doctoring style, let's compare distance management to the Six Skills of Lean Leadership.

- If you wish to **observe** the work of your subordinates, you must be there. It's hard to observe when you are one city, one state, one country or one continent away. The most important role is to observe and interact with your subordinates, and although emails and phone calls can substitute a little, there is no substitute for face-to-face dialogue, to create, improve and sustain relationships.
- For managers to **learn**, they need to question and listen carefully to the replies. Some of this can be done over the phone. It is difficult to learn when all you have are abstract models of reality. In the end, you must

go to the gemba and ask questions if you really want to learn, especially if you want to learn about your people.

■ To be an effective **change agent**, it is hard to be very far away. As you change, there are always unexpected results and unintended consequences, and these occur in the chaos that accompanies change. In this environment, decisions need to be made quickly; as a manager, this is your job. Once again, it is pretty hard to make quick decisions if you are a continent and 12 time zones away.

■ Just how does one **teach** from a distance? Web-based classes are surprisingly popular and they may be effective when the purpose is intellectual understanding. I personally doubt it is anywhere nearly as effective as advertised, not even close. Once again, webinars are surprisingly simple and extremely convenient, and to transfer intellectual knowledge, they are also both time and dollar efficient. Just one problem – they are not EFFECTIVE. Nonetheless, in the world of business, we are not satisfied by that which only creates intellectual knowledge … people need to be able to do things. They can't just talk about strategic planning and pontificate on its merits; they must be able to do it and even follow up and make it a reality. Business training is always behavioral-based and that cannot be taught in a webinar. Distance teaching to attain behavioral modification, although widely used … and even passionately believed to be effective to a large group … simply is not. Most professional football teams, whose success and failure is completely dependent upon the behavior of their workers (the guards, tackles, defensive backs, running backs, etc.) typically have 13 coaches for a roster of 53 players. These coaches see and interact with these players on a daily basis. It is pretty hard to extrapolate from that model to one where the coaches are interacting via the web, from another state using distant management … and still be effective. Distance management simply is not a model that works where the managers need to teach … and it never will.

■ Probably the most debilitating form of distance management is the lack of **role modeling** that transpires when your manager is a continent away … or even a city away. He's not there; as a subordinate, you cannot observe him. Role modeling stops except for his internet, webinar and emailing skills. It is the social equivalent of having one of your parents in prison, and no one seems to miss this as a problem in child rearing. What about "subordinate rearing", do you see any substantive difference??

- Regarding management's role to **support**, some of this can be done from a distance; however, the critical support your people need are the times things are NOT normal. They need the greatest support when the business is in crisis. In those cases, your presence is invaluable and there is no substitute for it.

Distance management, Toyota and Genchi Genbutsu

The final blow to distance management having any validity at all can be understood if we review the cultural principles of Toyota. As you recall from Appendix C, the entire culture of the Toyota Motor Corporation is built on Five Key Principles.

Think about that for a second. This is not some creed of some dealership or even one of their large factories. This is the creed for the entire world-wide corporation, encompassing all activities. Yet they reduce the guidance of all their values, beliefs and actions, their entire culture, to these Five Key Principles. Of those Five Key Principles, one of them is Genchi Genbutsu. They say,

> "We practice genchi genbutsu ... go to the source to get the facts to make decisions, build consensus and achieve goals at our best speed".

Parsing this:

- **Go to the source** ... They are talking about precisely where the specific item of current interest actually is. If it is a production problem, they expect their management to go to the production

> **PARADIGM SHIFT NO. 1C**
>
> The concept of distance management must be abolished and replaced with Genchi Genbutsu

floor, not just some conference room to discuss someone else's observations, spreadsheets and reports. If it is a customer satisfaction problem, you are going to visit the customer, not just some sales representative who has his filtered data.
- **To get the facts** ... They mean all the facts, not just the data output forms but information from the environment and especially input from the people. They wish to avoid using "filtered" data; they want the true story to surface.

- **To make decisions** … They are not looking to ruminate over this information and spend time listening to a bunch of people who seem to have a need to speak up at meetings and make no contribution. By going to the source and having the facts, they can ask the key questions, of the key people and finally make sound decisions.
- **To build consensus** … By having the facts and making good decisions, there is still the issue … "are all the key players ready to implement this?". If not, then consensus must be reached and that can only be done effectively using face-to-face dialogue.
- **Achieve goals** … That is what drives all the issues, and these goals are created using the Hoshin Kanri methodology. If the issue is not important toward meeting goals, the manager will want to know this.
- **At our best speed** … Only with the manager present and after the problems are analyzed and decisions made, after listening to all the discussion needed to reach consensus, can the manager determine if:
  – we are taking on too much work; or we are not taking on enough work; and
  – we are proceeding too slowly; or we are proceeding too quickly to be effective and efficient.

Distance management and false economies

However, I said earlier that the concept of distance management is very popular – and it is. Distance management is a part of a Western penchant to reduce indirect labor including supervision, management and all support functions – without looking at the purpose of indirect labor and specifically without looking at the effectiveness of the indirect labor. Recall that the purpose of most of the indirect labor is to make the direct labor effective and efficient. I find firms, time and again, ready, willing and able to slash the staff support functions without so much as a cursory look at the real impact on the entire business. Almost without exception, they are looking for ways to make immediate bottom-line impacts while ignoring the longer-term effects. It is a false economy of the worst sort as it not only destroys the long-term earning power of the company but it plays with the emotions and securities of all the workers.

Done this way, no cold, hard, dispassionate, introspective analysis can support this arbitrary reduction of supervision, management and support personnel as being effective. If for one moment you wish to ignore the issue of **effectiveness**, an argument can be made that it is **efficient**. Efficient in the sense that through the use of distance management you can probably reduce the total number of managers you need, but – if and only if -- you see no problem in eliminating effectiveness from the equation. It is a losing strategy and one that needs to change. Well, it needs to change if, and only if, you wish to survive and prosper.

Wrapping up managerial technical competence

The concept of the MBA gone awry, which has fostered and reinforced the incorrect belief that managers no longer need to be familiar with the details of their business, is such a debilitating and pervasive illness, it is at the very root of the failure of many businesses and even industries. When I grew up, we had RCA, Sylvania, Magnavox and Motorola TVs ... oh, ... we also had a Zenith. I am not sure these companies manufacture, much less even exist, anymore. Many people would like to lay this issue at the feet of import tariffs, lousy legislation ... or some other form of American manufacturing denial. Unfortunately for American management, there is simpler, and closer, although not quite so comfortable explanation

This concept of the MBA gone awry, and the dissociation of management's needs to understand the concrete details of the business, is a phenomenon starting in the '70s. At that time, the world of computing was done by large stationary devices, requiring complicated programming skills, and the internet was neither a viable communications tool nor was it an effective work tool. With the advent of PCs, good software and a litany of internet tools, distance management became a possibility ... but only because managers were released from intimately dealing with the people, the products and the plants. These traits of functionally ignoring many of the concrete details of the work, while at the same time largely disregarding the unique contributions and needs of the individuals, is so common among American management it is worthwhile to repeat the quote from *The Art of Japanese Management* (Athos and Pascale, 1981):

> "Japan is doing more than a little right. And our hypothesis is that a big part of that "something" has only a little to do with such techniques as its quality circles and lifetime employment. In this book, we will argue that *a major reason for the superiority of the Japanese is their managerial skill*" (emphasis mine).

Two powerful reasons these Japanese are better managers is that:

- They have the experience and background to be well versed in the concrete details of the processes and products, allowing them to make better decisions. The process of growth and development they went through to become managers prepared them for this.
- They avoid distance management; they go to the gemba staying in touch with not only the products and the processes but the people.

> **DELEGATION AND THE VALUE-ADD WORKER**
>
> If delegation is so important and the only people adding value are the hands-on-tools workers, why don't we **delegate** work to them?? Good question … and the answer is, "We did that long ago". We did it using a process known as standard work. The standard work document, coupled with the training in the executing of that standard work, tells the worker:
>
> - What to do
> - How to do it and
> - What resources are required

In both cases, they were trained much better and they continue to be better trainers.

The second lost skill – Delegation

In my days with Chevron, work delegation was a big topic. Often it was practiced and often it was taught to recently appointed supervisors. Particularly in my earlier years with Chevron, it was commonplace to get a new job along with the work well defined, desired results explained, guidelines you may need to be successful, resources defined, responsibilities enumerated along with consequences of success and failure. In my later years with Chevron, holding higher-level jobs with increasingly more responsibility, this type of delegation changed considerably. To this day, I am not sure if it was just something that diminished as I rose in the hierarchy or whether Chevron placed less emphasis on this important trait, over time. But what I can tell you is that: I saw good delegation, was taught good delegation and used it throughout my career with Chevron.

I have also seen, first hand, as a consultant, and can fully appreciate how supervisors and managers who practice poor delegation will have deleterious and lasting negative effects on engagement. On the other hand, good delegation is like a breath of fresh air and will markedly enhance employee engagement. Unfortunately, more and more, I see less and less delegation. What I frequently see is job assignment with assigned responsibilities inconsistent with authority, resources often overlooked completely and expectations either glossed over or not discussed at all.

I see very little good delegation.

What is delegation???

Assigning is much different than delegating work. Although all delegation starts with a work assignment in which the person is told in very general terms what to do, normally it is assumed: he knows what to do; knows how to do it; and has the necessary resources. Notice the carefully inserted phrase, "it is assumed". For example, when a supervisor or team leader tells his crew, "John, work at station one today, Cecilia take station two", etc., he is simply assigning work; there is no delegation involved – at that moment (see sidebar). In delegation, in addition to being assigned the work, the subordinate is given additional authority; authority that you hold. Also, when work is delegated, in most cases, it could have been done by the supervisor delegating the task. For this reason, delegation has the effect of shifting work off the supervisor and has a developmental aspect to the subordinate.

The power of delegation

Most importantly from a managerial standpoint, delegation is the manager's leverage. When a manager can invest 1 hour of effort and can produce 20, 50 or a 100 hours of productivity from his people through effective delegation, that truly is an asset. Effectively delegating to others is not only the single most powerful high-leverage management activity there is but it fosters growth among your subordinates. Proper delegation always contains some kind of challenge, and challenge is an intrinsic element of growth.

When to delegate??

While teaching managers how to delegate, often I hear, "It is just easier to do it myself and then I am also sure it is done correctly". Sometimes that is true, but the very same people who give me this feedback are the ones screaming that they don't have enough time in the day. I give them the following advice: unless you are the only person who has the skill inventory and access to the information to complete the task … plan to delegate it … or else get ready to get swamped and continue to be surrounded by people with inferior skill inventories.

The typical management errors in delegation

When delegating, as in all tasks completed by management and supervisors, you will want to make sure the task has:

- Superior results; and is
- Done as quickly as possible; and
- When implemented, it will be accepted well by those it affects.

Herein lies the genesis of the typical errors that lead managers to do the work themselves rather than delegating the tasks or decisions.

Many managers, particularly if they have a broad base of experiences, often think they know more than their subordinates. They often forget that their knowledge, while it may be experience-based, could now be out-of-date or even incomplete. In addition, many managers want to rush to a solution and since they have the power to approve and reject, they want to "just get this thing done". All too often, they then push forward to incomplete solutions that may not be well accepted. Quite frankly, the best managers, even if they know the technical solution, often guide their subordinates and allow them to learn just as they themselves learned. Finally, they make sure the subordinate has addressed the issues so the solution, once selected, will be acceptable to those most affected.

Work assignment versus work delegation

Unfortunately, what I see today among my Western clients, when managers are giving initial job instructions to their subordinates; it can seldom be called good delegation. More often than not, work is assigned, not delegated. Goals are loosely defined, little if any guidance is given, resources and accountability are not well thought out in advance and frequently only negative consequences are defined. When done in this way, there are normally two natural consequences, both bad. First, objectives and time targets are frequently missed. Second, both supervisor and subordinate leave the meeting with an appearance of calm. However, the reality is that management deep down does not believe that the subordinate is up to the task. Simultaneously, the subordinate is confused and neither confident of the job line up nor his ability to be successful. Both the supervisor and subordinate have a significant level of angst … yet both are unable to resolve it. However, with good delegation, not only is success much closer but most of the angst is resolved in the discussions inherent with good delegation.

The elements of delegating work

Whether you are delegating or assigning work, the same six elements should be involved. They are:

1. Definition of the work
2. Desired results including how to measure success
3. Guidance and guidelines
4. Resources
5. Accountabilities and "check-ins"
6. Consequences

When analyzed, the differences are not subtle but rather obvious, for example:

Work definition

Delegation is a two-way discussion with input from both the boss and the subordinate before the process is completed. Assignment is a one-way, top-down discussion where instructions are given to the subordinate with little opportunity for input.

Results

Delegation is focused on results instead of methods; it gives people a choice of methods and makes them responsible for results. In delegation "what" needs to be accomplished, with the specifics of how to measure success and "by when" conveyed along with the appropriate boundary conditions. The supervisor will ask specifically "How do you plan to achieve these results?" which the subordinate must explain. The methods used are largely left to the creativity and resourcefulness of the subordinate. In this way, the supervisor can perform a reality check on the methodology and also evaluate the "task readiness" of the subordinate. Using this "what-how" process, the supervisor can give the subordinate maximum autonomy and intercede only as needed to assure success. Due to the nature of the "what-how" discussion, often this takes more than one discussion to finish delegating. When assigning work, often both the end results and the methods are defined by the supervisor. The subordinate has less latitude and less input. It is uncommon for the "how" to get much discussion at all. When work is just assigned, often subordinates are left to "do it their way", even if they have little experience.

Guidance and guidelines

Assigning is often done because the supervisor has weak technical knowledge and cannot give the subordinate substantive guidance on best methods, guidelines or the various minefields to avoid as he approaches the task. I have heard more than one manager, while believing they are delegating, say "I just want you to get it done and I don't care how you get there". Yet another manager said, "Be a nice guy, bribe them or kick ass, I don't care how you get there, I just want results". When assigning work in this way, there is no check on the task readiness of the subordinate. There is no check on the willingness or confidence of the subordinate to attain success. He was given a simple dictate, nothing more. While the subordinate normally needs some latitude in selecting the methods to accomplish the task, taking it to this extreme is nothing more than laissez-faire management. This is simply technical and personal abdication of the supervisory role, all in the name of results. Allowing them the freedom to do it their way, even if it means failure, is hardly effective supervision or management. Recall that, as a supervisor, you wish to be a situational supervisor and that means you will do what is required to make you people successful.

Resources

In delegation, as part of the "what-how" discussion, there is a review of the available and needed resources and often a very substantive discussion of options. It is very common for the resources to be modified, from those originally supplied by the supervisor, to assure goal attainment. Often, to many people, this sounds like a negotiation – it is not. Rather, it is an iterative discussion to make sure the means and the results are aligned and attainable. Since there is no such "what-how" discussion in assignment, often resources are not rationalized until late in the project, leading to excessive costs and missed due dates.

Accountabilities and check-ins

As part of the delegation process, the supervisor needs to define "success" with meaningful metrics. In addition, since the supervisor now knows "how" the subordinate plans to proceed, the supervisor has some insight into when to accept feedback on the project or task. Consequently, they will jointly agree on a review frequency to allow the subordinate maximum autonomy while giving the supervisor the confidence he will have a chance to review and provide feedback in a timely fashion. In their rather concise little book, *The 4 Disciplines of Execution: Achieving Your Wildly Important Goals* (McChesney et al., 2012), McChesney, Covey and Huling unveil a surprisingly simple, yet extremely effective, format for review; they call it their Cadence of Accountability, and it has three basic steps:

- Account – report on last period's commitments.
- Review – learn from successes and failures.
- Plan – clear the path and make new commitments

I have found this format to be very effective and more importantly very efficient. I find we can complete a project review of even large projects in 10–15 minutes. However, this is only possible because of all the delegation that was done in the prior four steps. This type of "check-in" not only informs the supervisor but also gives him a forum to both learn and teach.

However, when the model is to assign rather than to delegate, I find these "check-ins" with the boss to be unfocused, disorganized, energy-draining and often with high anxiety experienced by both parties.

Consequences

Consequences need to be discussed on three levels. First, what will be the consequences to the customer (either external or internal to the company)? Second, what will be the consequences to the business overall? Finally, what will be the consequences to the leader and the team doing the work? When you delegate, you will need to specify what will happen, both good and bad, as a result of the results.

Hoshin Kanri as a form of delegation

There are several similarities between Hoshin Kanri and delegation as outlined above. Specifically, the catchball process is used to gain agreement and alignment on performance expectations (goals, targets, objectives, etc.), teams are given the freedom to figure out how to meet the goals, resource constraints are discussed and understood, visual management is used to monitor progress and establish accountability; in fact, the completed Hoshin Kanri process that includes follow-up, plan reflection improvement is a near perfect metaphor for the process of delegation

An example of poor delegation

I recently finished an engagement with an international firm who was world-class terrible in delegation; among the worst I have seen in quite some time. They are an international high-volume, low-mix producer for the auto industry and would launch 50–100 new products each year, in the US alone. Their new product launch process was reasonably well defined but poorly executed and very poorly managed. For each new launch, it was a disaster waiting to happen. Often, when the product was transferred to the plant to make the production validation runs (PPAP, the production part approval process), all too often there were serious unresolved problems in not only the process but the product as well. The plant, with a very small staff, and no design responsibility at all, was now expected to "pick up the ball" and make the launch a success. It seldom worked that way. Often, a product launch did not include much new equipment, but rather they only needed to purchase new molds and then incorporate these new molds into the existing equipment and processes. On the continuum of "launch complexity", these were not very demanding. Yet consistently they would fail to launch successfully. It was common to miss due dates, miss ramp-up quantities and very often the entire plant OEE (overall equipment effectiveness) would drop 10–15% for 2–8 weeks as the problems with this particular product were resolved. This effort sucked up all the plant's already-strained resources. With this client:

- the work, at the plant, was poorly defined;
- expected results at the plant level were not even reasonable;
- pre-launch tasks were normally incomplete and left for the plant to resolve;

- resources did not match the task at hand;
- yet the consequences of failure were severe.

When launches were not done well, the senior management still needed to find someone to blame and often the remarks were "Well, maybe we don't have the right guy in the job" and the plant manager was assigned the blame which belonged somewhere in the senior management ranks. Depending on how you looked at this problem, it was either a grossly inadequate launch process or improper plant support to account for this inadequacy. Both issues fall directly at the feet of the senior leadership, not the plant leadership. Yet the plant was "assigned" the task to make the launch successful and they alone bore the consequences.

A lesson in good delegation … A much-needed trait, but in short supply

My all-time favorite client is a small (~$5 million/year sales) manufacturing firm in El Paso, The ABC Company. They have many fine attributes and consistently make fine products to high-quality standards. The one attribute they have that is better than any client I have ever had – ever – is their flexibility. They can make decisions quickly, turn their production processes on a dime and ramp up or ramp down more efficiently and more effectively than any client I have ever had … or ever seen. None of those are the reason they are my favorite. They are my favorite due to the way the CEO, Wilson (yeah, his first name is my last name, neat??), deals with me when he wants assistance. I will get a call from Wilson three or four times a year.

Let me give you an example. Their major value stream is decorative street lighting. Their clients are typically cities doing downtown renovations and large-tract home builders. One day, Wilson gave me a call about an order of 120 lighting poles; for them, that is a large order. He called me Monday PM on his way home from work. After the normal catching up and pleasantries, he gave me my job instructions as follows. "Lonnie, we have an order of 120 poles we have been working on for 3 weeks and only have 20 completed. I am concerned we will miss our due date; they need to be shipped in 3 weeks. Brianne (the production manager) is out of town; can you come by, take a look and see what you could do?" I told him, "I am in town all this week, I'll be by in the morning". He continued, "Dave has the drawings, has all the needed parts and tools and he also has a full staff to work with. He and his crew are at your disposal. Just get them working the way you think is correct and I'll see you in the late afternoon. I have a doctor's appointment in the morning, a luncheon meeting with the Chamber and a board meeting in the afternoon, but I will be there later". Wilson had defined the work to be done, explained the expected results, gave me the necessary guidance and explained the resources fully, as well as told me when our next "check-in" would be. It was very effective delegation.

Furthermore, if you are a consultant, that is the type of work direction you simply love. "I got a problem, I need your help and just get going". No mentions of, "assess the situation and give me a proposal", nor any of, "put together a plan and we'll discuss when I arrive", or even "put together a plan and fill me in". None of that, simply: "I got a problem, I need your help and get going". This is no-nonsense delegation at its finest. More on that later.

Tuesday AM I showed up 7:30, and by 8:00 everyone was in full motion. The pole manufacturing process consisted of nine sequential steps:

1. First, the pole was welded to the base.
2. Bondo was applied to make a smooth transition at the seam of the pole to the base.
3. Following the Bondo application, this area was ground smooth.
4. From grinding, they went to bolt and screw application where dozens of attachment points had the female portion drilled and tapped into the pole and the base.
5. Then the poles with bases attached proceeded through a four-stage wash process.
6. Next, they were painted on the powder coat paint line.
7. Finally, all the attachments, including the top luminaire were assembled.
8. The pole was given a final inspection for quality and electrically tested.
9. The pole was wrapped and prepared for shipment.

By 9 AM I had done enough time studies to put together a process flow; it was a simple lean application. I immediately found the bottleneck. There were 16 poles in front of grinding, two in front of Bondo and four in front of assembly; grinding was the bottleneck. Counting wash and paint, there were over 35 poles in process. First, we attacked the unnecessary steps to reduce the total required work. The poles in front of grinding were due to excessive Bondo application, a manual process. We made a fixture to minimize excessive Bondo and made some minor changes to reduce the work at grinding, the bottleneck. Next, we balanced the work among the stations. With these changes, the bottleneck cycle time was 18 minutes, meaning we should be able to produce

3–4 poles per hour. Following this, we reassigned workers to balance the process. By noon we had the poles flowing, one piece at a time. Production immediately picked up, and by the end of the day we had 39 poles ready to ship. That day we finished 19 poles; we were now producing over 3/hr. Wilson arrived and after we counted the day's production, he was impressed but not surprised. His comments to me were, "I just felt we were going too slowly and whatever was the problem, I knew you'd sniff it out and fix it. We are a little blind with Brianne on vacation and this has helped tremendously. Now, can you keep an eye on this?" I told him we had

THE CRITICAL IMPORTANCE OF AUTONOMY

When I have discussions with workers, supervisors, middle managers and even C-suite managers, I hear the same types of complaints. Some are "If only we could …" or "I wish I was able to …" or "If I had the power I would …". All of these are some expression of wishing to have more control. It is in our DNA; quite frankly it is intrinsic, meaning it is part of our inner makeup. We want to have more control over the things that affect us. Quite frankly, one of the most powerful skills a manager can have is the ability to delegate well. Done well, it portions out the control to those who are best capable of utilizing it effectively.

81 poles to go; it would likely take 4 days to finish. Wilson summarized, "it took 3 weeks to prepare the first 20, now we can prepare 100 in 5 days. Please keep an eye on this and iron out any problems we might have".

The amazing thing was the response from the crew. All this week they were happy and focused on the work. Poles were flying through the system at a pace that more than satisfied their sense of accomplishment. By Friday we still had around 4 hours of work left to complete the order. The crew wanted to work through and finish the order. Rather, we came in Saturday and finished the last few poles and loaded the truck for pickup on Monday AM. We bought lunch for the team, bought a few cases of beer and sat around and just chatted. It was a home-run. The poles were shipped 2 weeks early, making both Wilson and the customer happy, and the workers were more than happy; they were fulfilled.

This looks like a success story in manufacturing as the customer got first quality poles, early no less. The ABC Company not only made a customer very happy but also made some very nice margins, and the workers walked away happy. Customer happy … company happy … workers happy … that is a tough triumvirate to beat. And although many things contributed to that success … do not forget that it all started with good delegation. Wilson, when he delegated this task, was clear on the work direction, the desired results, gave me guidelines to work with and told me what resources were available. Yes, good management laid the foundation for this success, and good delegation paved the way to a strong effort in employee engagement, not just for me, but for all the workers as well.

Why is this type of delegation not the norm??

Well, first and foremost, Wilson is lean competent, and we just discussed the relative scarcity of that trait. Second, he knows the skills of good delegation and he used them well. Not only did he find someone, but he found someone whose skill inventory made him feel very confident they could get the job done. To do that, you must have a grasp on the skill inventory of your people. Knowing the work and knowing the people are two issues in delegation. To properly delegate, both are needed. However, that is not enough. To delegate properly, as a minimum, two other personality traits are required.

- The manager must have sufficient **self-confidence** that he has a decent **understanding of the situation** and also a **good understanding of the people** involved, and:
- The people involved **must have a relationship based on trust**.

 With all these elements, good delegation is possible. If you are weak on one or more of them, the power of good delegation is compromised to the point that only work assignment is possible.

Technical competence, delegation, autonomy and employee engagement

Later, in Chapter 12 when we discuss Self-Determination Theory and again in Chapter 15 when we discuss the Intrinsic Motivational Loop, you will find out that autonomy (acting with a sense of volition and choice) is THE key element to achieving employee engagement (see sidebar). With no or lousy delegation, there is no autonomy, and with no autonomy, there is no engagement. Consequently, you can readily see that delegation and employee engagement go hand in hand. Hence, a critical management skill, as we move toward a fully engaged workforce, is the skill of delegation. Not surprisingly, the ability to delegate is predicated on a supervisor's ability to assess the work situation and the readiness of the worker. Both needs are dependent upon a supervisor's technical knowledge about the concrete details of the work. He cannot make either assessment well unless his technical knowledge is sufficient. Hence, technical competence is needed to delegate. So "voila", you need to be technically competent to delegate and you need to delegate to get autonomy and you need autonomy to create a fully engaged workforce. This makes these two managerial/supervisory skills *absolutely mandatory* if you want to create and sustain a fully engaged workforce.

The "kryptonite" to creating a fully engaged workforce – Micromanagement

You have probably all seen micromanagement in action with the manager hovering over his subordinates. While he is compulsively and incessantly checking up on them, interrupting them time and again for questions that are often trivial and frequently mistimed, he is sucking time from the subordinate's day, working against the employee's development and destroying whatever working relationship that still might exist.

The parenting metaphor to micromanagement in business is the helicopter mom popularized by Dr. Haim Ginott, the child psychologist. Helicopter parents hover over their kids in an ostensible effort to protect and develop them, and in so doing hamper: their personal growth; their emotional development; their move toward independence; as well as their need to develop an individual sense of responsibility. Likewise, micromanagers normally in the name of "getting the job done right", hover over their subordinates and in the end, they:

- Stifle their personal growth
- Stifle their emotional growth, especially in developing a sense of confidence
- Stifle their ability to work independently
- Steal their sense of responsibility and, worst of all,
- Steal their sense of accomplishment

What's at the root of micromanaging

Micromanagement consists of using three perfectly positive attributes – a caring attitude, an attention to detail and a hands-on attitude. Unfortunately, they apply these three otherwise positive attributes to an extreme. To such an extreme that they ruin their colleagues' confidence, hurt their performance and sometimes frustrate them to the point where they quit. Except in the all-too-common case where micromanagement has been normalized, most businesses will discourage micromanagement. Certainly, among the high-performing firms, it is not only discouraged it is actively sought out and remedied.

High-performing firms are interested in teaching and learning, with the attendant growth of the individual, growth of the group and the company growth as well. They know that micromanaging is antithetical to all these values. These same high-performing firms are aware that the proper amount of caring, attention to detail and staying in touch with the work are all management assets they wish to cultivate. It is only when it is taken to an extreme that it becomes harmful. Hence, it is an ever-present problem all supervisors must be aware of and they must carefully monitor their own activities so they do not take these traits and turn them – from assets – into liabilities.

The problem of micromanaging can be within the organization or within the individuals, or both.

Organizational issues fostering micromanagement

There are three common organizational problems which foster the growth and development of micromanagers. If, in the business culture:

- there is an inappropriate fear of, and intolerance for failure; or,
- the management team is obsessed with the short-term gains instead of a healthy balance of short and long-term gains;
- the behavior gets recognized (reinforced) in a positive way. Example: "that light post project got amazing results, it probably wouldn't have happened if Mike hadn't stayed right on top of it – great job, Mike!" and micromanagement gets a shot of steroids with that praise, signifying that this is exactly what management wants

then any of these issues will foster a group of micromanagers. These are common issues; hence, micromanagement, at some level, is common in many organizations.

How to create micromanagement – on steroids

If the organization is highly intolerant of errors, reinforces micromanaging and has an extreme focus on short-term gains, micromanaging will become a cultural norm and as such will become a desirable trait. It will be normalized. As I review my database referred to in Chapter 1, of 38 clients, micromanagement, as a cultural norm, was evident in 18 of them. In these companies, micromanagers were rewarded for being on top of the work at hand. These same firms also had very high turnover among the managers. In addition, especially in the technical and the management ranks, promotion from within was not the norm. Those firms that were very low on the micromanagement spectrum, without exception, had a practice of largely promoting from within.

Supervisory issues fostering micromanagement

Keep in mind that the characteristics that lead to micromanagement are, in and of themselves, good qualities. All senior executives want their supervisors and managers to have a caring attitude, attention to detail and a hands-on attitude. The problem in micromanaging is in the extreme nature that these quali-

WHAT'S A PERSONA?

A persona is an image you wish to project depending on your environment at that moment. It is often referred to as the "mask" we wear so we may "fit in". We have a different persona when we are at a social event than at a business negotiation, for example. We can have a persona and project who we wish to be at that moment, rather than who we really are. Or we can project what Kahn called "our true selves". There are two problem areas. First, if "who we are" is not what the job requires, and we are required to project a different persona, soon enough we are not performing well and we almost never feel "right" in the job. Second, if we are not careful, we actually believe that we are this persona, allowing us to fool ourselves. That sounds odd, but it is the rule rather than the exception. The way to find out "who you really are" is through challenge and the natural stress that comes with it. If under stress you perform admirably, likely that is "who you really are". C. G. Jung would say, "It is what you are called to do" and you are exhibiting "your true self".

ties are demonstrated. If you "care too much", "pay attention too much" and are "too hands on" you are simply too close to the work. The net effect is to steal the autonomy from those doing the work. Few things are more demotivating than being responsible for an outcome over which you have little control. The purpose of micromanaging is "to assure good outcomes, even if you must do it yourself"; and that hardly qualifies as supervising.

Micromanagement and trust

At the heart of micromanagement – at the individual level – is a lack of trust; both a lack of self-trust and a lack of trust in others. One issue is that the supervisor may misinterpret the attitude or the skill level of an individual. He may not trust the individual to get the work done, or he may not trust in his judgment to make that determination. If that is the case, he will then feel compelled to make sure things get done correctly and hence become over-involved and overly attentive.

Those are some of the behaviors of micromanagers, but what is driving those behaviors? At the root of these issues of trust is often a lack of self-confidence, and at the root of a lack of self-confidence is a low level of understanding of the work to be accomplished. So, this takes us right back to **Lost Skill Number One**, managers and supervisors who do not understand the concrete details of the work. When the managers and supervisors are not familiar with the concrete details of the work, this functionally eliminates their ability to be situational leaders, prevents them from delegating properly and, often, turns them into micromanagers. Once again, I cannot stress enough the debilitating effect of managers who are unfamiliar with the concrete details of the work.

Micromanagement and the persona – The pretenders

In addition to those with low self-confidence, there is yet another group that is poorly suited to be supervisors. These are people who have inordinate fear, anxiety, worry and even anger as part of their normal personality. I know they exist in many businesses, and in greater numbers than most people would like to admit. I have worked for several, both as an employee with Chevron and as a consultant. They are uniformly difficult to have as a subordinate or a peer and especially demoralizing as a supervisor.

Most people who wish to advance in their business know that fear, anxiety and anger are undesirable traits and not to be shown at work. Consequently, they develop a work-persona (see sidebar) that is consistent with the company norms. They develop what I call a "seems-to-be" personality. At their core, they harbor fears but "seem to be" very confident. They are natural worry-warts, but at work they "seem to be" cool, calm and collected. They have hair-trigger tempers, but at work they "seem to be" unaffected when others would normally get mad. They create a false persona to overcompensate for traits they know are antithetical to acceptance at work.

This persona, this false projection of who we really are, under normal circumstances, may allow us to perform. However, we cannot maintain this false projection forever. There are two circumstances that tend to expose those with this "seems-to-be" personality.

- First, in times of crisis and stress, they are unable to maintain this persona – as it is not who they truly are. Consequently, their less desirable – yet intrinsic – traits surface. Those managers you spoke with yesterday who "seemed to be" cool, calm and collected individuals become frazzled, rattled and disoriented when faced with a real crisis.
- There is yet another mechanism that will separate those with false personas versus those who are exhibiting their true selves – time. Maintaining a false persona is very effortful and in the fullness of time completely drains you as an individual and ends up damaging your working as well as your personal relationships. Being your "true self" may be uncomfortable at first, as you struggle to fit in. However, in the long run, it is both less effortful and more fulfilling than trying to maintain this false persona.

Situational leadership, micromanagement, intrinsic motivation and leader standard work

Keep in mind that a situational leader sets up those around him to succeed. Micromanagers, on the other hand, prevent employees from making – and taking responsibility for – their own decisions. But it's precisely the process of making decisions, and living with the consequences, that causes people to grow and improve. This growth process also feeds the intrinsic needs of both autonomy and competence. Good managers will not only guide and support their people as they set them up for success, but they will balance this with the independence to make decisions, and that involves the opportunity to fail. There is a balance that must be found by the manager, and it is different for each of his subordinates. It is a dynamic position that if managed too conservatively inhibits progress and individual growth, yet if handled too laissez-faire, will lead to project failure and fractured confidence.

If, as a supervisor, you wish to properly walk this tightrope, there is a simple solution; **talk to each of your subordinates on this topic,**

and do so frequently, openly, frankly and honestly in a two-way discussion. There is a very specific supervisory tool which should be used by all supervisors from the CEO to the first line supervisor which is designed for just this purpose; it is leader standard work. Leader standard work, with its two objectives of policy deployment and individual development, is the supervisory equivalent of standard work for the floor worker, as the name might suggest. If you are not familiar with this lean tool, it is nicely described, with details on our website at www.qc-ep.com.

Chapter Summary ... We explored three major issues in this chapter. First, we discussed the problems that arise when managers are not familiar with the concrete details of the work. We called this a lack of technical competence. This lack of technical competence is a fairly recent phenomenon; hence, it is the first of the lost traits. It was largely caused by the concept of "the MBA gone awry" starting in the '70s. The key problem was that managers were spending more time dealing with the "maps" than dealing with the "territory". This is largely correctable and not frequently found among the top performers. Also, I, for one, have not found it a problem in even one of my many Japanese clients. Next, we discussed the second lost trait, the ability to delegate. The loss of this management skill causes not only poor job execution but also steals the intrinsic needs of both autonomy and competence from the individuals. Finally, we addressed the natural outcome of these management skill sets that have become lost: the topic of micromanagement. Micromanagement is not a simple set of bad traits; rather, it is a set of admirable traits, including caring, attention to detail and a hands-on attitude, that have been taken to an extreme, with impactful and deleterious effects. The net effect of micromanagement is poor performance of your subordinates as well as a stifling of their professional growth. The cure to this is not a simple formula; rather, it requires frequent, open, honest, frank and two-way discussions between a boss and his subordinates so he can find the supervisory sweet spot between micromanagement and laissez-faire management.

What's next?? Wanna get to Management 2.0? Then you will need an awesome list of skills; here, we discuss two very critical ones. You can't get engagement without these skills described in Chapter 9.

Chapter 9

Management and Leadership – The Two New Skills

Aim of this Chapter ... to discuss two of the four "new" skills that need to be broadly used by the entire management team. They are the ability to create a learning, teaching and experimenting culture. The second skill is the ability to model the correct behaviors. Without these two skills, it is not practical to have even a Management 2.0 system. If you strive to be Management 3.0, you will need to be not just competent but very accomplished at these two skills.

The first new skill – Creating a learning, teaching and experimenting culture

"We get too soon old and – too late smart" Carolina Andreoletti Tam (my maternal grandmother)

From the work of Kahn (Chapter 3), we now know that engagement has components of cognitive (intellectual), physical (hard-working) and emotional (caring) commitment to the task at hand. When management focuses on creating a learning, teaching and experimenting culture, they are

PARADIGM SHIFT NO. 10

To learn effectively in a business environment, you must be able to not only comprehend the technical information, you must be able to apply it. Listening and regurgitating back information is not learning.

providing the fuel to engagement as they support the intellectual enlarge-
ment of the entire workforce. You will also notice that providing a learning,
teaching, experimenting work environment is one of the critical cultural
tools they need as they deal with the inevitable business changes that are
needed to survive and prosper. (See Wilson, 2015.)

What does a learning, teaching, experimenting culture look like??

All businesses spend some
time on teaching and learning,
mostly focused at the line operator. Scarce few have a training
program for management. When
does teaching and learning
become a true cultural norm?
Well, the culture is the "actions,
thoughts, beliefs, values, artifacts and language of a group of people" (Chapter
1). This means not just a few people but all the people in the group.

> **THE LEGAL TEST**
>
> I like to say, "If kaizen activity, PDCA or situational leadership were illegal activities, by taking a visit to your floor, could I find enough evidence to convict you?"

Again, in Chapter 1 we discussed the litmus test for creating and sustaining any cultural norm. If you wish to create a learning, teaching and experimenting culture, then your top managers must be exhibiting these traits. The
question is, "Are your managers, from the top-down, learning, teaching and
not only experimenting but fostering these behaviors amongst their subordinates?" If they are, you have a fighting chance to make this a cultural norm.
More specifically, are they studying their trade and their business? Are they
able to pass "The Five Tests of Management Commitment?" (see Appendix E).
Are they the gateway teachers to new and different skills? Do they teach their
subordinates, or do they expect some staff organization to do the teaching?
Does your organization just train your workers and then leave them alone to
do their work? Or do they continue to train and challenge them to expand
their competencies? If your firm is forever teaching and forever learning
and forever experimenting at all levels, then you have a culture of learning,
teaching and experimenting. When asked to assess this cultural element in a
company, I do not check out their training center nor do I check employee
records for classes they have taken; rather, I ask three questions and then go
to the gemba to find actual evidence. The three questions are:

- Are you practicing kaizen activity at all levels including management? and
- Is Plan, Do, Check and Act (PDCA) practiced at all levels?
- Is situational leadership practiced and taught?

So, if I can find these activities at all levels and in sufficient volume, then they have a culture which has a strong element of learning, teaching and experimenting.

Just where is the teaching, learning and experimenting occurring?

Even in an industrial setting, so much of what is called teaching occurs in the classroom and is normally dispensed using either Death by PowerPoint or distance learning via a webinar. Although this may be an EFFICIENT way to dispense this information, it is so wrong-headed it is hard to know where to start. In a sterile classroom, inundated by projected images, very little learning occurs. Perhaps the students learn a few new terms, but seldom do they come away with any new skills. A larger vocabulary does not qualify as learned behavior. It is a no-brainer that experimenting must be done on the floor. What is often not recognized is that most of both teaching and learning need to occur at the floor as well. Finally, the majority of the teaching should be done by your supervisor, punctuating his need to be technically competent. **It is this method of teaching, starting at the very top management, that not only creates the cultural norms but refines and changes them when necessary.**

If you doubt this last statement, just ask yourself questions like, "How did I learn my manners? How did I learn to interact in social groups?" Soon enough you will learn that much of what guides your behavior you learned by watching others and following their lead. I doubt many of us learned these traits by being locked up in a classroom, subjected to a stack of PowerPoint slides administered by a "staff expert". When it comes to learning behaviors as described above, we do not learn using this method … and the workplace is no exception. It does not work there either. We learn at the gemba, doing the real work under the guidance of a competent teacher.

> ## ACKOFF … ON BUSINESS SCHOOLS
>
> "Business schools do not teach students how to manage. What they do teach are (1) vocabularies that enable students to speak with authority about subjects they do not understand, and (2) to use principles of management that have demonstrated their ability to withstand any amount of disconfirming evidence. The only justification of these schools is the tickets of admission they provide to jobs where something about management can be learned" … Russell Ackoff (2010).

What are the key technical topics to train on first?

I have accumulated a lot of data from "reflections" of cultural changing activities over the last 29 years. From those reflections, I have gleaned a short list of skills that are needed in any culture-changing experience. This short list contains answers to the question, "If we were to do this over again, what would we focus our teaching/learning efforts on?" The list may surprise you; it is:

1. Standards as the basis of action and improvement
2. Leadership
3. Hoshin Kanri planning
4. Leader standard work
5. Problem solving
6. Statistical tools
7. Meeting management and facilitation

This list is adapted from my earlier book, *Lean Refining: How to Improve Performance in the Oil Industry*, (Wilson, 2017), where there is a great deal more explanation.

Kaizen activity

Kaizens are process and product improvements and they apply to all products and all processes. More and more, what I find when I go to the factory floor is some form of worker-initiated kaizens; this is very common. Unfortunately, and more often than not, the process of completing the kaizen is replete with forms and approvals, often delaying the kaizen and, worse yet, emasculating the work of those initiating the kaizen. Both the paperwork and the approvals need to be held to an absolute minimum or both the initiative and the autonomy (remember that word) of the worker are infringed upon. Neither of these issues enhances engagement. We have created many systems to complete kaizens and the one I like the best is "bureaucracy free". It is a simple whiteboard. Kaizens are written down by anyone, reviewed by other relevant workers and achieve supervisory approval or are explained why they cannot be done. The time cycle

> **PARADIGM SHIFT NO. 11**
>
> We learn by doing … and in no other way.

to approve and start work on the kaizen can easily be 24 hours and should not exceed 48 hours, for any three-shift operation. In this manner, all those affected can contribute.

Management kaizens

However, when I visit a facility and look around, what I do not find to be very common is kaizen of management activities. Most kaizens I see managers write have to do with processes other than their own, precluding learning, teaching and experimenting of those management processes – as a cultural norm. It also precludes changing and improving the management processes. When I do a system analysis of floor failures, like Dr. Deming has done, a causal study (looking for root causes of the failures), I find that over 90% of them are the direct result of what Dr. Deming called "the system"; it is just as easily called management processes. Some include the training process, the hiring process, the daily planning process, the strategic planning process, the problem solving process, the promoting process, the capital budget process, the process to select vendors, the bidding process … the list goes on.

Deeper problem solving is needed to learn

The anatomy of a typical root cause analysis of a production failure often only solves the surface problem, leaving the underlying situation there to crop up in yet another place. Let's say a customer returns some defective product. During the investigation, you determine that the "root cause" was a machine that had worn and needed maintenance. So, as corrective action, predictive maintenance was implemented. The problem is now thought to be resolved and no further work is done. However, several questions should be asked and answered. Why was this not addressed on the PFMEA? (the PFMEA is the *process failure mode and effects analysis* done on new processes to find and mitigate problems before they appear in process). Why did the current maintenance program not address this machine? Or more broadly you could ask: is our production preparation process adequate? Or, "Do we have the proper philosophy for maintenance? Are we looking at our Vision as we develop our maintenance program?" These are questions that dig deeper into the "root cause" question and more than anything they challenge the existing and underlying assumptions in the management system.

Single-loop learning

Managers, often with sincere passion, readily take on problems like the defective that leaked through the final testers and was found at the customer. Let's say an investigation was undertaken and it was found that the machine needed more frequent calibration. Often, the analysis stops at the point that the undesirable outcomes are mitigated. This is called "single-loop" problem solving.

The typical techniques used to solve a problem will lead to "single-loop" learning and we will learn "how to do these things properly". It will not answer the deeper questions of:

■ how did we get into this fix in the first place?
■ why did our normal processes not protect us and
■ why did it persist so long before we addressed it?.

The need for introspection

Unfortunately, when it is time to dig deeper and place the values, the motives and the behavior and the underlying assumptions that caused the failure to the complete scrutiny of the Six Questions of Continuous Improvement, the management team just does not want to be exposed to that level of scrutiny. This unwillingness – toward cold, hard, dispassionate and deep introspection – is a very common problem in businesses; as in life. The journey into "self-awareness" is often too difficult and too painful for many. Among my Top Seven firms mentioned in Chapter 1, venturing into self-scrutiny was only widely practiced by three of the firms. Not coincidentally, these three had the best overall performance, including the lowest attrition and had the three highest engagement scores.

Double-loop learning

Many of the problems we attack are not new. What is new is our awareness that they exist. Since many of the problems have persisted for quite some time, it is logical, and correct, to assume there are deeper issues that need to be addressed. These deeper problems are often buried deeply in the values, beliefs, motives and underlying assumptions we hold – or do not hold. And many of these values, beliefs, motives and underlying assumptions are not readily obvious. That is, not until we ask some deeper, penetrating questions. This review of values, motives and underlying assumptions to a problem is called "double-loop" learning and leads you to answer the question, "**At the management level, are we doing the right things?**". This review is a powerful and inciteful process and is often accompanied by plenty of angst for those participating. As you might expect, this technique accelerates not only your learning but your business improvement as well. (Single-loop and double-loop learning are terms coined by Chris Argyris, [Argyris, 2010].)

As we move to a fully engaged workforce, we will rely heavily on not only the increased awareness achieved through single-loop learning but also the increased awareness by using double-loop learning. This is the area that is most fruitful for management-level kaizens, yet I cannot give you even one company that does this regularly and rigorously.

Practicing PDCA

PDCA, the plan, do, check,

TEACHING AND LEARNING FAILURES

I have used and studied the Training Within Industries (TWI) methodology, and, in its original form, it is still the very best training delivery method for factory floor training I have seen. However, they make a basic statement repeatedly which I find incomplete. They say simply, "If the student did not learn, the teacher did not teach". Their implication is that if the student did not learn, then the teacher was deficient in some measure. By placing the burden on the teacher in this manner, I find a problem. I can give you many circumstances where, given the same training, some people learned and others did not. On the other hand, there is an old proverb that says, "When the student is ready, the teacher will appear". This adage then places the burden on the student to be ready. Likewise, I have seen many circumstances where eager and ready students were given instruction but not really taught. While both may be partially true, neither is helpful to improve the situation. Unfortunately, both are bad paradigms and focus attention on the people.

What I teach is: "the teacher will teach and the student will learn *when the system is ready*".

act cycle, is based on the scientific method, yet goes beyond the scientific method. The plan, do and check portion is largely the scientific method of creating a hypothesis and testing it. From the scientific process, we can learn a great deal indeed. When we teach PDCA, it goes beyond the experiment and the learning from the experiment; it takes you to the continuous improvement cycle via the "Act" step. By "Act" we mean **thoughtful action**, which may include consciously and responsibly deciding to not act at all. As you implement the "Act" portion, you now have converted spot learning into continuous learning and the cycle just goes on and on and on and the learning continues and continues and continues.

Acting on the results and the means

In the industrial setting, the actions following PDC should be of two types. There should be action focused on the "results". For example, if we met our specific results, do we now standardize or do we set another plan to improve further? In addition, again following the check, we should determine if actions regarding the "means" of our PDC were the best we could use. For example, did we plan well? If not, what should, or could we do next time? Did we have the right group of people involved? How do we do this better next time? The action steps should guide us to the next "thoughtful action". It is not only learning about the "results"; it is learning about the "means" – the process that created the results.

> "I shall assume that knowledge begins and ends in experimental data, but it does not end in the data in which it begins".
>
> (Shewhart, 1939)

PDCA and it imposters …

PDCA, plan, do, check and act has many imposters … and each of them falls far short of being a learning or a teaching experience. Each of these imposters not only fails to teach but it also makes the process worse, adding to the existing chaos. By initials, they include: PDHM; PDCI; PDCRAS; and PDCT.

PDHM

PDHM is plan, do, hope and move on. There is no real check and the only action is to hope things will work out. Any time that data on results are ignored, PDHM is usually the PDCA imposter.

PDCI

PDCI is a little more advanced as things are planned, checked and ignored. This is often the result with the bulk of computer-gathered data.

PDCRAS

PDCRAS is increasingly more common. It stands for plan, do, check and then record and store. This is similar to PDCI except the data is not totally ignored, just mostly. This includes a wide array of management reports replete with irrelevant and out-of-date information. In PDCRAS most of these data are collected not because they "should be"; rather, they are collected because they "can be". I find the main culprit here is that the facility really does not understand and use the Three Rules of Data Management as given by Dr. Ishikawa. They are:

1. Know the purpose of the data
2. Collect it efficiently
3. Take action based on the data

(Ishikawa, 1982)

PDCT

PDCT, to me, is the saddest of all the forms. It is plan, do, check and tinker. Tinkering is the term for adjusting a process when no adjustment is necessary. It is a direct result of not being able to distinguish common cause variation from special cause variation (Deming, 1982). The problem is that the worker is trying to do his best and the system, created by his management, is working to his disadvantage. He is attentive and acting. Unfortunately, the action he is taking is making the process deteriorate rather than improve. In nearly all cases, he has not been given the correct methods for process adjustment, which is clearly a management responsibility.

PDCA and prediction

Prediction and the factory floor … It is an ongoing experiment

Dr. Deming on prediction:

> "Management is prediction. The theory of knowledge helps us to understand that management in any form is prediction. The

simplest plan – how may I go home tonight – requires prediction that my automobile will start and run, or that the bus will come, or the train".

(Deming, 1994)

Toyota, among others, is known for its teaching–learning environment, and what is not commonly understood is that they all **have been taught** that their entire production system is a series of ongoing hypothesis tests. Engineers and managers have designed "specific activities" that should achieve "specific results"; these specific results are

HYPOTHESES AND HYPOTHESIS TESTING

A hypothesis is a scientific guess based on prior observations and theory. It is not a stab in the dark; rather, the scientist, based on theory, has made observations such that he believes there is some cause–effect relationship. Based on this, he makes a hypothesis which is a statement in the form of "If we do these specific things, we will get these specific results". Then he designs an experiment to test it. He controls "these specific things" and checks to see if he gets "these specific results" and either confirms or disproves his hypothesis. It is very interesting to many people that he generally learns ten times as much when he disproves his hypothesis. In lay terms, most people would say his experiment failed. The true scientist, seeking to learn, understands the power of disproving hypotheses and uses this new-found information to augment his knowledge base.

a prediction on their part. As part of the process, there are "checks" to see if the predicted results were achieved. If so, the hypothesis is confirmed, and if not, it is disproven. Once disproven, it is managements task to: make sure it is investigated; the weaknesses found and corrected; and have a new hypothesis created and checked.

In 1939, long before anyone heard of the Toyota Production System (TPS), Walter Shewhart, speaking of the mass production process in a plant, wrote:

"… specification, production and inspection, correspond respectively to making a hypothesis, carrying out an experiment and testing the hypothesis and the three steps correspond to the three steps in a *dynamic scientific process of acquiring knowledge*"

(Shewhart, 1939) and

"results of an experiment should be presented in a way to contribute most readily to the development of the knowing process".

(Shewhart, 1939)

The uniqueness of thinking of all production as a hypothesis, an experiment and a test is not new to American industry. But like much of what Deming and Shewhart taught, it got lost. Now as we study and learn from Japanese systems such as the TPS, we are re-learning the things we cast aside 80 years ago. My grandmother was right. As you recall, she told me, "we get too soon old and too late smart". At the heart of all this is what Shewhart called a *dynamic scientific process of acquiring knowledge".* As I study manufacturing systems like those at Toyota, Honda, Nissan and Mitsubishi to name a few, what sets them apart on the surface is their process stability and their cultural strength. However, below the surface when we ask, "what is the foundation they build upon?", the answer is that they cultivate and nurture an environment of continuous learning, teaching and experimenting, built on the PDCA model.

The hazards of experimenting

In all experiments, there is the danger of failure. Even though we learn the greatest amount when we fail, we seldom design an experiment to intentionally fail. Rather than failing, I like to say, "we just gathered more information on our way to success", and that is ultimately true if failures cease to be treated as failures but are treated as learning experiences. This is a highly desirable, extremely powerful, but rarely found cultural trait. Nonetheless, we almost always wish to confirm our hypothesis. Confirmation leads to direct progress and we now know what we can do with certainty. There is a simple way to improve our odds in experimentation on processes. That is to include the people with the most intimate process knowledge in the experimental design. No group has more intimate knowledge than the workers on the line. By including them in the experimental design, you achieve two very important objectives. First, you will improve your chances of success. Second, whether the hypothesis is confirmed or not, you have many eyes watching the process, so your subsequent actions can be even more powerful.

Kaizens and PDCA and risk

PDCA starts with plan; hence, it is a form of prediction and that prediction is part of the hypothesis. To make the prediction requires observation and this means that the observer must have some, if not intimate, process knowledge.

There is one extremely important aspect of management that cannot be understated as we work to create a fully engaged workforce. As it turns out, a key to improving employee engagement includes the concept that we will need to make improvement in the production process itself. Making improvements – interestingly enough – is both an antecedent to and a logical outcome of engagement. There is no such thing as improvement without change and there is no change without risk of failure. Now, if we really want people to be entrepreneurial and take risks, they need to know the boundary conditions to operate within and the consequences of both success and failure. And most of all, they need to know that having some experiments fail is OK as long as it is part of an overall learning experience. The alternative, which is all too common, is that most companies have a strong intolerance for failure. With this intolerance, you get not only a loss of initiative and a loss of progressive change but also a loss of trust.

JIT Training

Throughout this book, you have heard and will hear me discouraging the use of classroom training. I find most businesses favor classroom training because they view it to be financially and time efficient to get a whole bunch of people "up to speed". Quite frankly, I find most of this training to be pure waste … not all, just most. First, this is almost always a manifestation of a culture that has a very short-term perspective and is focused solely on financials as the key metrics to drive the business. They will think of efficiency first and ignore effectiveness. When it comes to training, efficiency means nothing if the training is not effective. Second, training is behavioral-related and scarce little can be taught in a classroom setting. It can be introduced, basics often can be discussed, but the changing of the work habits, the behavioral aspect, to be effective, must be taught on the factory floor using the real equipment in the real environment. Sometimes, if you have good simulators – and I don't mean computer models, I mean physical simulators – you can effectively complete a portion of the training in the classroom. Third, for learning to be effective, the student must want to, and be able to, absorb the materials. The student must immediately apply the techniques he has learned or they will soon enough be forgotten. This is seldom the case for most of the students in this classroom training environment. This further diminishes any learning that did occur and makes the training even less effective. Finally, there is nothing wrong with doing a little classroom training to explain the basic concepts of lean, and getting peoples' feedback is a good idea. It should be a 1-hour introduction with 1 hour for Q&A. It should not be 8 hours of "Death by PowerPoint", one of the more recent industrial epidemics. If Death by PowerPoint is no longer an option, just how do we get started?

Simply enough, you jump into action mode!! Quit talking and go grab your sensei, and consistent with True North (See Chapters 16 and 17), pick a problem, any problem. Start with the Six Questions of Continuous Improvement. As soon as you run into an obstacle that hinders problem solving, seek assistance from your sensei. Be ready for questions!!!!! And then when it has been determined you will need some cool lean tool, he can teach it. He can supply JIT (just in time) training. In this way, you have "pulled" in the specific tools you will need to be successful. Furthermore, since you want this tool to solve your problem and can apply it right now, you will very likely learn it. Following this, you then go back to the six questions and continue on your journey to becoming lean ... you are problem solving your way to the ideal state ... recall, this is part one of the "Means to Lean".

> "It is more obvious in acquiring motor skills than in acquiring intellectual knowledge—but no more true—that learning is an active process rather than a passive one. The necessary effort will be expended only if there is a 'felt' need on the part of the learner".
>
> (McGregor, 1960)

Let me share with you things I have learned that changed completely the concept of good teaching in my mind.

JIT training and questioning

After all, Socrates knew that. It seems like we forgot some of the real lessons of the past. We forgot the teaching of Shewhart and Deming, but even before that we forgot about Socrates ... go figure.

I have found that since most of the knowledge is already present, most of the learning needed can be drawn out. Questioning will do this. There are two other aspects of "teaching by questioning" that promote long-term retention. First, it requires you to meet the student where they are; they are the client, they are the focus. Second, as soon as you ask the first question, you can assess their current level of understanding. So, the system builds on what they already know. You can make a strong connection to their prior data and they will assimilate the new material much better. It will have greater context and make more sense to them and they will retain the information for a much longer time. JIT training is the essence of the "Initiative Mantra".

- *Start where you are*
- *Use what you have*
- *Do what you can.*

Growth and failure

I can tell you with certainty that the greatest learning experiences in my life have been when I failed. Almost anyone over 50 will tell you the same thing. Jerry Yeagley, the great soccer coach from Indiana University, once told me:

> *"The coach's two best friends are the bench and a loss".*

He went on to explain that success, if not balanced with humility, breeds complacency and even arrogance. In a student, those are not traits conducive to learning. However, failure has a focusing feature that gets everyone's attention.

> "If … 'post mortems' comprise no more than a search for a culprit in order to place the blame, they will provide learning of one kind. If, on the other hand, it is recognized that mistakes are an inevitable occurrence in the trial-and-error process of acquiring problem solving skills, they can be the source of other and more valuable learning".
>
> (McGregor, 1960)

In short, that means that you must make failure possible by challenging your people, but you also must make failing acceptable, at some level, or they will not accept the challenge. In many businesses, failure in any form is highly and openly criticized. This creates two compounding and very negative effects. First, when people encounter failure, they will hide it and no one learns. This then gets compounded by the fact that people then become risk-averse and won't accept the slightest of challenges. A double negative whammy to learning.

> *"Let's face it, we're all imperfect and we're going to fall short on occasion. But we must learn from failure and that will enable us to avoid repeating our mistakes. Through adversity, we learn, grow stronger, and become better people".*

> (John Wooden)

The second new skill – Behavioral modeling

As we discussed in the Six Critical Skills of Lean Leadership, Skill No. 5 was:

> **Leaders as role models:** They walk the talk. They are lean competent. They know what to do and they know how to do all of Lean that is job specific to their current function in the organization. There is no substitute for this. NONE.

Notice the final comments, "There is no substitute for this. NONE". Second only to recognition and rewards, modeling is, by far, the most powerful teaching mechanism that affects behavior. If you doubt this last statement, just ask yourself questions like, "How did I learn my manners? How did I learn to interact in social groups? Why is it that my son is more polite at school than he is at home?" Soon enough, you will learn that much of what guides your behavior you learned by watching others and following their lead. It is not only a strong form of learning in the workplace but in school, in social gatherings, at home and even sporting events. And it is not only social behavior we learn by modeling; it completely spills over into work behaviors and even technical competencies.

Why is modeling so important?

First, through their actions, when managers model behaviors in the workplace, they establish the acceptable standards. Managers are good role models when they impeccably exhibit the behaviors they wish to see in others, including both personal traits and technical abilities. **For many managers below the 3.0 level,** they expect those reporting to them to read about and practice new management techniques, but somehow, for them, their own personal plan for self-development seems to smack of weakness. They somehow think it is OK for them to take 2-hour lunches but reprimand others who do. When they introduce the Six Questions of Continuous Improvement, they expect others to use this powerful tool, but as they try to unravel the problems at their level, such as customer acceptance, compliance with the annual plan or hiring issues, they rely on gut-level intuition and tribal knowledge to make their decisions. They will frequently take shortcuts and violate rules when it is more convenient, yet they rule others with an iron hand. When it comes to values, **managers below 3.0** often exhibit a certain and convenient moral flexibility that they will not tolerate in others. Managers who say "don't do as I do; rather, do as I say" can only lead based on position power, and the 3.0 manager must be stronger and broader than that.

When management wishes to establish standards of behavior, what they say is important. However, what they do, if it not in harmony with what they say, will trump what they say – every time. It's like the adage, "Your actions speak so loud, I don't need to hear what you have to say". Consequently, when management wishes to change part, or all, of the culture, **the management changes in behavior must precede what they expect from others**.

Second, modeling is a particularly powerful technique because a great deal of what we learn by watching the behavior of others is learned unconsciously; that is, we are not aware of it.

The anatomy of modeling – Social learning theory

Social learning theory is the view that people learn by observing others and was popularized by Albert Bandura's work in the 1960s. Social learning theory explains modeling (imitation) and how people learn new behaviors, values and attitudes. Social learning requires:

■ paying attention to the person(s) observed;
■ remembering the observed behavior;

- replicating the behavior; and
- having a motivation to act the same way.

The power behind this concept in the workplace is a list of strong motivators that encourages people to "want to" model these "correct" behaviors. Motivators include:

- It improves your ability to be seen as a high performer by your boss if you "look like the boss".
- It improves your promotability if you are seen as "fitting in" (see sidebar).
- Social acceptance in the workplace, which will likely enhance your ability to work well with others and enhance teamwork.
- And the oldest one of all, "Imitation is the most sincere form of flattery". A little flattery of the bosses can go a long way so you might "be-seen-as" – even in the light of contradictory facts.

Too much imitation

While managers need to model the correct behaviors and should expect their subordinates to follow suit, taken out of context, this concept can be counterproductive. When the subordinates are imitating the bosses on which country clubs to belong to, which restaurants to eat at and where they buy their clothes … they are imitating behavior to curry personal favors, not support the business culture. This type of ass-kissing, while frequently successful when it comes to raises and promotions, is not what we are discussing here.

The key factor in modeling

Of course, the most important factor is that managers model the behaviors they want to see in others. While on the surface this seems obvious,

KANTER ON PROMOTABILITY

Sad but true …
"Rosabeth Kanter, in her analysis of factors governing managerial promotion and success in large corporations, found that personal chemistry was the key determinant. In her words, it boiled down to five factors: appearance, personality, aggressiveness, executive stature, and promotability. 'The interesting thing about these five essential ingredients', Kanter observed, 'is that they don't include professional competence'" (Pascale and Athos, 1981).

many managers are not good at this. They are not good at modeling, and not because they miss the concept. They are not good because they are not good observers of their own behaviors. When it comes to being self-aware, they have a blind spot. You will note that the No. 1 Skill of Lean Leadership is "leaders as superior observers". Being self-observant is a large part of that skill inventory. In fact, the gateway quality for any corrective action, for any change or really for any conscious response is awareness. If we are not aware of something, we always run the risk that, whatever it is, it will control us rather than we will control it. Such is the case here. If we as managers are not aware of our behaviors, it is very easy – even with the most sincere motives – to send the wrong messages.

Chapter Summary ... We explored two topics in this chapter: First, we discussed creating a teaching, learning, experimenting environment. The factory is a natural place for this as every part made is part of an industrial experiment based on a hypothesis and a hypothesis test. However, we will also go beyond the hypothesis and its test and into PDCA, which requires follow-up action on the "check" in an effort to continuously improve. Unfortunately, most firms employ some version of PDCA that falls short of this strong tool. Even fewer firms actively pursue double-loop learning, effectively allowing old paradigms to guide new actions. Second, we addressed the topic management modeling. This powerful trait is a key to learning for the organization and is second only to recognition and rewards as a motivator to create and sustain change. Equally important, modeling is the way a large number of standards and expectations are communicated to the entire facility.

What's next?? Wanna get to Management 3.0? Then you will need even more skills, and two of the really powerful ones are described in Chapter 10, our next discussion.

Chapter 10

Management and Leadership – The Two Key Skills

Aim of this Chapter ... In this chapter, we will discuss the two new skills preventing businesses from fully attaining a Management 3.0 system. The first topic is the need to create an environment that facilitates mentoring. This goes well beyond the management need to be good supervisors. The second topic: being inquisitive and integrative as opposed to being advocates and admirers of their works, a powerful set of management behaviors that not only feed the intrinsic needs which precipitate engagement but also work to facilitate whole person development. We will examine both concepts.

The third new skill – Promoting and participating in mentoring

What supervisory work are you doing to maximize the development of your people?

When I ask that question of most companies, I get a discussion that reduces itself to "the annual appraisal". If by now you do not know, let me tell you my opinion on the annual appraisal system ... it does more harm than good. I could go on for reams on the problems with the annual appraisal and rating system, but let me not rant. Rather, let me introduce you to a much better solution: one that works for both worker and supervisory development as a two-way tool and actually enhances individual growth and plant performance. Have your supervisors use the Five Supervisory Tools, which are:

1. Five-year business growth and staffing planning
2. Job succession planning
3. Individual performance planning (IPP)
4. Individual 5-year growth and development planning
5. Leader standard work (LSW).

Tools 1 and 2 are business tools to help the management better plan for the future and develop the entire work team. Tools 3 and 4 are specific development tools focused solely on individual development. Tool 5, leader standard work, relative to individual performance and development, is focused on frequent, timely and data-based feedback

Five-year business growth and staffing plan

This is a tool that lets us look at the facility's strategic plan over the next 5 years and ask ourselves, "Just how will we staff that in the future? What will our structure be, and what kind of skills will we need?" The process starts with the 5-year strategic plan for the facility. From this, managers can then create a hiring plan and a training plan for their respective groups. This is used in planning for promotions as well as personnel development and training.

Job succession planning

Here, as a facility, we look at job-specific attrition that may be caused by retirements, promotions and even those who might quit. We ask, "If Margarita left her job today, who is a capable replacement?" For each job, we create a list of potential candidates with the categories (1) Ready now, (2) Ready in one year or less with more job-specific skill development, and (3) Ready with more job-specific skill development; greater than 1 year of development is required.

Individual performance planning (IPP)

This plan addresses the growth and developmental needs in the current job. If the subordinate would have this discussion with his or her boss, the performance plan would be the documented answer. The discussion would start, "Boss, when you evaluate my performance, I want to be the very best employee you can imagine. To get that evaluation from you, what must I do in the next year?" IPPs are not an appraisal, they are a development plan.

Individual five-year growth and development planning

This is just what the title implies. And in this challenge, the supervisors address how they can assist each subordinate to improve, integrated with job succession planning (what can or should the supervisor do?). In addition, we challenge the individuals, so they grow at the maximum rate through self-development (what can or should the employee do?).

Leader standard work (LSW)

You will recall that the purpose of LSW is both policy deployment and employee development. Part of the process for LSW is routine feedback to all employees. For senior-level employees this should be at least monthly; for workers, first- and second-level supervisory, this feedback should be at least weekly.

Why is that not enough??

Quite frankly, for every company I have worked for that used two-way discussions in employee performance and development, I can show you ten that only do the annual performance review; and it is usually done each December – a message in itself. The firms that I see who strive to have a Management 3.0 system are more prone to have some of the Five Supervisory Tools, with LSW and IPP being common. Some even have ventured into Individual 5-Year Growth and Development Planning, and some are addressing the topic of long-term staffing as part of new product launches and Advanced Product Quality Planning (APQP). This is a process most automobile companies require of their tier one suppliers. However, the problem is that these are all company processes. No matter how well they are administered, they are company-initiated, company designed and company managed.

We need mentoring

More and more, people in business wish to have more say-so in the things that affect them. They are seeking autonomy. Individuals want to and benefit when they seek out and work on the areas of their life, including work, they wish to address. That is the inherent benefit of mentoring.

Mentoring misunderstood?

Much of the original concept of mentoring has been lost. It has gotten lost in the morass and misunderstanding of the concepts of teaching, learning, training, coaching and doing. Teaching is imparting knowledge to your student. It is intellectual in nature, and learning is the acquisition of that knowledge. Training and coaching go beyond intellectual understanding and are both behavioral in nature. They are beyond acquiring an intellectual base and they are about doing, not just thinking, talking and philosophizing about things. With both training and coaching, your objective is to get people to be able to do new things; it is education by doing. It applies to training the cell worker, it applies to supervisors, as you might train them to make and give feedback to their subordinates. It applies to managers, as you might

> **MENTORING**
>
> The concept of mentoring comes from the *Odyssey* of Homer. When Ulysses went to war, he turned over the care of his household and all he had to his trusted friend, Mentor. Most important to the Greeks was the raising of their male children. He entrusted this sacred duty to Mentor. And it was a serious trust indeed because as a minimum he would be gone for years or, in the worse case, get killed. It is this raising of his son that is the most important task for Mentor. It was not just making sure he had food and shelter, but Mentor's major task was to raise his son Telemachus to become a good Greek. That meant he not only needed to be a good warrior but reflect all that was great about Greece. In a phrase, he needed to make sure Telemachus was a complete person, in the finest Greek tradition ... and nothing less. Mentor clearly understood the breadth and depth of his job with Telemachus. It is this breadth and depth of the concept of mentoring that has largely been lost. Mentoring goes well beyond both teaching and coaching to the development of the whole person, physically, intellectually, emotionally and spiritually as well.

train them to do Hoshin Kanri (HK) planning, for example. Learning is mental; training and coaching are mental AND physical. Yet you can see in the literature, on the internet and amongst the consultants, much of coaching, training and even learning – is called mentoring. Mentoring is a very popular buzzword and consultants use it to describe what they do, even when it is not true mentoring. More often than not it is coaching and often just training. While coaching and training are beneficial at some level, they are distinguishable from mentoring.

What is mentoring??

Mentoring is teaching, training, coaching and even more. In mentoring, the objective is "whole person development" – in the environment of concern. Hence, when I mentor my students (mentee just sounds funny to me), we work on not only what they are doing but why they are doing it and how it affects them physically, intellectually, emotionally and spiritually, as well as how it affects those around them. Mentoring is very integrative by its very nature. My first question for my mentoring students is, "How are you doing?" and they have learned to understand that does not just mean "at work". The suffixes added also include, "with your family", "at home", "with your hobby", "with your health", "with your career"; the list is endless. To help them, I need to know what is on their mind. Then, depending on how they answer the first question, there are usually follow-up questions with a great deal of dialogue. In so doing, I try to help them. In truth, I seldom really help them in the traditional sense of helping them by giving them advice. If we are lucky, and we usually are, I can then ask them a series of questions which will allow them to help themselves; which, of course, is the real objective.

I have yet to see mentoring done properly in a business setting – in any business setting. I have worked in one facility that had what they called mentors, but mostly it was a sincere effort to get high-quality support for individuals. Although it was effective, in that people grew in their jobs and some even grew personally, it still fell short of true mentoring for at least two reasons.

■ First, it was required; there is no way mentoring can be mandated. To make the personal commitment to make the mentoring process work, it absolutely must be a voluntary process by both the mentor and the student.

■ Second, very often the mentor was the person's supervisor and the supervisory relationship got in the way of a more personal relationship.

A mentoring relationship is based on trust

If you have not already realized it, a mentoring relationship absolutely must have high levels of openness, honesty and trust. Often this is very difficult when your mentor is your boss, as in the company cited earlier. Most of what they did was coaching and, in and of itself, that was helpful. The program was successful, in that the students gained additional skills, work skills. It just was not real mentoring as it only focused on developing work skills – not skills in other areas of life. It was, however, the closest I have seen in an industrial setting. This location was a Toyota facility.

> **KANTER ON PROMOTABILITY**
>
> Sad but true …
>
> "Rosabeth Kanter, in her analysis of factors governing managerial promotion and success in large corporations, found that personal chemistry was the key determinant. In her words, it boiled down to five factors: appearance, personality, aggressiveness, executive stature, and promotability. 'The interesting thing about these five essential ingredients', Kanter observed, 'is that they don't include professional competence'" (Pascale and Athos, 1981).
>
> Yeah, I know you just read this in Chapter 9. I repeated it for a reason; don't miss that point.

I do see a decent amount of coaching and even some very personal and specific coaching. For example, I was working recently with a CEO who had hired a "coach" to help him and his direct reports deal with the issue of trust within the senior management ranks. But this was not mentoring, it was "about the topic of trust" rather than individual development. In addition, the coach, who would discuss this topic with all involved, would then report group progress back to the CEO. Hence, the trust and confidence needed for the mentor–mentee relationship was not adequate for open, honest dialogue. When the other members of the C-suite had their discussions with the coach, they knew they were not confidential. They were soon to be shared with the CEO, who quite frankly may have been the root cause of the trust issue in the first place. The entire effort turned out to be ineffective.

Mentoring is not coaching, and sometimes coaching is misguided as well

I also know of several cases where "mentors" were hired to work with young managers with lots of upward mobility to "prepare" them for future high-level management roles. This is not mentoring. This is simply coaching, and quite frankly most of what I saw was not about management skill development; rather, it was about the skills to **"appear to be a manager"**. (See sidebar … Kanter On Promotability. Yeah, it's the same sidebar as you read in Chapter 9. You might conclude that I find it not only relevant but revealing as well.)

Mentoring is a voluntary, confidential process

In mentoring, mentors are not assigned; they become mentors based on a joint decision of the mentor and the student. And there is absolutely no reporting at all; none. Your task as a mentor is to assist that person individually, and your sole responsibility is to them alone. I only know of one place that does mentoring as it was intended. That is, in several churches. Specifically, I have worked with some young pastors who have mentors, and these mentors are seasoned pastors who want to mentor. Their sole purpose is to help the young pastor decide if pastoring is his calling. In so doing, they need to explore all the issues the prospective pastor might have, and the mentors have no upward reporting obligations; in fact, they are sworn to an individual mentor–mentee relationship, no matter what they learn.

> **INTEGRITY AND DEFINITION DRIFT**
>
> Often, through misuse, the definition of words will drift. Integrity is one such word. In my 1954 *Webster's Collegiate Dictionary*, integrity means: (1) state or quality of being complete, whole, undivided or unbroken; (2) unimpaired state, soundness, purity. However, a newer dictionary, Webster's from the web, lists the definition as: the state of being honest or fair. When something has integrity, it is whole, it is complete. The act of integration is to bring together with the objective that all functions will benefit from the synergism of being "one". Most of us have heard of racial integration; that is one example of coming together. In a plant when the engineering, planning, maintenance and operations come together, are integrated, the synergisms will benefit the plant as a whole.

Mentoring is a skill management needs to encourage in the workplace. Mentors and students need to create, on their own, a mentor–student relationship. This relationship needs to transcend the business needs and focus on individual development and is based on the highest levels of trust. It is practically impossible for managers to mentor their direct reports or anyone in their organization. Yet, mentoring is a trait that management should encourage.

What should the management team do to promote mentoring?

In practically all businesses, there are people, usually young ones, who wish to have a mentor. Likewise, there are always some more seasoned managers and workers who wish to become mentors. If, within the company, mentees do not feel there is someone they can have a mentoring relationship with, they should seek out a mentor elsewhere. This should be encouraged. It is to management's advantage to connect these two groups. The management team should:

- Teach the difference between mentoring, training, coaching, teaching and learning
- Teach how to mentor for those wishing instruction
- Create a list of people who would like to be mentors with any caveats they wish to employ
- Make this list available
- Encourage people to become both mentors and mentees
- Make sure to keep mentoring a volunteer activity
- Do not allow mentoring to become part of the promotion or the performance appraisal system; all mentor–mentee discussion must be confidential

The fourth new management skill – Inquisitiveness and Integration

As I mentioned in the Preface, my initial interest was on management. However, the topic of engagement overcame me. Before I had this epiphany about engagement, I was well into preparing an outline and had a good start on a list of chapters to write. At that time, I had no idea what the completed book looked like, but I was sure I had discovered what I would later call the most powerful management trait. First, some background.

You first must cover the "givens"

As we are discussing these management and leadership styles in a typical business, we take certain concepts for granted. For example, the most important management trait is probably to make sure you pay your people. After all, you have a contract to work with them; they do what you ask and you pay them. The second most important trait probably is that you'll create no harm; if you don't have a safe workplace, that's a major problem. There are other concepts we almost take for granted. However, beyond this list of "givens", there is a list of management and leadership behaviors that are the answer to "How do I get the most out of my people?". At the same time, there is no "silver bullet". That is, "acquire a dose of this quality" and it will vault you and your company to greatness; there is no such skill. To create a fully engaged workforce takes a broad range of skills, massive amounts of sheer effort, and a little luck along the way never hurts. However, there are some skills which seem to have a larger impact, actually an exaggerated impact. This is precisely the trait to which I refer.

Toshi helped me out – I found this trait several years ago, by pure luck. It is inquisitiveness and integration instead of advocacy and admiration

When I interviewed Toshi Amino, my mentor, prior to gathering information for my book, *Lean Refining* (Wilson, 2017), we spent 3 intense and long days together as I picked his brain. However, each day, after dinner, I would return to my hotel, compile my notes and prepare for the next day. My first night in Marysville, Friday night, while recapping my notes, I was surprised at how little I had written down. I reflected on our discussions from the day, and it dawned on me that I had done most of the talking. I recapped in my mind some of our discussions and I found Toshi was asking me something like three times as many questions as I was asking him … yet he was the one I wanted information from. It was clear I needed to change this. For our discussion on both Saturday and Sunday, I consciously changed the discussion and got him to speak more; but I needed to be on my toes and needed to work at it. On our second day, I noticed that when I had something to say, he would often reflect it back to me, or ask me for clarification, seeking an example. Seldom would he disagree; rather, he would dig deeper into my thoughts. Interestingly, at no time did I ever feel he had an agenda to push upon me; rather, I was flattered that he wanted to hear what I had to say.

But soon enough, what I realized was that he often was taking a relatively small thought and enlarging it for the both of us ... and that was the point of it ... it was for the benefit of both of us. I thought about this dynamic and coupled it with some of my prior discussions and interactions with Toshi. I also thought about many discussions I had with others and found a stark contrast. It was truly an enlightening moment. One of those "Aha" moments when you are hit with the lightning bolt of clarity. Then I wrote down in my notes a summary of his behavior in our interactions, and my note was:

"inquisitiveness and integrity versus advocacy and admiration"

I found that Toshi wanted to question me further for **his and my** clarification. He wanted to then integrate the newness of our discussion into **his and my** knowledge base to make it larger and more complete. Keep that in mind as we go further; he made the thought larger and more complete.

During our discussion, it was obvious to me that he was teaching, without even appearing to be teaching, and that I was learning. However, what I was not aware of was, without knowing it, I was also teaching him and he was learning because of it. I was totally unaware that I was teaching. Furthermore, because of the atmosphere he created, through his questioning and listening, he had managed to increase the knowledge base of both of us. Both he and I had become larger; we were each more whole with a larger understanding of the topic. He had transformed the environment such that both he and I were simultaneously teachers of the topics as well as students of the topic of discussion.

Toshi's technique was one of asking questions, inquiring into your mind and experiences, at the same time as he shared his thoughts in a "what-do-you-think about" format. Then you and he could integrate these thoughts to come up with an enlarged and joint understanding

What do I hear from other senior managers??

I contrasted this with many discussions I had with others, especially those in the C-Suite. Too often, I could recall them almost pushing their ideas on you, expecting you to reinforce and recognize their approach as being a good one. Although they would often ask for advice, it is more like, "This is what I think, can you improve upon it?" Even though they may state their thought as a question, rather than being inquisitive, more often than not, they are looking for validation, they are looking for someone else to validate their observations and approach. It is like they wish someone to not only validate their ideas, they are looking for someone to praise them for the brilliance of such ideas.

They seldom wanted you to broaden the topic by interjecting new ideas, and least of all did they want any questioning of their ideas. All too commonly, the last thing they wanted to hear was a question like, "Well, on the floor I see this (giving them some example); how does that fit with your concept?" Rather than look for questions so you can jointly better understand the topic, they are looking for validation, if not admiration, for their wonderful thought … even if it's not so wonderful.

What is the typical reality?

Consequently, what I see more of, all over North America and certainly in the US, is a significant deficiency of inquisitiveness and integration in the workplace. I cannot think of even one facility that would not benefit from more of these qualities in the management and supervisory team. There are some very high performers in the Top Seven alluded to in Chapter 1, world class performers. Yet each one of them, too, could benefit from more inquisitiveness and integration from their management team. Of all the management qualities I can think of … this is the one that could help virtually all plants and it is the one that the workforce in many plants are screaming for … even if they are not quite sure what they are screaming about.

Let me give you a concrete example.

Strategic planning – A contrast in management techniques, a cultural example

Company A – HK planning done right

All the firms in the Top Seven (from Chapter 1) use HK-type planning. Company A is an example. I helped them develop their HK planning methodology and they did it following the Japanese design as outlined in Appendix F. In summary, the VP created the strategic objectives and then used "catchball" to create and deploy the strategic goals. They used catchball as catchball was designed. That is, they used the "what-how methodology" with full and open two-way communications (detailed in Chapter 8). This process was then cascaded through the entire organization vertically and horizontally until a final plan was reached with both means and results properly addressed. Along the way, many times the "whats" as suggested by the senior manager would need to be modified because the "whats that were hoped for" could not be accomplished, by the junior manager, with the resources available. The plan was then modified consistent with catch-ball procedures. Using this method, Company A was able to get full alignment and focus on the annual plan, and, not surprisingly, there was huge "buy-in" by all. Finally, they would follow up their plan with the hourly, daily, weekly, monthly and annual reviews. It was textbook HK planning and it worked.

At each level, the manager stated "what" was needed to meet the business needs. Then, the next level down was asked, just how do you intend to accomplish this? If they could not accomplish it, consistent with HK planning, the goals and/or the resources might be modified. All of these thoughts were then integrated into a strategic plan that was consistent with the needs of the business. Not coincidently this "what-how" process took a plan that was focused on the business needs, and with input from all levels, created an alignment and buy-in that made it a success. It was questioning and integration at the strategic planning level.

Company AJ – Pseudo-HK planning

On the other hand, Company AJ, one of the Bottom Seven, did not use HK planning but had an elaborate process with many levels of management involved. The CEO created the key performance objectives and met with his C-suite personnel and suggested possible strategies to achieve the objectives. Almost reflexively, and without much discussion at all, these strategies – and no others – became the strategies that were accepted with little fanfare. The C-suite members then discussed these with their general managers and asked them "how" they might execute those strategies. There was little discussion on the merits of the strategies. The asked question was, "What are you going to do to execute these strategies?" It definitely was not, "What do you need so you can execute these strategies?". The implication was clear and missed by no one. It was, these are the goals and your job is to assure they are attained. With a silent "or else" attached. These interactions had the appearance of a two-way discussion; however, they were anything but two-way. Later, the general managers had a similar discussion with their plant managers with the same degree of directiveness and with all veiled threats attached. Since the plant managers "already knew what the answer needed to be", little feedback was obtained. Finally, this was turned into projects for the entire corporation.

Later, after the PowerPoints were completed, presentations were made by each of the C-suite managers on their assigned strategy, complete with involvement and apparent support of the general managers in an almost carnival-like atmosphere that just screamed "kumbaya". The audience included not only the C-suite but senior managers, middle managers, staff managers and down to plant managers. There was a large audience in support. The presentations were met with loud acceptance and applause upon completion; ostensibly, this showed the unity and harmony one would like to see. A shared admiration for a job well done was the word of the day. All the presentations were videotaped and placed on the company intranet, and all plant managers were encouraged to share these videos widely at their plants. Well, even though the videos were available, they were used very little. Sharing with others was the hope of the C-suite but not the reality at the factory. And the follow-ups that are typical of HK planning were never done – except the monthly financials. You see, this company, with all its fanfare and effort, still only cared about the monthly bottom-line financials. All the planning and strategic effort was just noise in the system and an effort to "appear to be strategic" when in reality the lone thing that mattered was meeting the monthly financials.

If you observed the process of Company AJ, after the fact, and as documented, this process appeared to have had a great deal of interaction. **Superficially** it had a great deal of acceptance and looked like a joint effort … even if it was not. All the communication and all the interactions were one way – top-down. The question of "how" do we get this done made no allowance that the goal may not match the resources available, and the subordinate managers knew enough to not question their superiors, much less argue. Rather, they just went through the motions, exchanged the requisite amount of happy talk and could not wait for lunch and breaks. They all knew this would pass, and if they met their monthly financials, all this strategic planning would pass in the fullness of time.

The net result was virtually no alignment nor focus on the strategic goals, and corporate buy-in was only a fleeting hope of the C-suite. The subsequent reality was the plant and business unit managers and their teams worked very hard to meet the monthly budgets … even if they needed to apply creative economics and pencil-whip the data to do so.

The contrast

After working with both companies, I can tell you the difference is large. Company A, using Hoshin Kanri planning, was adept at asking the right questions, getting input from a broad range of people and integrating these ideas into a plan that was superior to what they had started with. But more importantly, because they questioned, listened to and integrated all these ideas, they had not only the proper focus with a strong plan but also they were aligned top to bottom and left to right and had strong aligned and buy-in from the entire workforce. First, their execution of the plan was excellent; second, their results exceeded the previous year's performance by a large margin. Finally, this firm not only performed financially quite well but they had excellent quality, delivery, safety performance and had engagement levels at world class levels; they were at 77% engaged.

On the other hand, Company AJ was a polar opposite. By the end of the first quarter, all the talk about, and the effort put into, the strategic plan was a distant memory. All energy was focused on one item alone, meeting the monthly budget numbers, at the cost of everything else. The balanced scoreboard created at the strategic plan had disappeared along with all the kumbayas. Virtually all plants were struggling to meet the goals set by top management – but not really agreed to by anyone. Financial performance was barely beyond survival numbers and certainly not meeting the lofty aspirations which were discussed at the strategic planning conference. Quality and morale problems were the norm and it was even common knowledge that trust among the top management team was a major concern. What you could see was managers working hard to pencil-whip the data into something that would make them look not-too-bad. They were not looking good and a good day was defined as one where you did not get your ass chewed. It was survival mode at its finest. Rather than ask questions to get input, they gave directives to the next level, and they knew enough to look like good soldiers and not question anything. It was a senior management expectation that they knew, at every level, what was needed and how to supply it. They just wanted everyone to get behind the plan and "we'd be alright"; they were looking for advocates, not contributors. And as could be seen at the annual strategic planning session, the senior management were not only looking for compliance, they expected admiraton and they expected the employees to be so proud of the business direction that they would be totally engaged in executing the plan. Well, none of that happened, regardless of their approach which fully expected advocacy and admiration for all they had done. The strategic plan was virtually all waste with lots of attendant noise. Finally, and predictably, this firm, based on their engagement studies, were less than 20% engaged. They had serious personnel losses and problems at all levels.

Inquisitiveness and integrity manifest on the plant floor, at the work cell

After looking at what inquisitiveness and integration looks like from the top of a corporation and how it is manifest in the entire organization as they do corporate planning, let's go to the plant floor and see it in action at a production cell, specifically the Theta cell.

Background on this plant

This plant had been selected to be an Alpha site to pilot-test a proposed corporate plan for a full-scale lean transformation. The history of the plant was that its profitability was a paltry 5%. It was a tier one and tier two supplier to the auto industry and had been in operation for over 20 years. They had a strong union. The key problems with the plant were low profitability and high turnover, even though there was not much local labor competition. The management style was a heavy-handed command and control style. We had done some recent work focusing on the management style and had taught them the Six Skills of Lean Leadership, as described in Chapter 9. This new style was getting great traction.

Background on the Theta cell

Earlier, in Chapter 6, we discussed the Theta cell, which was designed to produce a headrest for Toyota. This cell was one of five value streams in this plant. This cell was U-shaped in design. It was a tier two value stream and was staffed with 16 workers. The design of the cell was such that at modest defect rates, the profitability was very labor-sensitive. Target profitability required the productivity be 100 headrests/person/day (hpppd). Following PPAP and a brief start-up period, the cell leveled out at 65 hpppd. (PPAP is an abbreviation for the production parts approval process, which is a pre-production standard in the automotive industry.)

After 2 years and numerous efforts to improve, including visits from the home office support staff, the workers still struggled to reach a productivity level of 80; the cell was losing money. This is where the story of the Theta cell begins.

The kaizen event

First, we gathered the key plant personnel, including supervisors and engineers, and told them we would make progress using two types of kaizen. We introduced them to the concept of both kaizen events, which are large engineering- and management-intensive events, as well as smaller kaizens to be done by the workers. Today, we would start the large kaizen event. Immediately following this kaizen event, we would expect to continue the improvements with smaller kaizens. The workers, who are experts in their work, would be the best equipped and the best-positioned people to make improvements. Our job was to:

- explain to the cell workers "what" we wanted improved on the cell, the cell goals, and their job was to determine "how" best to do that
- provide them with the necessary boundary conditions and the training so they could execute these kaizens independently
- provide them with the guidance, support, and oversight to make sure the cell was making progress on its goals.

There was general agreement that the workers doing small kaizens was a good idea, but to say this was any sort of an epiphany would be an overstatement of galactic proportions. They had no idea of the power of 50 cell workers all focused on improvement. Their paradigm, as it was throughout their corporation, was that progress and improvement were a function of management and engineering … and no one else.

We then began our efforts by planning this kaizen event. We organized ourselves for a trip to the gemba to observe and gather data. The information we gathered was revealing. The spaghetti diagrams looked just like the plant, a total mess of disorganized activities. The utility operators (there were three) would move into areas that were falling behind to "help others". Operators would frequently leave their workstations to chase both parts and tools. The time studies were particularly revealing. Cycle times were all over the map, with many workstations showing large variation from the mean. We found that the work content at each workstation might change with the workers. In addition, work in progress (WIP) inventories would build up at a workstation, a utility operator would respond to assist the worker and, once done, would then move to the next accumulation. It was total chaos – a target-rich environment for lean activities. However, amid all this chaos, there was some very good news: this was a motivated group! The group members worked hard and really wanted to do better; they just did not yet know how to get better.

Early in the evening, we adjourned to the conference room to understand our data and observation. We combined our thoughts, plotted our measurements and reviewed our notes and spaghetti diagrams until very late in the evening, at which time, tired but optimistic, we adjourned for the evening. The following morning, while the cell was operating in its "normal mode", we made a quick visit to the floor and then met to reflect on all we had seen. After reviewing the data and combining the list of improvement activities, we embarked on a design review. We completed that work by midnight, and after rearranging the equipment and laying down some floor marking, we were ready for the day shift.

The next morning, when the operators arrived, the production manager trained them along with their supervisor, and we started producing with the new design. By the end of the shift, we were producing at a rate well over 100 headrests/person/day. The team met and did an informal on-site reflection, and we made some minor changes prior to the second shift's arrival. Upon arrival, the supervisor from the first shift, along with the production manager, met with the Theta cell team for the second shift. He told the team of the redesign and summarized the changes, including the new work rules, and the second shift started up without incident. The lead hand, Derek, kept all stations stocked, and work was flowing smoothly.

In the next 3 days, we made some minor modifications to the flow. We also trained the top management team on how to do kaizens at the cell level. By the end of the week, productivity had improved markedly. We had gone right past our minimum target of 100 and were producing at 188 headrests/person/day. Friday, I left for El Paso and felt good about what the team had accomplished – and we were just getting started.

Kaizens galore

Two weeks later I got a call from Dirk (recall from Chapter 6 that Dirk was the plant manager). He was concerned. Our redesign continued to show improvements. The operators had completed over 30 kaizens, and the cell was now overproducing so much they could get by working only 6 hours per shift, and he did not know what to do. We gave him some instructions, and following that, Dirk did some rough time studies, rebalanced the workstations and was able to reassign one person to another cell. Soon enough, after the operators had implemented more kaizens and people got used to the new work rules and flow, once again the cell began to overproduce. Again, Dirk called, and after doing some calculations and considering some options, he decided to shut down production at the seventh hour and assign kaizen activities to the team for the final hour of each shift. The operators implemented many kaizens, including upgrading their 5S standards and building a production-by-hour (PBH) board. At this time, we gave the assignment to the lead hand to initiate problem solving when production differed by ±15% from the target on the PBH board, but if production was in that range, to just keep producing – and smile. We effectively introduced the concept of "normal" versus "changed". Production smoothed even more, and the overall rate increased once again.

We reflect on the all the kaizens

When I arrived for my next visit, the operators consistently produced more than 225 headrests/person/day, and the productivity was still on the rise. I gathered the plant's leadership team, including some of the cell workers, and we reflected on it. **Now** the management team had an epiphany. It became particularly apparent when one worker, normally an agitator, said, "This is the best thing because now we can fix the things we know need fixing". Someone else said, "It's great to be able to contribute in a different way"; one of the union stewards said, "We have been arguing for this for 20 years; it's great to see it". The plant HR manager commented, "For some reason, attrition these last 2 months has dropped each month; I see a connection". All this and we all agreed that morale had taken a step-change improvement.

The cell productivity continues to improve

I continued to visit the plant, and the process continued to improve. After the second visit, we really had no more "kaizen events" where the engineers and supervisors locked themselves up in a room and redesigned the flow. However, each month, the number of worker-initiated improvements (kaizens) increased. The kaizens were too numerous to mention all of them here, and most were never formally documented. But they were all discussed within the cell, and before any changes were made, they were put up on the whiteboard to solicit the input from all three shifts prior to being executed. Each kaizen, although worker-initiated, was team-implemented.

It was a system that had a bias for action. This plant no longer had a bias for documentation, nor did it have a bias for the ritual of bureaucratic form-filling and higher-level review and approval; actions and improvements were the new game. The supervisors had an opportunity to review the whiteboard and get in their input, if need be. And if they had no input, they would sign off on the kaizens and most were implemented via the Nike principle, "Just Do It". Furthermore, if the kaizen required some engineering assistance, the workers would contact the engineer directly, get his input and then proceed. Everyone was focused and aligned on continuous improvement at this cell, and it was being done through problem solving, elimination of waste and a fully engaged workforce. The line people were engaged, the support staff was engaged, and the supervisors and managers were engaged.

In the ensuing months, literally hundreds of kaizens were done, and nearly all were done solely by the line workers. Eleven months after the initial kaizen event, this headrest model was discontinued when the new model was introduced. In its last month of production, the cell productivity was 304 headrests/person/day.

The Theta cell … Summarizing

The work at the Theta cell is an example of asking the workers to find ways to improve the productivity, quality, delivery and safety performance as they are executing their normal tasks. Earlier, many of these kaizens had been suggested to their supervisor or the process engineer, and most were choked out of existence by the internal bureaucracy. Upon written submission, they were being evaluated and decided upon by engineers and managers, who often knew less about the issue than the workers themselves.

Over the years, this plant had suggestion programs for the value-add workers and even had various awards program to spur interest, but soon enough these efforts ran their course and were abandoned as there was little or no participation. In the name of progress and improvement, what got done was only the ideas of the engineers and managers. Whenever an occasional idea came from a worker, by the time it saw the light of day, it had been massaged, manipulated by the internal bureaucracy and was often unrecognizable to the original creator; hence, there was no ownership by the workers and even less satisfaction. It turned out that the **advocacy** to get it done was management-initiated and ultimately these same managers would enjoy the **admiration** of their superiors for any gains. They might get an "attaboy" posted on the bulletin board or maybe they were the subject of an article published in the company magazine

However, as soon as the managers of the Theta cell changed and instead of **advocating** their own ideas, they **asked** for ideas from others and then rather than sitting back and **admiring** their new achievements, they **integrated** these ideas into the betterment of the cell ... engagement became a reality. The workers who had always been engaged physically, now become engaged with their hearts and with their minds. Going from advocacy and admiration to inquisitiveness and integration created an energy that not only facilitated engagement but business improvement as well.

Inquisitiveness and integration at three different levels: individual; at the cell; across the entire plant

At the individual level in my discussions with Toshi, I found he was always trying to learn from me and integrate my information and knowledge, with his, to create a greater understanding on his part. Seldom did he restate his position or advocate that he was right and I was wrong ... he never even came close to that position. In addition, reflecting on my career before consulting, I had one supervisor who used these skills. With Chevron, he was viewed as being indecisive and a weak leader. Long before he supervised me, he had been dead-ended into a mid-level management position. At that time and even to this day, some 45 years later, I still consider him to be the best supervisor I ever had.

The activities in the Theta cell were particularly instructive. The cell workers were given only minor training yet responded with immediate improvements. They were given a clear discussion of the goals of the cell, and metrics were posted locally.

Likewise, the HK planning done by Company A followed the same pattern, questioning to get to a solution and integrating it across the entire company. It all started with questioning to broaden the options and then discussions to integrate it into the best possible plan. Company AJ, on the other hand, also had a great deal of interactions with discussions, and finally, it was integrated into a solution. Forgetting for the moment all the kumbaya and backslapping, what's the difference?

The difference is really the revelation. The Top Seven used "inquisitiveness and integrity versus advocacy and admiration" **... from the very beginning and with sincere intent to inquire and integrate**. And that is one of the management traits that are key to creating a fully engaged workforce – inquisitiveness and integration.

Why is inquisitiveness and integration so powerful?

There are many common-sense reasons that asking people questions, listening to their response and incorporating it into the topic at hand is very powerful. People love to be heard, people love to be included, people like to be part of the solution and the list goes on. However, at the deepest levels, this technique addresses all four of the basic intrinsic needs.

■ First, is autonomy, which is the need to exhibit some control or volition over the things that affect you. When your ideas are sought out, taken seriously and incorporated into solutions, your need for autonomy is fed on three connected, but different, fronts.
■ Second, is competency. Again, when your ideas are sought out, taken seriously and incorporated into action plans, that is done because you bring and are recognized for some level of competency on the matter at hand.
■ Third, is relatedness. The very fact that someone is asking for your thoughts puts you in a walking–talking relationship with them.
■ Fourth, is meaningfulness. Once again, your ideas are being put to work and you are contributing in a real way to the overall welfare of the people and the business. You are contributing, and with it comes a natural sense of meaningfulness.

When all four intrinsic needs are satisfied, you have created a highly charged and motivated group of people. This is the formula for success. Motivated people, focused on a common goal, with a distinct level of ownership, of buy-in. It is hard to paint a better picture of a group headed for success. It all started with a management attitude to inquire of others and integrate their ideas into a comprehensive solution. The beauty of this approach is that even if the solution is not optimal, this motivated group, with high levels of buy-in, will make it work because of their personal investment.

Inquisitiveness and integration is such a powerful technique because it satisfies all four of the intrinsic needs. When this is done properly, the result is motivation on steroids. The Intrinsic Motivation Loop is fully activated and engagement is a natural outcome. And if this technique is done often and with everyone, a fully engaged workforce is the natural outcome. That is why this is what I view as the most important of management traits – the ability to inquire and integrate.

Why is this trait not "just how we do things around here"?

Why is this inquisitiveness and integration such an unusual trait, rather than a cultural norm? When I ask this question, the first answer I get is "We just don't do that around here". This is some form of excuse that says, we

---

THE POWER OF NAMING

S.I. Hayakawa, in his famous book *Language in Thought and Action* (Harcourt Brace, 1963), discusses the socially important topic of naming and classification. He says, "What we call things … depends upon the interests we have and the purposes of the classification". These processes, which the Japanese call hansei and nemewashi, have "names "because they are important to them and they describe specific procedures to follow to attain specific outcomes". Their "interest" in nemewashi is to improve the quality of their decision making, and their "interest" in hansei is to improve the execution of their ideas. They do both. But the linchpin that is making these two techniques effective is that they use a broad range of people; that is, they have a fully engaged workforce performing both.

I am sure some Western firms try to copy these techniques; I just can't find many.

---

simply do not value this technique. Which means that we don't value the input of many, just a few. Not many managers would own up to that conclusion, but it's hard to miss. Second, I would say the basis for that belief that we only want to hear from a few is that the management team is not very strong at situational leadership. If they were, they would know the strengths of their employees and inquire and integrate their thoughts from a much broader base, not just a few. Third, I attribute a great deal of their weakness in the situational leadership to their lack of understanding of the concrete details of the work. In addition, since many managers are more connected to the spreadsheets and monthly reports (the maps) rather than the people, processes and products on the floor (the territory) they prefer to "not let the details get in the way". Fourth, with a weaker technical and experiential base, they prefer to not ask questions they cannot process, for fear of appearing ignorant or ill-informed. Finally, I believe the root cause is that there is an insecurity many managers harbor of looking somehow inferior.

This overrides their desire to learn more. This drives the manager to ask fewer questions to get fewer people involved. The net effect is to truncate the quality of problem solving and decision making that is needed to reach Management 3.0 status.

Japanese on inquisitiveness and integration

I catch a lot of heat from my colleagues for using the term "Japanese management" as a metaphor for superior management. Well, as I have stated several times, I do. But not to any level of exclusivity. It is a stereotype I use, and like all stereotypes, they are not always correct, they just make discussion easier. However, here, I have examples of two very interesting techniques, which I have seen in several Japanese companies but not even once in my Western clients. The use of hansei and the use of nemawashi.

Hansei

Hansei is a Japanese term which roughly means deep reflection. It is a process they routinely perform following any project. It makes no difference if the project was done well or failed miserably. The hope is to learn more so next time it can be done better. I find this routinely practiced in many of my Japanese clients. In this process, all ideas are taken, questioned and discussed in a very open format. It is so open it often, to Westerners, appears to be very confrontational. However, my Japanese counterparts simply say, "That is just how we do it" The closest I can come to it with my Western counterparts is a celebration party following a successful new-product launch, for example. When projects have problems, the issue is more often than not "a search for the guilty and a reward to the uninvolved". Hansei has a number of similarities to the After Action Report (AAR) practiced by the US military, yet I have not seen even one Western company use this practice. It would not surprise me at all to find out that the Japanese learned this during the occupation following World War II, where they learned so much from the American military.

Nemawashi

This is a process that is often translated as "getting consensus" or "prior consultation" and is a process of decision making commonly practiced by the Japanese. In it, before ideas are decided upon, for example, a small corrective action to a customer complaint or a large decision on which stamping machine to purchase, the ideas are broadly discussed. First, it is discussed by all individuals in the group starting the decision. Then, it is discussed broadly and rigorously with all those affected, at each and every level of the hierarchy, until it is presented to be approved. The process is slow, but once completed, all issues have been discussed and addressed. It has some similarities to what we call consensus, but far more people, at each level, are engaged in the process. This too is a process with a great deal of both questioning and integration

The relevance of hansei and nemawashi

I mention those here because they are clear techniques using the techniques of questioning and integration of many thoughts and ideas from a broad scope of individuals. Not only are these practices, but they are common among Japanese firms and they are not only broadly practiced but they are significant enough to have been given a name.

Inquisitiveness and integration – Wrapping up

The inherent power of this skill is so sweeping, I almost find it hard to explain.

In scholarly terms, this practice works to satisfy all four of the intrinsic needs, activate the Intrinsic Motivational Loop and likely is the most powerful management tool to create and sustain a fully engaged workforce.

At the visceral level: Who that has an idea doesn't want to be heard? Who that does work, doesn't want to be recognized for their contribution? Who doesn't want to be asked to supply their specific level of expertise? Who doesn't want others to seek them out for advice? All of these are natural human responses which satisfy the basic human emotional needs. All that must happen is for someone of authority to ask pertinent questions, listen intently, use the information and recognize them for their contribution – such is the nature of inquisitiveness and integration.

Chapter Summary ... While there are many management techniques that are needed to be successful and to attain Management 3.0, there are two that stand out. They are the use of mentoring and the management skills of asking questions and integrating the information. Mentoring is a much-misunderstood technique, and many believe they are practicing it when they are just coaching or training, for example. The inherent power in mentoring individuals is that it is an intensely personal technique and allows the mentor and mentee to discuss the topics of interest to them, rather than topics of interest to the firm. The mentor and mentee are discussing topics of their own choice, based on their own interests; it is a manifestation of self-initiated self-development. The second management skill, inquisitiveness and integration, is contrasted to its more common management counterpart, advocacy and admiration. By inquiring rather than advocating, the manager can broaden the database of any problem, solution or choice. Asking questions is not normally a management forte. This skill of asking questions and integrating ideas is not strong within Western firms simply because they do not value it. However, few things can be more inherently motivating as this technique feeds all four of the intrinsic needs and can be useful in the work cell, in the C-suite and all locations in between. Many Japanese firms seem to have elements of this technique built into their culture as they practice two closely related topics, hansei and nemewashi.

What's next?? After that large dose of management, we are going to shift gears to the topic of motivation, basic motivation in the workplace. That is the subject we now turn to.

THE ROLE OF MOTIVATION IN ENGAGEMENT

In this section, we discuss the general concepts of motivation, including those of Maslow and Herzberg as well as McGregor's contribution to management motivation. In addition, we will discuss how these are incorporated into the management principles taught by them as well as taught by Drucker and others. We will discuss the crucial concepts of intrinsic and extrinsic motivation and make a critical and comparative analysis of how both intrinsic and extrinsic motivational concepts are employed in self-determination theory. We end this section with a seemingly unusual discussion of how managers can – or cannot – motivate their workers.

Part IV contains two chapters:

Chapter 11

On Motivation

Aim of this Chapter ... is to focus on motivation and how it relates to management theory. In particular, we will discuss the contributions made by three pioneers in the field: Abraham Maslow, Frederick Herzberg and Douglas McGregor. Maslow's theory is based on his principles of a hierarchy of needs. Herzberg's theory is an application of Maslow's theory and explains many concepts about motivation that are still widely misunderstood and hence misused. On the other hand, McGregor's work is focused on management belief systems and how they affect the behavior of the workforce. The specific works of all three authors were written more than 50 years ago but still directly apply to the workplace today. We will wrap up this chapter with the Three Rules to Motivate the Workforce.

Motivation

Motivation is what drives behavior. Motivation is the process that initiates, guides and maintains goal-oriented behaviors. It is the force that causes us to act, and it involves both the intellectual and emotional forces that activate behavior. In everyday usage, the term motivation is frequently used to explain why a person does something, and motivation is also that "thing" that causes you to persist in the face of obstacles; it is the key to "overcoming" whatever is holding your back. It is the key to "initiating", "doing" and "persisting". The concepts of motivation are largely misunderstood and consequently widely misused. Seldom does the management team know: how to measure it, how to create it or how to sustain it. The unfortunate irony is that many managers, while honestly and sincerely trying to motivate the workforce, end up using techniques that demotivate the workforce.

It seems axiomatic that a strong understanding of motivation and how to utilize this powerful concept would be very valuable information for a manager to have in his or her skill set.

So why don't managers have a better grasp on motivational concepts?

I can think of five reasons.

- The people these managers worked for did not emphasize and teach it to them. The countermeasure to that is to break that cycle and start teaching motivational principles and applications to your supervisors and managers.
- For many years, the behavioral sciences studied rats, mice and monkeys to create their theories and then extrapolated them to the human condition. Although there are generalities to be made, when animals are studied versus humans, there are, at least, three major elements missing.
  - First, animals really do not decide and act based on thinking of options and considering their environment; rather, they largely react based on their instincts, a hereditary trait.
  - Second, non-human animals have fewer "appetites" than humans, limiting the possible choices to make.
  - Third, since humans are less guided by instincts, there is increasing dependence on the environment and the culture as a factor in choice and adaptation.
- The study of psychology is largely the study of dysfunction and illness. There was not much thought on making people who are well even better until the positive psychology movement in the late 20th century. So, when managers want to create a positive change, there is simply less information available. Worse yet, many people make the "erroneous assumption of the opposites". For example, they believe the opposite of job satisfaction is job dissatisfaction. So, they might look at the causes of job dissatisfaction and say, "Ok, I will do just the opposite and then I can create a workforce that has high job satisfaction". As logical as this sounds, it is not correct. For example, let's say you appear unhappy and someone enquires about it and you tell them you have a

headache. They then give you an aspirin and your headache goes away ... Now, are you necessarily happy? Of course not. You may no longer be unhappy, but that does not mean you are automatically happy. We will explain this dynamic more fully in Chapter 12.

■ The overriding issue I find in my work is that managers minimize the importance of how their personal and individual daily activities impact workforce motivation.

■ Also, managers, as a group, are far more skilled and comfortable dealing with machines, spreadsheets and computer printouts in the quietude of their offices ... rather than going to the gemba and dealing with the people. The entire culture of the Toyota corporation is built upon two principles: continuous improvement and respect for people (Toyota, 2001). And my observations are that managers, far and away, prefer to deal with the continuous improvement principle, and most minimize the respect for people concept. They may say, loud and clear, that people are the most important aspect of our business. Unfortunately, way too often, when their actions are compared to their words, there is a large disconnect. Worse yet, there are often distinct actions which are in direct contradiction to those words. These actions include layoffs to reduce costs plus mergers and acquisitions to achieve short-term bottom-line improvements. Short-term bottom-line improvements have a very strong motivational effect on the managers, especially the most influential top-level managers.

Why study motivation??

It is often said that a major role of management is to motivate the workforce. Later, you will learn that this is not a meaningful statement; rather, people come to work motivated.

However, as soon as they come to work, they are subjected to a new environment. Possibly they have come from the military, high school, trade school or college and now want a job with you. Almost certainly, the environment, including the work demands, will be new to them and they will need to adjust. And it will be up to the facility management, and largely a responsibility of their direct supervisor, to prepare them for these new requirements. If the supervisor prepares them well, it is very likely these new hires will perform well and be highly engaged at work. On the other hand, if the supervisor does not prepare them well, **it is**

a certainty they will have problems in performance, and they will not engage or even worse they may become actively disengaged. So, it is the responsibility of the supervisor, of the entire management team, to create an environment where it is possible for these people to perform well and stay engaged.

Since they come motivated, it is not the responsibility of the supervisor to motivate the new employee; **rather, it is his responsibility to not demotivate the employee**, and, in addition, as the employee grows and develops, it is the responsibility of the supervisor to create an environment that will sustain their motivation.

Applicability of motivational theory

As we discuss motivational theories of Maslow and others, and their application, much of the literature is written to an American audience based on studies and data from an American environment. This presents a limited view of the theory. This should be understood. For example, if we are discussing engagement in countries such as the US, Canada, Mexico and most of Western Europe, very often there is strong applicability of these theories. However, if we were to discuss engagement in war-torn Syria or poverty-stricken nations such as Somalia, the discussion would be very different indeed. They would not be so interested in engagement and beneficent management of their businesses; their focus would be on survival. They would probably welcome some heavy-handed, command and control autocratic industrialist who was able to supply some jobs and an influx of money to be used for food, water, medicine and shelter.

While discussing this topic of "enlightened management" in his book *Eupsychian Management*, Abraham Maslow approached the applicability of some of these theories thusly:

> "The general principles … are for the most part far too general. Certainly, managing women is different from managing men. Managing children is still another story … all raise their individual problems for management. So also do the people who are fixated at the safety-needs level or who are stuck at the love level etc. … This point becomes clearer if we ask about the possibility

of applying these principles in Colombia, Iran, Syria, and South Africa. There are many places in the world where only authoritarian management, cracking the whip over fearful people, can work. Authoritarian characters confronted with human relations principles of management based on all sorts of beneficent and benevolent assumptions would consider the manager certainly weak in the head and at the very least sentimental, unrealistic, etc. ..."

(Maslow, 1965)
(Note: Maslow wrote this in 1965, and although the principles are sound, the exact examples may not be current.)

However, this book is written to managers in countries like the US that are not in war, are not struggling for survival and are not in political upheaval. I have used these principles all over the US, Canada and even in Mexico; I find they have blanket applicability. I have used them in South America as well, with excellent results. In addition, I have used them in Western Europe with great success. I would expect them to work very well in Japan. However, I have found them to be less effective in China, the only Far East country in which I have worked directly. In other low-wage countries such as Thailand, Bangladesh, Vietnam, I would not expect these principles of enlightened management and engagement to work well, if at all. The difference is that in these low-wage countries, satisfying basic survival needs and security may be their basic driving force; hence, they are at a different level on Maslow's hierarchy.

Types of motivation

In general, there are two types of motivation: extrinsic and intrinsic. Extrinsic motivators come from "an external locus of causality", that is, from outside of the individual. Examples are money, awards, prestige, power and social position, which all come from someone else or somewhere else.

Intrinsic motivators, on the other hand, are those that arise from within the individual. These include doing things for the pure joy of doing them. They are the motivators which cause people to take up hobbies, work for volunteer organizations and, for our purpose, the motivators which cause a natural enjoyment at work.

Maslow on motivation – His hierarchy of needs

The theory

In his classic book *Motivation and Personality* (1954), Abraham Maslow described a multi-level theory of human motivation (Figure 11.1). In it, he stated:

- To be motivated is to be driven (to act upon), to satisfy a need.
- Until the needs, at that level, were satisfied, those needs would push all other needs to the background.
- However, once that specific need was satisfied, it was no longer a motivating factor and the needs of the next level would be the "driver of interest" to the person.
- There was a natural progression up the hierarchy, and although there was some regression and return, the overall lifelong process of the individual was to ascend the hierarchy.
- Maslow said "man is a wanting animal and is never satisfied for very long", and

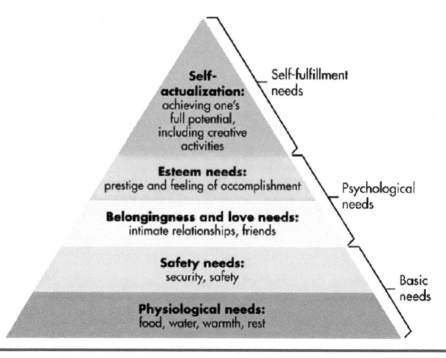

Figure 11.1   Maslow's hierarchy of needs. (From www.simplepsychology.com)

- "Humans are never satisfied, except in a one-step-along-the-way fashion and the wants arrange themselves in some sort of a hierarchy"
- There were five levels to his hierarchy of needs. Starting from the most basic, they were:
  a. The physiological needs of food, water, shelter; often called the survival needs
  b. The safety needs of protection, security and freedom from danger.
     i. Levels one and two, taken together are called "the basic needs".
  c. The belongingness needs including friends, relationships and intimacy.
  d. The esteem, or ego, needs of prestige and a sense of accomplishment.
     i. Levels three and four, taken together are called the "psychological needs".
  e. Finally, the needs of self-actualization, that is, becoming all you can be. Reaching your full potential.
     i. He called this level the self-fulfillment needs.

Additional thoughts on Maslow's hierarchy

Preconditions

There are preconditions for the "Basic Needs Satisfaction". These include: freedom to speak; freedom of expression; freedom to seek information; freedom to defend; justice; fairness; honesty; and order in the group. Stifling these preconditions then stifles the basic needs satisfaction, which in turn causes a lack of fulfillment of the basic needs. When these basic needs are not satisfied, this leads to illness, both physical and psychological, as well as causing people to get "stuck" at that level. For the purpose of our study here, this means that if the basic needs at levels one and two are not met, people are not motivated to ascend the hierarchy, and concepts such as teamwork and even engagement are out of their reach.

Level five – The need for self-actualization

Once the four prior levels are met, a new discontent and restlessness develops, unless an individual is doing what he is fitted for. An artist must paint, a coach must coach, a poet must write and a parent must parent if he is ultimately to be at peace with himself. What a man is "supposed to be" he must become or he is not at peace with himself. It is the human need for self-fulfillment, namely, to be actualized in what he is potentially. To become more and more of what one is capable of becoming. The emergence of these needs rests upon the prior satisfaction of the psychological, safety, love and esteem needs.

Like all needs, this need to be self-actualized, if not satisfied, produces both physical and psychological health impairment to some degree. On the other hand, the typical behaviors of the self-actualized individuals can be

ENTHUSIASTIC ... AND YOUR CALLING

Enthusiastic is a particularly meaningful word for me. The root of enthusiastic is the Greek word "theos", meaning God, just as theology is the study of God. "Entheos" is a Greek word meaning "possessed by (a) god's essence" (Wikipedia). I always think of people who are enthusiastic as being en-Godded. Simply put, they are responding to their calling. The natural response to following your calling is strong feelings of enjoyment, interest, satisfaction and even passion. Also, when finding and following your calling you have feelings of intense focus and an eagerness to repeat the experience. In a word, you are enthusiastic

described as more than happy, more than pleased and more than pleasant. Rather, they are excited, enthusiastic and energized. They are effervescent as they spread their happiness to all around them, and not only that but they seem to attract people to their particular area of expertise. They are contagious and make whatever topic they are interested in literally come to life. The self-actualized person is so energized they literally cause other people to want to get involved. They are contagious.

And this is because what they are doing is not just something they do; rather, what they are doing comes from their inner being and – it is who they are.

Self-actualization and "our calling"

Another way to look at self-actualization is to understand that self-actualized people are people who have found their "calling".

It is interesting to note, that another word for "your job" is your vocation. However, this word, vocation, is worthy of a little study. The word "vocation" comes from the Latin word, "vocare", which means: to call, to summon. Well, if you are called, there is someone who is doing the calling, and that is the "voice from within" which Jung called the subconscious. It is there; it is real, but since it is subconscious, we are not readily aware of it. However, if we listen hard enough and long enough we can "hear" this inner voice. In fact, sometimes this voice pops up in strange places at strange times and embarrasses us; like when we make a "Freudian slip" or when you are driving down the road and a particularly salient thought "appears" to you. Also, you get a lot of feedback from your subconscious in your dreams. There are various ways that this "voice from within" communicates with us.

The problem is that very often, our vocation, our job, **is not** our true calling. That is, we select a job that is not consistent with our "inner voice" but is more in line with social acceptance or the need for lots of material things. Rather than pursue our calling, which should be our vocation, many resign ourselves to "work for a living" so we can enjoy life. Then, for fun and enjoyment, we have a hobby, which we call our avocation, from the Latin verb "avocare" which means "to divert". Interestingly enough, the Spanish infinitive for "to have fun" is "divirtir", to divert.

So, in the end, if we are not careful and introspective, we pick a vocation, which we do for 50 or 60 hours per week and decide to "work" (read that as "pay the price") so we can "divert ourselves" and do what we really want to do for 2 or 3 hours per week. If that does not sound like crazymaking at its finest, it should.

For example, even though we enjoy teaching and working with children, we make a quick analysis and find that teaching does not pay very much. So, rather reflexively, we decide to practice law, so we might have a large salary and the perks that go with it, including a nice house, plush offices with secretaries galore and the prestige of being a lawyer. Unfortunately, going against your calling, while it may lead to some nice short-term perks as mentioned, will certainly cause some long-term problems. Recall that self-actualization is a NEED, not some superficial desire. And needs, when not satisfied, lead to physical and psychological illness. I can give you dozens of examples of men and women who did not follow their callings and, in the fullness of time, paid a severe price that went far beyond individual dissatisfaction, individual angst and individual lack of fulfillment but also included divorce and lousy relationships with their children as well.

Listening to that "inner voice", and finding your calling, is often a path to health and well-being.

The appropriate management response to Maslow's theory

First, teach and train all your managers and supervisors, including team leaders, about Maslow's hierarchy of needs. Incorporate it into your management philosophy. The senior management should not only read but comprehensively study Maslow's book *Motivation and Personality* (1954). It is rich in information that is not only helpful but intellectually stimulating. I know of no book that better captures the concept of motivation for the workplace, and mankind in general. It should be on every manager's bookshelf.

Second, recognize that in the US, most people have already satisfied the needs for levels one and two and are working on levels three, four and even five. That is not true of all countries; in fact, countries like Somalia and Syria are largely mired at level one, struggling to satisfy the basic survival needs of food, water, shelter and medicine.

Third, as we discuss the concept of engagement, it is resident in these three same levels. Hence, to try to apply the concepts of engagement and enlightened management which we will discuss in this book in countries that have not largely met the needs of levels one and two is not practical.

Fourth, even though, as a country, we have largely fulfilled the needs for levels one and two, poor management practices can drive the individual back to those levels. If we cause people to psychologically regress to the point that level two needs are not met, there is little hope for them to become engaged. That can easily happen if a plant is in distress and the management mishandles an expected reduction in force or if there are some safety issues not properly addressed by the management team. Recall that the growth up the pyramid is step-by-step, in order. So if someone is stuck trying to meet the needs at level two, there is little hope for them to "want" what level three has. It won't appear on their radar until level two needs have largely been met. Recall that,

> "Until the needs, at that level, were satisfied; those needs would push all other needs to the background".

> (Maslow, 1954)

Herzberg on motivation – His two-factor theory

The theory

Herzberg was the first to prove that the factors which create job ***satisfaction*** are a different list of factors than those that provide job ***dissatisfaction***. This dynamic is seemingly interesting to managers, yet at the same time, it frequently baffles them. Until his research, it was largely believed that if the presence of a certain factor would satisfy and hence motivate people, then, conversely, withdrawing or minimizing this same factor would demotivate the individual. It is as though if these factors, pay and working conditions, for example, were supplied in sufficient quantity, they would motivate people. Yet if these same qualities were supplied in a diminished quantity, this would lead to demotivation. His studies showed this was not the case.

As you study Herzberg's work, you cannot help but see that his work largely follows the work of Maslow. For example, Herzberg's hygiene factors are very similar to Maslow's basic needs. And as Maslow said, once a need was satisfied, it was no longer a motivating factor; that is precisely Herzberg's hygiene concept. In addition, Herzberg's motivators were largely the items Maslow called the psychological and self-actualization needs; the intrinsic motivators. There are many parallels.

Interestingly enough, what Herzberg found makes no sense to a lot of people, and even though it is counterintuitive, he proved it to be true. He was correct. He found that the opposite of job satisfaction is not job dissatisfaction. Rather, the opposite of job satisfaction is no job satisfaction. And the opposite of job dissatisfaction is not job satisfaction; rather, it is no job dissatisfaction. You might want to read that last paragraph again.

The "motivators"

This is because the factors which create job satisfaction are a separate group from those that cause job dissatisfaction. The first group he called motivators, and virtually all these factors were directly related to the work itself. They included items such as achievement, recognition, personal growth, the work itself and even the concept of job responsibility. They are all "intrinsic needs".

The "hygiene factors"

The second group he called "hygiene factors", and they really do not create job satisfaction. Rather, they are factors which, when supplied in sufficient quantity, become "non-issues". However, these same "hygiene factors" if not supplied in sufficient quantity, then become demotivators, usually large demotivators creating job dissatisfaction. The classic "hygiene factors" are pay and benefits. However, Hertzberg's list of "hygiene factors" went beyond pay and benefits to include working conditions, company policies and supervisory actions; all the "hygiene factors" were extrinsic to the individual.

"Not a lawyer but a teacher I should be ..."

A slice of life story about the dichotomy of job satisfaction and job dissatisfaction. Interestingly enough – John had neither. If that's confusing, I hope John can sort it out for you.

For several years, John, an accomplished lawyer, attended a Bible study class with me. On the surface, he was the consummate professional. I was later to find out this persona was not natural, was highly "forced" and he had to work hard to project this image. Although this persona served him well as a lawyer, it created several problems in his personal life.

At Bible study, we would meet each Monday. Although John and I never socialized outside of Bible study, we got well acquainted when after one class he asked me about some comments I had made in our discussion group. My comments centered on the concept of people finding and following "their calling" in life, a subject of passion for me which I had studied for some time. He said roughly, "Lonnie, I hear you talk about following your calling and I think I may not be". I simply asked him what he did, and he informed me he was a lawyer, and although he liked the profession, he was not really a happy person and especially not happy at work either. In the ensuing months, it became commonplace for us to discuss this in increasingly greater depth, after class, in the parking lot, frequently for an hour or more. This continued for several months. During these discussions, I learned that he was a very successful, high-profile litigation attorney. He was a partner in his firm and made a ton of money but reiterated many times that he was unhappy at work.

Early on, I asked him what his hobby was, and it was woodworking. After a tough day at work, he would adjourn to his garage and make furniture. He said that during the day the confrontation and arguing wore him down and he often needed to "recharge his batteries", which making furniture satisfied. He said, "In my woodshop, I am creating stuff. At work, it is a zero-sum game; my client can only win if his opponent loses so we are always looking for dirt, weaknesses, inconsistencies and all that is wrong with people. My job at work is to tear down; in the woodshop, I get to create".

I also asked him what he had previously done that he thoroughly enjoyed. He quickly replied he had coached both his son and daughter, in several sports, when they were younger. Both kids were from his first marriage. He also volunteered that he and his kids no longer get along well. Both are in high school, are generally upset with him and they don't really like Angela, his third wife. He also volunteered that he and Angela were having troubles and he was worried about their marriage as well.

It was clear to me he had a misalignment with his job and his true calling. I asked him why not try teaching, specifically junior high or high school woodshop. He laughed and said he could not begin to pay his bills that way. Later, we discussed this more, but he was not in any mood to take an 80% cut in pay. We had numerous discussions including discussions on Maslow's theory, Jungian principles and Herzberg's concepts as well, but mostly the discussion centered on him, his job and his family life which was rife with problems. This went on for most of the year. We might make a little progress, specifically that he should change jobs, but he would get stuck on that huge pay cut and the huge impact this would have on his life.

And then something changed. The discussion changed and his tenor changed. John approached me and initiated a discussion about possibly teaching. He had loosened up and was more willing to change. What had caused that was that Angela started talking about divorce, which John did not want at all. Well, the Bible study class ended for the year, and I did not see John for two more years.

Two years later, once again, John was back in Bible study, and he was also in my discussion group. After class, once again, he caught me in the parking lot and filled me in. He had retired from his law firm, gone to the University of Texas at El Paso (UTEP), earned a teaching certificate and was now teaching trig at a local high school. Next year there will be an opening in woodshop and he was looking forward to applying for it. With his reduction in pay, he and Angela had made some big changes. He had sold his 5600-square foot house with six bedrooms and five baths up on the hill and moved into a more modest 3200 square foot home in the valley. He had patched things up with Angela, and because they still wanted some of the old perks, she had taken a job as a special education teacher, something she had always wanted to do. And best of all, he and his kids were now on good terms and he was discussing colleges with both of them. John's life, especially his personal life, had improved dramatically. He told me he had not felt like this since his kids were little.

John was an all-too-common case of a guy who was locked into a job he did not like. In fact, as odd as it sounds, John had **no job dissatisfaction**, yet he had **no job satisfaction** either; and he was stuck. Recall from the discussion by Herzberg that job satisfaction came about by the presence of the motivational factors related to the work itself. And if they were absent, **job dissatisfaction** did not ensue; **rather, there was no job satisfaction**.

Likewise, job dissatisfaction was most often caused by the absence of the hygiene factors. And if these were present in sufficient quantity, **job satisfaction** did not ensue**; rather, there was no job dissatisfaction**. (You may want to reread that as it can be confusing).

In his case, John had no job dissatisfaction because he really liked all the perks of the prestigious offices, filled with perky interns and legal aids (the source of his second but short-lived marriage), and, yes, the salary was a definite perk. You will note that all of these are "hygiene factors" and all are extrinsic motivators; hence, **John had no job dissatisfaction**. And he had expressed it as such; when he said he liked the profession, what he really meant was that he liked all the perks and pay that lawyers received and generally how lawyers were treated.

Unfortunately, since he was not following his calling in life, **he had no job satisfaction** either. He was seldom excited, energized or enthusiastic about his work, at least internally. However, John was a "true professional" so he had mastered the ability to "seem to be" excited, enthusiastic, and energetic even if he was not. He knew how to create the proper façade, no matter how false it was. On the surface, almost no one could see this. But every day, John would go to work to face the battles of confrontation and the need to destroy people so his clients could prosper. It slowly and inexorably wore him down. John was not following his calling, which included: creating instead of destroying; teaching rather than arguing; and he wanted to be working with young malleable minds rather than arguing with intractable, emotionally-charged adults.

You see, even though John liked what lawyers looked like, he did not enjoy what they did. He was required to do things that were inconsistent with his "true self". This wore John out, completely. And since John was worn out by the time he had to go home, he had no energy and soon enough little inclination to fulfill his duties as a father and husband. When he came home, he was agitated, irritable, tense and often outright angry. His options were to vent on the family or withdraw to his workshop and avoid the entire family; neither are healthy responses. Consequently, John quickly went through two marriages and alienated not only his wives but his children as well.

This is neither a commentary on what lawyers do nor it is a commentary on John's strengths and weaknesses as an individual. Rather, it is a natural consequence of the decision John had made to become a lawyer. In the simplest sense, he had selected a job which required him to act in a way that was inconsistent with his "true self". You see, if you are not following your calling, if you are not working toward self-actualization, the net result is that your needs are not fulfilled and that is unhealthy for anyone. It is unhealthy both physically and emotionally. If you spend 12 hours a day doing something that is unhealthy for you, at some point there is a price to pay. It makes no difference if you are single or married with kids. John could have been a hermit and then the damage would still have occurred, but it would have been isolated to just him alone; but he wanted a wife and family. Unfortunately, he picked an unhealthy way to support them, and as much as he wanted a wife and family, he almost ended up with neither. That is, until he changed to a much healthier lifestyle. Now, John is excited, energized and enthusiastic about his new job and his new life. He confided in me that he no longer missed his time at the country club because now he saw it for what it was, a socially acceptable way to avoid his family obligations. However, he had always bought a new car every two years and would have to scale that back. He was fully aware of the financial compression he would have to undergo.

But on balance, with his marriage back on track and being able to properly parent his kids, he was a happy camper, a very happy camper, and he enjoyed his work. All because he found a healthier way to support his family – by following his calling.

More on Herzberg

In my work, I have found that Herzberg's motivators are strong drivers toward not only job satisfaction but employee engagement as well. I have also found the "Big Four Hygiene Factors" to be: pay and benefits; company policies; working conditions; and quality supervision. If these hygiene factors are not managed properly, as Herzberg predicted they will lead to job dissatisfaction. In addition to creating job dissatisfaction, I have also found they have a strong negative effect on employee engagement.

Herzberg was right. Unfortunately, many businesses still do not accept this.

To punctuate this point, you might want to read the *Harvard Business Review* (HBR) article on Herzberg's theory. The article is very good and much easier to read than his book. But the most interesting part of the HBR article is the subtitle, which nicely captures the essence of his theory in a pithy phrase.

"Forget praise. Forget punishment. Forget cash. You need to make their jobs more interesting".

(Herzberg, 2003)

The appropriate management response to Herzberg's theory

First, managers at all levels, down to and including the team leader, need to study and understand the implications of Herzberg's theory. Include these teachings into your management philosophy.

Second, for these "hygiene factors," especially pay, benefits, working conditions and quality supervision. We need to make sure they are satisfied to the level necessary, so they do not become demotivating. This means you will need to match the pay and benefits to the competitive level in your area. My recommendation is to pay at the 60th percentile or above. In addition, a special topic is supervisory quality. My work suggests this is a much larger issue than Herzberg predicts. What I have seen is that strong supervisory skills are paramount for the success of any business. Unfortunately, I seldom see a strong program of supervisory selection and development. This is a huge oversight needing correction.

The objective is to turn these "lightning rod" issues into non-issues. By difference, the entire facility needs to quit trying to use these hygiene factors as some form of motivation. Simply put – they do not work. Quit trying to motivate the people with "a trip to Peter Piper Pizza for your family if we reach the quarterly objectives". In fact, this type of "motivator" actually demotivates the workforce and sends the message that "you are not sufficiently motivated and need to be bribed". In addition, for work that is complex, requires creativity or involves problem solving, these bribes are demotivational and counterproductive.

Using these hygiene factors as short-term, extrinsic motivators reduces creativity, fosters short-term thinking and are quickly forgotten. They also extinguish intrinsic motivation, diminish performance, crush creativity and crowd out good behavior. If that is not enough bad news, you will find that this misuse of these extrinsic motivators also encourages cheating, shortcuts and unethical behavior. I know this flies in the face of a whole lot of prior and even planned management actions, but history has shown Herzberg to be right – time and time again. If you wish to study this further, I recommend you read *The Motivation to Work* (Herzberg, 1959) and also *Punished by Rewards* (Kohn, 1993).

Proper uses of "hygiene factors"

There is a lot of press and hype about benefits in the workplace that include such items as daycare for working parents, flex hours, freebie tickets to football games, Netflix subscriptions and ski passes. Some even have installed game rooms and provide free yoga classes. Depending on your circumstances, as a business, you may need to supply some of these benefits as they often help in recruiting new hires. However, none of them are motivators; they are hygiene factors. So supply them if you must, that is, if your competitors are … but don't expect them to motivate the workforce. They will not.

McGregor's Theory X and X

In 1960, Douglas McGregor published his seminal work, *The Human Side of Enterprise*. In this book, he posited that two different management belief systems created two dramatically different types of behavior from the workforce. He said:

> "Behind every managerial decision or action are assumptions about human nature and human behavior. A few of these are remarkably pervasive".

> (McGregor, 2006)

He then named these two belief systems Theory X and Theory Y and codified them as follows:

"Theory X

1. The average human being has an inherent dislike of work and will avoid it if he can.
2. Because of this human characteristic of dislike of work, most people must be coerced, controlled, directed, threatened with punishment to get them to put forth adequate effort toward the achievement of organizational objectives.
3. The average human being prefers to be directed, wishes to avoid responsibility, has relatively little ambition, wants security above all …

... Theory X explains the consequences of a particular managerial strategy; it neither explains nor describes human nature although it purports to ... (emphasis mine)

Instead, McGregor offers Theory Y, which rests on these assumptions:

1. "The expenditure of physical and mental effort in work is as natural as play or rest
2. External control and the threat of punishment are not the only means for bringing about effort toward organizational objectives. Man will exercise self-direction and self-control in the service of objectives to which he is committed.
3. Commitment to objectives is a function of the rewards associated with their achievement
4. The average human being learns, under proper conditions, not only to accept but to seek responsibility ...
5. The capacity to exercise a relatively high degree of imagination, ingenuity, and creativity in the solution of organizational problems is widely, not narrowly, distributed in the population.
6. Under the conditions of modern industrial life, the intellectual potentialities of the average human being are only partly utilized ... "

(McGregor, 2006)

Above all, the assumptions of Theory Y point up the fact that the limits on human collaboration in the organizational setting are not limits of human nature but rather they are limits on management's ingenuity in discovering how to realize the potential represented by its human resources".

(McGregor, 2006; emphasis mine)

The irony uncovered by McGregor

When we review this list of behaviors that result from managers who hold Theory X beliefs, they are a compilation of worker behaviors that managers do not want. They do not want workers who do not want to work and who need to be coerced. They do not want workers who need to be disciplined and punished. They do not want workers who need constant direction, surveillance and who avoid responsibility. These are the core of a litany of complaints that managers have about workers. Given these issues, any manager worth his salt would like to change then.

Yet McGregor is very specific, states very clearly that these behaviors are real, and is also quite pointed when he says,

"they are a natural response of the workforce that is caused by a style of management behaviors".

(McGregor, 2006)

Make no mistake, the irony is that these managers, through the best of their efforts, and the best of their intentions **are creating the very behaviors, they do not want**. Consequently, if we want greater contribution from the workforce, it is not the workforce which must change; rather, **it is the behavior of the management which must change**.

Now that is a real mouthful and a topic difficult to accept by most managers.

Furthermore, McGregor says these management behaviors are driven by a deep-seeded "belief system", (Theory X) which is the predominant guide to their behavior. And while it is possible to get the management behaviors to change, through training and executive follow-ups, for example, this will only lead to a superficial and strained form of improvement. These "forced" changes can have some short-term effectiveness but will ultimately unravel, and managers will regress to old heavy-handed methods, for example, in periods of stress or when the pressures of the "executive follow-up" is released. Unless the underlying belief system changes, the management behavioral change will be forced, superficial and short-lived at best.

To affect a true cultural change, the underlying belief system must change, and I am hard-pressed to find anything more difficult, in the world of management, than trying to change their belief systems.

A manager who has a Theory X belief system could best be described as a "command and control" type leader who uses that style at all times, regardless of circumstance. While there is an occasional time and an occasional place for this style of management, with today's workforce this is largely an antiquated style and is not an effective means to achieve a more effective and efficient workplace. Furthermore, the Theory X belief system is antithetical to basic employee involvement in the workplace and certainly not at all supportive of creating a fully engaged workforce.

The appropriate management response to McGregor's theory

First, all managers and supervisors, from the C-suite to the team leader, need to study and understand not only the theory but the implications of Theory X and Y belief systems. They must incorporate these beliefs and principles into their management philosophy and make sure all those promoted understand and comply with a Theory Y belief system.

Specifically, as a minimum, management needs to understand, accept and believe that workers:

1. are self-motivated and thrive on responsibility; hence, management needs to involve the worker in a participative relationship, but management must still retain appropriate control
2. have considerable untapped skills they naturally wish to embellish, and, hence, managers should encourage skill development and personal growth and also encourage them to make suggestions and improvements.
3. consider work as a natural part of life and all workers will solve problems naturally so management should educate them in and include them in the activities to improve their workplace

Motivation, and the role of management

It is pretty hard to pick up a book on management and not find that a significant portion of management's job is to motivate the workforce.

I could not disagree more!!

You have just hired people who came in the front door motivated at day one. If they were not motivated, what are they doing there? Now you are going to change their surroundings and you can then do one of two things. You can provide them with the things they need to stay motivated; or you can deprive them of the things they need, and demotivate them.

Consequently, some time ago, I developed my three rules to guide managers as they address the issue of workforce motivation.

Three management rules on motivating the workforce

Rule number one – Don't try to motivate people

First, they do not need it; at least, when they initially come to work they do not. Rather, I find that they come to work not only motivated but highly motivated. They not only want to learn about their job, they want to learn about their entire business. They want to excel at their jobs and more often than not, at day one, they have several ideas for improvements which they can readily see. Second, most efforts to directly motivate the workforce, although frequently very well-intended and thoughtful, are more often than not counter-motivational and should be avoided.

When I say that people come to work motivated,
I am in pretty good company!

This is a premise you will find in Douglas McGregor's famous book (*The Human Side of Enterprise*, 1960) also supported by the works of Fredrick Hertzberg (*The Motivation to Work*, 1993) as well as the writings of Abraham Maslow (*Motivation and Personality*, 1954). In fact, the great psychologist Erik Erikson (*Identity and the Life Cycle*, 1959) felt we had a natural innate motivation to perform and we would all, at a very early age, go through a series of "crises". Four of these "crises" were:

- trust versus mistrust (0–2 years old);
- autonomy versus shame and doubt (2–4 years old);
- initiative versus guilt (4–5 years old);
- industry versus inferiority (5–12 years old).

Furthermore, Erikson states that nearly all of us will have some success in overcoming these crises and this will give us, in order, a:

- certain level of hope;
- certain level of will;
- certain degree of purpose;
- certain level of competence.

All four of these personality traits: hope, autonomy, initiative and industry, motivate us in many ways; they drive us to do things. He therefore believes that we come to work both wanting to do a good job and wanting to improve the workplace. Furthermore, this penchant came to us at a very,

very early age, mostly before we even went to school and all, long before we ever went to work.

In *Maslow on Management*, there is an interesting insert. He says:

> "... reminds us of a story told about Peter Drucker, the legendary author and tireless teacher. He was speaking to a group of senior level executives and he asked them to raise their hands if there was a lot of 'dead wood' in their companies. Many in the audience raised their hands. He then responded, 'Were the people dead wood when you interviewed them and decided to hire them or did they become dead wood?".

> (Maslow, 1998)

Which takes us to our second rule.

Rule number two – Don't demotivate the workforce

Don't use Demotivator Number 1 – Fear

Nothing will demotivate a worker or an entire workforce faster than fear. Normally, when fear is used, an abuse of power accompanies it. When you are subjected to an abuse of power, your freedom and autonomy are negatively affected. Once fear is introjected into the culture, not only does it irritate people unbelievably but they withdraw. They withdraw not only emotionally but also physically and intellectually. Fear generates negativity, anger, frustration and most of all it generates wasted physical energy and wasted psychic energy. Management by fear takes the starch out of a workforce and they are no longer able to exhibit creativity or become engaged. This was such a large issue to Dr. Deming he included it as one of his Fourteen Obligations of Management; specifically, he said:

> "Drive out fear, so that everyone may work effectively for the company", Point No. 8.

> (Scherkenbach, 1988)

Fear in the workplace is almost always focused on work relationships and communications issues. The communications are either consciously or subconsciously intended to create fear. It is one of those very highly leveraged emotions where a little bit goes a long way, and when damage is done by the use of fear, it takes 10, 20 or 50 times as much effort to correct the damage that was done.

Sometimes the use of fear in the workplace is obvious. Considering that fear is a massive motivating force, managers will sometimes intentionally use it as a means to "get things going". Although conscious and often well-intended, it is almost always incorrectly applied. It often comes in the form of "If we don't step up our game, the XYZ Corporation is going to steal all our customers". If that is the entire message, then it is inappropriate. Rather than motivate people, not knowing what is wrong or what to do differently, they will simply withdraw and do nothing; it will be counterproductive as they are stuck with the fear and nothing else. On the other hand, if the statement were, "Even though their prices are higher than ours, XYZ corporation has stolen 7% of our business, because they have expedited overnight delivery and 100% on time delivery for regular orders. We need to step up our game. I want the managers of engineering, manufacturing, logistics and sales to jointly prepare and present a proposal to me by the end of the week, so we might get this business back and lose no more. Any questions?" People may leave both discussions with some fear; however, in the second one, they understand the context of the issue and with the opportunity to create some countermeasures, there is hope. If there is a balance with hope, then fear is something people can deal with.

Creating fear in the workplace comes in many forms. It may be an ornery, old curmudgeon who practices what he learned 50 years ago when it might have been more tolerated. Or it could be the insecure manager who knows no other way. The only "motivational arrow" he has in his quiver is to utilize fear and position power to get others to act. It could also be the frustrated manager who is at the end of his rope and really does not understand the problem in sufficient detail to provide a meaningful context that others can work with. I am sure there are other situations

For just a second, return to Maslow's hierarchy of needs. If you have a workforce that is engaged or marginally engaged and then start using fear as a motivational tool, people withdraw to the basic needs level and are only motivated by the extrinsic motivators. They fear for their safety and their security, even if it is emotional safety and emotional security. Engagement, creativity, cooperation and teamwork are no longer reasonable options. It becomes an every-man-for-himself culture with survival as the guiding motivator. Insufficient knowledge by managers, insecure managers, as well as frustrated managers, cover the bulk of the reasons that fear gets propagated in the workplace through subconscious means.

On the other hand, there are many things that are done on a normal and conscious basis that instill fear. These negatively affect motivation and engagement. They include unfair and open criticism, having others withhold information from you, not being appropriately included, being misled or lied to, unfair recognition, having hidden agendas, unclear instructions, inadequate resources, plus surprises and inappropriate consequences. Most of these are relationship and communications related, and although they are seemingly correctable, they are way too common.

On competition

However, the most common, conscious, fear-creating mechanism is competition. Comparing one plant to another is a sure-fire way to destroy intra-facility teamwork and sharing of information as well as promote jealousy and withdrawal. Having a contest for the fewest safety incidences is a sure-fire way to assure under-reporting of accidents. Also, imagine the fear and anxiety experienced by the one person who has his first accident in 30 years during the competition? Providing a picnic for the crew with the most improvement ideas is a sure-fire way to reduce improvement ideas in the long run. Not to mention, you are sending the message that, "We don't think you care enough or are motivated enough to come up with improvement ideas unless we bribe you". Not only does this pick away at confidence but it destroys trust.

You see, competition is the just the first cousin of conflict. In conflict, there are winners and there are losers; that is the nature of conflict. Whenever there are winners and losers, there is the fear of losing. Competition begets fear, always.

In conflict, two parties are vying for the same thing, whether it is all-out war for land between countries or intracompany competition trying to get the free picnic by having fewer accidents; it is still conflict. Competition is simply conflict … with rules. The rules are designed to make the conflict more

> **FUJISAWA QUOTE**
>
> Recall this quote from Chapter 1,
>
> "Japanese and American management is 95% the same and differs in all important respects" (Pascale and Athos, 1981)"?
>
> When it comes to making sure the hygiene factors and the basic elements are adequately addressed, this is where companies like Honda, Toyota and "the Top Seven" from my list stand out. They do that 5% that is missed by others. Rather than doing 5% more things, they do all the basics – 5% better.

humane, but at its core, competition is still conflict. So, whenever you create competition, you must be cognizant of the fact that you are creating conflict; this is unavoidable, so avoid competition.

Make sure the hygiene factors are adequately addressed

Herzberg taught us, if we do not supply the hygiene factors adequately, we will demotivate the workforce. The big four on Herzberg's list were pay, company policies, working conditions and good supervision.

I can think of a "thousand little things management and supervision does and says" to demotivate the workforce. Much of this falls under the topic of good versus bad supervision. They include such simple things such as being rude, worse things such as poor communications and withholding information, more serious things such as "playing favorites" amongst your workers, behaviors that are even worse, such as utilizing a certain "moral flexibility" in the enforcement of the rules and finally up to and including inappropriate and abusive use of power. This list is long and a great deal has been written about it so I will not belabor that point here.

Make sure the "basic elements" are adequately addressed

Rather, I wish to emphasize the **all-too-common-and-often-minimized** things, the basic elements, which management does not do nearly well enough; these all negatively impact motivation. There are four.

1. They do not adequately describe, specifically, what needs to be done. They need to supply good goals and objectives along with good work instructions.
2. They do not adequately describe, specifically, how work is supposed to be done. As part of supplying good instructions, they must have good work, process and product standards which people are well trained on. The clarity and enforcement of standards is so important it cannot be minimized
3. They do not provide adequate resources to get the work done. They must make sure all resources, including equipment, space and time, are adequate for the task at hand
4. They do not provide an atmosphere where it is conducive to be productive, detailed below.

Regarding items 1, 2 and 3, what management does do quite well is give a general idea of: what needs to be done; how it is to be done; and what resources are required to get it done. Most managers will balk at this statement; however, since the early '70s, following the writing of Dr. Deming and others, it has been documented that when control studies of quality and delivery, to name just two issues, have been done, it has been consistently found that around 94% of the root causes are directly related to the system supplied by management, and yet only 6% are directly related to worker deficiencies (see Chapter 3). Consequently, I say that management "gives a general idea", and, rather, they need to be more specific and thorough in the work direction, training and resourcing of the worker. The net impact of this on motivation is that deliveries are missed and product is scrapped or reworked, to name just two problems This reflects negatively on all who are manufacturing these products, and even if the workers are not at fault, two things happen. First, they get blamed for the "system" deficiencies. Second, no one likes to produce inferior work. Both of these are demotivating.

And don't forget the emotional needs

Regarding item 4, there are four basic human emotional needs that, if satisfied, will go a long way toward "creating an environment where it is conducive to produce". These are often called the intrinsic motivators; rather, I prefer to refer to them as intrinsic needs. They are: autonomy, competence, relatedness and meaningfulness. We will discuss them in detail in Chapter 12. In addition, there are three other emotional needs we will discuss here. They are: hope, challenge and initiative.

- You need to supply hope to the people. Hope that they can produce well, hope that they can produce safely and hope they will have a job tomorrow, to name just a few. This comes about first by good training; second, it comes about by creating a future that is promising and attainable. This is created by having local, as well as plant, goals and objectives which creates the possibility that there is a future state. It can be as simple as a production-by-hour board that shows we can make today's production or as complicated as discussing a 5-Year Developmental Plan with the individual. Hope is a positive motivator as contrasted with despair that demotivates.
- To most supervisors, they believe that creating job challenges is unfair. The truth is that almost all people like challenges. That's what makes many hobbies interesting; you can challenge yourself with little or no fear of failure. In Chapter 12, we will discuss this more fully.

■ You need to create an environment where initiative is rewarded. This means managers need to listen to ideas and support the actions of the workforce. Likewise, a certain tolerance for both bad ideas and mistakes must be maintained. If everyone is scared to death of making a mistake, no one will show any initiative.

Recall, these workers came to you, when they hired on, both motivated to do their job and motivated to improve the facility. Now you have introjected them into a new environment with new rules and requirements and all the possibilities to demotivate them. And it is your challenge to keep them highly motivated. This is not a simple challenge, and more often than not, it is done rather weakly.

However, when all four of the "basic elements", including the emotional needs, are satisfied, and not before, you will have made it practical to sustain the motivation they had at day one.

Now how do you sustain all that?

Rule number three – Manage to sustain this motivation

■ First, the most important factor in sustaining motivation is to make strong use of the intrinsic motivators on a daily basis. Herzberg taught us there were "motivators". He included such topics as challenging work, recognition, personal growth and responsibility. All these motivators give positive job satisfaction arising from "intrinsic" elements of the work itself. Later, in the 1970s, Edward Deci and Richard Ryan (1985) did studies regarding worker engagement and further validated the concept of intrinsic motivation.

■ Second, do not minimize the obvious. Both the hygiene factors and the basic elements will need updating and maintenance over time.

■ Third, you may need to add or modify some "perks" to stay competitive and supply your workforce with an appropriate package benefits to avoid employee dissatisfaction.

■ Fourth, make sure your culture has the proper "feedback" systems as outlined in Chapter 13. Soon enough you will find that the managing the "feedback" system is as important as making sure the basics are covered properly.

However, the real proof to me that the use of these "intrinsic motivators" is the major tool to be used by the manager to sustain worker motivation comes from my own personal experience, both as an employee and as a manager. Early in my management career, I used these intrinsic motivators extensively. Then, later, in one period of my managerial experience, I was taught to use other motivational tools thought to be more powerful. Unfortunately, while using these "other methods", I found myself to be less successful in both my managerial and supervisory roles; not to mention I enjoyed my work far less. Having then learned from that experience and those failures, and after studying even more, reflecting on what I have done well and done not-so-well and focusing intently on those intrinsic motivators once again ... I found they not only work, they are extremely powerful tools. Furthermore, the power of these intrinsic motivators has been reconfirmed during my consultancy of 29 years. In that experience, I have tried these principles and found them to be not just successful but wildly successful as I have not only used them but taught them as well.

Chapter Summary ... We discussed the serious problem where the management, often with the best of intentions, while trying to motivate the workforce actually ends up demotivating them. This is due, in large part, to a misunderstanding of motivation in the workplace. Maslow with his hierarchy of needs explained why the "basic needs" had to be satisfied before the "psychological needs" could be satisfied. Contained within the psychological needs is the concept of employee engagement. Hertzberg explained his "Two-Factor" theory distinguishing hygiene factors from work motivators. McGregor, while looking at management belief systems, debunked a great deal of current management thinking and stated very simply that workers' behavior was a direct response to the way they were supervised, and if you wished to change their behavior, you only needed to change the behavior of the management team. Finally, we discussed the Three Rules to Motivate the Workforce.

What's next?? Maslow, Herzberg, McGregor and basic motivation are interesting, but now we turn to the motivation that drives engagement, intrinsic motivation.

Chapter 12

Intrinsic Motivation

Aim of this Chapter ... First, we wish to discuss the concept of intrinsic motivation. Second, another principle that is part of the positive psychology movement, "flow", can teach us a lot about engagement, so we will explore that. Third, we will discuss a concept, known as self-determination theory (SDT), developed by Edward Deci and Richard Ryan, and its connection to intrinsic motivation. Fourth, we will explain how intrinsic motivation is the key element in both creative behavior and engagement. Finally, we will discuss the Big Question of "How can managers and supervisors motivate their workers?"

Intrinsic motivation – The basics

Motivation is that force which drives behavior. If we are motivated to do something, we generally will. As soon as we cease some activity, no matter how much we say we "want" to continue it, we are no longer motivated. Psychologists have created terms for the motivation that drives behavior depending upon the location of the apparent reward, and the location is always relative to the individual. The "reward" need not be a classic reward; it can also be an obligation or a demand, for example.

For those rewards that are outside the individual, the motivation that drives one to seek this reward is called extrinsic motivation. Examples are working hard to get a higher salary or a promotion. Grades in school are yet another example of extrinsic rewards. Very often when you find extrinsic rewards, they are not only external to the individual but normally they are tangible and they are also controlled or regulated by someone or something external to the individual. Examples of extrinsic rewards not only include tangibles such as salary, perks and grades, they also include items such as social recognition and acceptance.

On the other hand, there are rewards that are found internal to the individual. These rewards include such things as esteem, satisfaction, fulfillment and even plain old simple fun. The motivational driver for these activities is intrinsic motivation. When intrinsically motivated, a person is moved to act for the fun or challenge entailed rather than because of external demands, expectations, pressures or rewards. In pure intrinsic motivation, the regulation of the activity is self-controlled and the rewards are not tangible.

In a moment we will study Deci and Ryan's self-determination theory, where they distinguish between different types of motivation based on the different reasons or goals, the drivers, that give rise to an action. The most basic distinction is between intrinsic motivation, which refers to doing something because it is inherently interesting or enjoyable, and extrinsic motivation, which refers to doing something because it leads to a separable outcome or its instrumental value. A reasonable working definition of intrinsic motivation based on Deci and Ryan's SDT is that:

"Intrinsic motivation is defined as the doing of an activity for its inherent satisfaction rather than for some separable consequence".

There is some overlap in the definitions of intrinsic and extrinsic motivators and it is not a pure black and white thing. Deci and Ryan discuss this topic more fully in self-determination theory, to follow later in this chapter (see Figure 12.3).

Intrinsically motivated behaviors we have in common

To gain a common understanding of intrinsic motivation, as a concept, we can look at some experiences we all share. These include hobbies and volunteer activities. They are examples of behavior driven by intrinsic motivation. As such, they are done for the pure joy of "doing" them; there does not need to be a trophy, a paycheck, a grade or even an "attaboy" at the end of the activity.

There is yet another descriptive example of intrinsically motivated behavior that comes directly from the positive psychology movement. That is the concept of "flow". As we discuss "flow", I am sure you will be able to make some personal connections to this exhilarating experience.

The concept of "flow"

Mihaly Csikszentmihalyi (pronounced: me-high, cheek-sent-me-high) started studying the "optimal experience" in the early '60s. He first found this amongst artists and later studied a wide variety of other activities including chess, rock climbing and dancing. He was intrigued that under certain circumstances these people would work with incredible focus, energy and attention, oblivious to the entire outside world, focused intently on the task at hand. They would be so engrossed in their work they would forget to eat, never seem to get tired and would even forego sleep to stay engaged in the task at hand. It was not as if "time flew" such as when you are doing something you enjoy; it was far more intense. It was as if there was no such concept as time. In extreme flow, time was no longer relevant.

He expanded this research and created the concept of "flow" to understand the phenomenon of intrinsically motivated behavior during the creative process, where the activity itself was the reward. What he found, while studying the creative process, was that some conditions needed to be present for people to enter the state which he named, "flow" (Figure 12.1). They are:

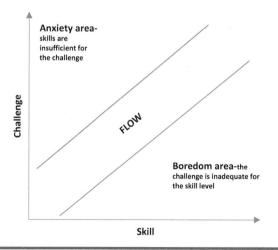

Figure 12.1   Flow: The challenge–skills relationship. (Adapted from Csikszentmihalyi, 2009.)

1. There must be a perceived challenge
2. The challenge must stretch, but not overmatch, the skills of the individual
3. There must be a definite goal
4. There must be an immediate and ongoing feedback system

When in flow, the individual is at "optimal capacity". However, this state can be quite dynamic. For example, if the challenge exceeds the skills, one first becomes vigilant and then if not rebalanced, becomes anxious. On the other hand, if the skills exceed the challenges, one first senses a level of control, then relaxes and if not rebalanced, becomes bored. This, in turn, speaks to the fact that as a person becomes more skilled, say, at rock climbing, to remain in the highly motivated state of flow, he must experience greater and greater challenge.

Later, so he could explain a broader range of emotions involved in understanding flow, Csikszentmihalyi created the model shown in Figure 12.2.

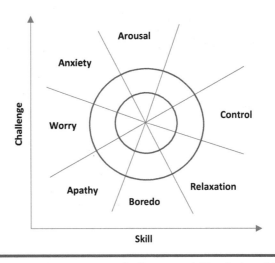

Figure 12.2 Flow: Detailed responses, challenges–skill relationships. (Adapted from Csikszentmihalyi, 2009.)

What is the relevance of "flow" psychology to engagement in the workplace?

There is a lot. Flow is the expression of extreme intrinsic motivation. Taken to its extreme, as described above, such as the artist who paints all day and all night and loses contact with both time and his external environment, I call it "obsessive engagement". As such extremes, "flow" is not a sustainable condition.

Think of the consequences. In extreme flow, people subconsciously deprive themselves of food, water and sleep as well as interaction with others; that too is not healthy. There is the danger of "blocking out your environment", and in the factory, this would not be healthy and certainly not safe.

It is often instructive to go beyond the limits of a concept to better understand the concept itself and explore how to exploit it more fully. For example, design engineers often run equipment to failure, and by understanding the weaknesses they uncovered, they can then make the equipment more robust. Studying flow has the same relationship to engagement. The extreme conditions of flow as "obsessive engagement" is engagement beyond healthy bounds ... but gives us insights to help us better understand and manage engagement. Each of the four flow conditions is instructive to that end. Specifically, if we want engagement, we will need to satisfy each of these four conditions.

There must be a perceived challenge

This is the first condition of flow, the challenge. **And without challenge, there is no engagement either.** This presents a problem to many managers. Not knowing how to challenge everyone at the same time, they normally throw up their hands or dive deeply into denial and rationalizations and say some things like, "Well, the union probably wouldn't let us do that" or, "If we pressure our people too hard, we will drive them away".

That is all poppycock, and a manager only needs to delve into his own personal experience to determine that work without challenge is simply boring. See Figure 12.1. Hence, managers who come up with these rationalizations to avoid challenging the workforce are just saying, "Well, I think I will go about making the work boring" for my workers. It is no more complicated than that. Exactly how does that sound when you are trying to create an engaging workforce? Do you want energized, excited enthusiastic workers ... or bored ones?

The concept of "challenging" workers at all levels is so basic to Toyota that in their seminal book "The Toyota Way, 2001" (Toyota, 2001) they documented the two overriding concepts to guide the entire culture of the Toyota Corporation. These are continuous improvement and respect for people. The very first element, yes, the first behavioral element is "challenge". They say,

> "Challenge – We form a long-term vision, meeting challenges with courage and creativity to realize our dreams".

> (Toyota, 2001)

If this is the first principle of the Toyota culture, I cannot make a stronger endorsement of the need to challenge all your workers. If Toyota's word is not sufficient, delve into your own personal experience and recall a "flow" experience you had, and you will find it only became a flow experience – because you were challenged.

This may seem like a huge management task, that is, to

> **KAIZEN**
>
> Kaizen is the concept of improvement. When the business has a culture of continuous improvement, the entire workforce is continuously active in making small improvements in the process and the workplace.
>
> Do not confuse kaizen with kaizen events, kaizen blitzes, kaizen projects or Six Sigma projects. These are discrete events, done sporadically by a select few and are focused on large events

make each job challenging to each and every individual. Yet to the lean professional, this is old hat. It is very simple, conceptually. Develop a culture of continuous improvement based on kaizen (see insert). When this culture of continuous improvement is created, then each worker is not only encouraged but trained to observe for and to implement kaizen in their work areas. This has a double-barreled positive effect. First, it fuels the concept of engagement, and second, it improves the business.

The challenge must stretch, but not overmatch, the skills of the individual

You can easily see from Figure 12.1 that as the work challenge overwhelms the skill level of the worker, worker anxiety is a result. On the other hand, companies must address the issue of worker boredom as boredom, with the resultant loss of concentration, which also leads to defects and customer complaints. I seldom see training programs working to assess the issue of "inadequate challenge", yet this will also lead to increased defects and decreased engagement. It seems like management is caught between a rock and a hard place. Train too little; get worker anxiety and defects. Or train too much and get worker boredom and still have defects. What should the management response to this dilemma be??

Again, the answer is to have a culture of continuous improvement based on kaizen. The beauty is that once you have an adequate program to assure the worker is properly skilled, to stay engaged in the work, the worker will self-regulate. That is, if the work is not stimulating and not challenging enough, the worker can satisfy his intrinsic needs by thinking more deeply about the work and creating kaizens. If, on the other hand, the basic work is challenging enough, he need not create any kaizens and will still be satisfied. It is a win-win scenario, and everyone stays engaged.

The hidden danger …

What happens when the challenge overmatches the skills of the worker? Hopefully this does not happen often, but when it does, it is imperative that this issue be addressed promptly for a variety of reasons including, safety, product quality and, of course, employee engagement. Unless the leader is like a helicopter mom and hovering over the worker, the leader will not quickly know if the worker is stressed by the challenge being beyond their skills. It is far healthier if the employee recognizes it and feels comfortable discussing this with his supervisor. This will not happen unless the leader has a trusting relationship with the worker and spends time at the gemba checking to see how the workers are doing. This is all part of creating an environment where it is possible for the worker to perform, creating yet another reason to have strong supervision. In addition, the topic of trusting relationships will be further addressed in Chapter 16.

There must be a definite goal

For anyone who has studied motivation, they know that people get motivated for "something". There is always a goal, and in flow, the goal is the task at hand as much as the end result. However, if you wish your people to be engaged, they must be engaged toward something. The goal needs to be tangible; it needs to be understood, and the workers' role in meeting that goal, likewise, must be understood. There must be a "focus" on something. To create a common and strong focus at your facility, implement Hoshin Kanri (HK) planning (HK planning is covered in more detail in Chapter 18). It is a common planning technique utilized at lean facilities, has proven itself and is easy to get started. HK Planning, done well, also has a double-barreled effect on engagement. The first effect is that everyone is engaged in the creation of the goals, so there is alignment, focus and buy-in by everyone. The second effect, feedback, we will discuss in the ensuing paragraph.

There must be an immediate and ongoing feedback system

For a worker to stay engaged in the work, just as in the flow experience, he must have a rapid feedback system which lets him know that what he has done was done well. This has the effect of confirming worker competence and keeping confidence high. Again, the management countermeasure to address the need for feedback is three-fold: HK planning; leader standard work; and transparency all provide feedback. HK planning is a feedback system, as it provides formal monthly and annual supervisory and management reviews that are shared with the workforce. To further accentuate the feedback process, all supervisors, including team leaders, employ leader standard work to assure that the policies are being deployed as well as worker development is occurring. Finally, to make sure all work elements are being employed, a system of "transparency" (sometimes called visual management) needs to be in place. Transparency will allow you to see, at a glance, if production is on schedule, if maintenance is on schedule and if training is up to date, to name a few elements. These are the all "short-term" feedback elements and for the most part address the process. In addition, to cover the long-term developmental and feedback issues regarding individual growth and development, administered jointly with his supervisor, each worker should have a 1-Year Performance Plan designed to make and keep him a productive worker, right now. And secondly, also in conjunction with his supervisor, each worker will complete a 5-Year Performance and Development plan, focusing on his longer-term performance.

Flow at work?

It might seem that since flow can be so intensive, it is not experienced at work. It seems that several studies have debunked that belief. For example,

> "As expected, the more time a person spent in flow during the week, the better was the overall quality of his or her reported experience. People who were more often in flow were especially likely to feel 'strong,' 'active,' 'creative,' 'concentrated,' and 'motivated'. What was unexpected, however, is how frequently people reported flow situations at work, and how rarely in leisure".

> (Csikszentmihalyi, 1990)

> "When people were signaled while they were actually working at their jobs ... the proportion of responses in flow was a high 54 percent. In other words, about half the time that people are working they feel they are confronting above-average challenges and using above-average skills. In contrast, when engaged in leisure activities such as reading, watching TV, having friends over, or

going to a restaurant, only 18 percent of the responses ended up in flow. The leisure responses were typically in the range we have come to call apathy, characterized by below-average levels of both challenges and skills. In this condition, people tend to say that they feel passive, weak, dull, and dissatisfied. When people were working, 16 percent of the responses were in the apathy region; in leisure, over half (52 percent)".

(Csikszentmihalyi, 1990)

Self-determination theory

Self-determination theory (SDT) was developed by Drs. Edward Deci and Richard Ryan starting around 1975. It was made more public in Dr. Deci's book *Why We Do What We Do* (1995) and further popularized in an article in *American Psychologist*, "Self-Determination Theory and the Facilitation of Intrinsic Motivation, Social Development and Well-Being" (Deci and Ryan, 2000). It is a widely accepted construct to explain human behavior and addresses both extrinsic and intrinsic motivational concepts.

It has gotten more attention and even more credibility as the positive psychology movement has gained momentum. As Dr. Deci writes,

"… people are assumed to possess an active tendency toward psychological growth and integration. Endowed with an innate striving to exercise and elaborate their interests, individuals tend naturally to seek challenges, to discover new perspectives, and to actively internalize and transform cultural practices. By stretching their capacities and expressing their talents and propensities, people actualize their human potentials. Within this perspective, active growth is complemented by a tendency toward synthesis, organization, or relative unity of both knowledge and personality. Moreover, the integration of that which is experienced provides the basis for a coherent sense of self – a sense of wholeness, vitality, and integrity. To the degree that individuals have attained a sense of self, they can act in accord with, or be "true" to, that "self".

(Deci and Ryan, 2002)

This paints a very rosy picture of human nature which is sometimes almost hard to believe; it is especially hard to believe considering all that is happening in the world today. The entire concept of SDT does have some critics, although research into SDT and its applications seem to be flourishing. I have not only read but extensively studied SDT, and I choose to accept it's concept and conclusions for three reasons. First, it makes sense. Second, it is gaining momentum and credibility daily amongst the scholars. Third, and most importantly to me, I can validate it from my experience not only as a manager in business and as a consultant advising businesses but also as an individual worker. I have lived it, I have taught it and I have seen people and businesses flourish when they accept and utilize it. I have little doubt that SDT is a sound explanation of human behavior in the workplace.

A basic premise of SDT is that to create and sustain both physical and emotional well-being and health, three basic psychological ***needs*** must be satisfied. These three are not desires and they are not what we call "wants"; they are basic ***needs*** for everyone. A need is something that if satisfied promotes health and wellness, and if frustrated promotes illness. These three needs are autonomy, competence and relatedness.

- Autonomy, acting with a sense of volition and choice. That is, having some control over your work environment and the things that affect you.
- Competence, being effective in your work and activities
- Relatedness, caring for others and being cared for

Work environments and activities which support the satisfaction of these needs will support and promote natural growth and personal development, including facilitating intrinsically motivated behavior and a healthier integration of extrinsic motivations. On the other hand, activities that are not supportive of individual autonomy, competence and relatedness, diminish motivation, diminish performance and negatively affect well-being. Furthermore, it is a basic precept of SDT that humans naturally strive for a state of high motivation and well-being. Hence, it is part of our nature to pursue both growth and well-being.

The key role of autonomy

Central to SDT is the concept of *autonomous* motivation, that is, self-determination. As contrasted to *controlled* motivation, which is controlled by others. Autonomous motivation is acting with volition, a sense of personal control and choice. And intrinsic motivation is a strong type of autonomous motivation. Hence, when people undertake and persist in an activity, simply because they want to, and for the pure enjoyment of it, they are intrinsically motivated and acting autonomously. On the other hand, being controlled involves acting with a sense of pressure, a sense of having to engage in the actions; this is associated with extrinsic motivation.

SDT states that autonomous and controlled motivations have different effects on the individual and fall on a continuum from amotivation to extrinsically controlled motivation and finally to self-determined, or intrinsic, motivation, the strongest form of autonomous motivation; graphically depicted in Figure 12.3.

SDT posits that autonomous motivation is typically associated only with intrinsic motivation, integrated regulation and sometimes identified regulation. All else is controlled motivation and largely driven by extrinsic factors.

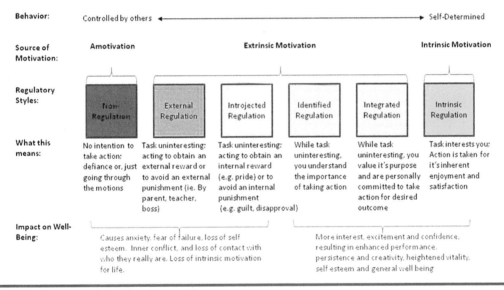

Figure 12.3 **SDT and autonomous versus controlled motivation. (www.physio-pedia.com)**

An example of the autonomy spectrum

Take, for example, the various choices an employee might have at work. Let's say the facility has a management philosophy of continuous improvement and has spent considerable time and effort to train the people in the many skills so they can recommend and implement process improvements. For a culture to sustain a philosophy of continuous improvement, **it is axiomatic that it must be a voluntary program**. In other words, the employees can participate or not; the choice is theirs. Nearly everyone, given the choice, will participate, but often for different reasons. Or, stated another way, the driving forces to cause them to act, to submit suggestions for improvement, can be very different. Hence, they are differently motivated with differing degrees of autonomy.

Controlled behavior ... acting due to undue external influence

For the person who acts based on **external regulation**, they might do it because the boss asks everyone to come up with at least one improvement idea, and you comply even though you don't feel you have the time to do it. You might do it just to get the boss off your back.

Let's say the boss keeps track of how many suggestions each worker submits. Someone else may complete several improvement ideas so he can appear to be the best worker. He is motivated by a social concern, he wants to be seen as being a good employee. This is called **introjected regulation**. It is external yet moving toward autonomous behavior in that he completed many activities, not just one. There is a larger element of choice involved. Yet it is still largely, but not completely, driven by external pressures. In this example, the external stimulus is the perceived social pressures.

Autonomous behavior ... Acting on your own volition

On the other hand, someone else completes several improvement ideas and does so because he is aware of the company objectives of continuous improvement and knows how important this is to the company. This is called **identified regulation**. Once again, it is extrinsic, as the company goals are the driving factor, yet there is recognition of the importance to the company goals and objectives, for example. This is generally considered the lower end of autonomous behavior, as part of the reason to contribute is an internal sense of awareness of being part of a larger entity.

Yet someone else not only completes many improvement items but they do it because they see themselves as an important part of the company. As a responsible member, they will always do their part to support the larger entity. They are aware of the impact and likewise have a clear understanding they must act responsibly. Although the driving force is still the company goals, the driving force has more to do with "who they are and how they act" rather than just "what they do". Deci labeled this **integrated regulation**. This is mid-range autonomous behavior and is getting close to intrinsically motivated behavior.

Finally, for the people who are **intrinsically regulated**, they will suggest and implement the improvements whether there is an external goal or not. They will do it because making the improvements is enjoyable – in its own right. By making the improvements, they can exhibit some control over their work environment, demonstrate their competence in yet another way and by working with others on the improvement, they are jointly improving their work environment. Very likely, the intrinsically motivated individual has no idea how many suggestions he has made and implemented; he is more than satisfied to just get them done. His scorecard is internal and not controlled by anyone or anything else, and very likely he has one or two additional improvements on his mind right now. It is the completion of the work itself, not meeting some external goal, peer acceptance or obligation that drives his behavior; this is autonomous behavior.

Is SDT compatible with, and reinforcing of, other theories??

If SDT sounds a lot like Maslow and his concept of people desirous of rising in the hierarchy of needs and striving for growth, it should. You will note that in Herzberg's theory, all his motivators (as distinguished from his hygiene factors) are intrinsic in nature. There is a tremendous congruence of SDT with the theories of Maslow and Herzberg. Also, McGregor's theories fit with SDT like a hand fits in a glove. For example, three basics of McGregor's theory are that:

- work can be as natural as play;
- people do not need to be threatened to bring about organizational objectives; and
- the capacity to exercise a relatively high degree of imagination, ingenuity and creativity in the solution of organizational problems is widely, not narrowly, distributed in the population. (McGregor, 1960)

One more thing … Meaningfulness

In my work, I have found that there is one more motivational factor to consider. That is the concept of meaningfulness. I find that workers are far more motivated when they are working on a product or service they consider to be meaningful. And by meaningful, I mean it serves a larger purpose than ourselves. For example, take the case where a worker is making a product and he has no understanding of what it is used for. When he asks his boss, "Just what is this used for?", and the boss says, "Got no idea, we just make 'em and sell 'em", experience shows me the worker is less than enthused, and this could negatively affect his motivation. On the other hand, if you are making safety devices for an automobile and you know you are somehow helping drivers and passengers travel more safely, I have seen this to have a strong motivational effect.

William Kahn supports this

From Chapter 3, it reads:

"He further goes on to define three psychological conditions whose presence influenced

> **THE SISYPHEAN CONDITION**
>
> Sisyphus was a Greek king who was being punished by the gods because of his extreme hubris. He was forced to roll a large boulder up a hill in Hades. However, as he reached the top of the hill, the boulder would plummet to the bottom and he was forced to repeat this action forever. It is a metaphor for doing meaningless work and the extreme emotional punishment that ensues.
>
> This impact on the worker in the typical factory is often subtly and unintentionally created, but it is devasting nonetheless.

people to engage and whose absence influenced them to disengage. They were meaningfulness, safety, and availability. He further said: '… members seemed to unconsciously ask themselves three questions in each situation and to personally engage or disengage depending on the answers. The questions were: (1) How meaningful is it for me to bring myself into this performance? (2) How safe is it to do so? and (3) How available am I to do so?".

(Kahn, 1990)

Not only is meaningfulness part of his construct, it is his first element. I have seen it, on the factory floor, to be a significant factor in engagement and hence include it and expand the list of intrinsic needs to four. To Deci and Ryan's needs of autonomy, competence and relatedness, I add meaningfulness.

Some more support for meaningfulness as an intrinsic need.

I recently read an interesting book by Professor Dan Ariely, *The Upside of Irrationality*. Professor Ariely does a lot of very revealing, very interesting, yet easy to understand experiments. In this one, he is evaluating the effect of someone diminishing the meaning in your work. In so doing, he tests two groups. The first group, the "meaningful" condition, are given materials to build Lego-based robots, Bionicles. They are paid $2 for the first Bionicle and the payment decreases by $0.11 for each subsequent Bionicle until the subject is no longer interested. Once built, the Bionicles were placed, intact, in a container. However, they were told that since everyone will use the same parts, they will later be dismantled. In the other condition, the "Sisyphean" condition, they were given the same pay and instructions except there were only two sets of parts. So, to keep the subject productive, while the subject was building the second Bionicle, the proctor was disassembling the first Bionicle, **directly in front of the subject.** When the subject then wanted to build Bionicle number three, he was handed the same set of parts he had assembled to make his first Bionicle. The difference between the two conditions was that in the meaningful condition, the Bionicles were stored to be dismantled later but in the Sisyphean condition, the subject saw his work dismantled, seconds after it was built.

What were the results? In the "meaningful" condition the subjects averaged building 10.6 Bionicles and received $14.40 in pay. In the "Sisyphean" they stopped after making 7.2 Bionicles and earned $11.52.

What does this mean? Well, Professor Ariely says:

> "What this analysis tells me is that if you take people who love something (after all, the students who took part in this experiment signed up for an experiment to build Legos) and you place them in meaningful working conditions, the joy they derive from the activity is going to be a major driver in dictating their level of effort. However, if you take the same people with the same initial passion and desire and place them in meaningless working conditions, you can very easily kill any internal joy they might derive from the activity".

Later, he also says:

> "… the translation of joy into willingness to work seems to depend to a large degree on how much meaning we can attribute to our own labor".

And he also said:

> "This experiment taught us that sucking the meaning out of work is surprisingly easy. If you're a manager who really wants to

demotivate your employees, destroy their work in front of their eyes. Or, if you want to be a little subtler about it, just ignore them and their efforts".

(Ariely, 2010)

In addition to the needs of autonomy, competence and relatedness, it seems reasonable to include meaningfulness, as a fourth need. It passes the common-sense test; I have seen it at work on the factory floor; Kahn includes it in his construct, and experiments like those done by Professor Ariely support it as well. In my model of the needs which must be satisfied to create an environment where people are intrinsically motivated in addition to Deci's three needs, I will include meaningfulness.

Motivation, creativity and a fully engaged workforce

Intrinsic motivation, extrinsic motivation and creativity

It is hard for me to imagine that extrinsic motivators would be effective when you wish to promote creativity of action or thought. First, it just doesn't seem to make sense you could walk up to some worker and say, "Hey, I'll give you 10 bucks for you to be creative". Bribing them to be creative, just does not seem to fit at all. Second, I always think of creativity as being somewhat spontaneous. The creative juices seem to flow when they want to flow. I have always thought of creativity as being one of the things that needed to be totally intrinsic and be a matter of happenstance rather than plan.
    I recently read an article on this subject, and the author said:

> "For more than three decades, psychologists have studied intrinsic motivation as a driver of creativity. The core assumption is that when employees enjoy the work itself, they process information flexibly, experience positive affect, and become willing to take risks and persist in efforts to develop and refine ideas".

(Grant, 2011)

The first works of Deci and Ryan I read were all about the possible negative effects of extrinsic motivators (pay) on otherwise creative and intrinsically motivated behavior. It was the story of the Soma puzzles that were given to students. **What they found was that for intrinsically motivated behavior, if *extrinsic* motivators were introduced, this had a negative effect on the naturally occurring intrinsic behavior.** If left alone with no extrinsic rewards, they found that a control group would outperform a group that had once been paid. Specifically, they paid people to work with puzzles and then would withdraw the pay. Those students would solve fewer puzzles than a control group that were never paid.

> **PARADIGM SHIFT NO. 5**
>
> In your position as a plant manager, or any management position, you are not able to "buy" creativity. If you manage and lead well, you are able to "encourage" and even "cultivate" creativity, but since it is intrinsically motivated behavior, extrinsic motivators won't work. Worse yet, trying to use extrinsic motivators is destructive of creativity. This requires a revolution in management awareness.

This is a monstrous statement and requires a significant change in the thinking of Western management.

It was formerly believed (and still is by the majority) that extrinsic rewards will guide behavior, all behavior. This is the prevalent thought in Western management and certainly the prevalent thought in all those who studied Pavlov's experiments. They became absolutely convinced that by using these extrinsic rewards they could create whatever behaviors they wanted. All they needed to do was to throw money, parking spaces, bonuses and country club memberships at the workforce and, like Pavlov's dogs, they could get the people to do whatever they wanted. They could also use techniques such as competition, surveillance and deadlines to motivate behavior; all behavior. The "golden rule" of extrinsic motivation that is used and overused by management today is; reward "it" with money, for example, and you will get more of "it". Not only is this inconsistent with common sense and the incredible works of Herzberg, Deci and Ryan flat out disproved it.

This concept of "buying creativity" or "forcing creativity" – while both highly prevalent and certainly convenient for management to believe – simply has been disproven. And now management must change.

Intrinsic motivation and engagement

You will learn that engagement is one of those outcomes, like creativity, that is a direct function of being intrinsically motivated. **Said yet another way,**

you cannot buy your way to a fully engaged workforce; rather you must create the environment where it is possible to occur – and then watch it ensue.

Motivation and the "big question"

The big question that managers frequently ask and want answered is, "How can managers and supervisors motivate their workers?". All too often, we see on television the example of the coach giving to his team the "locker room speech". He gets them motivated to a feverish pitch and the team then goes out and "gives them one more for the Gipper". True enough; you can get a certain type of behavior from individuals with this dose of intensive, extrinsic motivation. Unfortunately, it is very focused on the event at hand and is extremely short-lived. Five minutes after time runs out in the game, the motivation disappears. This is not the type of motivation we need in the workplace. We need people with drive for the entire shift, day in and day out. The motivation can't come in fits and starts; it must be omnipresent.

To repeat the question, "How can managers and supervisors motivate their workers?". In the workplace, the answer is "they can't". Sounds discouraging, but don't despair. This is the wrong question.

Specifically, in Chapter 11 we gave you the Three Rules for Motivating the Workforce with a whole list of to-dos and caveats. Yet the answer to "How can managers and supervisors motivate the workforce?" can be addressed by a much better, but seemingly, indirect question.

The correct question

The proper question is **"How can supervisors and managers create an environment where the workforce will be self-motivated?"**

The answer lies in learning how to manage the four intrinsic needs of autonomy, competence, relatedness and meaningfulness. Specifically, **create an environment where these four basic needs are satisfied on a daily and hourly basis.** Then the workforce will be intrinsically motivated and you will be on your way to creating full engagement with all its attendant benefits.

Chapter Summary ... As we discussed the topic of intrinsic motivation, it is helpful to look at why we are so motivated to work at our hobbies and are also motivated for volunteer activities. This introspection will give us basic insights into intrinsically motivated behavior. An example of "obsessive engagement" comes from the research on "flow". Flow is of particular relevance as it is created by the proper handling of challenges, skill levels, goals and feedback, all elements of engagement as well. This took us to the Deci and Ryan's self-determination theory, which nicely explains the concept of intrinsic needs and employee health and well-being in the workplace as well as its relevance to creative behavior. Their major and revolutionary point is that the intrinsic needs, especially the need for autonomy, are not niceties; they are emotional and physical needs that if met will lead to health and well-being and if frustrated will have deleterious effects to both physical health and emotional well-being. Finally, we explained, that the "big question" regarding motivation is not "How do we motivate the workforce?" but rather "How do we create an environment where these four basic needs are satisfied on a daily and hourly basis?".

What's next?? Now we will switch gears from the psychology of engagement to the "systems approach". Do you know how engagement is a system and acts as an integrated whole with a specific purpose? Read on.

CREATING A FULLY ENGAGED WORKFORCE

V

In this section, we will introduce you to the concepts of systems, system elements, systems thinking, system diagrams, causal loop diagrams and engagement as a system. We will define the elements of the engagement system and explain the process of getting your workers engaged, including some needed cultural changes and the elements of engagement. Following this, we will then explore the strong impact all these elements have on the "engine" that drives the entire engagement system, the Intrinsic Motivational Loop. Once again, we will emphasize and discuss the critical role of management. We will then discuss what we must do to further activate the system of engagement, which is a matter of improving the levels of management engagement, including the four types of management feedback that are needed to drive engagement to world class levels.

Part V contains four chapters:

Chapter 13

Systems and Systems Thinking

Aim of this Chapter ... is to introduce you to the concepts of systems, system elements, systems thinking and engagement as a system. We define the system of engagement with a system diagram and introduce you to the two causal loop diagrams, the engagement loop and the disengagement loop.

Systems

> *"You think that because you understand 'one' that you must therefore understand 'two' because one and one make two. But you forget that you must also understand 'and' – Sufi teaching story."*

What is a system??

> System: A set of elements or parts that is coherently organized and interconnected in a pattern or structure that produces a characteristic set of behaviors, often classified as its "function" or "purpose".

(Meadows, 2008)

Your body is a system, composed of many sub-systems. You have your cardiovascular system, your digestive system, your renal system, and these sub-systems, have sub-systems of their own. Wherever there is a purpose to be obtained and it takes multiple, interconnected elements to create the purpose, likely we have a system. And if you then think most "things" are a system, you're right. Your car is a system whose purpose is to get you from point A to point B. And the car has sub-systems such as a powering system, a braking system and even an interior cooling system. We used to call that interior cooling system air conditioning, but now in some cars that is no longer accurate. Now, the interior cooling system might also include a seat cooling system and even a steering wheel cooling system. Systems within systems to create larger systems that synergize to create even larger systems, the concept is almost without limit.

Systems have some very distinctive properties

1. Each element has an effect on the behavior of the entire system. Your body will not function properly without all its parts. Take out the heart and the body stops functioning, remove a leg and the body cannot run.
2. The behavior of the elements and their effects on the whole are interdependent. No element has an independent effect on the system. All are interdependent. If you have problems with your stomach, it affects your blood pressure, your cardiovascular system and many other elements.
3. While a system has identifiable parts, it is a whole that cannot be divided into independent parts. If you line up all the parts of an automobile, you do not have a car. Which highlights two essential properties of a system; first, every part of a system has properties that it loses when separated from the system, and second, every system has some properties that none of its parts do, and these are the essential parts of the system that make it useful. To be useful, a system must have a purpose. For example, an engine is part of an automobile but cannot function outside the automobile as it is missing its ignition and fuel sources. Likewise, the automobile can transport people, its critical purpose, while an engine or a frame alone cannot.
4. The essential properties of a system derive more from the interactions of its parts than from their actions taken separately, and these properties will persist over time in a wide array of circumstance.
5. Therefore, when a system is taken apart, it loses its essential properties.
6. **Because of this, a system is a whole that cannot be understood by analysis**. It can only be understood by observing and measuring the entire system, dynamically. (This list was largely adapted from *Ackoff's Best: His Classic Writings on Management* (Ackoff, 1999).)

A system isn't just any old collection of things. A system is an interconnected set of elements that is coherently organized in a way that achieves something. If you look at that definition closely for a minute, you can see that a

PARADIGM SHIFT NO. 7

Creating and sustaining engagement is not done in a simple linear process; it is done in a complex dynamic system.

system must consist of three kinds of things: elements, interconnections and a function or purpose.

System elements

These are all of the "parts" of a system and include not only tangible things such as training and kaizens but also intangible concepts such as pride and feelings

Interconnections

These are the relationships that exist that hold the elements together, normally in a causal relationship of some kind.

Purpose

All systems have a purpose. The purpose of the system known as your car is normally to transport you from point A to B. However, some systems have multiple purposes. For example, to some people, the purpose of the car is to express social status. When it has a different purpose, even if it has the same name, assuredly it is a different system. In addition, think of two purposes for a university. A true learner might want to use the system to learn and gain knowledge; someone else might only want a diploma and the recognition that comes with having good grades. If someone wants to just get good grades, they take easy courses and cram for exams, for example, while the true learner will seek out both challenging courses and challenging professors as well as study hard and consistently. In the end, both have a degree and a diploma, but the path they took, the "system" they used, not only had a different purpose but they used different methods along the way.

The purpose of a system can be measured by its behavior. For example, a company may have a quality system but allocates few resources or effort toward that goal, so quality is not its purpose. Purposes are deduced from behavior, not from rhetoric or stated goals. To discern a system's purpose, watch for a while to see how the system behaves.

What is "not a system"?

To find out if something is or is not a system, ask yourself four questions.

1. Are the parts identifiable?
2. Do the parts affect one another?
3. Do the parts together produce an effect different than the effect of any of the parts?
4. Does the behavior persist over time?

If the answer to these questions is "no", very likely you do not have a system.

So, a pile of sand is not a system. The grains are not distinguishable. Remove one grain and you still have a pile of sand. There is no connectedness of the grains of sand; not to mention, it probably has no purpose. However, the human body is clearly a system with its identifiable parts each affecting one another, reaching a desired result, and this behavior will persist in a wide variety of circumstances. Likewise, any business is an incredibly complex system with many sub-systems and sub-sub-systems. There are systems embedded within systems that are further embedded within other systems and so on.

We will focus on the specific business system whose purpose is to create engagement. We will find that it has identifiable parts, these parts work together and together they can create an effect, engagement, that cannot be a result of just one or even a few of the parts. And when all the system elements are in place, it will persist and even grow over time.

Systems thinking

Most management thinking is of the "if-then" quality, and most of the time, it is very good thinking.

■ For example, **IF** we pay attention to our client and supply them with good products, **THEN** they will let us bid on the next project. **IF** we underpay our workforce, **THEN** we will likely have high employee turnover. Most of the time "if-then" thinking works. However, there are two problems.

■ First, the implication in the **IF** statement is that this statement is not only necessary **but it is sufficient** to create the desired outcome, the **THEN** statement. I wish life were so simple; it is not. Rather, **IF** we do these things, **THEN** this outcome is more likely is a better statement of reality. For example, "if we supply workers with training and personal protective equipment, then we will have fewer accidents" is a statement any manager would like to make. Unfortunately, that is not always true. The problem here is that people, while they understand some of the problem, do not have a complete understanding of the entire problem.

■ The second problem is a furtherance of the first in that people have a misunderstanding of the real cause of the problem. For example, let's say your workers are quitting for reasons other than low pay; then improving the pay situation will have little effect on the employee turnover.

On the other hand, let's just say for the sake of argument that the managers doing the thinking do have a solid grasp on the cause–effect relationship of any given situation … there can still be large problems. And most often the root cause of this problem is using linear thinking when systems thinking is required.

The key benefits of systems thinking are to not only see the IF-THEN relationships but also to see the interactions. Then you can see the dynamics and ultimately see the patterns that exist in systems. To achieve systems thinking, it is usually best to describe your system in graphic format.

Linear thinking…

Information ⟶ Actions ⟶ Results

Analysis

To understand processes, or things, using linear thinking, we use a process that is known as analysis. Analysis is a three-step process which is:

1. breaking down the whole into its components
2. understanding and explaining the behavior of the parts, individually, and
3. attempting to optimize the parts in an effort to optimize the whole.

Unfortunately, using analysis in this manner makes it difficult to understand many phenomena. Take the dynamics of stopping a car, for example. On dry roads, with good tires, a typical car will take 30 meters to come to a stop from XX mph. However, if the tires are worn, on dry roads it may then take 40 meters to come to a complete stop. On the other hand, with good tires but a rain-covered road, the stopping distance may be 45 meters.

However, if we combine these two conditions and change the system to one where the road is wet AND the tires are worn it will take over 90 meters to stop. Since wet roads increased the stopping distance 15 meters and worn tires increased the stopping distance 10 meters, it seems reasonable that with both conditions, the stopping distance would be 40+15+10, or 65 meters, but it does not; it takes a full 90 meters. Linear thinking does not explain this phenomenon. This is because the reaction between the tires and the road is no longer linear. The two conditions INTERACT to create a condition worse than the sum of the two. This is very hard to find using the three-step process of analysis. Until we consider all the conditions – simultaneously and dynamically – we cannot understand these interactions. To understand these interactions and other dynamics, we need to use systems thinking.

Systems thinking …

Uniqueness of systems thinking?

There are three significant differences when using systems thinking:

- First, we start with an eye toward optimization of the system's purpose, and rather than take things apart, we put them together; we synthesize
- Second, is the emphasis on the dynamics of the system. The simple linear process is seldom a good model for many processes, especially social processes like engagement
- Third, is the combination of synthesis with analysis. Both are necessary. Very often, analysis is viewed as cause and effect. Systems thinking is effect–cause–effect.

Systems thinking is not just synthesis, it is also analysis.

- Analysis focuses on structure; it reveals how things work. Typical analytical thinking is reductionist in nature. We try to break down everything by "taking it apart". By seeing how the parts behave and by improving them, we look to make improvements.

■ Synthesis focuses on function; it reveals why things operate as they do. Synthetic thinking puts things together, i.e., it "build things" into a cohesive functioning whole.

The "key" paradigm shift in systems thinking

In a hospital, we were asked to assist in the preparation of the annual capital budget. Of particular interest was expanding their magnetic resonance imaging (MRI) capacity and one new MRI was proposed at an investment of $2,500,000. The present condition was they were completing four images per shift, and interviews with physicians confirmed that there was the potential for at least another four images per shift. We performed a complete process study using process mapping, process flow, workstation loading, processing cycle time analysis in addition to waste analysis using Yamazumi charting (time study charting showing activities that are waste or value-added). We found the MRI had the capacity to do ten images per shift and was adequately staffed. The process bottleneck was not the MRI or the imaging process in any way. Rather, the bottleneck was the ability to transport patients to and from the MRI. Frequently, the MRI would be "waiting" for patients and just as often, patients would be "waiting" after the MRI to be transported back to their rooms. There was clearly an understaffing issue. That was the technical problem – inadequate transportation to and from the MRI.

However, this was created by a much larger and much deeper organizational and system issue: the group in charge of the transport personnel was trying to be "efficient" and wanted transport personnel to be actively moving patients. This sounds imminently logical ... when based on a narrow view of attempting to achieve a local optimum. Unfortunately, working to optimize this sub-system "patient transportation", caused the overall system "patient MRI" to be severely underutilized with an overall large negative effect on both patient service and financials.

To mitigate the losses and create a better system, we embarked on a group problem solving effort. After sorting through the system's time and motion statistics and a thorough review of both facility and local KPIs, we added transport personnel and improved the queueing process.

PARADIGM SHIFT NO. 6

The system optimum is not the sum of the local optima. To assure you will not achieve a system optimum, work to achieve local optima.

This, with other process improvements, increased the MRI usage to over nine images per shift. The net gains, at $4200/MRI, was over $40,000 of revenue per day (the MRI was only staffed two shifts). There were, at least, three other benefits. First, the investment for the second MRI was delayed. Second, patient satisfaction improved as they no longer had to wait, and third, the doctors were pleased as well with the improved capacity of the diagnostic services.

In this case, the purpose of the MRI was as a diagnostic tool for the physicians, and the measure of effectiveness was "images per shift". We found this "system purpose" was limited by transport personnel; which on the surface seemed to be the problem.

However, what was missed by the entire management team was that the real and deeper problem was a lack of systems thinking. Even after this incident, the long-standing process of local optimization through the use of management by objectives continued just as before. (See double-loop learning in Chapter 9)

Other issues to consider in systems thinking

- A key issue that makes linear thinking inferior to systems thinking include the belief in linear thinking that the information is all known at day one. This is never the case; the more you work on a problem, the more you learn.

> **GENERAL EISENHOWER ON PLANNING ... AND SYSTEMS THINKING**
>
> "In planning for battle, I have found that plans are useless, but planning is indispensable".
>
> I believe it was also he who said, "No battle plan survives contact with the enemy" and "Everything changes as soon as the first shot is fired".
>
> Bits of wisdom in their own right.

- Second, linear thinking presumes that the information, even if it is all known, is static. This is never the case. As soon as you begin to study a problem, the very fact that you pay attention to this problem will cause it to change; sometimes in large and strange ways.
- Third, in linear thinking, we tend to think of actions as being independent and simply additive. This is seldom the case. Actions can act and interact in such a way that the sum of the results is either greater or lesser than the sum of the individual actions.

- Fourth, many results will be affected not by what we do but by what the people in the system believe we are trying to do. This is especially impactful in social systems such as engagement.
- Fifth, for any stimulus in linear thinking we normally assume there is a single response. This is seldom true as there are not only multiple responses but also both intended and unintended consequences from those responses.
- Sixth, as we learn more about the problem, our initial objectives may change, affecting all we had done before, causing us to rethink the entire situation.

Our system – the simplified view

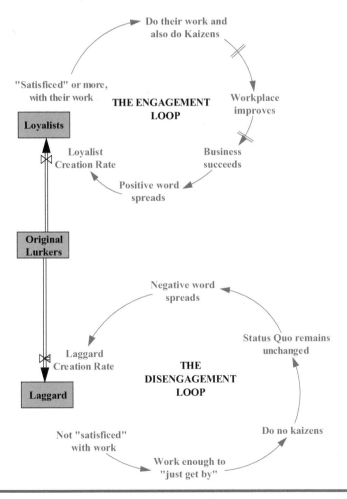

Figure 13.1   **Engagement system diagram, simplified.**

Systems are described and studied using systems diagrams

If a systems diagram is good, it will be a learning and teaching tool and allow you to reach your system goal more rapidly. In addition, if you can study it (by which I mean that you change it and through the use of the scientific method, with hypothesis testing, either prove or disprove your hypotheses with data) then you will gain a deep and abiding understanding of your system.

To achieve systems thinking, it is usually best to describe your system in graphic format. The key benefits of systems thinking include the ability to see interactions, to see the dynamics and ultimately to see the patterns that exist.

Chapter Summary ... We discussed the concepts of systems, system elements and focused significant effort to differentiate between classic and systems thinking. Systems thinking requires the use of not only reductionist-analytical thinking but also synthetic-analytical thinking focused on overall system goals and objectives. We explained how engagement is a system and requires systems thinking to properly analyze and improve. The one overriding concept of systems thinking is that we are striving to define and manage a system, and in so doing we wish to find the optimum of the system, not local optima. We introduced you to a simplified system diagram showing the two causal loop diagrams, the engagement loop and the disengagement loop (Figure 13.1).

What's next?? The concept of engagement as a system is pretty amazing. Now, in Chapter 14, we'll explore how all the system elements including stocks, interconnections, delays and the power of negativity all work together to create ... or destroy ... engagement.

Chapter 14

System Dynamics and Engagement

Aim of this Chapter … We will define the system of engagement with a system diagram and explain the two causal loop diagrams (CLD), the engagement loop and the disengagement loop. We will define the various system elements, the dynamics and interactions involved as well as the counterintuitive nature of system's behaviors. This counterintuitive nature frequently confuses managers and causes them to not act in their best interests, even if they are well-intended. As part of this, we will look at the specifics of the engagement and disengagement loops and their intricacies. We will examine the "positivity–negativity" dynamic. Finally, we will explain the complex role of communications and the power and the critical importance of the cultural network as a change mechanism. We will discuss the power of the cultural network and its important role in creating engagement.

Our system of engagement

Returning to our definition of a system

> System: A set of elements or parts that is coherently organized and interconnected in a pattern or structure that produces a characteristic set of behaviors, often classified as its "function" or "purpose".
>
> (Meadows, 2008)

The simplified view

I have repeated the simplified system diagram later as Figure 14.1 so you may refer to it as we discuss this system and its elements and interconnections as well as the system dynamic (see sidebar) concepts of stocks, flows, interconnections, delays and feedback.

Engagement system elements

Our system of engagement has six main physical elements. They are stocks, flows, actions, interconnections, delays and feedbacks.

SYSTEM DYNAMICS

The study of systems dynamics was started by Jay Forrester at the Massachusetts Institute of Technology. It uses the concepts of stocks, flows, relationships, delays and feedback loops to create mathematical models of complex systems, especially social systems. The models are often very complicated with even fifth order differentials required to explain the system's behavior. This also helps to explain why social systems are not well understood. System dynamics also showed that many social systems behave in a manner that is counterintuitive. His most read article is "Counterintuitive Behavior of Social Systems". It is a great read; I recommend it to everyone.

Stocks

Stocks are the elements of the system that you can count, or measure, at any given time. The general stock we will deal with in this book is people, and it is shown in a dark box. There will be three specific stocks: Loyalists; Lurkers; and Laggards.

Flows

Stocks change over time through the actions of a flow. Flows are represented by pipelines with an arrow showing the direction of flow. There is a valve on the end of the pipeline indicating the flow rate can be changed and at some level controlled. In our simplified system, we have two competing loops, each trying to enlarge itself. One loop will try to get Lurkers to flow and become Loyalists; the other one, a balancing loop, will try to get Lurkers to flow and become Laggards. We will try to increase the stock called Loyalists by converting two other stocks, Lurkers and Laggards, and getting them to "flow" and become Loyalists by properly managing the engagement and disengagement loops.

Actions

These are actions, activities and even interim results of people or things described by short phrases. They can be thought of as factors that influence other actions and are connected by arrows. For example, "do their work and do kaizens" is an action by people. Whereas, "workplace improves" is an interim result of a thing, and "positive word spreads" is an activity of your cultural network, a "thing" made up of "people".

These are all the parts of the system. They include not only the people but all they do. Kaizens are an element, as is the communications network that spreads the positive and negative word. The communications network has other elements such as notices, speeches and meetings. Also a part of the communications network is the informal communications network which includes such powerful elements as discussions around the coffee pot and the rumor mill.

Interconnections

Interconnections are often called causal connections, and they show the relationship of one action to another. The arrows leaving the causal connections can be unidirectional or bidirectional. The solid arrows represent a direct relationship, dashed arrows represent an inverse relationship and dark arrows represent a very strong relationship. The arrow can be read as "influences" such as "the negative word spreads and this positively influences the laggard creation rate". Or, referencing the engagement loop, starting at kaizens, you would read it as: "People do their work and also do kaizens, and after a delay, this will influence the workplace to improve, and after another delay, this will influence the business to improve, and these improvements will have an influence on spreading the positive word".

A simpler, but misleading, way to read system diagrams is by "if-then" statements. For example, "If the workers do their work and do kaizens, then, after some delay, their workplace will improve". While this is simpler, there is a problem in that it implies a direct and simple relationship while there may be many other factors at play. And business improvements, such as financial gains, while they may be influenced by workers doing kaizens, do not necessarily improve by this activity alone. "If-then" logic, can be interpreted to be a situation where the "if" is both necessary and sufficient; that is seldom the case and using the word "influences" is a better description of reality.

Delays

A delay represents a time gap that occurs between the interconnections. One problem with delays, they cause system oscillations. With no delay, the cause–effect relationship is much easier to both see and manage. Think of the delay in the temperature control of the water when you take a shower. If there is no delay as you adjust the flows, you can quickly make the sec-

> ### "SATISFICED"
>
> I like the word "satisficed" to describe many people's description of what constitutes "work satisfaction" to them. I suspect many people are never really "satisfied" at work, at least when work is compared to going fishing or lounging on the beach. Words seem to have different meanings when they describe work conditions versus conditions at other locations. Take "clean" as a concept. If you are a machinist, your workplace may be "clean as a whistle" ... but I doubt it would ever meet the standards for "clean" that a surgeon might use for her operating room. It may not satisfy a surgeon's standards of cleanliness for an operating room, but for your conditions at work, it will suffice. So **satisficed** is a cross between "satisfied and sufficient"; you might, like me, find this word useful.

ond adjustment and get the correct water temperature. On the other hand, if there is a delay, very often you will need to make several adjustments. This is why delays cause oscillations in systems and lots of false information to flow if decisions are made too quickly. Our system has two delays, both in the engagement loop.

Feedback

At the heart of system dynamics are feedback systems. These are mechanisms that either reinforce or counteract the previous actions in the system. Feedback systems will create an exaggerated response as compared to a simple linear response. Wherever there is feedback, you will find a loop. In systems dynamics, "feedback is the breakfast of champions". In fact, within the system of engagement, you will find that the interactions are often stronger than the main effects themselves. Interactions, dependencies and interdependencies are a reality of life and need to be understood, acted upon and properly managed.

A commonly understood feedback system is compound interest. As the interest grows, the principal grows, creating even more interest. For example, with 10% simple interest, if you reinvest the interest, the principal will double in 10 years. With annual compound interest, the principal will double in a little over 7 years. The general equation for simple interest at year N is Stock New = Stock Old + (Stock Old* i *N); where "i" is the interest rate and N is the number of years). For $1000, earning 10% simple interest will yield $2000 after 10 years. However, if the interest formula is based on compound interest, the equation is Stock New = Stock Old $(1+i)^n$, and after 10 years your investment will have grown to $2593. The same dynamic occurs when the system has feedback on itself. The formula is the same and "i" is the incremental improvement for each cycle and "n" is the number of cycles.

In our system above, the engagement loop is a reinforcing feedback loop. That is, as employees do kaizens, then the workplace and the business improves and the positive word flows then more Loyalists are created – who do even more kaizens with even better workplace and business performance – resulting in yet more positivity, creating even more Loyalists and the cycle goes on … that is the nature of a positive, reinforcing feedback loop. Likewise, the disengagement loops is a reinforcing feedback loop.

The dynamics of creating a fully engaged workforce – The players and the purpose

We have discussed the science of engagement, the motivation behind engagement and a practical model of engagement. That affects people at the individual level as well as the group level. Now we will explore the dynamics of that system. We will explore how "this system" works.

Who are the players?

In any culture-changing event, there are three groups. The first is a core of people I call Loyalists. Loyalists are those people who are highly engaged and "acting like they own the business". They would score very high on our engagement evaluations. They have bought into the management philosophy, see the benefits, are out on the floor productively performing; these are the movers and the shakers … and they are engaged. Next are the Lurkers;

they are not resistant, they are just observant. They are not engaged, they are waiting to see what will happen. They may be sleepwalking through the day, or even less, but generally they do enough to "get by". For the most part, they are doing a good job, get mid-range scores on execution and mostly are "doing as they are told". They do not exhibit high initiative when things are not as planned, but when things are normal, for the most part, they do a good job. These people are not engaged. While they are "doing as they are told", they are only really engaged physically. The intellectual and emotional commitment is just not there yet. Many are "on the verge of engagement", but for some reason are not yet willing to exhibit the initiative to "act like they own the business". The third group is the Laggards. They are not only not engaged, in Gallup terminology they are actively disengaged. They are negative and non-committal at the very least but can easily be irresponsible and disruptive at the worst. Without question, at the drop of a hat, they can point out every management mistake, near mistake and missed opportunity, over the last 10 years, at least. Some are just lollygagging around: trying to look busy; staying out of the way; hoping not to get noticed. They use this time to actively prepare the excuses for why they are not getting much done. There are always "others" to blame and they can find them in a heartbeat. Within this group are the ROAD Warriors (a military acronym for retired on active duty). But among the Laggards, there are some who are preaching about all the company ills, arguing about trivialities and generally being actively disruptive. They do just enough to not get fired. Excepting that, rather than "acting like they own the business", they are acting like they work for the competition as they confuse, create chaos and drive morale down.

The stocks

Stocks are the elements of the system that you can count, or measure, at any given time. The general stock we will deal with in this book is people, and they are depicted by a dark box. Remember that there are three specific stocks: Loyalists; Lurkers; and Laggards, as described above.

Who's engaged and by how much??

If we use the jargon of Gallup:

- the Loyalists are "engaged",
- the Lurkers are "not engaged" and
- the Laggards are "actively disengaged".

What's our purpose and how large is our challenge?

We want to reach world class levels of engagement; that means we want over 70% of the workforce to be engaged.

There are two processes at work, simultaneously and in opposition (see Figure 14.1). The engagement loop is working to create higher levels of engagement. In systems dialogue, it is trying to get the "stocks" known as Lurkers and Laggards to "flow" and become Loyalist, which is the "stock" that is engaged. The second process is largely influenced by the Laggards. They are working very hard to sustain the status quo, or worse; this is the disengagement loop. Their objective is to get the workforce actively disengaged. They are working in opposition to the Loyalists. And in the middle are the Lurkers, looking for the best place to land. Many Lurkers would like to join the Loyalists, as they seem to have the most fun, but there are issues, so they hesitate.

In terms of numbers, at the start of our effort towards achieving a fully engaged workforce, we will have about 25% Loyalists, 50% Lurkers and 25% Laggards. However, to get the benefits of a fully engaged workforce, we will need to exceed 70% Loyalists. 70% of the workforce engaged is normally enough to be highly productive, and Gallup refers to this as world class levels of engagement. If we look at the causal loop diagram, Figure 14.1, we see two competing processes, each trying to win the hearts and minds of the Lurkers.

Let's examine each of these loops in turn.

The disengagement loop

The disengagement loop is the simplest; let's look at it first. **It is the default position.** If management just manages following the status quo, disengagement will ensue. In a minute we

THE NORMAL STATE IS DISENGAGEMENT – REALLY??

By now you may be challenging the concept that "disengagement is the normal state". After all the discussions we have had about intrinsic motivation and its inherent power, that statement seems contradictory. Well, read the rest of the sentence ... "for any entity that must be managed and led". The truth is that **being engaged, by the worker at day one ... is the natural state of the worker.** In this concept lies both the answer to the problem of disengagement and the absolute hope that achieving a fully engaged workforce, while it may be effortful, is absolutely achievable and a direct function of improved management will discuss why **disengagement of the workforce, while not the natural position … is the <u>normal</u> position … for any entity that must be managed and led.** However, make no mistake about this, as normal as it may be, it is not healthy. Keep in mind that arsenic, although it is normal, is not healthy to ingest.

First, in any business, even the best managed and led businesses, you will find some disgruntled workers. In poorly managed businesses you find a lot more than just a few; they may be the majority. They are the Laggards, and they are not "satisficed" (see Figure 14.1). Generally, to these Laggards, things are OK, at least OK enough so they do not quit, but certainly not good – and Laggards by their nature are a hard lot to please. This causes

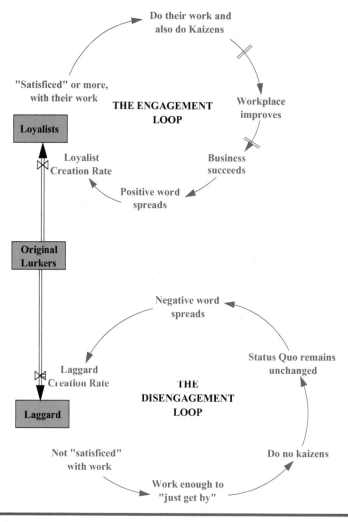

Figure 14.1   **The engagement system, in simplified format.**

them to do just enough to "get by" and hence they do no extra work and certainly no "kaizens" (aka, process improvements). In turn, this causes the status quo to remain unchanged, which reinforces that "nothing has changed, just the same damn old place". This then allows whatever level of negativity there was to at least persist. If shouted loud enough and long enough, this negativity will increase. When this negativity is transmitted by the cultural network, you will capture some of the Lurkers and they will "flow" and enlarge the ranks of the Laggards. Now there are more Laggards to spread the bad news and the cycle just repeats itself. This is the nature of a reinforcing feedback loop. This is a feedback loop based on "negativity", and if it is the dominant cycle, the net "flow" of Lurkers will enlarge the ranks of the Laggards. This we do not want.

The default nature of the disengagement loop

Although the disengagement loop, on the surface, appears rather straight-forward, there are three major issues which magnify its strength. All three issues are serious problems requiring management attention or very quickly the disengagement loop will completely overwhelm the engagement loop, and you will have lost the battle to achieve a fully engaged workforce. These three factors are: entropy; Hertzberg's hygiene factors; and the inherent power of negativity. We will discuss each.

The normal forces of entropy

All systems deteriorate, and the engagement system is no exception. As we discuss further, you will find that many sub-systems are required to create and sustain engagement. The four that I have found to be most impactful are:

- Worker training systems. And by this, I mean a training system that can deliver trained and validated workers to the workstation. To send new employees with a basic introduction to company policies to the line to be trained in a "buddy" system is woefully inadequate. The worker is not competent and he is not confident. This type of "training" is disrespectful to the individual, and not only is it a disservice to the worker but also his co-workers, the process, the value stream and the business suffers as well.
- Employee development systems, and by this I do not mean the appraisal system. The appraisal system should be discarded.
- Supervisory, including management, training and development systems.
- The promotional system.

Of the last 50 companies I have worked for, the majority do not even have one of these systems. This is an error of galactic proportions. Of the "Top Seven" referred to in Chapter 1, all seven had at least three of these systems, and three had all four.

The solution to the problem of entropy is to maintain these systems. That means they have a clear and measurable purpose and that metric is evaluated over time.

Hygiene factor effect

Herzberg taught us there were hygiene factors, which are those things that if supplied in sufficient quaintly are non-issues when it comes to motivation. However if not supplied in sufficient quantities they can become strong demotivators. His big four were:

- pay and benefits;
- company policies;
- working conditions; and
- supervision.

He also reminded us that, consistent with Maslow's principles, the quantity of these hygiene factors which would be sufficient to be non-factors would increase over time. Recall that Maslow said, "Man is a wanting animal", and his needs are never satisfied for very long. This means that if you wish to keep any level of motivation of the workforce, you need to improve worker's conditions over time. You must continually improve not only pay and benefits but company policies and working conditions as well as the level of supervision supplied. If these levels remain the same for any period of time, and do not improve, this will create more negativity and provide fuel to the Laggards driving employee engagement down. The power of negativity has such a large impact, we will discuss it in its own section.

The inherent power of negativity

The third and by far the largest factor that multiplies the words of the Laggards is the inherent power of negativity.

The dynamics and the power of negativity is something that affects each of us every day, not just at work but in everything we do. Yet somehow, when a manager's plan changes, they ignore this dynamic almost fully. There are at least three factors that, when taken together, can make negativity an overpowering force if not properly addressed. These factors are: the presence of negativity; the limits of negativity; and the imbalance of negativity.

The presence of negativity

Think about the news; just how much positive news do you read? The editor's mantra is "If it bleeds, it leads". In other words, blood and gore on the front page or the lead story on the TV news guarantees more followership. Well … blood and gore, to most of us, paint incredibly negative pictures. Another example, think of the power of gossip. Seldom is the

BETTER MANAGEMENT IS REQUIRED

"More simply, they will need to manage better … period" (Athos, 1981).

That is a tough concept for many in management to swallow.

And the bad news is that you have seen the numbers on engagement, nationwide and worldwide, and they are not good. Around 30% engagement with no appreciable improvement since they have started gathering data. This means we have not changed our management style by any appreciable amount. The message is clear: if you want to get higher levels of engagement, you will need better management … pure and simple.

topic positive. And the speed that it gets passed on is amazing. People will drop what they are doing to pass a "juicy bit about Evalyn and Harry having an affair" to anyone who will listen. Start some gossip and everyone's ears perk up. Negativity surrounds us, it piques our curiosity and always catches our attention. We seem to have a pathological need to hear some bad news.

We are preoccupied with negativity, not only individually with news and gossip but the academic and, in particular, the psychology community is likewise heavily imbalanced toward the negative. In our vocabulary, we have 3–4 times as many terms to define negative emotions and situations than we do for positive ones.

Although the study of psychology is around 140 years old, there was no positive psychology movement until:

CHURCHILL ON LIES

"A lie gets halfway around the world before the truth has a chance to puts his pants on".

(Winston Churchill)

"… in 1998, Seligman picked up the mantle of those who came before him, Maslow, Menninger, Drucker, and many others such as Marie Jahoda, Beatrice Wright, Albert Bandura, and Don Clifton, and paired scientific zeal with good timing to make positive psychology come alive and round out psychology".

(Snyder and Lopez, 2009)

"One reason that positive emotions may have garnered so little attention is that, relative to negative emotions, positive emotions are few in number ... we can identify only one positive emotion for each three or four negative emotions".

(Fredrickson, 1998)

What are the limits on negativity and positivity??

The "truth" ... powerful in the long term ... but limited nonetheless

There is also another dynamic that gives negativity even more power. If you are "spreading the positive word", you are almost assuredly going to deal with the truth only. First, if you are trying to get a fully engaged workforce, the truth is both powerful and your ally. However, most people are skeptical when change is the topic of discussion and often "want some proof". This takes time, but if you make and keep commitments, **in the long run**, the truth may ... and I mean may ... win out. Finally, we are in this for the long term, and eventually, lies and untruths will surface with their resultant negative impact. However, make no mistake about it, ... the truth has limits. It is the truth, nothing more.

Exaggerations, half-truths and lies – Powerful in the short term, yet with no limits

On the other hand, if you want to "tear down" an issue such as engagement, exaggerations, lies and falsehoods face no such limits. There can be partial truths; "sometimes" truths; exaggerations; information taken out of context; and even outright lies. But "the truth is the truth" and it has definite limits. For the people with their own agenda, whether it is: some type of revenge for a previous wrong; some type of power struggle; an issue not supported by the union; the fact that they just don't want to change; or even if they sincerely believe it is not the best thing for the plant ... for any and all of these reasons that they wish to take a negative stance, they have far more latitude to "sell" their position. So, when someone is trying to "tear down" the concept of engagement, he has far more latitude than the person who is trying to "build it up". The person supporting the creative position of reaching a fully engaged workforce needs to deal with reality; the person who is trying to destroy this with negativity is only limited by his imagination and his specific level of moral flexibility.

A "reality check" on exaggerations, half-truths and lies ...

To reality test the power of negativity, you need go no further that the world of politics. The unscrupulous politician can promise anything. He can exaggerate, lie and "spin it" (half-truths and lies), only limited by his imagination and moral flexibility. Even if he gets elected and then cannot deliver on what he promised, once again he can "spin it" (more lies) and very likely blame (lies) the people he ran against, who just might have been telling the truth. However, the honest politician is stuck with the truth, and quite frankly many people don't want to hear the truth; they want to hear something very positive ... even if it is impossible. The use of exaggerations, half-truths and lies can have a powerful magnifying effect on the use of negativity. This dynamic that you see in governmental politics is the same as you might see in any culture-changing process in your plant.

The "imbalance" that grossly favors the negative

Now, couple the latitude to embellish the negativity with our pathological interest in negativity and the impact is even stronger. You will note from the CLD in Figure 14.2 that there is a term, "Intensity of Positivity", which is a multiplier for the effect that is causing Lurkers to convert to Loyalist. Likewise, there is a term, "Intensity of Negativity", which is magnifying the effect, causing Lurkers to convert to Laggards. You will also note that the arrow going to the negative effect is bolder. This means it is much stronger. In this case, it may be as little as four times as powerful, but under other circumstances, it can be over 50 times as powerful. If the negativity is much stronger than the positivity, engagement is in serious danger of not improving.

The needed shift

The management team must learn to deal with the fact that negativity is a much more powerful concept than positivity with far-reaching consequences. In addition, the negativity can have multipliers that make it even worse than first envisioned. (These multipliers are so important we give

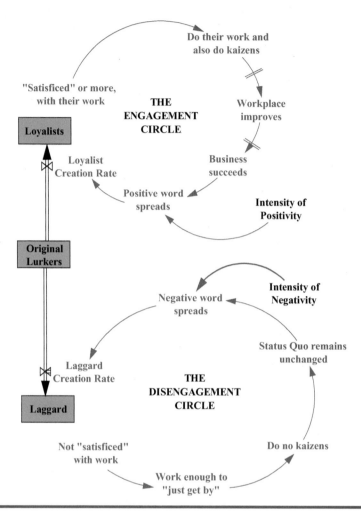

Figure 14.2 The engagement system, in simplified format, with a little more detail.

them a chapter of their own; they are called High Leverage Points, and we will discuss them in Chapter 17).

How to manage the negativity and the positivity

The linear approach

The all-too-typical approach to creating a better balance between the positivity and the negativity is to:

■ Send out more positive information in the form of memos, postings, meetings and "attaboys" to bolster the positivity

■ And to counter the negativity, maybe we'll "talk to" some of those "not on board", or worse yet, threaten them in the hope of squelching the negativity.

This appears to be a very logical and straightforward approach to improve the positive to negative balance. Unfortunately, as logical as that sounds, it is not only a bad idea it is a somewhere between a horrible idea and a galactically horrific idea. The bad news is that: this will not work, and the even worse news is that this approach will be counter-productive, making the situation worse.

PARADIGM SHIFT NO. 8

Both "negativity" and "positivity" are powerful change forces. However, neither can be created directly; both will "ensue". Almost exclusively they will ensue from the actions of management. So, do not try to create positivity directly or try to counter-act negativity directly; you will be thwarted even with the best of efforts. Rather, manage the system properly and you will indirectly "inflate the balloon of positivity" and "deflate from the balloon of negativity".

Problems with the linear approach

The first problem with the linear approach is that you are dealing with a circular-interactive system yet using linear thinking. Second, the real causes of the negativity are seldom known. Quite frankly, even if you knew, you likely could not fix them. Some of the Laggards who are so ardently pushing the negativity have been harmed in the past, some are looking for power and even some might be well-intended. In addition to this lack of cause–effect relations, there are three "systems reasons" this linear thinking approach is not going to work, as described below.

Systems thinking and counterintuitive behavior of systems and people

The father of "systems dynamics" is Jay Forrester of MIT (Forrester, 1991). He developed the science of system dynamics starting in the '50s, studied it and wrote about it extensively. One of his most influential articles is entitled, "Counterintuitive Behavior of Social Systems". The title alone highlights the root of the three system reasons that linear thinking is not effective when applied to complex systems, especially complex social systems, of which engagement is one.

First, most systems respond counterintuitively

For example, Forrester writes:

> "Our first insights into complex social systems came from corporate work. Time after time we went into corporations that were having severe and well-known difficulties. The difficulties would be obvious, such as falling market share, low profitability, or instability of employment. Such difficulties were known throughout the company and were discussed in the business press. One can enter a troubled company and discuss what people see as the causes and solutions to their problems. One finds that people perceive reasonably correctly their immediate environments. They know what they are trying to accomplish. They know the crises which will force certain actions. They are sensitive to the power structure of the organization, to traditions, and to their own personal goals and welfare. When interviewing circumstances are conducive to frank disclosure, people state what they are doing and can give rational reasons for their actions. In a troubled company, **people are usually trying in good conscience and to the best of their abilities to help solve the major difficulties.** Policies are being followed that they believe will alleviate the difficulties. One can combine the stated policies into a computer model to show the consequences of how the policies interact with one another. In many instances, it emerges that the **known policies describe a system which actually causes the observed troubles**. In other words, the known and intended practices of the organization are sufficient to create the difficulties being experienced. Usually, problems are blamed on outside forces, but a dynamic analysis often shows how internal policies are causing the troubles. **In fact, a downward spiral can develop in which the presumed solutions make the difficulties worse and thereby cause greater incentives to redouble the very actions that are the causes of trouble**" (emphasis mine, in all cases).

(Forrester, 1975)

Second, since system response is often counterintuitive, more often than not, to improve the system, most managers work on the wrong parts of the system

In this case, seeing the power of the positive word, they go to great efforts to spread all the news about the successes in the system. They have bulletin board postings galore, every meeting is opened with an "engagement success story", they start an "engagement newsletter" and they create the "engagement idea of the month", and the winner gets a front row parking spot. They have a monthly meeting of teammates to discuss the "best engagement idea in each cell", giving out tickets to the local baseball team for the winners. And finally, on the corporate intranet, they create a webpage to "Share Engagement Ideas". They do all this, but somehow the battle to improve engagement levels is being lost. The semi-annual engagement survey, along with other indicators, shows no improvement. Engagement is the word of the day; everyone knows it, it is plastered on every bulletin board, it is discussed at every meeting – yet it is not getting any traction.

Then someone says, "Hey, in our teachings on systems dynamics, we were taught you often get more leverage if you work on the balancing loop", so someone says, "OK, let's focus on the balancing loop".

In the system to create engagement, the engagement circle is a "reinforcing loop" designed to "Spread the Positive Word" and create more Loyalists. These New Loyalists, added to the old Loyalists, then cause even more "positivity", which creates more Loyalists, and the system spirals up. That is the nature of a "positive reinforcing loop" and, in this case, this is what we want. And to drive the desired improvement, the management effort was focused on the engagement circle, especially getting the positive word out. However, working in opposition is the disengagement circle, driven by negativity, and it is called a "balancing loop". And it just so happens that, very often, the best strategy to get maximum system growth is not to strengthen the reinforcing loop but to weaken the balancing loop.

Third, since system response is often counterintuitive, to improve the system, even after they have found the correct spot, more often than not, managers push in the wrong direction

Having decided we need to work on the "balancing loop", we address issues in the disengagement loop. Since negativity is a key point, we look to reduce that. So, we try to quell the negativity using the linear thinking outlined above; specifically, we'll "talk to" some of those "not on board". For example, one of the Laggards, Old Harry, a senior employee with credibility amongst the rank and file, is spreading the negativity. He is a charter member of the cultural network, and, although he has no official position power, he is extremely influential; Old Harry is relevant. To "on board" him and get him to support the engagement effort, he is approached by his supervisor, politely and professionally. A discussion ensues attempting to get Old Harry to embrace the changes needed to achieve a fully engaged workforce. Following the discussion, the supervisor thinks he has made some inroads when old Harry says, "he'd think about it". But in reality, he is unable to change Old Harry's mind. Meanwhile, two Lurkers overhear this discussion. Soon enough on the rumor mill is the discussion that Old Harry had a discussion with his boss about the engagement effort and Old Harry "really took it to him". This rumor goes on that, "Old Harry must have 'nailed it' if the boss decides it is important enough for him to pull him off the job for a discussion 'on this engagement thing'". And the word spreads and the Laggards are emboldened, and the net effect is that some Lurkers are now leaning toward becoming Laggards.

When Old Harry's supervisor reports back, the production manager says, "Nice effort. But you know Old Harry, he's pretty hardcore. Let me give it a shot. I'll talk to him and maybe I can sway him". The next day, the production manager pulls Old Harry off the line and talks to him once again. They have a polite, professional discussion, but Old Harry is not to be swayed. Now, the rumor mill, tuned into the fact that Old Harry "has some juice", is watching intently when the production manager shows up. And the message in the cultural network is, "Now they are sending out the big guns, geez, Old Harry really has it right and we need to get behind him and fight this engagement thing". The Laggards are getting pretty cocky, some Lurkers join their ranks; and the level of engagement drops a little.

Well, nonplussed by the fact that the production manager made no real headway, and feeling Old Harry is worth saving, the plant manager decides to talk to him. As he pulls him off the line, the word literally flies around the plant at light speed, "Old Harry is right, the management team is scared of him and we need to join him and fight this engagement thing".

By their actions, the management team is sending the message that they are afraid of what Old Harry might say. "That they must get him under control" is the message sent … unwittingly, but that is the "true message" on the floor. The second problem is that management has forgotten that the rumor mill is several times more powerful than any oral or written message management can send. Yet since managers believe in the power of their own communications (naively so), when it did not work at first, they decided they needed to do it "more and better". In effect, they were pushing in the wrong direction, and since they were blind to this reality, they decided to "push more", and in so doing, the harder they worked, the further they got from their goal. By paying undue attention to him, they strengthened rather than weakened his negative position, and by using more and more influential people, they exacerbate that negative response and cause the entire engagement effort to spiral down. So by doing exactly what they want to do, they are creating exactly what they DON'T want to create – negativity. They are pushing in the wrong direction

The proper way to deal with this issue of negativity

Recognize that the negativity and the impact of the negativity is part of a system. In this case, the proper management response to the negativity should be "Note it, understand its magnitude and do nothing more directly about negativity". The more attention given to it in terms of interacting with these Laggards (the naysayers), the more it validates their positions, right or wrong. Certainly, it is prudent to discuss the issue of engagement with everyone and get their input. The problem with the naysayers is that, very often, they are looking for a platform from which to air their complaints, both present and past. I consider it prudent management to listen to everyone and understand their points, then absorb what they have to say and integrate it into the solutions you need. The management team should spend their time judiciously working on problems. Furthermore, to maximize the engagement, they should work on the problems with the greatest impact, first.

> ### CONCEPTUAL HIGH LEVERAGE POINTS
>
> The most impactful High Leverage Points (HLP) are the conceptual HLP of paradigms and goals. And you will also note that throughout we have listed a number of paradigms that will need to change to reach your goal. Also, we have been very clear about our goal: to improve engagement until we have "a fully engaged workforce", which on a standardized study would be >70% engaged.

Positivity and Negativity are not directly created; rather, they "ensue" from other actions. Yet these two factors can control the power of the loops and either create or destroy engagement.

And what are those actions??

The bottom-line issue on how to strengthen the intensity of the positivity and weaken the intensity of the negativity is surprisingly simple. Management simply must do the jobs of managing and leading and do it well. Recall the earlier quote from Athos:

> "Japan is doing more than a little right. And our hypothesis is that a big part of that "something" has only a little to do with such techniques as its quality loops and lifetime employment. In this book, we will argue that *a major reason for the superiority of the Japanese is their managerial skill*".
>
> (emphasis mine, Athos, 1981)

And just how does management do their job well? Chapters 6–10 went a long way to describe good management and good leadership. Now, as we discuss the engagement loop and later discuss the High Leverage Points, we will answer that question with more specificity

The engagement loop

Now let's take a look at the engagement loop. It is manned by the Loyalists, and at the end of the day, they are satisfied and generally in a good mood (see Figure 14.2). They do their work, plus they also do "kaizens", process improvements, on a routine basis. Not only does this improve their morale, but the workplace improves because of their efforts, and later they can see the business improve as well. This is a feedback loop based on "positivity". All of this system creates positive news and the word spreads; and if shouted long enough and loud enough you just might get a few Lurkers to take a leap of faith and become Loyalists. This enlarges the group of Loyalists, so this too is a reinforcing feedback loop.

In the engagement loop, there are six elements. First, is the Basics and Beyond. Second, is the work with the need to do kaizens, process improvements which are done at the worker level. Third, is the Intrinsic Motivational

Loop (IML) (Figure 14.3). Fourth, are one internal and two external feedback loops which both have some feedback delay. Fifth is the inherent power of positivity in the workplace, and sixth, is the ability to spread the word

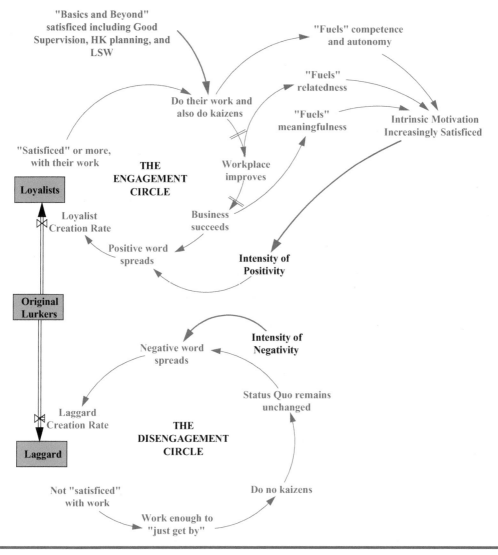

Figure 14.3　**The engagement system with the IML included.**

The elements to the engagement loop

The first four elements: the Basics and Beyond, the work with kaizens and the IML are so important they have a chapter of their own; Chapter 15 is "Activating the Engagement System", where we discuss these three elements. Likewise, element four on feedback systems is so important it also has its own chapter: "Completing the Engagement System", Chapter 16. The power of positivity, the fifth element, was discussed with the power of negativity in the previous section. Now we will focus on the critical nature of how the positivity (and negativity) is transmitted throughout the organization to activate the engagement loops, it is the sixth element, the cultural network.

Closing the loop ... The cultural network

Surprisingly enough, the sixth element, the factor that closes the engagement loop is the cultural network. This informal and seemingly innocuous network, is what controls the effect of both loops. Word of mouth is what affects the Loyalist creation rate and the Laggard creation rate!!

Never underestimate the power of peer information, peer pressure and peer acceptance. At the end of the day, if people become Loyalists, it is almost always after they have heard a few positive things and seen several positive things, but they will not change until they have discussed it with their peers. Almost never will they convert without this discussion in some form. The same dynamic applies to Laggards and Lurkers; they too are driven by the cultural network, the peer discussion. However, due to the nature of the dynamics of negativity, there is a large difference in the amount of information it takes to convert. To make a change to a Loyalist, most people need overwhelming positive evidence; yet to stay as a Lurker or to become a Laggard, a little negative evidence goes a long way. Yet another manifestation of the impact of negativity.

The communications issue ... Pay very close attention!!

In all businesses and all plants, there are two communications channels: the formal communications network and the informal network, the cultural network

The formal communications network

In the formal communications network, you find the company bulletin boards,

> **PARADIGM SHIFT NO. 9**
>
> The cultural network is a more powerful change mechanism than all the meetings you can hold, all the memos you can write and all the webexes you can produce ... combined. Hence, to "arm" the cultural network, don't send memos and hold meetings – create transparency, share information and discourage secrecy. Furthermore, only the cultural network is effective enough to create cultural change.

memos from the boss, management reports and even formal letters sent to each employee. The formal channel also includes meetings, with its use of slide presentations, flip charts, statistical analyses, decision matrices and risk analyses. And then there are the meeting notes, project report-outs and follow-ups. Also, as part of the formal communications network, there exists a structure, normally a very formal structure, that is used to transmit the information. In most cases, information travels down the structure, making sure no levels are passed. The VP discusses it with his division managers, who in turn discuss it with their plant managers, and so on down the power structure. Sometimes this is automated with technological tools that aid in the efficiency of the communication. While these technological tools may improve the **efficiency** of communication, almost always they detract from the **effectiveness** of the communications as it all tends to be one way with no real opportunity for dialogue. The formal channel is large and very structured indeed.

The cultural network

On the other hand, there is the informal communications network, the cultural network. This is where the "real" communications occur. Unlike the formal network, the cultural network includes everyone, ties together all parts of the company, is highly efficient and carries the "true" as well as the stated meaning of the communication. For example, a recent announcement says that Bob, a senior plant manager, is taking over the Biloxi plant. The real message on the cultural network is that Bob hasn't done a lick of work for the last 2 years and the Biloxi plant has a government contract and will make 12% with or without Bob. Furthermore, the cultural network learned from its union contacts that the Biloxi plant will likely be shut down in 2 years. The real message is that Bob is being transferred so he can be put out to pasture and will retire in 2 years; and an embarrassing firing will be avoided. The interesting part is that this information was available, circulating and widely understood long before the formal announcement; all due to the power of the cultural network.

Comparing and contrasting the two networks

The cultural network is much more effective and efficient. The information is focused, communicated face to face, done in real time with a realistic opportunity for dialogue.

Rather, the information in the formal communication network comes in long, windy documents that discuss multiple topics or in long drawn-out meetings with tons of unnecessary discussions and posturing. The formal network is just that, formal, and as such, it is not personal, it is not face-to-face and it is not directed to you. Most of it comes in written format, is written to everyone and requires that you spend a good deal of time sorting through the verbiage just to get to your item of interest. Seldom is there an opportunity for dialogue, but the memo usually ends with, "and if you have questions, direct them to your supervisor", who probably has fewer answers and more questions than you do. And finally, it is anything but fast.

However, nothing is faster than your teammate leaning over and saying, "did you hear about____?", and then giving you the real story, in real time. At that point, you are now "in the know".

When people are gossiping, most people understand it is information that is nearly always incomplete, frequently inaccurate and normally negative. They intuitively know it is almost never very accurate nor complete information, yet they are drawn to it like moths to the light. Even the most humble and honest people will take notice when they hear some juicy gossip. Because then you are "in the know", are "part of the scene" and have some information that maybe others do not have. With this gossip, you get "news", "inclusiveness" and "the power of information" all in one short discussion. Gossip is a powerful concept and is a key part of the cultural network.

The reality management must accept

Finally, the cultural communications network is not only more powerful, **but if you want to make a cultural change, managers need to recognize that the formal communications network, while necessary to carry certain messages, cannot make the culture change occur.** Only the informal, the cultural, network is powerful enough. For example:

> "We think that 90% of what goes on in an organization has nothing to do with formal events. The real business goes on in the cultural network"
>
> (Deal and Kennedy, 1982)

And as a result, you will see that the final step in the engagement loop, just prior to increasing the "Loyalist Creation Rate" is the "Positive word spreads". Likewise, the final step in the disengagement loop, just prior to increasing the "Laggard creation rate" is the "Negative word spreads". It is this communication that makes the cultural change possible.

A huge communications paradigm shift is needed

To create engagement there must be a huge paradigm shift in management so they will understand the type of communications that is needed to achieve a fully engaged workforce. Management must learn three things. (See paradigm shift no. 9, earlier in this chapter)

■ First, the cultural network is immensely more powerful as a communication tool than the typical formal communication network

■ Second, to create a cultural change, the necessary communication will be done through the cultural network. As discussed earlier, the formal communications network is totally ineffective in this process.

■ Third, as the management tries to influence the workforce to create a fully engaged workforce, they must realize the ineffectiveness of their own communications and learn to arm the Loyalist, and the entire workforce, with the information necessary to activate the cultural network. Properly arming those in the cultural network with the information necessary to create a fully engaged workforce is a key change strategy.

Now we are on our way to a fully engaged workforce

It would now seem that we can fulfill the Basics and Beyond, do a little HK Planning, make sure we have strong supervisors using leader standard work, get the workers to implement kaizens and we're well on our way. **Whoa, dynamite!!** (my dad used to say) ... **Not so fast**. We have some more ground to cover, and Chapters 15 and 16 will give us the information we need to complete the engagement loop.

Chapter Summary ... We learned about system elements and discussed the six elements in our system that were designed to understand the dynamics of employee engagement. The purpose of our system is to increase employee engagement by transforming Lurkers and Laggards into becoming Loyalists. To do this, our engagement circle must be more powerful than our disengagement circle. Unfortunately, our disengagement circle has three very strong normal effects that all work toward disengagement. The strongest of these three is the inherent power of negativity. Nonetheless, we will use clear systems thinking to strengthen the engagement circle which will help us achieve our goal of a fully engaged workforce. (Forrester gave us wonderful insights on how to handle three counterintuitive management behaviors which we are so prone to follow.) Finally, we discussed the inherent power of the cultural network, the relative weaknesses of the formal communications network and our need to properly manage it so we may attain a fully engaged workforce.

What's next?? All this theory is cool indeed, but now we are going to get into action mode as we explore how to activate the engagement system by working with the engagement loop.

Chapter 15

Activating the Engagement System

Aim of this Chapter ... is to explain the process of getting your workers engaged. To that end, we will explain how to activate the engagement loop. First, we will discuss three needed cultural shifts and then the five Basic Elements of engagement. This list of five includes those elements supplied by the workers and those supplied by the management. Next, we will discuss yet another five elements we call, "Beyond the Basics". Following this we will then explore the strong impact all these elements have on the "engine" that drives the entire engagement loop, the Intrinsic Motivational Loop (IML). Fourth, we will discuss the criticality of the role of management, the need to change this role to one of lean leadership, the special role of the first line supervisor, and finally, the structure that is needed to not only perform well but to create a fully engaged workforce.

Getting full engagement – We will need three large cultural changes

To get a fully engaged workforce, so your employees "act like they own the business", there are three precursors that must be understood and addressed by management. We will discuss each in turn, and they are:

- Addressing the three operational modes and making "normal" normal. This is nothing more than operating your system to a set of standards – at all times. This sounds simple enough, yet it may be one of the hardest parts of operating a manufacturing system.

- Creating a "new normal", that is, creating a culture of continuous improvement so progress can be made beyond the standard situation.
- Creating a culture where all workers "know the context of the business".

Each item taken alone is a large cultural change for most companies, and each one must be addressed in an effort to change the culture to one of a fully engaged workforce.

Precursor no. 1 – Addressing three operational modes and making "normal" normal

Full engagement is not JUST getting all the people engaged to the work as designed. Although a significant accomplishment, there is yet another dimension to engagement. They need to be "situationally engaged". If we truly want engaged employees and if we want them "to act like they own the business", then we need to address a number of "circumstances" which they will need to respond to as they make the decisions they are charged with on a daily basis. This can be called the "predictability dimension", and it has three levels;

- normal mode
- normally not normal mode
- abnormal mode

Normal Mode

The first set of circumstances is the "normal mode". In this mode, the entire manufacturing system, including the work cell, is performing as designed. That is, all the materials are there, the tools are all in good working order, the people, including the management, are all properly trained and the support systems are all functioning as designed; everything is normal. At least, it is operating as we had hoped it would operate. The system is predictable. In addition, all employees, workers, supervisors and managers alike, are thinking about and making improvements. They are continually analyzing the process to see if there are ways to do the job better, faster and cheaper. This is the normal mode that is needed.

Under the "normal" circumstance, life is pretty simple. Engaged people are "nose to the grindstone" working to keep pace with takt or customer demand. They are attentive, doing their job, and the process is flowing smoothly.

Normally not normal mode ... (see sidebar)

Unfortunately, what we "hope for" and what we get are often very different. The second mode of operations occurs when things are "normally not normal" (NNN). For example, this would include all the things that happen way too often – but should not. Some "predictable unpredictability" has entered the picture. This could include people being late for work and not calling in; some materials coming to the cell that are substandard; and occasional machinery breakdowns. They are not "as designed" but happen often enough to be "NNN". In a nutshell, NNN is a mode you thought you had covered in the design but really did not. Usually, these conditions have lingered on without proper attention and sometimes people have figured a "workaround".

For example, let's say that at shift start Ralph is not there

NORMALLY "NOT NORMAL"

"Normally not normal" is a mode familiar to many good observers. And this is all too common in many factories I have visited. You can see it on the first visit as they give you your first tour. For example, you see a workstation waiting for materials and your guide says, "Well, that normally doesn't happen". Later in the walk around, you see the production-by-hour board at a cell showing it is well behind schedule ... with no corrective action taken. And your guide says, "That's not normal; the team leader is on vacation". You walk further and see an empty cell and the shadow board shows two missing tools. You inquire and your guide says, "That's odd, that seldom happens". Soon enough you learn that "not normal" is their "normal".

"Normally not normal" – for the aware and engaged worker – presents a "target-rich environment" for kaizen activity.

and that is not a terribly unusual circumstance. Your cell of six people now only has five. You can wait for Ralph, and if you do that and no one seems to worry that Ralph has held up work, for say 15 minutes, then waiting for Ralph is normal. Well, not really, but what do you do? After all, as a cell worker, it is not your job to take care of staffing. With impunity, you could wait for the boss to show up and inform him. Well, those people who are in "wait until told mode" are severely "initiative challenged", are not engaged and almost any employer has a right to expect more. At the very least, someone should seek out the boss and tell him "Ralph's not here and we've got a problem". On the other hand, someone can take some initiative and say, "let's change to a counter-clockwise rabbit chase until the boss shows up". That would show some initiative, and that is what a business owner would want. Specifically, if you were asked, "Would it be better to produce 83% of capacity or zero capacity?" , the disengaged person would say, "That doesn't sound like my problem". The engaged worker would not need to answer the question because they have taken the initiative to get the cell into production mode.

During the NNN circumstance, the engaged employee really has a solid opportunity to shine. Frequently, these problems occur because some aspect of "the standard" is not sufficient to cover frequently occurring circumstances which may not have been seen as "frequently occurring" to the engineer or supervisor who originally designed the system. However, in the fullness of time, problems such as yield and quality issues surface. Now, the worker who is right there can assess the situation and "improve the standard" by suggesting or implementing solutions. The cognitively and emotionally engaged worker welcomes this situation as it gives him an "opportunity to shine" and the opportunity to contribute gets his motivational juices flowing.

The basic cause of the NNN situation

Normally, the reason a system deteriorates to an NNN situation is due to a lack of management attention and a lack of management support. Looking the other way, problem avoidance and problem denial is a slippery slope, with no upside, yet many have fallen culprit to the trap of current convenience and/or procrastination. I would classify it – looking the other way – as an industrial epidemic.

Abnormal mode

Then there is the truly abnormal mode of operations, where something unexpected and unplanned happens. A customer, at the last minute, doubles his demands. The only steam boiler you have fails completely. The truck carrying the just-in-time (JIT) shipment of critical parts is stuck in a Midwestern snowstorm. These are abnormal, and they are unpredictable.

The abnormal circumstance is a lot different than the NNN mode. In the abnormal mode, there has been a major disruption of materials, machinery or work environment that was not considered in the design. By comparison, the NNN mode, the standard exists, someone just chooses to ignore it often enough that you create a new normal. However, under these "surprise circumstances" of the abnormal mode, to keep producing requires significant thinking and caring so you can act to minimize the impact of, if not solve, the problem.

The abnormal circumstances present a totally different opportunity for the engaged worker. The situation is abnormal because, even after serious process design and review, this circumstance was not expected; it was unpredictable. And as such, how can he handle this with only his basic training? By their very nature, these "abnormal" circumstances present a new challenge, something he has not been trained to handle. If the basic training in the first three elements is all he has … the answer is simple, he may not be able "to respond as if it were his business"; hence, he really cannot get engaged. Therefore, since management wants him to be fully engaged, management must give him some additional "training and tools" to arm him to handle these more difficult circumstances. We call these training and tools "Beyond the Basics"; there are five, and they are all management supplied and will be discussed later in this chapter.

Let's say you are the supervisor and your shipment of JIT parts did not arrive as planned, and you now have ten people with nothing to do. The disengaged supervisor will blame the outside circumstances and probably tell his people to hang around while he goes to yell at someone to expedite the parts. On the other hand, the engaged supervisor will ask himself, "If this were my business, what would I do?" Faced with no parts, he could do some much-needed cross-training; he could work on his 5S issues; he could maintain tools and workstations; or he could update standards. The engaged supervisor will always have a few of these projects in the back of his mind. Whether he is a supervisor or not, under these abnormal circumstances, there are two things the engaged worker **does not do:**

- he does not wait to be told and
- he does not blame others.

The countermeasures that create "normal mode"

Through the use of standard work, clear job descriptions and training, it should be made clear what is "normal". Then the management must both support and audit these three techniques to make sure they are properly prepared, properly delivered and properly maintained. Leader standard work, executed at all levels, will go a long way to accomplish this

However, until you get there, whether the situation is "normally not normal" or "abnormal", the expectation is for the engaged worker (meaning value-add worker, supervisor and senior manager as well) to address it actively and not remain in "wait until told mode". What he does – always – is show initiative and "act like he owns the business" and try to get the business back to "normal" mode.

Precursor no. 2 – Creating the "new normal", a culture of continuous improvement

In most businesses, what they consider "normal" is: to ship 100% good product; attain 100% full-load, non-expedited on time delivery; safely following established procedures; and in so doing, make a profit along the way. Today, that is a large stretch for most businesses; nonetheless, that is their objective.

To achieve a fully engaged workforce and to remain competitive in today's marketplace, that is no longer sufficient; we need the "new normal". In addition to supplying sufficient quantities of high-quality product, on time, safely; suppliers must work toward continuous improvements – and that means

> **PARADIGM SHIFT NO. 4**
>
> The "new normal" for EVERYONE in the business, worker and manager alike, is to: first, execute their job as designed; and, second, to work on kaizens for product, process and service improvements. Or in leanspeak, create a culture of continuous improvement

that improvements need to be a part of everyone's job. Yes, everyone – from the cell worker to the team leader, to the group leader, to the section head, to the manager, to the VP, to the CEO and to the board members as well. **EVERYONE must be working to improve the processes, products and services. Quite frankly, many American firms do not have a philosophy of continuous improvement of products, processes and services; consequently, many American firms are being replaced by those who do.**

There are two major reasons for this.

- ■ First, if you wish to survive, this is mandatory in any competitive situation.

■ Second, if that is not enough, **you will never get an engaged work-force without working on improvements**. A culture of continuous improvement makes the job more interesting, it makes the job more exciting, it gives the worker an opportunity to make improvements; to improve his work environment; to establish some control over the things that he must do; to be creative; to put his personal stamp on the process; and literally to own part of the process. It is an absolutely critical aspect of engagement. Making improvements is the one thing that is common to all jobs that can satisfy the intrinsic needs of competence and autonomy. It is the "trigger" that activates the Intrinsic Motivational Loop (IML). That loop starts with doing kaizens as a part of regular work. This activity, properly executed, satisfices the basic needs, which in turn further activates the intrinsic motivation to work, and then people are truly and deeply enjoying their work and it creates an excitement and enthusiasm that is contagious. This is one of the major factors which causes "The Positive Word To Spread". This will then cause Lurkers to join the Loyalists and the entire Engagement system will spiral upward with positive results for the customers, the processes, the products and the employees as well.

The countermeasure to making "normal" normal

The management countermeasure to the "new normal" is to create a culture of continuous improvement. It all starts with all employees doing kaizen, improvement ideas, but there is a great deal more. (For more information, creating a culture of continuous improvement is a process that is described in great detail in *How To Implement Lean Manufacturing*, 2nd Edition (Wilson, 2015)).

Some kaizens are more impactful than others

The three drivers   There are three different drivers for kaizen activity. First, the Hoshin Kanri (HK) planning process (discussed in just a minute) is putting pressure on the system to find improvements; these are management-initiated kaizens. Second, during the normal course of work, some process fails to perform as planned and the worker is asked to fix it. This is process-driven kaizen. Third, the worker sees an opportunity to improve upon a work or process standard and takes the initiative to make the improvements; he is engaging in worker-driven kaizen.

It seems strange, but when you evaluate the actions of the workers as they implement these kaizens, driven by different factors, the outward behavior of the workers is virtually identical. Whether the kaizen is initiated by part of the annual HK plan; or driven by a process failure; or driven by observations by a value-add worker … the actions of the value-add worker are the same:

■ they go through the Six Questions of Continuous Improvement
■ they satisfy whatever company requirements there might be to initiate kaizen activities
■ then they change the system

You cannot distinguish the way the kaizen was initiated by the subsequent behaviors.

The three different impacts on engagement   Although all kaizen activity has a positive impact on employee engagement, some kaizen activity is more impactful than others. The hierarchy is:

■ management-initiated kaizens, normally an outcome of the HK planning process, have the least impact on the Intrinsic Motivational Loop (IML).
■ process-created kaizens have more impact than management-initiated kaizens
■ the kaizens with the greatest impact on the intrinsic motivation, and hence the IML, are those kaizens initiated by the value-add worker

And there is a simple, yet not broadly understood, reason for this. As you may recall from Chapter 12, "Intrinsic Motivation", when the intrinsic need of "autonomy" is satisfied, this has the largest effect on motivation. You might say that satisfying the need for autonomy is the "gateway condition" to activate intrinsic motivation. Conversely, the opposite of autonomy is anything that falls on the scale that starts with being cajoled; through being enticed with "things"; to being instructed; to being ordered; up to being forced with fear of reprisal … to do something.

While the outward behavior of the value-add workers may appear the same, what is happening internally, and hence driving intrinsic motivation, is dramatically different. His thinking is something like this:

■ <u>For the management-driven kaizen</u> – the worker is thinking, "This is a pretty good idea, but we wanted to do this a long time ago; why was management so slow in doing this? Oh, well, we are at least getting it done; it will make things better, and, after all, we submitted this during the annual HK plan development. Just wish we could have done it sooner".

– The level of worker autonomy: both the timing of the work and the creativity to design the fix is imposed on the worker; he has little autonomy.

– Impact on the IML: the relative impact of this type of kaizen on the IML is 1.

■ For the process-driven kaizen – the worker is thinking, "Sure glad we caught that so we could improve things a bit. But I had planned to fix the rotorback and this interrupted my plan, and, by the way, we'll need to work a little overtime to make up for the time we lost. I am glad the problem found us, as we are the best ones to fix it, and all the team will benefit".

– The level of worker autonomy: the autonomy to fix the problem and implement the fix – the timing of the problem is imposed upon the worker

– Impact on IML: the relative impact of process-driven kaizens is approximately 2, a significant increase over management-driven kaizen.

■ For the value-add worker-driven kaizen – the workers is thinking, "This was an ultra-cool thing to find. We can now produce more, do so more safely and we have contributed to the bottom line. And we found it, we fixed it and it made life better for everyone".

– The level of worker autonomy: here the worker had far more control. He controls not only the fix but the implementation of the fix, as well as the overall timing of the work.

– Impact on IML: the relative impact of worker-driven kaizens is 10. These are the kaizens that provide nuclear fuel to the IML.

Precursor no. 3 – They need to know the context of the business

The natural precursor to "wanting" your employees to be engaged, that is, to "act like they own the business" is that you as the owner, or you as the manager, or you as the supervisor, must advise and train all your workers on precisely what the business needs and wants. This is absolutely necessary if you want them to situationally respond to the three aforementioned operational modes.

This is not commonly done, and the only people I have seen that does this well are those who employ HK planning. We will introduce you to HK planning later in this chapter.

And to the worker, that means he must be informed of what is needed at various "levels" of the business. These "levels" include:

- the workstation level;
- the cell level;
- the value stream level; and
- the facility level.

You can see that it is pure folly for the manager to expect his workers to "act like they own the business" unless they know what the cell is "supposed to do" and what the value stream is "supposed to do" and what the facility is "supposed to do". So, you can see that there is a large responsibility upon management to provide this training and information before they can expect to have a fully engaged workforce. Luckily, that entire topic is discussed later when we explain the five management-led efforts we call Beyond the Basics.

Now, with all three of those cultural precursors understood and addressed, we can turn to what more it takes to achieve a fully engaged workforce.

> **IF YOU WANT THEM TO "ACT LIKE THEY OWN THE BUSINESS"**
>
> Treat them that way. If you owned a company, you would know who works for you, what equipment you have, you would have metrics and KPIs to reflect your business and you would have the financial reports such as a P&L for your company. If you want employees to act like they own the business, lead and manage them like they do. Give them a P&L, let them create their metrics and KPIs, ensure they know exactly who works in their company and what equipment and footprint the company owns.

Activating the engagement loop

There are six behavioral elements to the engagement loop. The first element is a little complicated. It includes a group we call the Five Basics as well as a second group we call Beyond the Basics. The name of the first element is "The Basics and Beyond". The second element is simply "The work being performed, along with improvement activities, kaizen". When we accomplish these first two elements, they activate the third element, the "Intrinsic Motivational Loop" (IML),

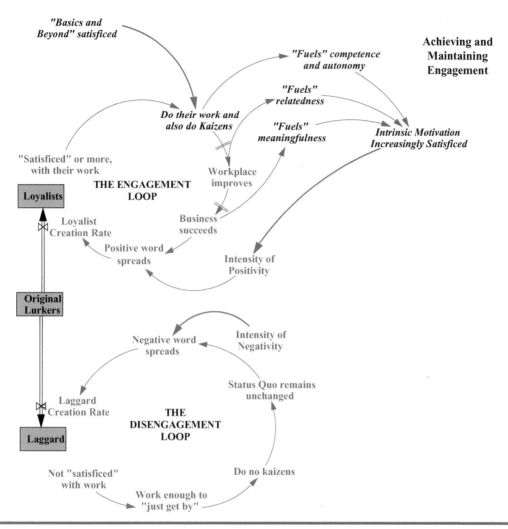

Figure 15.1 **The engagement system diagram, in simplified format, with even more detail.**

which is the engine that drives the entire system. The fourth element is the feedback loops that are both part of and augment the IML. The fifth element is "The Power of Positivity" and the sixth element is the "Ability to Spread the Word"; this is the cultural network, which we previously discussed in Chapter 14. We will now discuss each element in turn. You can see the engagement system diagram, with a little more detail, in Figure 15.1.

The Basics and Beyond

The Basics are a group of five elements that are often recognized as the five Basic Elements of engagement. Most businesses make some effort to address these, and almost all businesses feel they do a good job on the three they are responsible for … even though they often have a great deal of contradictory information.

A separate group of five, which we call Beyond the Basics, are a set of planning and communications tools. For many businesses, this list of five is often thought to be important to only the management ranks. However, if you want to have a fully engaged workforce, you must develop and teach these behaviors to everyone, not just the management team. Likewise, all employees must participate and be practiced in these five Beyond the Basics behaviors.

In our engagement system, all these tools have been subsumed under the name, the "Basics and Beyond", and they comprise the first element.

Activating the Five Basic Elements

To achieve initial engagement, there are some basic criteria which must be supplied. There are five; we call these "The Basic Elements". These are the minimum "opening conditions" which must be met to get your employees engaged; and I make no distinction between hourly workers and salaried personnel. Nor do I make a distinction between line

> **PARADIGM SHIFT NO. 3**
>
> Creating engagement is not a **new thing**. Although there are some new techniques and skills, a full 95% of the work is just doing what you do now do, **but doing it better.** Your existing management system will need to change.

and staff workers. From the cell worker to the first line supervisors, through middle management, to the C-suite and even in the boardroom I make no distinctions regarding these five Basic Elements of engagement – they apply to all jobs.

Two of the elements are supplied by the workers, three are supplied by management. We will discuss each in detail as we go forward. The Five Basics are:

1. Knows what to do to accomplish the task at hand.
2. Knows how to do the job.
3. Has the resources to do the job.
4. Wants to do the job.
5. Wants to do the job better.

Worker-supplied elements

Element 4, "Wants to do the job", and Element 5, "Wants to do the job better", are supplied by the workers themselves. These are the elements that most managers think are missing from their engagement programs.

They could not be more wrong!! **Workers come motivated ... at day one.**

Rather, the vast majority of workers who enter your facility have tons of "want to", at day one – maybe not so much later, but at day one they are stoked. Be they factory-floor workers, engineers hired right out of college, line supervisors hired from the outside or recently appointed or promoted managers – they all act the same. They want to do a good job, and, furthermore, they instantly have ideas about how to improve their new work; hence, they want to do it better. That is not the problem with engagement. I state it axiomatically, *your workers come to work both wanting to do a good job and wanting to do it better.*

The "want to" very often subsides   Yet I will fully agree with you that later in their working lives they do not have the same "wanting" as they did early on. The reasons for this deterioration of "wanting" are very simple to understand, but a bit more complicated to correct. The common thread is a lack of management understanding of worker motivation.

In simple terms, these workers who are motivated at day one, do not get the initial support they need to "get going" and, almost immediately, their "want to" begins to subside. The first three of the five "Basic Elements" are the management-supplied support that is required to "get going". When this support is not supplied properly, they suffer from a lack of understanding and are uncertain as to what is the best thing to do. They try to make some changes, often get in trouble for this, and then they withdraw and "just do as they are told". They see other possible improvements, but "once burned, twice cautious" and just keep quiet. Soon enough, any initiative they once had is completely subdued, and with it, their intrinsic motivation is fully stifled. They are now "working for the man" and have a clear and simple transactional understanding. That is, "I'll come to work and follow your rules, and I expect you to pay me"; certainly nothing more, often something less.

Maybe the "want to" lasts a while and they get frisky and make suggestions   On the other hand, maybe the information they received early in their training set them up well to perform and they were very satisfied and even thinking of new ideas. Then they submitted a process improvement idea to their supervisor and he said, "Great idea, Joe; I'll talk to the boss and get back to you". And after 2 weeks, he still hasn't responded. So, one day when the boss comes by, they ask him, "Hey Jorge, what happened to my idea to redesign the workbenches?". And he replies, "Oh yeah, I'll have to get back to you". Two weeks pass and they again ask their supervisor, who is piqued because the cell is having material delivery problems and responds rather abruptly, "Joe, why don't you get this cell working well, rather than wasting your time trying to improve a place that is not even doing well as it is?". At which time they now learn that their job is to "keep your nose to the grindstone and quit bugging your bosses". So even though they received good support and training at day one and remained engaged for some time, there is no real management support to sustain their engagement. As they try to stay intellectually engaged by making improvement suggestions, their ideas are ignored. They are now "stuck". Their motivation naturally become more superficial, and as the fuel to the intrinsic motivators diminishes, so does their enthusiasm and their engagement. Once again, they go into "wait until told mode". It does not mean they do not try to do a good job. But, once again, the motivation is to "get by", and nothing more. They have been mistreated and are confused. They are not sure what is the best thing to do, so they withdraw and their motivation is characterized as "pain avoidance". Once again they get to the transactional situation; "I will do this for you and you will pay me for that".

This takes us to the management-supplied elements.

Management-supplied elements

There are three basic management supplied elements. They are:

1. knows what to do;
2. knows how to do it and
3. has the resources to do it.

Most management teams think they supply these three well … seldom is this the case   Although these sound like simple things that are routinely supplied, I can tell you with certainty that is not the case. Rather, what I find is that these three elements are supplied by management, in some degree, but it is normally not adequate to get a fully engaged workforce. If the way management had supplied it perfectly, you should be able to get 100% yield and 100% on time delivery. That is simply not the case with most firms. My experience is that while a great deal of effort is expended so the worker knows what to do, how to do it and has the resources to do it, this three-fold task is only about 70% complete in most firms. Hence, work remains to be done in these areas to achieve a fully engaged workforce.

When a serious "causal study" is done on the reasons for these quality and delivery problems, most of the "root causes" of the problems are NOT found to be due to deficiencies in the workers. Well over 90% of the deficiencies, are found in the "manufacturing system", which is the system that is created, managed and owned by management. For example, there is the famous quote of Dr. Deming when he says:

> "I should estimate that in my experience most troubles and most possibilities for improvement add up to the proportions something like this: 94% belongs to the system (responsibility of management), 6% special".
>
> W. Edwards Deming

I have done several causal studies myself and all have shown that over 95% of the root causes are created by the system which management created and owns. Unfortunately, when businesses have problems with quality and delivery, for example, they almost reflexively ask "Who is to blame?" and focus on the worker. Well, Dr. Deming is correct. Ninety-four percent of the time, the worker needs no correction; rather, the management system supplied to the worker is the source of the deficiency and needs to be improved. A full 94% of the problem is management controlled and can only be corrected by management. There are large weaknesses in the system supplied by management, and, hence, the worker, through no fault of his own, frequently:

■ Does not know what to do and/or
■ Does not know how to do it and/or
■ Does not have the needed resources

We will discuss each of these three elements in turn.

Knows what to do   That is, they understand and can execute the major steps to their job.

If you use Training Within Industry (TWI)-type training, these are the major steps on the Job Breakdown Sheet or the major steps on the Standard Combination Work Sheet. For him to know what to do, he must have received training. By training, I do not mean some type of "buddy" system or, worse yet, where he is "thrown into the fire" and expected to learn as he goes. Training means structured training done by an expert in the task, using documented procedures which we call "standards". Performance to these standards can be objectively evaluated to assure training is successful. This can include work on simulators, but it must also be hands-on training. The training should be "stepwise" with each step evaluated for success. Only after successfully completing step one can the person be expected to learn step two. The purpose of the training is to "**simultaneously create competence with confidence**". Only when we have assurance he can be successful, will we schedule him to work on the line. Furthermore, when "placed on the line", someone is watching, supporting and providing guidance in case the training was deficient in some respect.

Also, they have a defined method for process improvements (kaizens), and all employees are trained in this methodology. In addition, they are encouraged, but not forced, to engage in process improvements. After all, they are the experts in their area of work.

Knows how to do the job   That is, they have the skills, techniques and talent to produce a quality product safely and efficiently. If you use TWI-type training, there are three circumstances which need to be trained for each major step. First, how do we do this step

> **PARADIGM SHIFT NO. 1B**
>
> Management must rid themselves of the mental model that engagement is "worker thing" only. The workers will only become engaged – after the management team is engaged.

safely? Second, is there a "make or break issue" in this step? Third, are there efficiency techniques? These are then taught to the worker. When the worker can perform these skills and techniques, he can work on the line.

Has the resources to do the job   They have not just the physical tools but the training, time, work direction, support and leadership as well. The resources also include such items as a plantwide support system of just-in-time problem solving, JIT management support and JIT maintenance, to name a few.

Going Beyond the Basics – Five other elements

The purpose of the five elements in Beyond the Basics is to share the needs and the status of the business so they may respond to the unusual circumstance and so they can respond "like they own the business". It is a combination of five planning and communications techniques to share the context of what the business is trying to accomplish in the larger sense than just the daily production and quality numbers. In addition to discussing workstation, cell, value stream and plant performance, future goals and business directions are also undertaken. The whole point is to prepare the workforce so they understand the business better and hence are far more likely to become and stay engaged. The fifth of the Beyond the Basics is the concept of system transparency. It is hard to understate the importance of this communications technique, and you will find it is instrumental in making the intrinsic motivational work. The IML is the driver that makes the entire engagement loop work and is discussed in detail later in this chapter.

Hoshin Kanri (HK) planning

It is difficult for someone to "act like they own the business" if they are unaware of the business plans. HK planning uses the concept of "catchball", which gets all levels of the organization involved in plans, including the comprehensive 5-Year and 1-Year plans. Catchball looks a lot like a negotiation – it is not. Rather, catchball provides a mechanism to align the goals with the means so goal achievement is a practical reality. Once the HK plan is created and posted, each member of the business has the opportunity and needs to understand the important metrics and, specifically, why they are important. It is extremely important to discuss the HK annual plan via catchball, down to the last person, going through the structure from top to bottom. This will apprise everyone of not only the goals but the means to those goals and how they interact with daily activities. A simplified version of HK planning is attached as Appendix F.

Don't miss both the emotional and intellectual impact on engagement when everyone plans

For those who **do not** use HK planning or a similar process that engages the workforce using the process of catchball, they miss what Russell Ackoff calls "effective planning". He says,

> "Effective planning cannot be done to or for an organization; it must be done by it. Therefore, the proper role of the professional planner, whether inside or outside an organization, is not to plan

for others, but to encourage and facilitate their planning for themselves. All those who are part of an organization and all those external to it who are affected by it (except competitors) should be given an opportunity to participate in its planning. The professional planner should provide all these stakeholders with the information, knowledge, understanding, and motivation that can enable them to plan more effectively than they would otherwise".

(Ackoff, 1999)

And then when leader standard work (described in just a minute) is applied to the HK process, you get what I call "policy deployment on steroids" and you are well on your way to facility-wide focus, alignment and execution with absolutely large and wonderful results.

Information sharing on a continuing basis

Standup, tiered, start-of-shift meetings

CATCHBALL

Most planning models are very weak on deployment. This leads to poor alignment, poor focus and weak "buy in" – except for the top few. A countermeasure to these problems is HK planning using the process of "catchball". In catchball, a goal is established by the folks at one level, answering the question "WHAT is to be done?" Then those at the next level down are asked, "HOW can we accomplish this?" A dialogue ensues around these two questions and continues until the results, "the WHATs", are compatible with the means, "the HOWs". This is done from the top to the bottom and entirely across the organizational structure; everyone is involved. This sounds like a negotiation; it is anything but. Rather, it is a method to align the goals with the means and use the knowledge experts at each level to participate. For more information on HK planning and catchball, refer to *Lean Refining*, (Wilson, 2017)

To stay apprised of what is happening on each shift, and as part of the HK planning review process, a critical element is "daily review of plan". In addition, the business who wishes to keep its people engaged works hard to keep them "in the know". Part of this is to have a standup meeting each shift start. It is normally 2–5 minutes covering any last-minute changes to the plan or business situation. This should be coupled with "tiered meetings". In a "tiered" meeting, key process indicators (KPI) are discussed. Key production, quality, delivery personnel issues are first discussed at the cell level with the team leader and the supervisor. Immediately following this, the supervisors get together and discuss the key issues at the next tier, the value stream level. Later, the value stream managers meet and discuss these same topics at the plant level. Tiered meetings:

■ Are done standing up
■ Use a posted agenda
■ Take less than 10 minutes
■ Are designed to highlight problems, not solve them; rather, who is to resolve it and by when
■ Occur at the job site
■ Use the visual display board with space for actions and due dates documented.

The bottom line: the business who wishes to keep its people engaged works hard to keep them "in the know".

Business metric reviews

Once the people are apprised of the HK plan, they will see it in action, due to the system of "transparency" in the plant. This will include that the business metrics and status of the HK plan are kept updated monthly and available for everyone to view. This keeps all teammates updated on the progress at the plant.

The monthly business review is a meeting normally held, at the value stream level, so the management can apprise the crew of "how we are doing compared to plan". It is normally held after shift, once a quarter, taking 20 minutes plus 10 minutes for Q&A. Everyone is invited.

Not only that, a key element of HK planning is daily and even hourly monitoring of key targets and means. These are posted at each cell so that all workers are apprised of how their work is affecting the entire HK planning and execution process.

Leader standard work (LSW)

Leader standard work is the parallel to standard work used at the workstation but focuses on leadership activities. The purpose of LSW is twofold:

1. Policy deployment. That is, are we working on and accomplishing the HK plan? And

2. Personnel development. The leader reviews how each of his people are doing. Checks on successful completion of activities, completion and success of training and routinely discusses job performance and all of its outcomes. Team leader's LSW would involve hourly interaction with all workers. Supervisor's LSW would include at least daily interaction with workers, while plant manager's LSW would more likely involve a minimum of weekly personnel development review with his subordinates.

   Done properly, LSW effectively assures constant alignment and focuses on workstation, cell, value stream as well as plant goals and objectives. LSW simultaneously formally addresses personnel development and, as such, eliminates the need for the annual performance appraisal. It applies to all people in leadership positions, starting with team leaders and does not end until the CEO is also using LSW. It is a technique of documenting routine and even non-routine activities of leaders. It provides a reminder and documents completion using a checklist format that normally covers a weekly cycle. For more information and background on LSW, I refer you to *How To Implement Lean Manufacturing*, 2nd Edition, (Wilson, 2015). You can also find examples on our website at www.qc-ep.com. (You will find it on the Lean Manufacturing pull-down menu.)

> **VISUAL MANAGEMENT**
>
> I prefer the term transparency. Many people use the term visual management, and more often than not I find they are very long on the visual and very short on the management. Their systems are replete with all kinds of charts, tables and graphs on the cell walls and at the information center. This "technical wallpaper", while it is impressive to the uninformed, has no informative power to the line worker.

LSW done poorly

At the heart of LSW is a unique checklist of activities to be accomplished. It needs to be dynamic, so what is checked upon by the leader will change from time to time depending on the needs of the business and the needs of the people. On the other hand, if LSW is simply a non-changing, check-the-box checklist, it will not be helpful. When it is done poorly, LSW is simply micromanagement at its worst, which is entirely counterproductive and worse than doing nothing.

High-quality supervision

At the heart of all of this communication is a strong relationship with the supervisor. We have previously discussed the needs and the qualities supplied by the supervisor periodically throughout Chapters 6, 7, 8, 9 and 10. In that regard, this discussion seems superfluous. However, it is impossible to understate that the supervisor needs a strong complement of relationship skills and talents to properly handle the employee interactions, including the HK planning and other communications. The supervisor needs to be skilled in employee assessment and especially observant in the ability to see if training is needed. Furthermore, the supervisors need to be accomplished in the five supervisory skills noted in Chapter 10. The supervisor is the person who either supplies or makes sure all the "Basics and Beyond" are supplied to the worker. Their contribution cannot be understated.

Simply put, you do not get engagement until you have good supervision.

Visual feedback systems – Transparency

By far, the most effective feedback tool is system transparency. Done right, it is both informative and empowering. It provides to the entire workforce the information on how the plant, and all parts of it, are performing. This feedback is real-time and is honest, unfiltered information. It is specifically this information that provides the feedback to the worker to show that he is performing; that his cell is performing; and his plant is performing. Each of these feedbacks supports employee engagement. The true power of system transparency is that it provides the worker confirmation as to his competency, his autonomy, his relatedness and can provide meaningfulness to him in his work. A well-designed system of transparency will address four questions, at least.

- "How am I doing?",
- "How is my cell doing?",
- "How is the plant doing?" and
- "Can I get the support I need when I need it?"

The concept of transparency

A system of transparency has four salient features. It is objective feedback; it is honest feedback; it is fast feedback and it is readily available to everyone.

It is not data that has been gathered today to be sent to the computer, digested, stratified and then puked back days or even weeks later as some unintelligible graph or metric. Transparency is real-time, honest, visible, not-manipulated data and it represents exactly what you are doing.

The purpose of transparency

Transparency is designed to tell you, at a glance, if the system is performing as designed. The primary function of good transparency is to distinguish "normal from abnormal" **so you can initiate real-time problem solving.** Transparency is the visual "check" on the production system. All processes in lean manufacturing are based on the Plan, Do, Check, Act (PDCA) cycle. The "check" is the confirmation that the process is performing as designed. And many elements of transparency are "the check step" of PDCA. For example, a production-by-hour board will list the production from the cell every hour. Furthermore, it "checks" it against the plan and records the accumulated production during the shift. Hence, each and every hour the cell workers, the team leader, the group supervisor and everyone in the plant who might want to know can tell if that cell is performing as designed. And if not, they can initiate real-time problem solving to fix it. With good transparency, feedback is rapid, non-emotional and accurate.

The "scoreboard" metaphor

Transparency is a concept in which any given situation is obvious and easily diagnosed by the worker, supervisor and manager. The metaphor for good transparency is the "scoreboard effect". That is, at a sporting event, you can enter the stadium, look at the scoreboard and in two seconds understand if your team is winning or not. The question is, can you look at your plant, a process or a workstation and in two seconds evaluate if things are normal or abnormal? If so, you likely have good transparency. If not, it's time to get better at transparency.

In a properly designed system that is "transparent" to the worker, anyone familiar with the work can see at a glance if all the resources are there and determine if the system is performing properly. Looking at a cell, for example, it is obvious if the materials are there, such as seen in a Kanban system. The shadow board will tell you if all the tools are present. It is obvious that the equipment is properly maintained or in need of maintenance by a red/yellow/green indicator system. By use of a production-by-hour board production, you can see, at a glance, if the cell is meeting the plan. Looking at the red containers to segregate defective parts, it is obvious if the product is good quality. Use of andons can signal if there is need for help, for example. All of the elements of production are readily understood at just a glance.

Motivational power of transparency

With a good system of transparency, the worker is now "in the know"; he can readily discern if he is doing a good job, confirming his sense of competency, which is so important to engagement. A properly designed system of transparency will give the worker direct, accurate and fast feedback, just as we discussed in the "flow situation". When it comes to the question, "Boss, how do you think I am doing?", with a well-designed system of transparency, the system will answer the question – any time and every time the worker wants to know – rapidly, directly and accurately. This has not only an empowering impact, it has a far-reaching, positive and uplifting impact as well. Workers don't even need to ask; they know, they know right now and they know for sure exactly how they are doing.

The worker can see at a glance that the system is performing well, he can also conclude that he TOO is performing well. He can conclude that he "knows what to do",

MOTHER NATURE HATES A VOID

People hear the term "power structure" and they cringe; they should not. Power is just something you use to get things done. The problem with power is not power itself; rather, it is the abuse of power. However, I frequently see businesses that are missing the key elements to have a healthy power structure. Simply put, power should ensue from competence and integrity for 99% of the decisions that need to be made in a business. However, if there are deficiencies in competence, someone must make the decision, or nothing gets done. Although this is problematic, it does not necessarily create the moral and operational dysfunctions of secrets, lies and gossip. These problems are rooted in a company's poor system of values. When a company does not have a:

- clearly stated,
- uniformly understood and
- widely practiced set of values,

it is hard to lead with integrity, and "other methods" will creep in to fill the void in the power structure.

he "knows how to do it" and he "has the resources to do it". This "knowing" fuels the intrinsic motivation and further improves his engagement and sense of well-being. He is doing his job well, and he knows it. He has dispassionate confirmation, on a routine basis, of his competence and his contribution.

Transparency also improves supervisor efficiency

There is yet another factor in transparency I wish to discuss. I have found a key benefit of good transparency is that it markedly will leverage the supervisor's time. I have done studies of several types of supervisors in many plants and routinely find that over 90% of the decisions they make are NOT because they have: some special skills; some special talents; or even some special training. Rather, 90% of the decisions they make are because of the information they have. When this same information is given to their subordinates, most often they can then make the same decisions, certainly faster and frequently better. Sometimes, some minor work rules need to be established, but the basic reason they are not making the decision is because they are lacking the information and/or they are not empowered to make this decision. So, when we make this information available with a system of transparency and get into the hands of the workers, they can then make many of these decisions probably better and certainly with less delay. It has the effect of leveraging the supervisors as well as enlarging the job of the worker. You get employee empowerment, faster decisions, better decisions, and this, in turn, frees the supervisors for higher level work. Pretty hard combination to beat.

Transparency and secrets

Keeping secrets is the opposite of transparency. In transparency, relevant information is openly and easily available to everyone. By secrets I do not mean the specific techniques, patents or materials you may use as a company that leverages you over the competition.

Most of the secrets that destroy motivation and undermine engagement have to do with power retention by supervisors, managers and staff member. Certain people, to enhance their power in the company, will intentionally withhold otherwise normally shared information. I see production managers not sharing the production schedule and hence the work schedule. They rationalize (read this as **rational lies**) this by saying, "Tell people what they need to know when they need to know it", for example, ignoring the fact that the worker might have only been trying to see when it might be best for him to take his vacation.

A revealing story about system transparency and secrets

On one occasion, we were implementing a culture-changing transformation in an old facility of an established company that had a particularly dysfunctional culture. At one of our steering committee meetings, as part of the discussion, I mentioned the upcoming addition of a new furnace and the 12 new jobs it would create when John, the VP, became immediately enraged. In a New York nanosecond, he jumped on me and very aggressively asked, "Wilson, where did you get that information? That is not to be released. I want to know!" I thought for a moment and could not recall, but had I recalled, under those conditions, likely I would not have revealed it. I told him, "I do not recall, but what I do recall is that no one told me it was to be kept confidential in any way, shape or form". Before I could finish my thought, John jumped on me even further and told the group, "That information must stay in this room and I expect it to go no further, are we clear?" I looked around the room and all of John's direct reports looked more like they were embarrassed for me than anything else. They certainly did not, nor were they about to, say a word. Mostly they just stared down at the large oak table in the room, avoiding eye contact. However, one of the young union stewards bravely entered the fray and said, "John, I am not sure how I know, but I knew that as well". Again, not a peep from any of John's direct reports. Just as John was about to jump on this young man, another of the union stewards joined in following some paper shuffling. He said, "John I knew about the additional jobs and I know where I heard it; it was in the company newsletter from 2 months ago" and then, to punctuate his point, "you know, the one we mail to all employee's homes". Well, John neither apologized nor said much; we just went to the next item on the agenda. This incident highlights one of the inherent weaknesses of any culture using secrets or lies. You absolutely must have a good memory so you can keep them straight in your mind … obviously, John could not.

This was a culture with a highly dysfunctional communication system where information was withheld routinely as a means to retain power and "secrets" were a key cultural power tool. In addition to secrets, lies and gossip were prevalent in unhealthy amounts. That combination is not unusual; if you have one of the three, very often you have the other two in abundance as well.

One final point about this company. It had a values statement; it was clearly written as well as widely and visibly posted. However, it was openly and frequently violated, with no resultant consequences. And this, too, was widely understood but never talked about openly. The fact that it was not enforced, at all, was "undiscussable" (see sidebar in Chapter 1). On one occasion, I was observing a team working to solve a local problem, when one member spoke up, emboldened probably because I was there. He mentioned that it was a common practice for John's direct reports to bring in their boats, motorcycles and motorhomes to the shop for repairs. The work was done on company time with company materials and using company money. This practice was in direct violation of company policy, both local and corporate. Once I had been told this, I had to discuss it with John. His total response was to make a bulletin board posting reminding all employees of the policy. I told John I could no longer work with them as it violated our agreement, which required "open honest communication". He was furious, but I had terminated our relationship and moved on.

By the way, this was one of only two companies I have worked for that had single-digit engagement levels.

The Intrinsic Motivational Loop – Its structure

The concept of meeting the intrinsic needs

Keep in mind the concept of intrinsic motivation and especially the concept of intrinsic needs. A need is something that if satisfied promotes wellness, and if frustrated promotes illness. There are four: competence (being effective); autonomy (acting with a sense of volition and choice); relatedness (caring for and being cared for); and meaningfulness (contributing to something larger than yourself).

The concept of intrinsic motivation is simple. It is intrinsic; it is natural. If the needs are satisfied, the motivation is reinforced, and then we just naturally want to do more.

Needs not just wants

What is often overlooked in this concept is the concept of "needs". These are not "intrinsic wants"; they are fundamental biological and emotional needs. If they are not satisfied, worker illness ensues and worker well-being is compromised. And we are not just talking about emotional well-being but physical well-being as well. They are only optional if well-being at the workplace is optional. Unfortunately, due to misunderstanding and other factors, looking at the actions of management, they frequently treat worker well-being as if it is optional. However, if you want a fully engaged work-force, and you want the huge list of benefits that naturally flow from a fully engaged workforce, worker well-being is not an option.

The dynamics to create engagement starts with needs fulfillment. This includes satisfying the needs of autonomy, competence, relatedness and meaningfulness. Once the needs are fulfilled, the people are likely to be more intrinsically motivated. And when workers are intrinsically moti-vated, they are freed to be both creative and engaged at work. It needs to be clearly understood that creating an environment where people are intrinsically motivated is not just a nice thing … it is both a productive and a healthy thing. With needs fulfillment, both physical and emotional health and well-being are fostered. Workers are both happy and satisfied. Consequently, as a manager, if you satisfy the intrinsic needs, you not only get a healthy, happy and creative workforce – but one that is engaged as well.

Driving the entire concept of engagement is the IML. It must be fully understood and properly managed if you wish to create a fully engaged workforce. The good news is that it is pretty straightforward to do … the bad news is that very few do it well … the really bad news is that most busi-nesses think they are doing it well – so they are not inclined to improve it.

The elements to the IML

The first step … The IML starts with the work itself and kaizen activity

The activity that starts the IML is the work itself. First, is the basic work as it was originally designed and the work for which the worker was properly trained. Make no mistake about it, it is not just the work but it is the work **after the Basics and Beyond have been fully supplied**. Second, is the opportunity for the worker to make improvements (kaizens) in the work in his area of responsibility. Doing the work and being able to make improve-ments is where the topic of worker engagement starts. It is where the intrin-sic needs of autonomy and competency get their first jolt of positive energy.

Once the work gets done, the intrinsic need of competence is satisfied at some level. However, the stronger and more important intrinsic need is the need for autonomy. When workers, of their own volition, start making improvements to their work area, to their environment, they are exhibiting control over the things that affect them and they are fueling their needs for autonomy. Of the four intrinsic needs, autonomy has the most impact when fulfilled. And this is satisfied as soon as they have the opportunity – to implement kaizens. Given the opportunity, they will respond with kaizens; it is as certain as day follows night. In 49 years of working with this concept, I have not seen a single exception.

It should come as no surprise to those who understand Herzberg's theory of worker motivation and motivators/ hygiene factors that the work itself is at the heart of engagement. Not only Herzberg but also McGregor's Theory Y showed that workers not only

HOW TO DO KAIZENS

The very best kaizen program I have devised consisted of operators entering "kaizen proposals" on their information center, a simple whiteboard. All operators in the cell and those on other shifts were able to comment on the proposed kaizen. After all shifts had an opportunity to comment and the supervisors from all three shifts initialed the whiteboard, the kaizen would be implemented. No paper, no bureaucracy and – good or bad – no records, just action and results.

enjoyed the work but also the responsibility that came with it. And further, both Maslow and Drucker not only echoed these comments but amplified them as well. When given the opportunity to creatively improve their work area and processes, **using kaizen, we now have successfully introjected the concept of challenge into everyone's work regardless of job or skill inventory**. Each person is empowered to make improvements. Keep in mind that, just like when we are achieving "flow", challenge is a key issue toward achieving engagement. And the beauty of this, by implementing the concept of kaizen in their work area, since everyone has a work area, this simple concept provides challenge for everyone regardless of the job and performance level.

So, regarding kaizen activity, what should management do? They only need to create the opportunity to make improvements. To do this, they must practice two overlapping behaviors:

■ create a culture of continuous improvement and
■ exhibit the Six Skills of Lean Leadership

and then, for the most part, stay out of the way!!!

Yes, if they do those two things, the kaizen activities will flow naturally; they will flow intrinsically. Once the Basics and Beyond have been properly addressed, kaizen activity will ensue following these two management behaviors; nothing more need be done.

This is not without some "issues"   Unfortunately, this almost unbridled desire, by the worker, to feed this intrinsic need of autonomy and express their willingness to do "extra" work, creates a problem for management. This is a very tricky part which we will discuss later, once we have completed the discussion of the IML. Keep this in mind.

The second step … Strong, internal, feedback

In Figure 15.1, you will see an action "Do their work and also do kaizens". This connects with "Fuels competence and autonomy", which later connects with "Intrinsic Motivation Increasingly Satisficed". Of course, those that are motivated are the workers who have done the kaizens. We can read that as part of the engagement loop as "workers do their work and do kaizens and this positively satisfices their intrinsic needs of competence and autonomy which increasingly satisfices their motivation". This is the first of the feedback loops and it is internal to the worker as no one else is involved. You will also note there is no delay and it is felt by the worker as soon as he finishes his kaizen. Note, this feedback is not just feedback but it also fuels the most basic and most powerful of the intrinsic needs, autonomy and competence. Once he has done this kaizen, he has not only demonstrated his job competence at a higher level but he has also done this work of his own volition.

The third step … Two feedback loops, external and delayed

Now, if we follow the engagement loop, we next find a delay and the action "workplace improves". Once the kaizen is instituted, there is sometimes a short delay both to complete the kaizen and also to have the kaizen's impact show up on the cell's production-by-hour board, for example. However, as soon as that is seen, a second feedback loop is activated and the worker(s) who instituted these kaizens gets to see the improved performance of their work area. This feeds the intrinsic need of "relatedness" as everyone is affected and probably many people contributed to this kaizen.

Following the engagement loop, we now see another delay, and this is the time it takes for the information from these kaizens to show up in the value stream process and in the facility metrics. At this time, those who have completed kaizens can see their impact on the business success. This feedback is normally felt at one of the communications meetings covered in "Beyond the Basics". Now those who have completed and contributed to kaizens know for sure they have had a positive impact on the business success and that they are an important part of a bigger entity, and this then fuels their need to make a meaningful contribution.

Integrating the IML into the engagement loop

This strong set of feedback to the individuals initiates and perpetuates a great deal of discussion. This in turn, via the informal information network, has a large impact on the "Intensity of the Positivity" which amplifies the spreading of the "positive word" and improves the "Loyalist creation rate", completing the engagement loop.

The Intrinsic Motivational Loop – Its inherent power

It would be a management mistake of galactic proportions to not recognize the power of the IML. And I do not mean just as it applies to creating a fully engaged workforce; specifically, I mean as it applies to everything that is done in your facility. It is the major knob that management can turn to improve workforce motivation.

As I did the research on engagement, and especially when I was introduced to the self-determination theory of Deci and Ryan, it has become obvious to me how important the IML is. Its importance in creating engagement cannot be minimized. However, in typical first-world cultures, it is the basic reason that people do what they do. Most people in the developed world are no longer striving for survival and are no longer at level one on Maslow's pyramid of needs. Nor are their motivation drivers at the security level, those of level

> **"NEW THINGS??"**
>
> In my book *How To Implement Lean Manufacturing*, 2nd Edition, (Wilson, 2015), I made this statement …
>
> "Lean is not so much a 'new thing', rather it is a 'new way', to do the things you need to do anyway".
>
> This truth applies to most facilities which aspire to create a fully engaged workforce. Achieving engagement is not so much in doing "new things" as much as doing them better – much better.

two. The majority find their motivational drivers at levels three, four and five as described in Chapter 11. It is therefore paramount for management to understand that the satisficing of workers motivation needs, especially at the workplace, is a matter of proper handling of the IML. A careful review of the dynamics and results of the IML will allow you to understand: how to improve your plant's quality performance; how to improve on time delivery; as well as how to reduce costs. The beauty of the IML is two-fold. First, it is simple; second, it is absolutely and wonderfully natural. And to many in management, there is another benefit. To implement the IML, management needs to do very little that is new; there are few new tasks for them to perform. However, what they will do, they will need to do much better.

So how can management turn this powerful knob to improve the motivation

This is the tricky part I referred to earlier. First, management must not tinker with the "natural" stuff. Second, with the possible exception of leader standard work, most facilities will not need to do anything new. However, they will need to do a whole slew of current management activities … and do them **much better**.

The things they need to do much better

The IML really starts with the Basics and Beyond being done … not just done but done well. I find that of the Five Basics, the three management-supplied tasks must be improved immensely. The heart of supplying this list of three is largely a matter of having: (1) good work descriptions, (2) good job descriptions and (3) good training. This is hardly an earth-shattering explanation. But in my experience, while working with over 100 firms in the last 49 years, I find that these three "Basics" are seldom done well and frequently are simply inadequate – even to the mildest scrutiny. Second, of the Beyond the Basics group, even though planning is normally done, as I stated earlier, it needs to improve dramatically. Both normal communications and communications via a system of transparency will need to improve both in quality and quantity. Most importantly, any company wishing to get serious about employee engagement will need to improve the supervisory selection, training and development process. None of these are new "things", but in most firms, they must be done better, much better. (See sidebar.)

How does management "tinker" with the natural stuff?

The tricky part, as I mentioned earlier, is tricky indeed. It is counterintuitive as well. If the management team does not understand the dynamics of what is happening at the individual worker's level, they can, even with the best of intentions, destroy the engagement effort.

Management must understand that the desire to do kaizens to do "extra work" is not simply a desire to do some more things; rather, it is a process of needs fulfillment. It is a desire to "step up" after our survival and security needs have been satisfied. Maslow said that that "man is a wanting animal" and once the needs at one level are satisfied, they are no longer motivated and the next level up holds the motivational power to drive us to action. Societally, that is where we are. The "natural" motivators are in levels three, four and five. So this current desire to "do more work" can be more accurately stated as the need to satisfy the needs of autonomy, competence, relatedness and meaningfulness. The management predicament surfaces when they first get the inkling "that the troops want to do more"; that is a red flag they have trouble both understanding and reacting properly to.

So what should management do:

- First, getting the workers to execute kaizens cannot be a mandate or a program of any form; **it must be voluntary.** These kaizens must come directly from the autonomous motivation of the individual … and nothing else. The worker must be self-regulating. Go back to Figure 12.1 and note that they must attain the proper balance of challenge and skill; only they can do this.
- Second, the minute managers see the manifest power of kaizen activity, they will want to intervene and encourage them to create more. They will want to keep track of not only how many kaizens were done but the benefits achieve. For the most sincere and altruistic reasons, they will want to encourage kaizen activity using scorecards of some type. They will want to recognize kaizen activity in many forms and come up with the kaizen of the week, the group with the most kaizens and other forms of recognition. **All this must be stifled.** This infringes directly on the ability to self-regulate. Return to Figure 12.3 and you will see that it turns what was originally intrinsically motivated behavior into some form of extrinsically motivated behavior.
- **Management must not "tinker".** Unfortunately, at this point, their instincts start to lie to them and they can't help but "try to improve it". In so doing, with the best of intentions and often with the best of designs, they will surely screw it up. Whenever and however the management team gets involved, they will diminish the volition of the worker. Management "things" like baseball tickets for the team with the largest number of kaizens, or a preferred parking spot for the "kaizen of the month", although sounding good, are all aspects of control that chip away at the autonomy the worker needs. **Although it seems intuitive to "reward the behavior you wish to see repeated", this is not true of intrinsically motivated behavior; it is its own reward and needs nothing else.** Both of these natural responses: (1) to make it a program and (2) to encourage the activity with rewards are very

common and also well-meaning. **Yet they are not only direction-ally wrong, they are destructive, and the urge to do them must be quelled**. And I mean quelled completely. In short order, both of these activities will undermine employee engagement and kaizen activity will become superficial and not helpful to either the company or the individual. You see, all these are extrinsic motivational techniques, and when applied to creative activities, they will demotivate, rather than motivate, the workforce.

■ From a management standpoint:
  – First, learn, and I mean learn thoroughly, the dynamics and the psychology of the IML
  – Next, do your job well; that will present a very large challenge in itself to most management teams
  – Third, they should work on activating this same IML in their activities, such as: planning and budgeting; staffing and organizing; plus controlling and problem solving.
  – Fourth, they should provide the support that is necessary to activate, sustain and maintain the system to create a fully engaged workforce, as described later in this text.
  – Finally, just lean back, watch, marvel and enjoy the Intrinsic Motivational Loop at work.

Challenge

Although it does not rise to the level of being one of the intrinsic needs, the topic of challenge cannot be ignored, as it impacts employee engagement, and many other business aspects, in several ways. It is a powerful concept that management can utilize to not only keep motivation high among employees but it also has a unique "filtering" concept. I recommend you return to and reread the topic of "flow" in Chapter 12.

First, it is a way to enhance the ability to demonstrate competence and satisfy that need. For those who have developed the skill level to do their regular work, the issue of boredom needs to be addressed. Although you can cross-train and satisfy those who want additional challenge, soon enough aggressive learners get fully cross-trained. Recalling what we learned from the theory of flow in Chapter 12, when an individual's skill level exceeds the job challenge, boredom is the natural result. And boredom is not compatible with engagement, not at all. Engagement requires vigor, dedication and absorption, all completely and totally antithetical to boredom (see

Chapter 4, Schaufeli et al.). However, for any job – any job – **it can always be done better**. Any job can be done with less effort, it can be done to higher quality standards and it can be faster. If the workers are encouraged to forever improve their workplace, improving their individual workplace can then become an ever-present challenge. Attacking and overcoming these challenges is one of the finest ways to "fuel" the need to demonstrate competency.

Second, challenge builds competence and competence builds confidence. With this new-found confidence, workers are more likely to take on more improvement activities, that is, they will do more kaizens. Such is the nature of challenge; it reinforces this loop (IML) within the larger engagement loop. Challenge has a double effect; it not only provides the incentive to act in the first place, it also can provide the motivation to do even more.

Third, challenges have a filtering effect. If any manager wants to improve his worker retention, that is no problem. Pay them more, give them more benefits, improve the workplace; that is easy to do. However, those things attract EVERYONE, the good worker, the mediocre worker and the poor worker alike. This then places a lot of emphasis on the entry-level process to screen and find the best workers. My experience is that screening is very difficult, and I see lots of "good talkers" make it through only to become "weak workers" when they have to perform. Hiring is a very inexact science; the more skilled the workers are, the more inexact the process is. On the other hand, if you make it known that "challenge" is part of your company's value statement and you will "challenge" all workers, the weaker ones will shy away while the stronger ones will relish the opportunity. Letting everyone know that "challenge" is a key value has a filtering effect that naturally strengthens the workplace ... from day one.

Activating the engagement loop and the role of management—Especially the supervisor

In my 2012 article, attached as Appendix B, I stated,

> "Since your employees come to work with No. 4 and No. 5 – and if you as a manager supply No. 1, No. 2 and No. 3 – that covers all five. And "voila" you get engagement not just at day one but long-term engagement that works to the benefit of not only the company but the employees and stockholders as well.

Or, as I so often like to say:

'It's all about the management. The rest is just details'".

I cannot say it more clearly; employee engagement is all about management. With good management, you get it; without good management, you won't get it. A simple litmus test.

What kind of management is needed???

There is frequently a paradigm of the manager, surrounded by computers and spreadsheets, making decisions with his management cohorts while they are sequestered in a mahogany-paneled, carpeted meeting room. They are sitting in the room, isolated from the actual work, puffing on a large cigar as they "strategically determine what the next moves should be". Using primarily "good business judgment coupled with decades of tribal knowledge" – which somehow these managers have magically been blessed with. Collectively, reveling in their successes and blaming others for their failures, they try to carve out the road to success for the enterprise. This is frequently not only the image we see in our mind's eye but the reality we experience when we hear the words of "manager and executive".

Unfortunately, this paradigm is way, way out of date. No; managers today must discard this paradigm and accept their new role, the role of lean leadership. In an earlier book, *How To Implement Lean Manufacturing*, 2nd Edition, (Wilson, 2015), I wrote:

> "I call the new model of leadership—well, it is not really new; many Japanese firms have been using it for 70 years that I know of. It is called lean leadership. It has six basic qualities (the Six Skills of Lean Leadership), which are as follows:
>
> 1. Leaders as superior observers: They go to the action—they call it the Gemba—to observe not only the machines and the products but also to spend significant time with the employees. They strive to be aware of not only the products and the processes but more importantly the people. They also are in contact with their customers. A much-overlooked leadership skill they have in abundance is the ability to be an empathetic listener.

2. Leaders as learners: They do not assume they know it all. Rather, they go to the floor to learn. They are in 'lifelong' learning mode. They are masters of the scientific method. They learn by observing and doing, but most importantly they are superior at asking questions, they learn by questioning.

3. Leaders as change agents: They plan, they articulate and sell their plans, and they act on their plans. They are not risk averse, yet they are not cavalier. They do not like to, but are not afraid to make mistakes.

4. Leaders as teachers: They are 'lifelong' teachers. When something goes wrong, their first thought is not "Who fouled up?" but "Why did it fail?" and "How can I use this as a teaching opportunity?" They teach through the use of questioning rather than just instructing.

5. Leaders as role models: They walk the talk. They are lean competent. They know what to do and they know how to do all of Lean that is job specific to their current function in the organization. There is no substitute for this. NONE.

6. Leaders as supporters: They recognize they mainly get work done through others, so they have mastered the skills of 'servant leadership'".

The special role of the first line supervisor

The role of the first line supervisor is absolutely critical to keep employees motivated and engaged. It is almost impossible to understate their importance. It is such **a strong leading indicator of engagement**, I can spend as little as a few hours with a firm's first line supervisors and predict with amazing accuracy the engagement levels they will have ... before they do the first survey.

Just how important is the first line supervisor?

When Gallup was doing their seminal work to create the Gallup Work Assessment, the Q^{12} document, recall their focus:

" ... We asked them questions on all aspects of their working life, then dug deep into their answers to discover the most important needs demanded by the most productive employees ..."

They did something very powerful; they tried to find:

> "Which elements **will attract only talented employees** and keep them, and which elements are appealing to every employee, the best, the rest, and the ROAD warriors?"

By the way, ROAD warriors, I learned, is a military term and is an acronym for "Retired On Active Duty"; it is a very descriptive metaphor. We used to have a few of these when I was in industry. We just said they had retired but not yet filled out the paperwork. And Gallup was investigating "how to attract the best without getting the rest".

> "Our research yielded many discoveries, but the most powerful was this: Talented employees need great managers. The talented employee may join a company because of its charismatic leaders, its generous benefits, and its world-class training programs, **but how long that employee stays and how productive he is while he is there is determined by his relationship with his immediate supervisor** ..."

They go on to say,

> "Once a year a study is published entitled 'The Hundred Best Companies to Work For.' The criteria for selection are such factors as: Does the company have an on-site day care facility? How much vacation does the company provide? Does the company offer any kind of profit sharing? Is the company committed to employee training? Companies are examined, and the list of the top one hundred is compiled. Our research suggests that these criteria miss the mark. It's not that these employee-focused initiatives are unimportant. **It's just that your immediate manager is more important"** ....

(all emphasis is mine and all references are to Buckingham et al., 1999)

There is no question what Gallup concluded. That is, improving employee performance and improving employee retention is a direct function of the quality of their immediate supervisor.

But what is really happening in the workplace??

As important as this job is, you would think the senior leadership would pay particular attention to this topic. That is not the case, not at all. When discussing areas of plant operation, I seldom find any areas that are as universally neglected as creating, selecting and developing supervisory talent. I find it to be a glaring void in many companies … despite the protestations of management. Most supervisory training is simply not there, not in any form. Firms frequently take the strongest worker and somehow conclude that will extrapolate into being a good supervisor. I seldom see even as little as a simple break-in. Rather, one day they are a worker, the next day they are a supervisor with the attendant responsibilities and increased pay.

The typical supervisor is more of an attendance monitor, traffic cop, quality inspector and material expeditor than he is a coach, teacher, trainer and people developer.

Sometimes, as you watch them at work, if you don't know their names, it is hard to tell the supervisor from the other staff functions. You will find them more often expediting some parts rather than working on someone's development. You are more likely to find them driving a forklift than teaching a new skill to a worker. And when it comes to problem solving, they are seldom performing this task but are incredibly adept at workarounds and firefighting, largely because these might have been the skills they exhibited as a worker … leading to their promotion.

In the last 15 years, I have only worked with two companies that have strong first line supervisors; they are Robert Bosch and Toyota. Of the other five of the "Top Seven" referred to in Chapter 1, all had adequate, if not strong, first line supervisors. On the other hand, for the Bottom Seven, when it comes to creating, selecting and developing first line supervisors, to call their efforts inadequate would be an inordinately kind description of their paltry efforts. Woefully inadequate or, and in most cases, non-existent would be more accurate. Not surprisingly, this supervisory weakness correlates very strongly with all aspects of the facility's performance from bottom-line financials to employee morale and customer satisfaction.

How does Toyota develop supervisors?

Toyota is particularly focused on supervisory training. In their work structure at the plant, they have around five cell workers who report to a team leader. His primary tasks are training, implementation of standard work and assisting in problem solving. Normally, three team leaders report to a group leader who then is to perform the remainder of the standard supervisory tasks. The team leaders, if the facility had a union, would be a represented position. To qualify to be a team leader, they must be skilled in the five cell workstations and then complete 160 hours of specific training to become a team leader. Once he is a team leader, he must complete another 120 hours of training to be able to post to become a group leader. This is the first level of management. The training is very goal oriented and consists of classroom study, role-playing, as well as practical applications. All needed skills are tested and evaluated against standard criteria. The training is supplied by certified trainers who are not only trained in the specific work skills but have taken the "train the trainer class" and are accomplished at training. Some of the most prestigious jobs at Toyota are in the human resource field, training being one of them.

And, by the way, they have been producing excellent cars for decades. Toyota has been able to ride through the ups and downs of the economy and do so while they are making record returns on their investment … and, not surprisingly, one of those investments is in their people; this is but one example. That is Toyota; and how does your first line supervisory training compare to theirs?

The needed structure at the floor level

Very few businesses have a manufacturing floor and support structure that is conducive to having good supervision. Frequently, the supervisor has too many things to do. Worst of all is lots of paperwork to feed the system bureaucracy. Things such as timekeeping, calling out overtime, routine evaluations of tool and materials conditions are all things that are normally not necessary, and if necessary should be done by a staff person. In addition, supervisors spend undue time expediting parts,

OPTIMUM??

An often overlooked maxim is that "the system optimum is not always the sum of the local optima". This is yet another example. As these companies drive to optimize direct labor percentages, they not only drive labor costs up but overall production costs rise as well. They are trading a system optimum to create a local optimum, the reduction of indirect labor. One of my earlier supervisors would say, "They are losing more on the peanuts than they are saving on the bananas".

expediting drawings and work instructions as well as expediting tools. If that is not enough, they are often found communicating with both upstream and downstream processes to maintain materials flows which by their very nature are unpredictable. If that is not enough, they get involved in solving process problems that repeat on a daily basis. Well, they really don't solve anything; through workarounds and firefighting, they find a way to make the undesirable effect go away … for the moment. And they are surprisingly well equipped for this "bubble gum and bailing wire" approach, not because of some special skills or training. Rather, they are adept at this "temporary symptom removal process" because they have seen these issues many times before … and they were never solved.

Almost none of these issues are things supervisors should be doing. Supervisors should spend their time planning, teaching and supporting their people, as well as improving the process. Undue amounts of paperwork should first be minimized, and what remains should be handled by a clerk. Scheduling should be transparent, and everyone should know the status of materials, tools and flows. A system of transparency, done well, will take care of this issue nicely. Expediting is just "problem avoidance". Any expediting that is necessary should be highlighted as a problem and solved until once again the process is predictable, and the problem solving should continue until all processes are in statistical control. As for problem solving, the plant **should be structured so they have time to address these issues and get to root cause problem solving.**

Two large problems … created by the structure

It is very common to see two very large problems that prevent supervisors from being effective, and by effective, I clearly mean being able to comply with all Six Skills of Lean Leadership. The problems are that (1) supervisors have too many direct reports and (2) they are not structured for problem solving. I frequently see supervisors "trying" to supervise 15, 20 and even as many as 50 people. This is not possible. To properly comply with the Six Skills of Lean Leadership and execute leader standard work, floor supervisors should have 5–8 people.

Many businesses try to increase this ratio from say 1:7 to 1:15 under the guise of reducing indirect labor percentage. And they do improve this ratio. While they gain on this metric, each of the 15 people they are supervising soon enough loses enough efficiency that the net effect is to reduce overall productivity, with rising costs, reduced engagement and decreasing morale

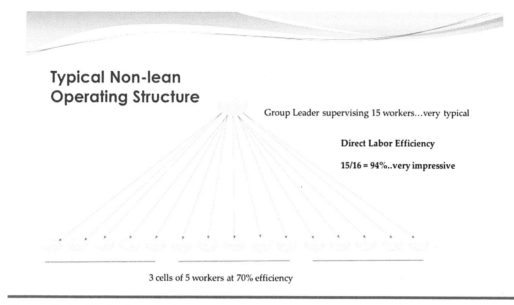

Typical Non-lean Operating Structure

Group Leader supervising 15 workers...very typical

Direct Labor Efficiency

15/16 = 94%..very impressive

3 cells of 5 workers at 70% efficiency

Figure 15.2 **Typical operating structure.**

… for certain. (For a detailed treatment, including the mathematics of the net productivity losses and gains, I refer you to *How To Implement Lean Manufacturing*, 2nd Edition (Wilson, 2015).

At least one structural solution

The inefficient and ineffective structure looks like (Figure 15.2), and direct labor efficiencies are high, but the individual workers are at 70% efficiency, at the very best, (I normally see efficiencies in the 30–50% range in these structures).

When supervisors are well trained and capable of executing the Six Skills of Lean leadership … and they have a structure that is conducive to properly executing their job, then the efficient and effective structure looks like Figure 15.3.

In the Toyota structure, they have 90% labor efficiencies compared to 40, 50 and 70% at the very best. When this gain is integrated across all 15 value-add workers, it more than justifies the added support, and, in fact, if you do the math, you will find there is a net gain of 39%.

This structure with team leaders is needed to keep the value-add workers focused on the tasks. This structure is not only more productive, it will improve all aspects of plant performance including quality, customer service, safety performance, costs, morale, employee retention, and, not surprisingly, it will also provide improved employee engagement.

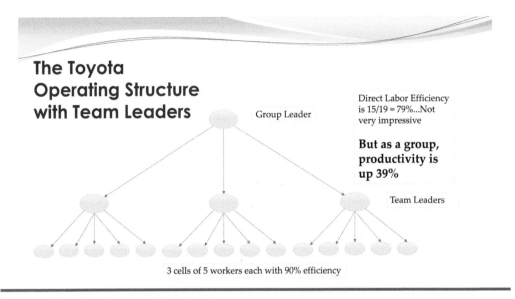

The Toyota Operating Structure with Team Leaders

Group Leader

Direct Labor Efficiency is 15/19 = 79%...Not very impressive

But as a group, productivity is up 39%

Team Leaders

3 cells of 5 workers each with 90% efficiency

Figure 15.3   Toyota operating structure.

Chapter Summary ... In the process of getting your workers engaged, we will first need to make three cultural shifts. First, we discussed the need to create a standards-based "normal". The second shift was the need to create a culture of continuous improvement so those standards were always being improved up. Third, the management team would need to improve the quantity and the quality of communications so workers could understand the context of the business. We discussed the five elements of the engagement loop, although elements four and five were developed in Chapters 11 and 12 when we discussed motivation. The first three of "the Basics and Beyond, "the work and kaizens" and the "Intrinsic Motivational Loop" were all developed in detail. Of particular importance to the entire engagement loop is an understanding of the Intrinsic Motivational Loop (IML), which is the engine that drives the entire engagement effort. In the midst of this was a warning to management that they must curb the use of several motivational tools they use frequently as they are antithetical to the IML. Finally, we ended that the important role of lean leadership must be employed with particular attention to supervisory skills as well as an alternative to the typical organization structure. One that is more conducive to good management and engagement as well.

What's next?? We got the engagement loop in action and are now increasing our engagement levels. Next, we will examine how we not only sustain these gains but how we also accelerate the rate of engagement; I call it engagement on steroids.

Chapter 16

Completing the Engagement System

Aim of this Chapter ... is to explore precisely what we must do to further activate the system of engagement. First, the workers will be very excited about what has transpired. They will also recognize it is now in the hands of management to improve the levels of engagement. Largely this is a matter of getting the managers more fully engaged, and their actions will, in turn, spur the rest of the organization to higher levels of engagement. First, we will discuss some cultural shifts that management will need to initiate. Then we will discuss the critical nature of feedback and the four types of feedback that are needed to drive engagement to world class levels.

We have been making great progress ...

After we have worked hard to supply the Basics and Beyond and have worked hard to create a culture of continuous improvement and everyone is active in kaizen activity, this alone will give engagement a huge shot in the arm. You will get some early and strong gains. You will be both pleased and amazed. Not only will this improve any level of engagement you currently have, but it will also improve quality, on-time delivery, profitability and all key business metrics. If the "Basics and Beyond" are done well, especially if HK planning is started, communications channels are improved and LSW is implemented, engagement will improve.

You can be ***absolutely certain*** it will improve for at least 3–9 months if just "The Five Basics" are done. It will continue to improve for maybe as long as 12 to 18 months as long all the "Basics and Beyond" are done and done well. If you do these well, complete engagement surveys and watch the other key indicators of engagement, they will all track positively for some time, like I say, maybe as long as 18 months.

However, the lifespan of this effort is capped – if that is all you do.

Why is this not enough??

At this point in your engagement effort, if you do it guided by your "gut feel"(as opposed to the recommended approach outlined in Chapter 18), you have spent nearly all of your management time focused on "The Basics and Beyond" as you have worked to support the value-add worker. But, make no mistake, you are not disappointed because the response from the workforce has been incredible. Morale is up noticeably; the plant metrics are improving and the 1-year engagement survey probably showed a 10–12% increase in engagement. You are ecstatic. However, now is the time to become aware. If you do not do more, and do it soon, this engagement effort is in real trouble.

What's the problem??

Whenever the levels of engagement are improved, one of the logical outcomes is the new "openness" of the culture. Communications have improved dramatically, and new and different topics of discussion ensue. Some items that used to be "undiscussable" (see Chapter 1) are now frequent topics, and not just on the cultural network. They are discussed at meetings regularly, and with this openness, other questions get asked. Things like, "If we are to use the Six Questions of Continuous Improvement as our standard problem solving tool, why does not management do the same with their issues?" Other topics surface such as, "Since this first wave of training and awareness has spawned a great deal of improved engagement, what is next??" The workforce is saying they like what has happened. Like all Herzberg hygiene factors, they now want more. They go on, "We are not sure what more we have to give to make it better, and it seems like it is up to the management to make some changes so we all can get to the next level".

At this point, it is up to the management team to respond

As you might expect, not only did Maslow, Drucker, McGregor and the harbingers of the past predict this, the auditors of the present do as well. In their 2013 report on the "State of the American Workplace", Gallup said:

> "Employees in manufacturing and production are among the least engaged, perhaps owing to the fact that the management culture

in these companies tends to focus on process ahead of people. An investment in managers' engagement in all industries, but these in particular, could go a long way in boosting employee engagement. **Gallup finds that managers continue to be the most powerful influence on workers' engagement levels**".

(emphasis mine, Gallup 2013)

Also, in their 2016 survey they say:

"Employees in manufacturing jobs are the least engaged. Equally discouraging is the alarming number of actively disengaged employee in manufacturing roles. The manufacturing industry has as many actively disengaged workers as it does engaged workers. **The traditional management mentality in this industry tends to put process ahead of people,** possibly accounting for some of the engagement obstacles".

(emphasis mine, Gallup 2017)

What is the needed response?

They are right; it's now up to the management "to do some stuff". When they supply the "Basics and Beyond", management is doing what they are normally charged to do; what they are supposed to do. Even if they supply these elements very well, management still needs to change more, and, specifically, they need to get more engaged themselves. For the most part, the changes that have occurred have mostly been changes by the rank and file workforce. They are the ones who have taken a leap of faith. The onus is now on the management team to step up, and they must change their behavior … or your engagement effort is doomed. Just what are those changes? As you might expect they are changes in what management does – or should begin doing – each and every day. Those four changes, all forms of management feedback, will be the topic of the rest of this chapter.

Management feedback systems

There are visual feedback systems and systems of management action that provide behavioral feedback. The visual techniques are designed to feedback process and other plant information on a routine basis. (see Scoreboard effect in Chapter 15). Some hourly, some daily, some weekly, some monthly and yet others annually. The management's behavioral feedback is what they do daily. Their actions send all kinds of messages to the workforce, and, specifically, their actions signify what is culturally acceptable and culturally unacceptable.

Our studies have shown that, beyond those feedback systems already discussed, there are four systems of feedback that management must both develop and actively participate in to create a fully engaged workforce. It is these four systems of feedback that send consistent and honest signals to the entire workforce that the management team is supportive of creating and sustaining a fully engaged workforce. It is these four systems of feedback that confirm the management team is committed – and engaged themselves. Before we dive headlong into these four issues, we will address the broader topic of feedback.

The power of feedback

I recall a discussion with my mentor from long, long ago. I had just gotten my first promotion and he took me aside and discussed the role of supervision with me. I recall one particular piece of advice he gave me. He said:

> "Wilson, people will tell you that Wheaties is the break-fast of champions. Not true. Feedback is the breakfast of champions".
>
> (Wendel Larson, personal discussion, circa 1974)

Obviously, the metaphor he used made a lasting impression. More importantly, he was correct. I have found the concept of providing feedback to be a very important motivational tool; and not just

FEEDBACK AND SYSTEM DYNAMICS

At the heart of system dynamics are feedback systems. These are mechanisms that either reinforce or counteract the previous actions in the system. Feedback systems will create an exaggerated response as compared to a simple linear response. Wherever there is feedback, you will find a loop. In system dynamics "feedback is the breakfast of champions". In fact, within the system of engagement, you will find that the interactions are often stronger than the main effects themselves. Interactions, dependencies and interdependencies are a reality of life and need to be understood, acted upon and properly managed.

in the workplace. Honesty in giving feedback is paramount, and the most honest feedback is your actions over your words. Make no mistake about it, in the world of feedback, your actions speak much louder than your words.

Lack of feedback is harmful

With no feedback, you neither know if you are in trouble or not; in addition, you are not able to discern the consequences of what might ensue. Given negative feedback, at least you know where you stand and can likely chart a future path. Said another way, even with negative feedback, you understand the present and can possibly chart the future. With no feedback, your present condition is unknown as well as what might ensue in the future. You are left with present case "not knowing" and future case "not knowing".

Workers "not knowing"

There are many questions and concerns to the average worker. "Will we have a job in a month?" "What will my new schedule be?" "Will we make the monthly numbers?" "Will we ship on time?" "Will I do my job well, day in and day out?" And even, "Will the boss come by and chew on us for whatever?" These are all reasonable questions that can gnaw away at both a worker's attention and his motivation as well. If management wishes to improve productivity and morale, it is incumbent upon them to address these and other issues and bring them into the light. In a phrase, a transparent system creates a much healthier work environment.

Squelching the "not knowing"

These issues are largely squelched if the environment has a set of goals and values and a system of feedback that shows if the goals and values are being attained (addressed by the Basics and Beyond). If there is no system of feedback, these issues not only create anxiety and fear, they have a negative effect on productivity, quality,

EMPLOYEE FEEDBACK

There are many types of feedback an employee should be given. Here, we are talking about daily performance feedback. We have already discussed the Five Supervisory Tools including the Personal Development Plan, the 5-Year Development Plan and routine feedback via the normal activities of leader standard work. Yes, employees deserve feedback not just on daily activities but on their future as well.

safety, delivery and morale … as well as fester and become worse as they are left unanswered. "Not knowing" is a powerful concept with extreme and negative consequences if not handled properly – yet with calming and empowering effects when handled well.

The countermeasure to "not knowing" is feedback. Feedback can come in a variety of ways, and the faster and the more objective it is, the better. Strangely enough, when I discuss the concept of feedback, managers almost reflexively think of their feedback in either written or oral form. They default to memos, postings, emails and announcements in meetings. Seldom is top management feedback of this nature influential; when we are trying to sustain engagement, meaningful feedback comes in other forms. (Recall the discussion on the Cultural Network in Chapter 14).

The most meaningful and most influential feedback is the most objective and the fastest. Recall the concept of "flow" and how critical the fast feedback is required to sustain flow. Another example, maybe closer to home that demonstrates the manifest power of fast feedback is video games. If you have a son or daughter who plays them, notice how much feedback there is, how fast it is delivered and how graphically it is delivered. This concept of rapid feedback, coupled with a little challenge, will keep people of all ages glued to their video games for long stretches.

What is "typical" feedback?

When I ask managers, "What type of performance feedback do you give your employees?", the default answer is the annual performance review. The second response given to my question is usually about some management feedback systems such as quarterly plant performance reviews and even sometimes plant metrics posted at the information centers.

Why is this inadequate?

These two are not powerful feedback tools. The annual performance review, as we discussed earlier is both counterproductive and should be discontinued. Nor is the quarterly management feedback of plant performance meaningful feedback. They are not directly related to the worker; they are not timely; frequently unintelligible; and often they are subject to a lot of interpretation.

What is needed? (See sidebar)

Recall from Chapter 15 that what is needed is a feedback system that answers the following questions for the worker:

- "How am I doing?",
- "How is my cell doing?",
- "How is the plant doing?" and
- "Can I get the support I need, when I need it?"

Visual feedback techniques – Transparency

By far, the fastest feedback tool is system transparency. Done right, it is both informative and empowering. It provides to the entire workforce the information on how the plant, and all parts of it, are performing. This feedback is real-time and is honest, unfiltered information. It is just this information that provides the feedback to the worker to show that he is performing, that his cell is performing and his plant is performing. Each of these types of feedback supports employee engagement. Transparency provides the worker confirmation as to his competency, his autonomy, his relatedness and can also provide meaningfulness to him in his work. A well-designed system of transparency will address the four questions above. The concept of transparency and its many benefits were discussed in detail in

MOTHER NATURE HATES A VOID

People hear the term "power structure" and they cringe; they should not. Power is just something you use to get things done. The problem with power is not power itself; rather, it is the abuse of power. However, I frequently see businesses that are missing the key elements to have a healthy power structure. Simply put, power should ensue from competence and integrity for 99% of the decisions that need to be made in a business. However, if there are deficiencies in competence, someone must make the decision, or nothing gets done. Although this is problematic, it does not necessarily create the moral and operational dysfunctions of secrets, lies and gossip. These problems are rooted in a company's poor system of values. When a company does not have a:

- clearly stated,
- uniformly understood and
- widely practiced set of values,

it is hard to lead with integrity and "other methods" will creep in to fill the void in the power structure.

Chapter 15 as one of the five elements of Beyond the Basics. Consequently, we will not repeat that here. Rather, we will focus on the role of management in this important feedback system.

The role of management

The role of management in system transparency is two-fold. First, there is the typical roles of management of: planning and budgeting; organizing and staffing; as well as controlling and problem solving while the system is being built, maintained and supported. Second, management can have an even greater impact, and that occurs when **they actually use this system**. When they go to the floor, do they bring their spreadsheets, or do they use the production-by-hour (PBH) boards to get their information? When they look on the PBH boards and they see an hourly production that has fallen short, they must not ignore this abnormality; rather, they must respond to it. One of the better questions the manager could ask of the line supervisor, would be: "How can we help you so you can better meet the production goal?"... and then just listen. Then the manager should take this information with him, digest it with the value stream manager and then get back to the supervisor with "exactly how you intend to help him meet his goal". Recall, the purpose of system transparency is to facilitate real-time problem solving … and the role of everyone in the facility is to support the value-add workers. This is one way that management can send an unmistakable message about transparency, recognizing normal from abnormal and showing the willingness to act. In this manner, the manager can use system transparency to assist the supervisor and the value-add worker. It is a clear message of management use and support of both this system and the workers as well.

Behavioral feedback techniques

As was discussed earlier, once engagement is improved and people become accustomed to it, in concert with Herzberg's hygiene theory, people will want some more. At this point, it is incumbent upon the management team to lead the engagement effort even more vigorously. Normally there are several behavioral traits they will need to work on. Since these are hygiene factors, when used, they create little or no motivation to engage. However, if these same tools ARE NOT used at all or are not used properly, they have a powerful and negative effect on motivation, with resultant disengagement. When they are not properly satisfied, they act like Herzberg's "hygiene factors on steroids" with extremely large and negative impacts. There are three such large factors. They are: "management must walk the talk"; "supervisory feedback"; and "workers must trust management".

Management "walking the talk"

Of all the issues that will create engagement, this is NOT one of them. When management "walks the talk", there is little positive effect on the workforce; after all, everyone has a right to expect that the leaders will abide by their own rules and will practice what they teach. On the other hand, once an initial level of engagement has been reached, there is no issue that is more **destructive to sustaining engagement** than when "management **does not** walk the talk".

When management is creating rules, policies, procedures and cultural change of any form … the one straightforward way to assure that the rules, policies and procedures will not be followed is to punish those who comply. Sounds strange, but it happens in many forms (see sidebar). Next to this dysfunction, when the management team does not walk their own talk, when they do not follow their own self-made instructions, when they expect everyone else to change and yet they themselves refuse to change, that is a sure-fire formula to assure that others will not remain engaged. Next to punishment … nothing is more destructive to the engagement of everyone else, nothing. In the fullness of time, when management fails to "walk the talk", this will destroy any culture-changing event.

Management denial is at the root of this issue

The power of this concept is often misunderstood, either intentionally or not. If it is properly understood, it is frequently minimized by the entire management team. Too often when change of any form needs to be made, top management sees it as a change to be implemented at the "next level down". They are in denial that "they need to change also". For anyone who truly understands cultural change, they know this is EXACTLY the wrong response. Rather, the first people who need to change are the top managers. And the higher they are in the power structure, the faster they must change; and the higher they are, the more consistent they must be in the changes they make.

When you review The Six Skills of Lean Leadership below, you will find that to not "walk the talk" is an egregious violation of Skill 5. However, with only a little review, you can see that it is in direct contradiction to all six qualities.

I have repeated this list from Chapter 7 here, so you can review, skill by skill, and ask, how is "not walking the talk", a violation of this skill?"

The Six Skills of Lean Leadership

1. **Leaders as superior observers:** They go to the action—they call it the Gemba—to observe not only the machines and the products but also to spend significant time with the employees. They strive to be aware of not only the products and the processes but more importantly the people. They also are in contact with their customers. A much-overlooked leadership skill they have in abundance is the ability to be an empathetic listener.

2. **Leaders as learners:** They do not assume they know it all. Rather, they go to the floor to learn. They are in "lifelong" learning mode. They are masters of the scientific method. They learn by observing and doing, but most importantly they are superior at asking questions, they learn by questioning.

3. **Leaders as change agents:** They plan, they articulate, and sell their plans, and they act on their plans. They are not risk averse, yet they are not cavalier. They do not like to, but are not afraid to make mistakes.

HOW DOES MANAGEMENT PUNISH THE BEHAVIOR THEY SEEMINGLY WANT?

It seems odd that management would punish the very behavior they want, but it happens all too often. Seldom is this the intention. Unfortunately, a lack of awareness is usually at the root of the problem. The classic case happens in any process improvement effort, when after the rank and file make a number of process improvements and then when efficiencies improve ... management lays off workers. A lesser version of this punishment is "job creep" as described later in this chapter (see Trust). It does not take the workforce long to figure that one out. Less subtly, you can work hard to promote teamwork as a business strategy with work teams and small group problem solving and then undermine this by basing your entire system of recognition and rewards on individual performance. Those are some common examples of management shooting themselves in the foot; there are others.

The book *Punished by Rewards* (Kohn, 1993) is filled with all kinds of seemingly good and well-intended actions, which, rather than reward people, punished them. It's good reading for all.

4. **Leaders as teachers:** They are "lifelong" teachers. When something goes wrong, their first thought is not "Who fouled up?" but "Why did it fail?" and "How can I use this as a teaching opportunity?" They teach through the use of questioning rather than just instructing.

5. **Leaders as role models:** They walk the talk. They are lean competent. They know what to do and they know how to do all of Lean that is job specific to their current function in the organization. There is no substitute for this. NONE.

6. **Leaders as supporters:** They recognize they mainly get work done through others, so they have mastered the skills of "servant leadership" (Wilson, 2015).

For example, look at some simple examples. What do you suppose happens when, as a manager, you routinely show up late for work? Soon enough, others are late. What happens if you go out on the floor and never bring your safety glasses? Soon enough, safety glasses become "optional" or, more appropriately, just not enforced. Let's presume that as a manager you have decided that you will use the Six Questions of Continuous Improvement as the facility-wide problem solving tool. Then in your management meetings, you still make decisions by gut feel, using tribal knowledge as your information basis. Well, maybe initially no one notices. But soon enough, while touring the floor, you discuss a problem with a worker and he says, "By rule three of our Six Questions of Continuous Improvement, we need to address …" and you interrupt him and say, "Tell me again, what is rule three?". At which time, you have been found out, you are fully exposed and he, along with everyone he tells, now fully understand you neither understand nor use the Six Questions of Continuous Improvement. Then he asks himself, "If the boss doesn't use them, why should I?". Soon enough the entire problem solving initiative winds down and everyone regresses to using gut feel decisions driven by tribal knowledge, just as the management team does. If as a manager you and your entire management team are not "walking the talk", there simply is no hope to sustain whatever engagement you get, beyond your early gains.

What is the real test of "Do we really want to change?"

Anytime you embark on a cultural change, the one thing that everyone is watching, is: "exactly what will management do?" It is not unusual for many of those in the rank and file to "stick in their toes" and test the waters of change and make some positive change. But if they do not see some change from the management team, that is more substantial than just talking; soon enough, they will say, "Wait a minute; let's see what's really up here". And if management does not start to walk the talk, the rest of the place will forever be in "wait and see mode". If the management team does not change, the engagement transformation is over. That is the true test; does the management lead the transformational change by personally changing their behaviors … or not?

And what is the "acid" test?

However, once management passes the test, of actually changing, there is one more test. I like to say that there is no true test of your values until you are faced with a crisis. In the midst of smooth, stress-free operations, it is easy to wax philosophical about your val-

---

A HARSH REALITY

What do you do when managers don't change? It requires that those managers will have to be removed or reassigned. Often these will be the most senior of the management. The transformation will fail if they are not replaced, because they are the guardians of the "old" way and are the most resistant to change. They have been rewarded by the old system, and often cannot change, even if they wanted to.

In the end, these managers who can't or won't change don't meet your minimum standards of performance, which are to:

■ Understand the objectives
■ Accept the objectives and
■ Execute the objectives.

And if you fail to get them to change and then fail to change them out, you are guaranteeing the failure of the engagement effort.

---

ues. When life is a "cocktail" party, where talk is cheap, it is easy to espouse values. However, it is much different when you are faced with the difficult choices in the midst of a crisis. I like to say the crises do not create character so much as they reveal it, and it is a measure of character to be able to hold your standards in the midst of adversity.

So exactly how will they react in a crisis? Soon enough there will be a crisis. Maybe a major customer has a serious complaint. Or some major equipment fails, endangering the entire production schedule. Does the management team ignore all the work they have done to get engagement? Do they toss aside the skills of lean leadership which they worked so hard to learn and revert to their old ways of command and control leadership? Do they stick their noses in where they swore they would not and revert to old directive, autocratic behavior? If they do – the jig is up. The conclusion, and the correct conclusion, the workforce will draw is, "This engagement thing is not real; they'll do it only when it is convenient". Soon enough, the skeptics will send the message via the cultural network that "this engagement thing is not for real"… and they will be right. Engagement will unwind from there.

More on the need for supervisory skills-relatedness issues

As mentioned earlier, in Chapters 7 and 8, supervisors play a large role in not only engagement but production, quality and delivery as well. Workers, next to their co-workers, have more interaction with their direct supervisor than anyone else. It is their supervisor who makes sure they are properly trained, properly equipped and have all the necessities to perform their task. It is the supervisor who makes sure the parts and tools delivery systems are properly servicing the work cells, as well as making sure that all the instructions and information the workers need are available when they need them in the quantity they need and in the quality they need. In short, the supervisor is the element that makes the worker both effective and efficient.

Yet another element of supervision is to stay in constant contact with his workers. He is simultaneously required to be the "voice of the worker to management" and the "voice of management to the worker". In so doing, he is readily available to field questions and provide both support and feedback. One concept I regularly teach in my supervisory training classes is that workers want to hear the most important information directly from their supervisor in a face-to-face discussion, and they want personal materials discussed not only face-to-face but individually. When the worker gets the proper support from his supervisor, usually a strong bond is created. Typically, the strongest bond the worker has with management is the one he has with his direct supervisor.

> "Our research yielded many discoveries, but the most powerful was this: Talented employees need great managers. The talented employee may join a company because of its charismatic leaders, its generous benefits, and its world-class training programs, but how long that employee stays and how productive he is while he is there is determined by his relationship with his immediate supervisor".
>
> (Buckingham and Coffman, 1999)

When we are discussing meeting the key business objectives of supplying good product on time to your customer, it is very hard to understate the importance of the first line supervisor. Likewise, when we are discussing the topic of attaining and sustaining a fully engaged workforce, there is no practical way to overstate the importance of the role of the first line supervisor. You will note we have discussed their importance when we train and equip the workers with "The Basics" and when we arm them so they can go "Beyond the Basics". Later, in Chapter 17, you will learn that strong supervision is a High Leverage Point in the system to gain engagement.

DEFINITION DRIFT AND "INTEGRITY"

Often, through misuse, the definition of words will drift. Integrity is one such word. In my 1954 Webster's Collegiate dictionary, integrity means: (1) state or quality of being complete, undivided or unbroken; (2) unimpaired state, soundness, purity. However, a newer dictionary, Webster's from the web, lists the definition as: the state of being honest or fair. To me, integrity goes beyond honesty and fairness.

It is no exaggeration to say that the key personal relationship at work is the worker–supervisory relationship. Therefore, the feedback directly from the supervisor is so important to not only productivity but engagement as well.

Trust in management

The anatomy of trust

The basis to trust anyone is two-fold.

- First, you must have certain strong personal traits such as honesty, fairness, humility, reliability and others, which I lump into the quality of integrity. Included in integrity I also add bravery and trusting yourself. I cannot recall a single person I could trust, that was not courageous and trusting of himself.
- Second, to be trusted, you must be competent.

Hence, you do not blindly trust people; rather, you "trust them to …". For example, I would trust my son to watch my grandkids, his nieces and nephews while they are swimming in our pool. He can swim, and he is mature enough to keep a close eye on them. However, I would not trust him to fix the water heater. Not because he lacks the necessary personal traits; he has them. Rather, I cannot trust him to fix the water heater because he lacks the requisite skills. For example, he does not know a box-end wrench from a pair of water-pump pliers. He certainly is honest, with high integrity, but he fails to be a competent plumber. We do not blindly trust; rather, we "trust to …".

Some problems creating trust with management … Are the managers aware of the concrete details of the work??

An increasingly large impact on being able to trust managers is the ability of managers to know about the concrete details of their business. We discussed this in detail in Chapter 8 where we spoke about the "lost skills".

I am reminded of a discussion I had with a prior client. The CEO was a retired Navy SEAL. He was very interested in making his company successful but was uncomfortable with his level of "business skills". At one point I asked him if he had high trust with his SEAL team. He responded, "Of course". I probed further and he mentioned the training they had all suffered through together as well as the natural camaraderie built as a result of being in battle and having to depend on each other. I probed further. Finally, he said, "It doesn't matter what happens on a mission; even if one guy goes down, everyone else can fill in". And "voila" a large part of their trust for one another was that each SEAL had been trained and was competent as a medic, as a radioman, as a demolitions expert, as a sniper, and they could all do all the activities needed on a mission – and every other SEAL knew that. In a phrase, the trust they had for one another was built upon the basis that all team members were competent, and everyone knew that. A large part of their bond of trust was based on competence. Maybe the stakes in a manufacturing plant are not as high as with my SEAL friend, but the dynamics are the same. If you wish to be trusted, be competent.

Trust – The basics

Making and keeping commitments is the bread and butter of creating trust. It is not possible to have a trusting relationship if promises are not honored. However, there are some subtle ways to pick away at a trusting relationship; one is to fail to accept responsibility. These can include blaming others, especially the ambiguous "they". Another bad habit that undermines trust is to "pass the buck". Regarding making and keeping promises, I found the following advice in *First, Break All the Rules*:

"And especially important: Never pass the buck. Never say, 'I think this is a crazy idea, but corporate insists'. Passing the buck may make your little world easy, but the organism as a whole, sorry, the organization as a whole, will be weakened. So in the long run, you are actually making your life worse. Even worse are those who find themselves always promising things that don't come to pass. Since you never know what corporate might spring on you next, I recommend living by this simple rule: Make very few promises to your people, and keep them all".

(Buckingham and Coffman, 1999)

More egregious things which work to destroy trust include reductions in force, spin offs and mergers, with the resultant changes in structure. In addition, the rank and file have seen the management act in their own best interest, to the detriment of the rank and file and even the business in general. All these are huge trustbusters.

In my 49 years in industry, I cannot cite more than a handful of facilities that had a trusting relationship between the workforce and the management. Not one of them "talked" their way to a trusting relationship; each one "behaved" their way to that result. They all had six things in common:

■ First, the managers made no promise they could not keep. And if circumstances changed and they could no longer honor their commitments, they explained why.
■ Second, the managers exhibited personal integrity at work and in their personal life as well.
■ Third, the management spent significant time on the floor creating relationships and staying in touch with the workers.
■ Fourth, expectations were made clear and consequences were followed up.
■ Five, when they made a mistake, they apologized sincerely and made efforts to correct it.
■ Sixth, the management team were competent in their jobs and respected by their subordinates.

The fragile nature of trust

Trust is gained by making and keeping commitments. It is one of those things that is very hard to gain, yet very easy to lose. If you make and keep a number of commitments, people will start to trust you. If you continue to honor your commitments, that trust in you will gain. However, if you slip, that error has a multiplying effect, and one missed commitment is not erased by one or even ten honored commitments. Early in my career, a salty old maintenance manager spent some time mentoring me. He had a sign on his wall that said:

> "As a Chevron employee, your job is to solve problems, and improve things. In so doing we expect you to be creative, innovative, and entrepreneurial. However, it is in your best interest to survive; so never forget that it takes 100 attaboys to cancel one 'aw sh_t'.

Such can be the nature of trust: hard to earn, easy to lose.

"Knowledge workers" want to contribute more … but lack of trust is an impediment

---

HOW DO WE LEARN?

Using the scientific method to "test" and learn, you start with a hypothesis, which takes the form of, "If I do these things, I should expect these results". Then you carefully define the "things" and the "results". And when you measure the results, you can either get positive results and "accept" the hypothesis or get negative results and "reject" the hypothesis. When you confirm the hypothesis, you simply affirm what you already knew. There is no new learning. Much more learning is achieved when the hypothesis is rejected, or, in lay terms, when the experiment "fails".

However, rather than failing, you have just gained additional information that can be used to improve your level of understanding.

Following my graduation from college, I entered the workforce with Chevron. At that time, it was not unusual to find maintenance workers and even operators who did not have a high school diploma. They had been hired in the '30s, '40s and '50s, and the hiring standards, as well as the work, was much different. By the time I worked in Chevron's refinery in New Jersey, we would easily get 500 applicants for our typical class of operator candidates, which was only 16 individuals. Of these 500, 30% would have a 2- or 4-year college degree, and that was between 1977 and 1980! While I was with Chevron at their El Paso refinery (1980–1990), in a typical hiring class, 40% would hold 4-year degrees. We were getting better-educated people year after year. I do not believe we were unique; rather, I believe the educational level of all manufacturing workers is increasing, maybe increasing exponentially. In short, the typical talent pool, particularly amongst the hourly workers, in almost all businesses is growing.

With this increase in intellectual muscle, you also get a natural interest in making greater contributions. People want to express their ideas. In short, they want to make improvements. Like we discussed in Chapter 12, it is a natural desire; it is intrinsic. As early as 1960, Peter Drucker coined the phrase "knowledge workers" to signify the change from those workers whose only previous need was to supply physical labor. Today, in manufacturing, virtually everyone is a knowledge worker ... **if they are allowed to be**. Drucker made that observation in the '60s and it has not been understood, nor fully exploited, to this day. These knowledge workers are a national treasure we have not even recognized, let alone utilized.

And now, increasingly, companies are trying to create a culture of continuous improvement. Improving quality, improving on-time delivery and reducing costs are all part of the typical business strategy. It used to be that continuous improvement was a ***strategy to accomplish growth*** so businesses could become larger. Fortunately for the consumer, those days are over and continuous improvement has become a ***survival strategy***. Now the growth strategy is "accelerated" continuous improvement. If your competition is improving bottom-line performance, customer satisfaction and product quality by 4% per year, you must do at least that much – just to survive. If you wish to expand, you need to improve 4% every 6 months, not just 4% per year. You absolutely need to accelerate the improvement.

However, make no mistake, continuous improvement, the implementation of a kaizen mindset, is purely optional; unless, of course, you wish to survive.

With added intellectual muscle, you'd expect a flood of kaizen activity   With this backdrop of an increasing intellectual strength at all levels in a business driving people's natural desire to create improvement projects, coupled with the need for continuous improvement in business, you would expect a literal explosion of companies who are bursting at the seams with kaizen upon kaizen. But that simply is not the case; there is no explosion of kaizens in manufacturing in general. There is an explosion of technology; there is an explosion of web-based activity; there is an explosion of sending jobs offshore, but when it comes to an explosion of kaizen activity ... it just is not happening.

Why??

Where's the creativity??   No secret here. To perform kaizens takes innovation and creativity ... that is not the problem. There is no such thing as "error-free" innovation or creativity; there is always some form of risk. Both innovation and creativity have the specter of possible failure attached; that is the problem. It causes people to hesitate. If the management sees the positive gains and rewards those efforts yet somehow "punishes" the failures, soon enough the innovation and creativity and the improvements themselves will come to a halt. The punishment can be outward, with a slap on the wrist, or by joking about it in a mock-serious mode or simply ignoring it. Those are all forms of negative reinforcement and soon enough will put out the creative fires you are trying to sustain as you work to create a fully engaged workforce. Some of the matters that destroy trust can have to do with the engagement activities themselves, such as Macey says here:

> "… trust (in the organization, the leader, the manager, or the team) is essential to increasing the likelihood that engagement behavior will be displayed. Trust becomes important even for intrinsically motivated behavior, as the conditions that contribute to the investment of self, require what Kahn (1990) identified as psychological safety. This is the belief people have that they will "not suffer for their personal engagement". One example of punishment

BUREAUCRACY – IT'S DOWNRIGHT UNHEALTHY

I recently had a discussion with a young man I am mentoring. Part of our discussion centered on his growing job dissatisfaction, which stemmed in large part from the fact that his job was rife with bureaucratic paperwork. We discussed how a bureaucracy did not foster autonomy, because you are doing most of it because you are told to and it always requires higher level reviews and approvals. It does not foster competency because, in his case, it was lots of forms and reports that no one even read. Nor did it foster relatedness, and most of it was meaningless work. In fact, a quick review will reveal that these are the four intrinsic needs and each one is being negatively affected. Well, if filling these needs leads to health and well-being … failing to fill these needs will deny the worker health and well-being. We ended our discussion with a question I had for him, "Do you want to work for a company that negatively affects your health and well-being".

I wonder how many managers ask that question as they create these policies, rules, procedures and red tape that make a bureaucracy … a bureaucracy.

for extending oneself is "job creep," where, "discretionary contributions become viewed as in-role obligations by supervisors and peers". Job creep does not yield trust, so it does not yield engagement behaviors. A second example would be performing above the norms of a group and then being socially punished as a rate buster".

(Macey, 2008)

Bad risk to reward ratio   That is the problem; the risk to reward ratio is not sufficient to spur the motivation to make improvements. When it comes to making improvements, the risk issue causes hesitation at the least and inaction at the worst. And the only thing that will make the risk to reward ratio acceptable is for those involved to know in their head – and in their heart – that they can make mistakes and be treated fairly, with reasonable mistakes taken in stride.

For anyone to take such a risk, they absolutely must trust those in charge … therefore,

- You cannot have engagement without kaizen activity
- You cannot have kaizens without using creativity and innovation
- Creative and innovative activity always introduces risk
- No one will take a risk unless they can expect to be treated fairly should it fail
- No one expects to be treated fairly unless they can trust those in charge …
- Hence, there is no engagement without trust …

Trust has litmus test power when it comes to engagement; there is no getting around this point.

How management shoots itself in the foot, damaging trust

Creating bureaucracy

When we are trying to get engagement, recall that one of the needs to fuel intrinsic motivation is the ability to relate with others (Chapter 12). Relating is being cared about and caring about others; it is all about relationships. A key element to all relationships is trust.

To the manager who wants to trust his people, it is necessary he trust them and that they be worthy of trust. When the trust is weak or lacking, the management team is forced to protect itself and the company by creating structure, rules and policies. These get in the way of creativity and innovation. Structure, rules and policies – beyond the minimum necessary – create bureaucracy, wiping out any hope for engagement as well as hindering productivity and profitability.

Acquisitions, spin offs, reductions in force and restructuring

These almost universally have a large negative effect on trust in the management by the worker. These are routinely handled very poorly from a human relations standpoint, focusing almost exclusively on the bottom line and are very unsettling to the workforce. The resultant lack of trust felt, by those who remain, is often long-standing and deep. These massive changes in the business are very hard to erase in people's minds. With careful, honest, sustained and serious work, fully using Hoshin Kanri planning, that trust that was lost can possibly be regained, if not totally, in part.

That takes me to reductions in force. Sometimes they are euphemistically called restructuring or rightsizing – they are neither. What they are, more often than not, is a crude way to try to correct a litany of management mistakes that were made over the years. Almost always, these are simply methods to reduce operating expense. In so doing, they simply treat the workforce as an expense to be minimized. If that is the case, admit it, don't do it again and work hard to get the trust back. It will take some time. If, on the other hand, you really believe the workforce is just an expense to be minimized, go forward but do not expect any engagement. Rather, with that belief, you have created an "every-man-for-himself" culture based on survival and you will most certainly have a Theory X culture and no more. But at least you will be honest.

Management bonuses

Even though the theme of this entire book is based on the power of intrinsic motivation, there is nothing intrinsic about bonuses. They are the poster child for extrinsic motivation and they are incredibly powerful in determining management actions. Let me give you just one example. In a recent engagement, I was assisting a company to implement a Lean Sigma program. I really don't like to do Lean Sigma programs, but it was an oil firm and I was writing a book on the oil industry at the time. We had been very successful in creating many large projects for the refinery green belts and black belts. With my refinery background, I was able to find several very attractive projects. I was amazed at the huge financial opportunities these managers had been blind to, but considering the inward-looking nature of the oil industry, in retrospect, it is not surprising. It was in early May that I approached the operations manager with these projects, as it was his job to nominate a "project sponsor" from the management team. As I presented the three projects in summary format, he listened intently and then said, "Those look great, but let's hold them until later in the year, November or December". I was a bit surprised and reiterated the earnings which were in the millions of dollars per month range and reminded him of such. As I recall, the potential earnings could easily have been $10,000,000 this year alone. He was nonplussed and said, and I quote, "The refinery has reached its maximum profitability for the year". I was stunned – I did not know what to say – I took a deep breath – I caught my composure and said, "Maximum profitability??? I do not even understand that concept, can you say some more about that?". At which he said, rather dispassionately and without hesitation, "Well, we have reached the maximum profitability improvement that is figured into the management's bonus equation, so let's just save these projects for next year. Maybe kick them off in November and assure next year's earnings". And, of course, he meant "as it applied to their bonus calculation".

It reminds me of the power of one adage which I routinely teach to management:

■ Tell me how a man is measured, and I will tell you how he will behave

Management distrust of other managers

In many companies which have done employee engagement and workplace health surveys, I often see a treatment of trust as an issue. When I first reviewed these surveys, I expected to find that the labor–management gap in trust would be the largest. I found this not to be true. Rather, more often than not, the greatest gap in trust is in managers not trusting other managers. This has an extremely toxic effect, as this distrust is telescoped down the power structure within a division. Pretty soon, supervisors from divisions that must cooperate, for example, maintenance and operations, simply have little trust or even respect for one another. When this happens, teamwork and engagement are only distant hopes.

Some unfortunate but real issues you'll need to address in creating trust

You'll start with skepticism as you try to change the culture

The paradigm of trust is a powerful business and personal concept. To effect a change, people will need to believe what they hear and what they see. They will need to believe that what they hear is the truth and what they see will persist over time. They need to believe that the management team will actually change – or they themselves will not change. Unfortunately for you, this is probably not the first culture-changing event they have seen. Likely they have seen the management team be very energized and seemingly very involved in the initial stages of an event, only to see that same energy and interest wither in the fullness of time. They will be skeptical.

You'll inherit trust issues due to prior culture-changing efforts that failed

If there are issues such as "the last Operational Excellence" program that failed, those issues need to be openly and honestly addressed by management. In addition, management needs to make sure they explain to everyone why the last improvement program did not work and what they intend to do differently so this one focused on creating a fully engaged workforce will work.

Trust, as a major problem … Some uniqueness

This is the fourth of the management feedback tools, and trust has some uniqueness that the others do not have.

- First, it is always the slowest to change. With a little thought, this makes sense because with low levels of trust, people will need to see if the promises that are made are honored in the fullness of time. Coupled with the "once burned, twice cautious" adage, we can understand why this is slow to change.
- Second, when people's trust has been damaged in the past, if you are in management, you must bear the brunt of the errors of your predecessors. Past efforts that have damaged trust, whether they are individual or collective, as in union bargaining, get attached to the entire company. Consequently, all the management, current and future, need to deal with them.

■ Third, if you are in second, third or higher levels of management, you must bear the brunt of all the errors of your subordinates as well. I personally have heard it a thousand times, and it goes like this. As a refinery manager, after discussing a personnel issue with one of my mechanics, said to me,
  – "Lonnie, I know I can trust you, but on the graveyard shift, I don't deal with you, I need to talk to Elmer and you know how old school and hardheaded he is. So, until Elmer changes, not much else will change; and I'm not holding my breath on that one".
If you are a CEO, everyone in the C-suite, all the regional VPs, all the general managers, all the plant managers, all their functional managers and especially all the first line supervisors can directly impact your trustworthiness. Well, in reality, they do not affect your trustworthiness; that is a function of your individual actions. But they do have a direct and strong effect on the "impact of your trustworthiness".

■ And fourth, largely due to the impacts of the first three listed above, there is no management trait that requires such a high degree of consistency if trust it to be maintained. The consistency will include consistency up and down the power structure, as well as across the power structure. All the players need to be consistent. It will require consistent actions in the easy times as well as the times of crisis. Nothing is the better test of values than a good crisis. A good crisis will separate the posers from the performers. Furthermore, all these supervisors and managers, working in harmony, will need to exhibit consistency over time. You have heard it said in a folksy way, "When I am right, no one remembers; when I am wrong, no one forgets". Such is the nature of promises made, promises kept and promises that are not kept.

What should management do about trust issues in their organizations

First and foremost, the management team will need to understand and accept the manifest importance of trust in the workplace. Second, the management team will need to accept that history is against them when it comes to getting trust from the workforce. Third, they will need to understand that what they say will not garner trust, not at all; only their actions will do that. Fourth, as a start, they need to adopt the six common behaviors listed earlier. Then they will need to repeat these six items over and over and over.

They will need to make each one of them a value statement to be practiced by all of management. Listen for it on your gemba walks, cultivate the issues that come up innocently or subconsciously. Attack all problems.

Be the role model by honoring all your commitments.

The power of positivity and the essence of good management feedback

So often we look at the negative side of a behavior, such as trust. On the other hand, it is often instructive to look at the positive side. In the case of the four key elements of feedback, when we do this we can readily see the "essence" of the power of each of these feedback dynamics. We will explore each.

- **Transparency**
  We need look no further than the concept of "flow" to see the manifest power of feedback on the individual. As I told you earlier, "any action you wish to see repeated, reward it". Well, there is no stronger reward than a system that tells you time and again, all day long, that "you have done well". The **essence is that it clearly and continually reinforces that you are competent and you are contributing, feeding the sense of meaningfulness.** This is the essence of the message of transparency.
- **Management "walking the talk"**
  This message is simple, direct and sweet. When management models the right behavior, when management "walks the talk", it says: I am on your side, I have your back, we will do this together. **The essence is the message of teamwork, relatedness and support.**
- **Trust**
  With trust, I know I can take a risk and try some new ideas. I can be creative and innovative. If I screw up, I will not be punished either physically or emotionally. This allows me to create and execute kaizens. The **essence of trust is that I can be autonomous, as well as creative.** With trust from my supervisor and trust from my management team, I can use all the skills I have.
- **Good supervision**
  I have a person who will support me. We are in a serious work relationship and I can count on you and you can count on me. By being a link to upper management, and their link to me, the supervisor is

strengthening that relationship as well. The supervisor plays many important roles to his workers, but the most powerful one, when it comes to engagement, is that he provides a contact who cares about him, and just as likely the worker cares about the supervisor. **That is the essence of relatedness.**

As you look over this list of the attributes that are supported by these four feedback systems, you will see that they are the four basic intrinsic needs of autonomy, competence, relatedness and meaningfulness. This is the precisely the reason these four feedback systems are so important in the creation of a fully engaged workforce.

Chapter Summary ... Executing the tactics and skills as outlined in Chapter 15 has gotten your workforce excited and energized and they are looking for more. This now must come from changes that the management team will need to make to keep the entire workforce "in the know" and to let them be aware that the management team itself is engaged. We covered the typical feedback that is supplied and compared this to what is actually needed, including the Five Supervisory Tools. Beyond that, there are four types of management feedback, which are: First, to build, use and manage a visual feedback system, a system of transparency; second, there are three other feedback systems that have no scoreboards and are not visible but are strictly behaviors of the management team that must be practiced consistently and include the need for management to "walk the talk" (that is, they must behave as they expect others to behave), the need for supervisors in particular to give strong, timely and productive feedback; third, the need for cultivating not just a relationship with the entire workforce but a trusting relationship; and finally, we wrapped up the chapter with a discussion of how the four types of management feedback can develop a strong positive atmosphere that will foster engagement in the workplace.

What's next?? What about improving our system? Learn about the RES "knob" and about the Five High Leverage Points (HLP), the HLP Grid and how you can use all these things to further improve your engagement system.

IMPROVING ENGAGEMENT

In this section we discuss how to put all to use, all that we have learned up to this point. We will introduce you to a method, so you can improve your engagement system and in particular how to find and exploit the "high leverage points" and show how you can use them to calculate your Residual Engagement Strength (RES). Next we will explain how you can improve your engagement levels and how you can put together an action plan with the three steps of preparation; execution and improve. We will end this part, and the book itself, with some final thoughts.

Part VI contains three chapters:

Chapter 17

Engagement and Your RES

Aim of this Chapter ... is to introduce you to a method so you can improve your engagement system and, in particular, how to find and exploit the "control parameters". In systems language, these control parameters are called "High Leverage Points" (HLPs). We will explain how you can use HLPs to improve your system of employee engagement. We will explain how to calculate your Residual Engagement Strength (RES), and then by reviewing two case studies, we will demonstrate how you can use your RES as a problem solving tool to improve employee engagement.

Improving engagement

While operating a process, it is very convenient to have "knobs" to turn so you can adjust the process. For example, if you want the heat on your oven to increase from 350°F to 400°F, you simply go to the correct knob and adjust it to get the desired result. When you want your car to speed up, you press the accelerator pedal. Well, unfortunately, when we wish to "adjust" some aspects of human relations such as morale, loyalty or engagement, their "knobs" are not so straightforward.

But wouldn't it be nice if we had such a knob?

There are hundreds of such variables (knobs) that can influence engagement. Unfortunately, most of these variables have very little impact. It just so happens that by study and analysis we have found five that are very influential. And by influential, I mean: that for any given amount of input (change on our part), we will get a substantial amount of output (increased engagement of the workforce). In systems jargon, we call these High Leverage Points, and they are:

1. kaizen activity;
2. system transparency;
3. management walking the talk;
4. good supervisory feedback; and
5. trust in management.

You will recall that kaizen activity was the "trigger" to the Intrinsic Motivational Loop. The other four items are the four types of management feedback we discussed in Chapter 16. The engagement model, updated with these five High Leverage points, is shown in Figure 17.1.

"Turning the knobs" – Simple to discuss, but a little more complicated to do

HIGH LEVERAGE POINTS – WHY FIVE? WHY NOT SIX?

You may recall that I called inquisitiveness and integration the most powerful management trait. So why is it not an HLP also? Good question, and I knew you would ask it; that's why I wrote this sidebar. I would have included it as the sixth HLP, but, try as I may, I was not able to quantify it. In a couple of models, I got close, but I found I was not able to separate its pure value from its interactions. You see, it had a positive effect on the other five. It got really complicated, and I recall some advice I once received on modeling … simpler is better … as long as it is equally useful. Recall the advice of Stuart Hunter when he said, "All models are wrong, some are useful". Well this model has served me – but I know it can be improved. So when you are ready and have some data to share, give me a call and we will, together, improve this one.

Now if we can "turn these knobs" in the right direction, we can influence engagement. Well, it's not quite so simple as that, because the "turning of the knob" is often a process in itself, with the need to change many aspects of the business, especially the need to change management behavior. We have discussed each of these "knobs" and the process behind them, in detail, in Chapters 15 and 16. So please be mindful that although the Residual Engagement Strength, which we will discuss in a moment, is a simple equation, getting there is very complicated. It is not only complicated, it is effortful, but it can be done, and the results more than justify the effort involved.

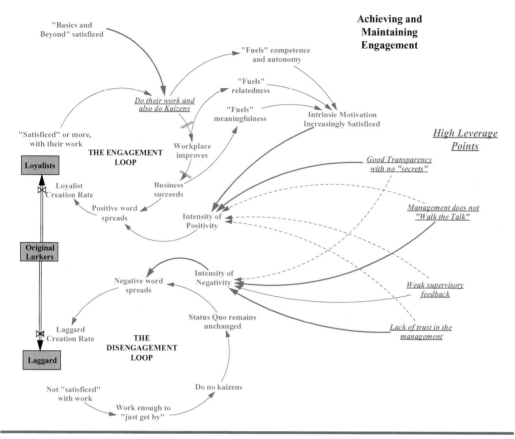

Figure 17.1   **The engagement model.**

The "key knob"

We have found five "knobs" and each has a process of its own with some unique characteristics. If you can properly manage these five knobs and turn them in the right direction, you can influence the levels of engagement at your facility. These five knobs are inter-related in an equation which results in one "key knob", I call it the Residual Engagement Strength, RES. Adjust the RES knob by increasing its value and it is very likely that engagement will improve.

We have empirically determined the relationship of RES to engagement, and it is shown in Figure 17.2. Here, each data point represented by an alpha character represents the value of a given plant. You will note some data points have a numeric component; that represents yearly evaluation of that plant. You will note that the data on the far left, with very low engagement values, are the Bottom Seven (firms AD through AI), and likewise, those on the top right are the Top Seven (firms A through G), which were discussed in Chapter one.

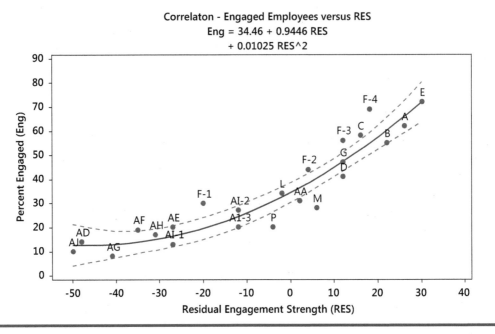

Figure 17.2 Correlation of RES with employee engagement.

The line of regression on the graph is the dark, solid, central line. The formula at the top of the graph is the equation of this line. This line of regression is flanked by two dashed lines which represent the 95% confidence interval for the line of regression. And you can see that a full 30% of the data falls outside these confidence limits. Normally, this would not be good; however, since we are typically working to improve engagement levels that start in the 25% range with the goal of achieving 70%, given this huge window of opportunity, the level of confidence is robust enough.

The purpose of most correlations is for their use as predictors. This correlation is no different. It is designed to guide you to answer the question:

> "If we want to improve employee engagement, which HLP should we work on?"

What is the meaning of this correlation??

This correlation is designed to be a model of "how to improve engagement". The great statistician Stuart Hunter once said, "All models are wrong, some are useful". So I am sure the model I will show you here is wrong. However, I have tested it many times and have found it to be useful when working to improve employee engagement.

The concept of the Residual Engagement Strength

In the system of engagement, there are always two forces at work. The first one is the engagement loop, whose purpose is to increase engagement. However, balancing the engagement loop is the disengagement loop. It is working to force disengagement. These two loops are fighting each other by trying to get employees, mostly the Lurkers, to join their ranks. The engagement loop is working to make Lurkers become engaged and join the ranks of the Loyalists, while the disengagement loop is working to encourage Lurkers to become disengaged and join the ranks of the Laggards. The more powerful loop will win in the long run, and the force creating this flow is called the Residual Engagement Strength, or RES.

The RES is a driving force creating a net flow. It does not imply anything like one-way flow. When changes occur that alter the value of the RES, that does not imply there will be a flow in that direction only. Quite the contrary; since the entire system is striving for some type of dynamic equilibrium, workers will flow from any stock to any other stock. However, as the RES gets larger, that will favor a flow to increase the levels of engagement and cause a net increase of Loyalists. On the other hand, should the RES become smaller, this will act to decrease the levels of engagement and cause a net increase in Laggards. The entire system of engagement looks like Figure 17.3.

We have completed the entire engagement model with the addition of the concept to show how Laggards can become New Lurkers and likewise how Loyalists can become disenchanted and join the ranks of the New Lurkers and possibly become Laggards.

Calculating the Residual Engagement Strength (RES)

The RES is a function of the strength of the engagement loop (S_{EL}) added to the strength of the disengagement loop (S_{DL}).

$$RES = S_{EL} + S_{DL}$$

The equations for the strength of the engagement loop, S_{EL}, and the disengagement loop, S_{DL}, are:

- S_{EL} = P*K* (sum of the positive HLP feedback values)
- S_{DL} = N*(sum of the negative HLP feedback values)

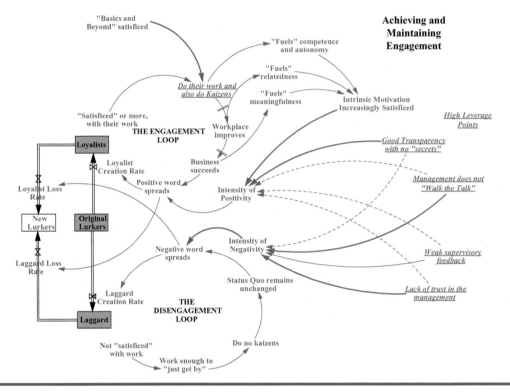

Figure 17.3 The entire engagement system.

- P = strength of positivity, a constant, 1.0
- N = strength of negativity, a constant 4.0
- K = strength of the kaizen factor
- Other HLPs are graphed on the High Leverage Point Grid. The greyed in areas show the range of the values for the High Leverage Points (Figure 17.4).

Getting the data for the HLP Grid

The HLP Grid is designed to give a graphic picture of the strength and relative impact of the five HLPs. Only the kaizen factor is always positive; all others have both positive and negative potential. Whenever a value is positive, it will work to augment engagement. Conversely, if a value is negative, it will always work to increase disengagement.

When we are looking to improve employee engagement, we will want to find those HLPs that will create the greatest impact. If the value of the HLP is on the far left of any shaded area in any HLP, it is a likely candidate

High Leverage Point Grid														
HLP	Range of Values													
	-6	-5	-4	-3	-2	-1	0	1	2	3	4	5	6	7
Kaizen														
Transparency														
Walk the talk														
Supervision														
Trust														

Figure 17.4   **The HLP Grid, blank.**

for process improvement. You will see the dynamics of this when we go through the examples later in this chapter.

The kaizen factor

The kaizen factor is one of the more powerful factors in the RES equation, and you will note it is a multiplier.

The data for the kaizen factor chart is straightforward (Figure 17.5). Calculate the average number of kaizen submitted each month. In most situations, you will quickly find that 90–95% of them are actually completed, so don't worry about the number *actually completed*. Early on, people worry about this, but if the "Basics and Beyond" are done well, you **will not find** many frivolous or irrelevant kaizens. If and when frivolous and irrelevant kaizens appear, it is a clear sign that the "Beyond the Basics" have not been done well or have lost their traction, and that should be addressed immediately.

Calculating the transparency factor

Transparency is not just having the information present, but in addition:

■ it must be in the right place, readily visible to the relevant people;
■ it must be kept current; and
■ it must pass the "scoreboard effect" test.

That is, if the question is "are we producing to plan?", by looking at the element of transparency **you must be able to answer that question in**

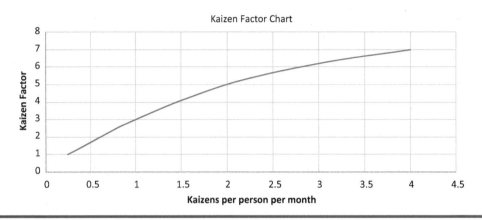

Figure 17.5   The kaizen factor calculation.

two seconds. When you enter a football game, for example, you can look at the scoreboard and you can tell in 2 seconds who is winning and who is losing and how badly. By looking at the clock on the scoreboard, you can quickly calculate if the losing team has a chance to catch up. It only takes two seconds.

For the factory floor, and especially for the performance of the work cell (or workstation) and its workers, the most important information is the information that is required to be at the cell itself, in the line of sight of the worker and always current. There are other trend indicators that are not needed on an hour-by-hour basis that can be kept at an "Information Center". This Information Center should be near the cell and on a well-traveled walkway, like on a normal path to the lunchroom, for example.

Information at the cell, in the worker's line of sight

1. **Does the worker have the tools, materials and information immediately available to him, so he can properly execute his duties?** For tools, this is frequently done with shadow boards and place labels. For materials, this is frequently a Kanban system. And for instructions, this often comes in a routing slip or kit package. For highly repetitive tasks, instructions are often not necessary. The work schedule, including a training plan, needs to be at the cell. If all this information is present and current, a value of 1.5 is scored. If some is missing, appropriate deductions are made and kaizens are submitted to correct them. (Maximum value 1.5)

2. **Is the cell producing at the correct cycle time and producing the proper mix?** This is normally done with a "production-by-hour" (PBH)

board which not only tracks hourly production but accumulates the values to show if production is on plan; it is normally filled in by the team leader. A heijunka board can also provide the same information. However, a PBH is often a whiteboard and provides additional information. If you have all this information and the board is kept current, score 1.0. If it is not current, the score is 0; no partial credit here, this is the key motivating factor to the cell workers. If a whiteboard or its equivalent is used, there should be a place for operators to write important comments such as equipment needing maintenance, problem solving that

MAKING YOUR OWN SURVEY

As a consultant, I have made and evaluated hundreds of surveys for a number of topics, including workplace health, customer satisfaction and, of course, engagement. Even though I have a strong background in statistics, I found a simple little book that helped my customers prepare, evaluate and even statistically validate their surveys, if they so wish. The book is *Measuring Customer Satisfaction* (1992) by Bob Hayes. It can be understood by anyone in your facility who understands statistical process control (SPC) for example. I know this will rankle some of my consultant friends, but making the survey perfect is a distant second, or third or fourth, to sharing and acting on the data.

is underway, kaizens they propose or other forms of communications. If this communications concept is present, add another 0.5 point. If the production data is transmitted via computer onto a terminal, even if it is real-time data, subtract 0.5. It is no longer "my data" and I am not sure I can own it. (Maximum value of 1.5)

3. **Is the produced quality good?** If there is a lot of rework or scrap, a special quality board should be used, very similar to the PBH board. It should be filled in by the team leader. If, however, scrap is only a couple of pieces per shift, "Red Containers" should be used to accumulate scrap. The team leader should check these hourly and respond accordingly. If the quality information present in the cell is data that has been sent in earlier, manipulated by the computer and returned to show up on a spreadsheet or a computer screen, score 0.0; this is not real-time information (Maximum value 1.0)

4. **Is the worker getting the support he needs to handle the unusual situation?** For example, a machine might need some special

maintenance or the parts that were delivered had defective units. Under these circumstances and others, the worker needs a system so he can get the support, normally resources, he needs, right now, and remain at his workplace and still be able to produce. Typically, this is covered with an andon system of some type. Another benefit of the andon system is to signify any safety concern. Having the andon system is only half the equation; unless there is a support system to respond to the andon, the score will be zero. (Maximum value 0.5)

5. **Is there a 3 minute, standup, start-of-shift meeting?** Although technically this is not an element of transparency, it provides the team leader and the cell workers an opportunity to address the four items above and any issues they see prior to shift start. In addition, this short meeting allows the team lead, or supervisor, to advise the cell workers of any unusual circumstances. (Maximum value 0.5)

Information at the Information Center

6. At the plant Information Center, there should be information that is not needed today but is useful to track progress. Here we should include all the trend data such as monthly production, plan completion, costs, profits, productivity, quality, safety, upcoming projects and other pertinent value stream and plant information. There should be routine meetings at the information center, run by either the supervisor or management. If the information center has this information and it is conveyed in routine meetings available to all, then the worker can answer the question "is my workplace improving and is our business succeeding?" The key information must be present, up to date, and meetings that include a Q&A format must be routinely held. (Maximum score 0.75)

Getting the value for transparency

To get the value for transparency as a High Leverage Point, you simply add up the values obtained from the six items outlined above. However, do not fail to recognize that although this factor has little downside, there is some. Make no mistake, a lack of system transparency has a negative impact. Sum up the six items and add them to -1.0. That is your score to plot on the HLP Grid. For example, if the sum of the six items was 5.2, you add that to -1.0 and the plotted value would be a rather healthy 4.2.

Calculating: Management walking the talk;
supervisory feedback strength; and trust

Keep in mind that to get this far, you, of course, will need a completed engagement survey such as the Utrecht Work Engagement Survey (UWES). If you have the UWES, the Gallup Q^{12} or any validated engagement survey, that is very good. Since the correlation of both metrics to engagement is very strong, these surveys will work just fine. Recall that most companies have engagement values in the 25% range and we want to reach 70%. With this huge "window of opportunity", you really don't need a very sharp knife, so to speak. If you have a survey you have already used, the continuity of the survey will allow sound comparisons of past results; this is far more important, at this point, than being "engagement pure". Consequently, it is very likely that from your current survey you can extract questions that focus on these three HLPs: management walking the talk; trust; and supervisory feedback strength. If you do not have these data in your current survey database, you could either add this to your survey or do a separate survey (see sidebar), addressing just those issues. Most surveys use the Likert 5-point or 7-point scale, to normalize them to the HLP Grid, simply make a linear conversion.

For the two case studies discussed later in this chapter, in addition to the basic engagement survey, we created a smaller survey, to address the issues of management walking the talk, trust and supervisory strength. These surveys were tailored to each specific company and followed up by individual interviews of a large cross-section of the workforce, as well as a critical review of leader standard work (LSW) which gives insights into supervisory activity and floor presence. The LSW review was particularly insightful.

Plotting data on the High Leverage Point Grid (Figure 17.6)

The RES calculation

- RES= S_{EL}+ S_{DL}
- S_{EL} = 1*3.4* (4.2 + 1.8) = 20.4 (1 is the relative power of positivity, 3.4 is the kaizen factor, 4.2 for transparency, 1.8 for supervision)
- S_{DL} = 4 *[(-3.1) + (-1)] = -16.4 (4 is the relative power of negativity, -3.1 for walking the talk, -1.0 for trust)
- RES = S_{EL}+ S_{DL} = 20.4 + (-16.4) = 4.0
- You will note this is the data point on F-2 in Figure 17.2 and:
  – The predicted level of engagement was 39%
  – The measured level of engagement was 44%

High Leverage Point Grid														
HLP	Range of Values													
	-6	-5	-4	-3	-2	-1	0	1	2	3	4	5	6	7
Kaizen										3.4				
Transparency											4.2			
Walk the talk			-3.1											
Supervision								1.8						
Trust					-1.0									

Figure 17.6   HLP Example with data entered, (this is the data for Point F-2 in Figure 17.2 above).

Two case studies

Case study no. 1 – Early gains and then loss of management focus and support, Company AI

Background

While working with a client wishing to have "a fully engaged workforce", one of the focus areas was their assembly operations. To evaluate progress in engagement, we utilized a self-report engagement study that was given and tracked over a 3-year period. Also, of particular financial and capacity importance to the client was labor productivity in their labor-intensive assembly operations. To measure this, we chose a large assembly to benchmark, as it was produced several times per year. This allowed us to acquire data, labor productivity, which could be compared over time. They were curious to see if labor productivity would track with engagement levels.

This was a firm well over 30 years old. It had a strong but very inflexible culture with many dysfunctions. Average seniority exceeded 20 years and there were many "old hands". Much earlier, the company had created a significant technological advantage that gave them a huge economic advantage over their competition. The tales of past earnings and bonuses were impressive indeed. They rode this technological advantage for many years, making few if any improvements in work processes or investment in either people or equipment. Over time, the competition caught up. Not only did the competition catch up but it passed them. It became obvious that changes needed to be made, and the board finally made changes in the senior leadership. Soon, new senior management was hired, and they made many changes in personnel and some relatively minor process changes. However, little was done to change the culture. This is where we get involved; we were hired to begin the transformation to a lean operating system. It was obvious to us, at a glance, that engagement levels were very low. I did simple productivity studies and found that productivity in the 15-20% range was typical. The place was a physical mess with no apparent flow and little organization. Morale was low: there were many personnel conflicts, job execution at many levels was hard to evaluate and there were many personnel problems. It was equally obvious that their supervisory concept was virtually non-existent.

We do the initial engagement survey in 2015 .. and act

We completed the first survey in 2015. The data were statistically analyzed and a report was forwarded to the management team. Together with the management team, we formulated a plan for feedback and created several small projects focused on supervisory support and development. This plan was in turn discussed with the supervisors, and they were given training (role-playing sessions) on how to explain the survey and its findings. Then, feedback was given promptly to the employees, directly from their supervisors in small group meetings with the opportunity for dialogue. In addition to the supervisory development, the management created several small projects to improve the engagement. Over the next 12 months, the supervisory development continued and the small projects were attended to. My interviews showed there was a new level of enthusiasm in the plant as for the first time in a long time, the supervisors were paying attention to the rank and file workers. We anxiously awaited the 2016 survey.

The 2016 survey results were very positive

During the previous year, it was obvious we were making headway. The improvement in the general attitude and attention to work was palpable. Not only could I sense the engagement levels were up but many morale problems diminished as well. We also had hard data that confirmed we were making progress on labor productivity. Predictably, the survey results in 2016 showed a significant increase in engagement from a paltry 16% to an industry-average-like value of 27%. This was widely celebrated and publicized. That quarter, the facility enjoyed its largest bonus in 8 years and everyone was on a high.

Then the management team loses its way …

However, after the 2016 survey, follow-up actions by the management team was much different. There was no plan created to improve the areas of opportunity found during the survey. Management gave the supervisors quick feedback and advised them to share the results with the team. Unlike the previous year, there was no plan, no supervisory training, no action items and little fanfare about the survey. They seemed satisfied to bask in the results from the prior year and were more interested in other items. They did little. After several months had transpired, and not one supervisor had discussed the survey results with his employees, the regional VP had a company-wide meeting where he explained the results of the survey. It was both a well-attended and a well-intended effort – but it was too little and too late. This sent an unmistakable message to the workforce, and the results showed in the 2017 survey. During the year, you could feel the "air come out of the balloon", and in the 2017 survey, engagement dropped to 20%, well below the 27% achieved the year earlier. Once again, the management team did nothing with the 2017 results. We were soon to part company with this firm. If you look at Figure 17.2, you will see these data; they are points AI-1, AI-2 and AI-3.

The results of the engagement data

What is the significance of these data? The key was that engagement rose from a low of 16% in 2015 to 27% in 2016 and then dropped to 20% in 2017. It was also significant that the percentage of "actively disengaged" dropped from 38% to 32% then rose back to 37%. In addition, there was an 84% participation in the 2015 data and only 72% participation in the 2017 survey (Figure 17.7). It was clear the workforce was disenchanted. I suspect the percentage of "actively disengaged" would have risen had more people participated in the 2017 survey. The workforce response was a direct result of the actions – and lack of actions – by the management team.

What about the labor productivity data??

They had a large assembly which they would produce as many as 12 times per year, which we were using to track labor productivity. This provided us with great trend data, and these data turned out to be representative of the cultural response as well.

In 2015 the average number of manhours to complete this assembly was 984 hours. In 2016 the average manhours had dropped to 708 (Figure 17.8). This was due to a concerted effort to improve labor productivity, well beyond the work earlier mentioned, that was specifically associated with the engagement effort. We were improving many aspects of this labor-intensive task, including materials ordering, materials delivery

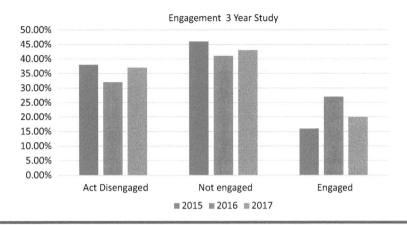

Figure 17.7   3-year case study results.

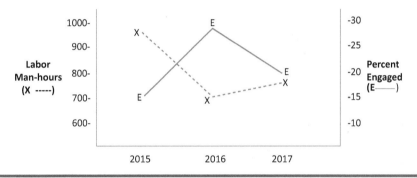

Figure 17.8   Engagement impact on labor productivity.

and work cell support. Hence, we were not surprised to see the data drop as we progressed through 2016, and at the end of the year, we averaged 708 hours. However, to our surprise, the time to make this assembly in calendar year 2017 rose to over 750 hours. The surprising part was that the improvements during 2016 had been continued and there was little reason to believe this assembly would take longer. Certainly, there was no technical reason for the increase, as all process improvements remained in place and others were added. Yet they did. The time to increase can only be explained by a change in the attitude of the workers, which was obvious as based on observations.

The engagement and the productivity numbers track almost perfectly. When engagement made a large improvement, so did labor productivity; and when engagement dropped a small portion, labor productivity did as well, confirming the trend we discussed in Part 1.

What I learned from this case study

Although these data, in volume, do not compare to the Gallup database, I was able to observe the plant operation during this period. During that time, we not only executed many projects to improve plant operations, we also gathered other information, including both formal and informal time studies and audits. In addition, I make it a practice to frequently interview employees. Each year before the survey is distributed, I made predictions based on these other parameters which I had gathered each year. My predictions were very accurate.

As to the direct question, "What did I learn from this study". Other than the specific results for this firm, the answer is I learned nothing new. However, it reinforced, what I already knew.

- If you wish to improve a business metric, first you must measure it
- Improvements in engagement will only occur if management is directly involved
- Improving engagement will improve other business metrics
- The supervisor is the key member to achieving worker engagement
- Working directly with and assisting people will improve engagement; ignoring them or treating them poorly, will hurt engagement
- And about 100 other things

Case study no. 2 – Engagement improvement done well, Company F

Year one – Baseline survey

Company F had started a lean transformation 2 years ago. They had decided to embark on an effort to improve employee engagement. They had completed their first engagement survey and were not quite sure how to proceed from there. Their internal lean consultant contacted us; this is where we started with them. The first engagement survey, done recently, showed they had 30% engaged employees (F-1 on the graph in Figure 17.2). It was an internally created survey and we were skeptical of the 30% value; our data would have predicted a lower value. But that is where we started. Since the all-manufacturing average, as advertised by Gallup, was 25%, we were not starting in a bad place. The facility goal was to exceed 65% engaged employees, so there was a lot to do. We analyzed their data, created an HLP Grid (see Figure 17.9) and completed a number of employee interviews.

High Leverage Point Grid														
HLP	Range of Values													
	-6	-5	-4	-3	-2	-1	0	1	2	3	4	5	6	7
Kaizen								1.3						
Transparency											3.4			
Walk the talk		-4.0												
Supervision						0.8								
Trust				-2.6										

Figure 17.9 **HLP Grid, Baseline data.**

Year one – Action plan

The data we found most compelling was the extremely low kaizen factor. Accordingly, we focused primarily on "the Basics and Beyond". The first thing we did was implement a training program based on Training Within Industries (TWI) methods. At the same time, we converted the management by objective (MBO) planning and goals system and adapted it to the Hoshin Kanri model. Later in the year, we implemented leader standard work for all supervisors, starting with the CEO.

Year one – Results

By the end of the year, all three improvement plans were mature and showing gains. We had made progress. Interviews and interactions during the year showed a significant change of attitude in the workforce. Employee attrition had dropped from a rate of 9%/year at the beginning of the year and had trended down to 4%/year. They had initiated operator-led kaizen activity as part of their lean program 3 years earlier, but now it really took off. The hard work on the Basics and Beyond had paid dividends and were evident by the sizable improvement in the kaizen factor. Kaizens had improved from 0.3 kaizens per person per month to 1.2, a four-fold improvement, and the quality of the kaizens improved as well. Supervision had been a relatively strong point, but now they felt a new level of management support. Not surprisingly, the score assigned to supervisory abilities rose, probably due to the strong training focus. Both walking the talk and trust rose, either sympathetically or possibly the workforce was convinced the management team was serious and responded appropriately. Talk on the cultural

High Leverage Point Grid															
HLP	Range of Values														
	-6	-5	-4	-3	-2	-1	0	1	2	3	4	5	6	7
Kaizen											3.4			
Transparency												4.2		
Walk the talk				-3.1										
Supervision									1.8					
Trust					-1.3									

Figure 17.10 **HLP Grid, Survey beginning of year two.**

network was increasingly positive and there was a new-found energy in the plant. People were smiling.

And it showed in the engagement survey. Our year two survey showed engagement had improved to 44%, a full 14% improvement, validating the hard work. Not surprisingly, many other factors had improved, including facility quality, morale and employee retention. After 1 year, the HLP Grid looked like Figure 17.10.

Year two – Action plans

Again, we analyzed the survey data and interviewed employees at all levels. Guided by these data and the HLP Grid, the management team reached consensus. All the actions listed below were incorporated in the HK planning process and one key metric added to the list of HK Key Metrics, was "% Employee Engagement".

■ First, we instituted a maintenance plan for all ten of the Basics and Beyond. Even though the kaizen factor improved markedly, the team felt we needed to do more in the area of HK planning and communications of the plan. Earlier, we had quarterly feedback meetings with the workforce. We had received a lot of positive feedback and decided to improve that further. We converted to bi-monthly meetings, adding two feedback sessions each year.

■ The obvious place to improve was in getting management to better "walk the talk".

- We started out by having roundtable discussions on "going to the gemba" using the "go see – ask why – show respect" model. We wanted to distinguish this management learning experience from the typical floor walks which are designed to "find what is wrong and fix it". We also had training sessions, including many sessions of role-playing to emphasize the "management learning" rather than "critique and repair" that is so typical of management visits to the floor. Included in this were training sessions on questioning and listening.
- An important aspect of management improving "walking the talk" was to get the manager to become more aggressive in doing kaizens in their areas of expertise
- The normal interviews highlighted a problem we had previously missed. Although the supervisors had a very impressive score of +1.8, we found they needed to focus on career planning for their subordinates. We modified our plan and initiated 5-Year Developmental Planning, starting at the CEO
- In addition, we found the maintenance manager, the planning manager and several of their supervisors were drowning in paperwork and simply did not have time to go to the gemba very often. We decided we needed to reorganize the production floor. We planned to install the system of team leaders.

Year two – Results

Year two was both a joy and a large source of frustration. It was a joy because the plant was a much more pleasant place to work. Workers seemed more content. With much more information and far better communications all around, tensions were down. Earlier there had been many blowups, particularly between management and the floor workers and even at management meetings. These and other forms of conflict seemed to diminish. Like I said, it was just more pleasant. The presence of management on the floor, to just observe and learn was obvious. At first, there was a certain curiosity by the rank and file, as this was a significant change. But later it became a non-issue as it became more routine. In addition, although cautiously and very slowly, the managers started implementing kaizens for their systems. The first one was a critique and change to the HK planning system. Also, the maintenance manager instituted several kaizens to reduce the paperwork for his supervisors. These were two examples, but several managers did not even have one to show. Nonetheless, things were beginning to change. Our engagement levels rose from 44% to 56% a nice improvement.

It was frustrating because we had not made as much progress with the management team changing their behavior as we had hoped for. Our interview data suggested that we might not show much improvement in this area. Looking at the plan for this year, virtually all efforts were focused on improvements among the supervisors and managers, and they were changing slower than we had hoped for. There was not the same "level of change" we felt in year one, although plant metrics of quality, delivery, build to schedule, employee retention and cost containment continued to improve. Since many systems were slow in changing, the entire effort lagged, and as a result we did not get to implement the team leader concept, a large item we needed. We were skeptical that the survey may not show much improvement. So, like I said, we were more than pleased to see the improvement to 56%. Some, like me, were surprised the improvement was so large; it simply did not feel that way as we progressed through the year.

However, after 2 years, the engagement levels had improved to a rather healthy 56% and are the results shown on the HLP Grid in Figure 17.11.

The explanation of year two results:

■ Although the focus of the entire year was on walk the talk, it did not rise much: Note that in walk the talk, the first year we improved by 0.9 units, yet we had no targeted action items to accomplish this gain. When we did focus on it in year two, after considerable effort we only rose by 0.7 units. Even though we had no items targeted directly for management change, in year one, the management team provided a

High Leverage Point Grid														
HLP	Range of Values													
	-6	-5	-4	-3	-2	-1	0	1	2	3	4	5	6	7
Kaizen												4.6		
Transparency												4.1		
Walk the talk				-2.4										
Supervision								1.6						
Trust					-1.1									

Figure 17.11 **HLP Grid, Survey beginning year three.**

great deal of both leadership and support to entire engagement effort. It is not as if they were absent; quite the contrary, they were very involved and supportive. Upon reflection, we also felt that the first year was such a change – a large positive change – virtually everything improved sympathetically.

- On the other hand, this year we did little to improve the Basics and Beyond, yet we were pleased to see the large improvements in kaizen activity. Kaizens rose from 1.2 to 1.7 kaizens per person per month. Possibly the effort to provide maintenance for the Basics and Beyond focused attention on this. On the other hand, we have seen this often. That is, once the intrinsic needs of autonomy, competence, relatedness and meaningfulness are satisfied, they tend to increase of their own accord – consistent with the theory of intrinsic motivation.
- Supervisory feedback took a small hit. This could easily be just random variation, or it could be that we had a project to implement the team leader concept but were not able to get this done; that could have affected this value.
- Trust in management rose a small amount. Probably due to the management presence on the floor. Or it might be just noise, but nice to see none the less.

We reflected on why we were so worried we might not be making progress. Simply put, we just did not "feel" the same change had occurred during year two. Part of this might be just mathematics. When you change from 30% to 44%, relatively that is almost a 50% improvement. When you then change from 44% to 56%, relatively that is around 25%. So while the absolute change (14% vs 12%) is very close, relatively, the change in year two is only half what we saw in year one. Also, our expectations simply may have been too high. Make no mistake, the bottom-line issue was that for the second year in a row, engagement had improved by double digits. We had just improved to 56%, and for that we felt good. We were pleased.

Year three – Action plans

An uncomfortable reflection   A review of both the first- and second-year plans led us to believe that we had exaggerated expectations of management's ability to change. This was discussed directly with the management team in a group format. Although they spent considerable time trying to justify the slowness of their change, our consulting firm was not convinced. However, this is not unusual. We normally find the rank and file are both more able to and more willing to change. Interestingly, the reason they are more able to change is precisely that they are more willing. This conclusion was not met with full acceptance but was not rejected totally either. It was an interesting, if not comfortable discussion. However, the net effect was that the management team seemed somewhat more flexible as we put the third-year plan together.

The plan

Prior to making the plan, in addition to our interviews, the management team wanted to perform their own employee interviews. They decided that each manager would interview five employees, all from other divisions. We felt this was an excellent idea and facilitated the process. Not only that, once completed the managers were amazed with the feedback as being both insightful and helpful. We combined their information with ours. Following this, we put together the year three plan, which had only three items. They were largely repeaters from the year two plan. Following our "uncomfortable reflection", they decided that "just maybe" some of the items in the year two plan had not been given enough effort and they wanted to improve upon what they had done. These items were:

- Complete the implementation of the team leader concept
- Increase manager's time at the gemba with more coaching on how to "go see – ask why? – show respect" and add a kamishibai system (routine management audits).
- Increased kaizen activity by the management team.

Year three – Results

While year two was both a joy and a frustrating event, year three was fun. Not only were all employees more content, they were more confident. The plant took on a whole new air of cooperation. Nearly all metrics improved, and the plant had its best safety year. Several customers commented on the cultural change during their visits; it was obvious to everyone. The increased presence of management on the floor showed clear results. At first, there was a certain curiosity by the rank and file as this was a significant change; later, they clearly began to appreciate it. The team leader concept allowed the supervisors to spend more time supervising, and now we had the team leaders to give even greater support to the line workers. In all the interviews, it seemed the common item was that floor workers saw that managers were just more engaged, and many management systems were

High Leverage Point Grid														
HLP	Range of Values													
	-6	-5	-4	-3	-2	-1	0	1	2	3	4	5	6	7
Kaizen								1.3 ———————→				5.1		
Transparency										3.4→4.0				
Walk the talk			-4.0 —————→			-1								
Supervision								0.8→1.4						
Trust				-3 ———→		-1.0								

Figure 17.12 **HLP Grid, Survey ending year 3 (starting points and year 3 values).**

improving as well. These included better scheduling, making the plant more predictable, as well as improved support from several staff functions. Even HR had several kaizens they could point to. We had created a culture of continuous improvement.

Employee engagement had risen to a very robust 69% and exceeded our stated goal of 65%. The results shown on the HLP Grid are shown in Figure 17.12.

Summarizing the progress of Company F

Overall engagement and benefits   The level of employee engagement had risen from a very average 30% to a very robust 69%. Meanwhile, every plant performance metric improved as well; that is no surprise. Not only did quality, delivery, employee retention, morale and safety performance improve but all the financials improved as well. The engagement effort provided a shot in the arm to the lean transformation, and the plant, as you might expect, prospered.

Kaizen activity had been initiated in their lean transformation 2 years before our arrival. However, it had not realized any traction. It took a focused effort on the "Basics and Beyond" to catalyze the kaizen activity. Before that improvement, considering all the effort expended on the lean initiative, the facility was averaging a modest 0.3 kaizens/person/month. From that point forward, they quadrupled their improvement activity in the first year alone. Then over the next two years, they increased the number of kaizens around 2.3 kaizens/person/month with many workers averaging one per week. This increase in kaizen activity occurred intrinsically as the engagement effort was focused on all parts of the plant.

Transparency   As part of their lean effort, they started off with a good system of transparency, and they had the right concept and were using it to distinguish "normal" from "abnormal" as they problem solved. Their system was good enough to provide the type of feedback necessary to support engagement.

Walk the talk   This was a significant problem from day one. The lean effort had this issue as well. The management team felt that engagement was a "worker thing" (Paradigm Shift No. 1B, Chapter 15). It took more than 1 year and considerable effort to convince them that it required more than management effort to make the system of engagement work; it would also take management engagement. Once that connection was made, progress was strong. It is not too difficult to raise the engagement levels the first 10 or 15%. But to go beyond that, and to sustain those levels, it is imperative that management not only lead the effort but they must engage themselves. This is not commonly understood and was not understood here. Once it was both understood and accepted, progress was strong and predictable.

Supervision   This facility had a strong supervisory ethic. They started strong before we arrived and maintained high values throughout. Our efforts to help them install the team leader concept not only strengthened their current position but provided greater training and support to the cell workers as well.

Trust   This plant had a mid-range level of trust between workers and managers. During this effort, progress was made on this metric, and there are still improvements to be made. The problem with this metric is that it is a lagging response and people are very reluctant to be trustful of any management. It is a metric that is hard to improve and with even a little negativity will quickly regress to former lower levels.

What's next for Company F and their engagement effort??

Our parting words to the senior management of Company F were, "Don't let your guard down". They planned to continue to work on engagement, and they kept it as an HK Annual Goal and wove it into their 5-year plan as well. They set new targets, which were to achieve 80% engagement in the next 2 years. In addition, this facility of Company F prepared a post-mortem of their activities that included a training program and execution outline, so the other seven facilities had a blueprint to follow.

Chapter Summary ... We explained how to improve engagement by use of some "knobs" to turn. The strongest knob is the Residual Engagement Strength (RES), which is a model comprised of the five High Leverage Points (HLPs) and a strong predictor of engagement. We discussed each HLP and their ranges and relative strengths, as well as how they fit on the HLP Grid. Not surprisingly, the strongest one is the level of kaizen activity. Finally, we reviewed two case studies showing how engagement levels can be improved ... or not.

What's next?? We now know how to create engagement; how do we get prepared for and execute this engagement system? Or what does our action plan look like? Chapter 18 addresses that very topic.

Chapter 18

The Action Plan

Aim of this Chapter ... to explain how to implement a plan which will improve and sustain engagement levels in your facility. We will discuss the three aspects of preparation, execution and improvement. In preparation, we will discuss what to do, as well as what to avoid and the specific task of how to prepare the management team. On the topic of execution and improvement, we will discuss the need for external support, the first survey and how to turn this information into a viable action plan.

Get prepared

You are about to embark on the most demanding of business challenges. You are about to embark on a large, enlightening and uplifting cultural change in your business. Not only is it a large change but once underway you will see benefits to your customers, your stockholders, your employees and even to you yourself that will exceed your wildest expectations. You will not only see the present leaders, at all levels, take a stronger role in improving the business. But you will also see those who formerly were very quiet and subdued step up, take charge and make changes that will improve not only their work environment but improve the competitive position of the company. You will see initiative explode. You will see creative and imaginative ideas come from people you hardly even noticed before. With this revelation, your list of future team leaders, future supervisors and future managers will grow exponentially. You will literally see the potential of each and every person expanded, and you will be able to bask in both the improved productivity and the improved work satisfaction that is a natural result of unleashing the potential of each worker, from the newest hired floor worker to the CEO. All will benefit. And this will all follow the effort you and your team put forth when you are truly capable of fully exploiting the Intrinsic Motivational Loop and strengthening the engagement loop.

This is all accomplished by making the huge cultural change that will end in a fully engaged workforce. Recall that culture is the combined thoughts, beliefs, actions, artifacts and language of a group of people; or, more specifically, "just how we do things around here". We are going to change how we train, how we write, how we teach and how we deploy job instructions. We are going to change how we plan, how we problem solve … and especially who and when we do problem solving. We are going to change how

CULTURES … THE STARTING POINT

Mental models, paradigms and stereotypes are all generalizations we use in everyday life. They guide our information gathering and our decision making. They are a form of thinking and talking in shorthand. When broadly understood and accepted, they provide psychic economy. For example, when I speak of an "open culture", my mental model is one where: data is readily available to everyone; discussions are open, frank and honest; and information is widely shared. It is much easier to use the use the term "open culture" than redefine that term each time it is used. However, it only works if we have the same mental model for "open culture".

When we have a shared set of mental models, discussion, problem solving and decision making is much easier; this is psychic economy. However, mental models, paradigms and stereotypes have two problems, at least.

- First, as generalizations they are not always correct. Tall guys make better basketball players; that's generally but not always true.
- Second, they are largely unconscious. As such, they can guide our behavior and we may not even be aware of it.

Hence, they can control us and we will make unconscious errors. We will gather biased data and make incorrect decisions. And just where do our mental models begin?? … in our beliefs, that's where. As such, our beliefs then dictate "just how we do things around here" which is the operational definition of our culture.

we supervise, how we develop employees. We are going to change how we communicate. But most of all, we are going to change how we both manage and lead.

Prepare for what? We will prepare for the huge cultural change that is on the horizon. And as we do that, there are both things to do and things to avoid doing.

> **PARADIGM SHIFT NO. 3**
>
> Creating engagement is not a **new thing**. Although there are some new techniques and skills, a full 95% of the work is just doing what you do now do, **but doing it better.** Your existing management system will need to change.

What not to do

Almost without exception, the approach to management as they embark on an effort to improve employee engagement is to have a "program", an "initiative" or a "transformation". Avoid all that. Avoid the announcements and the speeches; avoid the meetings and bulletin board postings; avoid the new banners declaring a "new approach" – avoid all that. After all the banners have faded and the speeches have been forgotten, you are left with what you started with … getting the work done and meeting your customers' demands. So start there.

These programs, initiatives and transformations are a bit like the latest fad diet you might use to lose some weight. They predictably work very nicely for some time. But then in the fullness of time, they lose their staying power and the weight you previously lost comes back, but now with the guilt of failure attached. These diets – much like your initiatives, programs and transformations – fail because they are not integrated into all you do. They fail because all you changed was part of who you are and what you do. You changed **part of your actions** – but that is all you changed.

Ok then, what do we need to do?

We talked about this before; recall from Chapter 6,

> "The essence of strong, effective – or weak, ineffective – management largely flows from the belief systems the managers hold. And by no small margin, the managers at the top of the management pyramid are far and away the most influential. It is their belief

system that literally drives the entire management system. Their belief systems are reflected in their paradigms, often called mental models, they both use and expect others to use. For example, a common mental model we need to overcome is the definition of what we call "a problem". In many businesses – most actually – problems are viewed as something undesirable and should be avoided. Consequently, and unfortunately all too often, problems are intentionally hidden. If that is your mental model, you will never be able to implement lean because lean is all about finding and fixing problems.

The strength of mental models, of how they end up determining not only actions but destinies for people and businesses alike, is reflected in the following logic attributed to Mahatma Gandhi:

'Your beliefs become your thoughts,
Your thoughts become your words,
Your words become your actions,
Your actions become your habits,
Your habits become your values,
Your values become your destiny'.

This is true not only in business but in virtually all aspects of life as well. While you may not have total control over all the variables in your life, you can have a very large impact on them. It is as my mentor, Toshi Amino, once told me, "Lonnie, you can believe that you can or you can believe that you can't; and you will probably be right". **Your success – or failures – be it in business or another aspect of your life is greatly affected by your initial beliefs; that is where it all starts**".

The cultural change must start by changing the beliefs, the thoughts, the words and then the appropriate actions will follow

But where do we start??

We start by reviewing how we can change a culture.

There are three key sources that work together to form a business culture. First and most importantly is the business environment. If you happen to be a massive player in a small niche business, you may be able to control the business environment. However, for the vast majority of us, that is not the case. Rather than controlling our business environment, it controls us. We must learn how to understand it and respond to it. If we wish to effect change, we cannot start there; it's unlikely we can change the business environment. The second key factor in creating a culture is the history of your business and your facility in particular. Since the history is already written, this too we cannot change, even if we wish we could. That leaves the third source, the few very influential people at the top – the senior leadership. These are the policy creators, these are the rule makers and these are the trendsetters. These are the people who control all the written – and unwritten – norms of the business. Sometimes they are called the senior leadership, the executives or the C-Suite. But changing them … is where we start.

Often this is a tough pill for management to swallow

All the management team will need to take to heart the new paradigms they must operate from. Very likely, at this point you will re-evaluate your Mission and your Vision, and almost certainly you will change your Company Values. The paradigms that need to change are described throughout this book, and as a management team you will need to understand their impact, you will need to accept the need for the cultural changes, and ultimately they will need to change. But before any change can be made to the facility, they must make changes in what they believe and how they act. This is not easy, due to a variety of reasons, some technical, but more so the reasons are emotional. These managers and leaders are the pillars of the company, literally its vitality, and to some degree they must now admit that what they have done so far must change. They must admit that the prior path is no longer healthy. This is not easy at a group level, and it is even more difficult at the individual level. The group must become its own critic, and its own support structure, as you work to process these paradigms and work through the minefield of change.

The real test is if the management team is capable of cold, hard, honest, dispassionate and introspective analysis. Without this, change will be difficult. Go back now to Appendix E, "The five tests of management commitment to creating and sustaining a fully engaged workforce", and review the questions one by one. First, place yourself in the position of the senior leadership. And as you are doing this, ask yourself, "Just how easy is it to respond positively to each question". If you perform a cold, hard, honest, dispassionate and introspective analysis, you will see the difficulty in being totally committed to this massive culture change.

If acceptance is tough, executing the change is even more so

With the senior leadership is where we start, and don't even try to start anywhere else. **If you want to start in some area other than senior leadership, my recommendation is to drop this effort and do something else to improve your business.** If you do not start with the senior leadership and make changes at that level you will fail completely. I don't mean that things won't work out perfectly. I don't mean you will only get 60% of the benefits. Not at all. What I mean is that it will be a failure of galactic proportions. As you embark on the effort expectations will be raised. Even if you approach this halfhearted, you will get some early gains and those expectations will appear to be met. But soon enough the people will see through the thin veil of "management change" and recognize that the important things that need to change … simply are not changing. When the dust clears, your employee engagement, along with your business metrics, will have all digressed. Worse yet, the workers will retreat and become hardened by the unmet promises and unmet expectations.

Better management preparation is required

To refresh and/or teach these new thoughts, beliefs and actions to the management team, we will use four techniques. They include interactive teaching, group discussion and dialogue, gemba walks and in-field coaching.

Interactive teaching

This teaching will need to be done by a proficient expert in the field of employee engagement and cultural change. You will later learn, when we discuss the specific action plan, that you need to bring in a cultural change expert; he will be your initial teacher. As members of the senior leadership become proficient in these topics, they should then teach lower level managers these concepts. A starter list of topics include:

1. Engagement as a system and how the system works
2. The inherent power of negativity

3. The Basics and Beyond with an emphasis on supervision
4. The kaizen mindset
5. The Intrinsic Motivational Loop
6. Understanding the cultural network
7. Motivation basics covering Herzberg, Maslow, McGregor and Drucker, as a minimum
8. Intrinsic motivation, flow and self-determination theory
9. The power of intrinsic motivation and the limits of extrinsic motivation
10. The five High Leverage Points
11. Using engagement concepts to design systems of recognition and rewards

For each topic, first, outside reading will be assigned. Next, in the classroom, the teacher will give hypothetical situations to solve individually, in small groups and by role-playing. Third, after the hypotheticals have been completed, each hypothetical will be discussed by the group format. Fourth, the senior leaders will be asked to relate this hypothetical to real problems in the plant, and this will also be discussed in a group format. Finally, the teacher will respond to any questions the senior leaders have on the assigned reading. Each session will take approximately 4 hours.

Once the senior management has completed this training, they should train their direct reports. Initially, they may need support from the cultural change expert.

Group discussions

Following each training, and after applying these concepts in practice, the senior leadership should meet to discuss each training topic. Relative to the subject matter taught, the senior leaders should ask and answer the following questions:

■ What should we start doing that we are not now doing?
■ What should we stop doing that we are now doing?
■ What should we do better?

These may be of any length, but if they are not at least 2 hours, people are not really observing and questioning. Again, each senior managers should follow this up by holding discussions with his direct report.

Gemba walks

There is a great deal of misunderstanding about gemba walks. The gemba is the place where the actual work is occurring. Most of the time, people think it is at the production floor. It is if that is where the actual work is occurring. However, for accounting, for engineering, the actual work is probably in the office. If so, that is the gemba. The primary purpose of going on gemba walks is to improve management awareness. Managers should prepare themselves to ask questions and then just listen. They are to learn, not teach. The walk is designed to provide input to the manager, not create a platform for his output. Gemba walks are not to critique processes, products or people; they are to provide awareness to management. The best formula I heard for a gemba walk is provided by Jim Womack, and his advice is to "go see, ask why and show respect". I recommend daily gemba walks of 30–45-minute duration, cycling through all aspects of the business.

In-field coaching

To some, it is surprising how weak many managers are at interviewing and listening. In-field coaching consists of going on gemba walks with your coach; probably your cultural change expert can be the initial coach. As with other topics, as proficiency is gained by others, they should learn to coach. I would recommend that at least once per month each senior manager should go on a 1-hour gemba walk with a coach. The coach should not intervene, simply observe the interactions on the walk. Then, following the walk, the coach can give feedback to the senior manager. This should be done once per month for the first year, as a minimum. As with all other trainings, the senior leaders will expect this of their direct reports, and when they feel ready, the senior leaders should coach their people.

Creating and executing the plan

Find a skilled change agent – an outsider for sure

Once the management team has decided they wish to improve engagement, the first move should be to hire a cultural change expert. After the CEO has read and educated himself to some level, he can interview candidates and select a consultant to assist you in the effort. The change agent must be an outsider. Anyone who has been a part of your culture has too many blind spots and will not be able to give you guidance. This needs to be done early on. The consultant will provide support in many ways, but two aspects are invaluable. First, a great deal of what many managers believe about engagement is incorrect and much of what is correct is both counterintuitive and counter-cultural. You need a subject-matter expert; there is no substitute for this. Second, you will be blind to many aspects of your culture; this is unavoidable by those within the culture. An external agent will be much more observant and skilled in assessing the real inner workings of your culture. For this, there too is no substitute.

Complete your first engagement survey

There are three approaches to completing an engagement survey. The easiest way is to contact Gallup. For a reasonable fee, they will supply you with their standard survey and the analysis. Second, if you wish a purer measure of engagement, you can use the Utrecht Work Engagement Survey, available on the web. Third, you can create your own. There are several good books available to teach you how to create and validate a survey. I recommend *Measuring Customer Satisfaction – Development and Use of Questionnaires* (1992) by Robert Hayes. Creating your own survey is not as difficult as you think, but it is time-consuming. It does have the benefit that you can easily include questions that allow you to evaluate the High Leverage Points (HLPs). However, the most important part is, whichever path you choose, use the same survey year after year. This is crucial. This allows for meaningful comparisons of progress. Fourth, there are other surveys available, and some are quite good. If you wish to check the market, that is another avenue. Normally I recommend the Gallup survey, even with its issues. It is easily completed, intuitive and they provide fast feedback. While the Gallup is out for analysis, we could complete a smaller survey and interviews to get information for the HLP Grid.

Analyze your engagement survey, create action items

Along with the engagement levels reported in the survey output, plot the values of the five High Leverage Points on the HLP Grid. You can now create a gap analysis comparing the level of engagement you have to the level you wish to attain.

What is a reasonable improvement goal?

I find that improvements of 10–15% per year are reasonable to accomplish and readily sensed. Larger changes are very difficult. If you are at the average levels of all manufacturing, e.g. 25%, and increase to 40% in 1 year, it will be immediately obvious. Your eyes and ears will tell you that something very wonderful has happened, and the next survey will only better quantify what you see, hear and sense. A change of that magnitude is obvious to even the untrained observer. Even a change from 60 to 75% is easily felt, although not as dramatically. Again, a survey will quantify what you already feel.

What's the strategy to improve?

That is pretty simple: which High Leverage Points(HLP) will give us the greatest impact and which is the easiest to improve?

Focus on creating kaizen activity.   As for the first part, it is clear that we have two very powerful impacts on the RES equation. Note that the strongest factor which works to make the disengagement circle dominant is the power of negativity factor with a value of 4.0; this is largely unchangeable. This strong and natural influence, working to decrease engagement, is one reason it is so hard to get an engaged workforce. Yet of the five HLPs, the one with the largest potential for impact on the engagement loop, and hence improvement, is the kaizen factor. If kaizen activity can exceed 1.5 kaizens/person/month, the kaizen factor will exceed the magnitude of the power of negativity of 4.0 (see Figure 17.4 in Chapter 17), effectively neutralizing this natural phenomenon. Then if even more kaizens are done, the kaizen factor can reach 7.0.

As for the second aspect, ease of accomplishment, implementing kaizens is orders of magnitude easier than making an impact on any of the three people-related High Leverage Points of: management walking the talk; improving supervisory feedback; and improving system trust. All of these require a great deal of change by a large group of people, certainly a large and difficult undertaking. Improving transparency is easier than the three people-related issues but not as impactful as the kaizen factor.

The kaizen factor is the most powerful tool you have to improve the RES; this must be your first priority when you are thinking of improvement.

Kaizens will only "ensue"   An extremely important point to remember is that you cannot directly create kaizen activity. Recall from our discussion of motivating intrinsic behavior, this cannot be done with the extrinsic rewards.

In fact, if you try to use extrinsic rewards to motivate kaizen activity, it will backfire and demotivate the behavior you wish to see. Rather, kaizen activity will naturally "ensue" when three conditions are met. First, you must pay close attention to and properly deliver the Basics and Beyond. Second, you need to make sure everyone knows that the management team wants and will support kaizen activity. Third, the management team must act in a manner to support those principles. That done, kaizens will flow.

The "Intrinsic Power" of kaizen activity – Satisficing the intrinsic needs   The engagement loop starts with Loyalists doing their job and also doing "kaizens", improvement projects (see Figure 17.1). This combination is the essence of paradigm shift no. 3, discussed in detail earlier in this chapter. Doing the "normal" work, plus incorporating kaizen activity, provides the fuel to activate the Intrinsic Motivational Loop (IML), and this IML is the "heart" of the engagement

> **PARADIGM SHIFT NO. 4**
>
> The "new normal" for EVERYONE in the business, worker and manager alike, is to: first, execute their job as designed; and second, to work on kaizens for product, process and service improvements. Or in leanspeak, create a culture of continuous improvement

effort. When they are designing and executing kaizens, the workers are:

- autonomous (working of their own volition),
- improving the workplace (demonstrating competence)
- making life better for themselves and their teammates (showing relatedness) and
- improving the business overall for the customer, employee and employer (demonstrating meaningful work and contribution).

These kaizens, when encouraged and supported properly, satisfice the intrinsic needs, thus providing the fuel for the entire engagement effort. **Notice that it all starts with kaizen activity done right.** In doing the voluntary kaizens, especially when the workers see the benefits manifest in the system transparency, this:

- satisfices the four intrinsic needs, which
- fuels the intrinsic motivators,
- activating the IML and this, in turn,
- improves the "intensity of the positivity".

You will recall this is only one of two positive modifiers to the "Intensity of the positivity" in the RES equation.

Other natural benefits of working to improve the level of kaizen activity   Do not forget for one second that to get the ball rolling with kaizen activity the Basics and Beyond must be delivered and delivered well. So if all the above is not good enough, some wonderful synergisms occur when you pay close attention to and properly manage the "Basics and Beyond". Several things – simply and naturally – get better. For example, to properly supply the new information, training and resources associated with the "Basics and Beyond", the supervisors must themselves become better in the delivery of these items, hence improving supervisory skill levels. In addition, they also must get closer to and pay greater attention to the value-added workers, thus improving relatedness. Second, to make sure this work is done well, the managers simply must spend more time on the floor checking, auditing and just going to the gemba. Third, the system of transparency will get a real shake-down cruise as a result of the supervisors and the managers being on the floor and reviewing this information on a daily/hourly basis. And finally, since the managers, supervisors and value-add workers are all communicating more and having more direct contact, trust will naturally improve. If you haven't already noticed, that covers the other four HLPs.

This is why, as a first effort, the attention should be almost exclusively focused on improving the kaizen factor … it seems to have a strong positive effect on all the HLPs.

Next look at the other High Leverage Points   A quick look at the relative positions of the values for the HLP will guide you nicely. Once you find you need to improve an area such as transparency or management walking the talk, the solutions are normally straightforward and are well outlined in the previous chapters. Follow the examples in Chapter 17. Like I say, solutions are the easiest part of problem solving; defining the problem takes you to 90% of the solution and working with engagement level is no exception. Finally, as you progress through the year and implement the improvement plan, keep an eye on the number of kaizens completed. Almost surely, if you have done your job right up to this point, the number of kaizens will increase. If, for some reason, kaizen activity does not rise, go back to the Basics and Beyond and re-evaluate how you are doing. But most likely you will see kaizen activity increase, and your engagement levels will increase and be quantified in the next engagement survey. The engagement survey should be completed annually. In some cases where you start with very low levels of engagement, say 15%, you might want to do engagement surveys every 6 months.

Digging deeper-analyze your losses

Analysis using the five HLPs will give you great guidance, but you will also need to dig deeper. Creating a fully engaged workforce is almost always a matter of doing what we already know, just doing it much better. It is about: training better; about having better job definitions; about having better work instructions; it is about scrupulously evaluating the level of resources supplied. It is about providing better plans, improved supervision, better information sharing and a scoreboard quality system of transparency. It is about better involvement and presence of the management team. Almost all companies have these elements – to some degree. Yet most are deficient in a variety of areas, and the next question is: just how do we find those areas? Well, that's not complicated at all. Where are your losses?

Finding the opportunities.
Where are your quality losses? Where are your financial losses? What is the source of your safety incidences? What is causing your employee attrition? What are your formal and informal grievances and complaints? Not just those by the hourly workforce but by the supervision and management as well. Put another way, you can ask and answer, "If everyone knows what to do, how to do it and has the resources to do it, why do I have these problems?", whatever and wherever they might be. And if you default to "because the workers don't want to", then go back and reread Chapters 11 and 15. Then if you still default to "because the workers don't want to", give me a call and I would be more than willing to discuss it with you. If you are still stuck on "because the workers don't want to", give up your engagement effort and move on to some other method to improve your business; and you can stop reading as well. On the other hand, if you can accept that these deficiencies in your system are largely owned by management, then you can make changes.

Once the losses are found, the majority of the time, the solutions are straightforward. In our teaching on problem solving, we teach that a problem once defined is 90% solved, and problems in engagement are no different. If you find the quality defects are a result of loss of concentration, institute workstation rotations and/or install poka yokes. If you find rate variations in your labor-intensive assembly line, institute standard work and improve your training. If you find that you have high attrition in your engineering staff, institute the Five Supervisory Tools. If you find that machinery downtime negatively impacts performance, implement a total productive maintenance program. Most of the solutions are known once the problems are found.

Taking action

This is not a revolution

The changes should look more like an evolution rather than a revolution. Initially, the obvious efforts of the management team will focus on providing support and guidance on "The Basics and Beyond". Later, the behaviors of the management team will be both more pronounced and more visible. As they become fully engaged in supporting the five High Leverage Points, their presence will be felt directly. At this point they are going beyond just providing guidance, support and resources … they are visibly changing their behaviors in what they do to fulfill their management and leadership roles.

We want the change in engagement to be slow and consistent. Ten percent improvements per year are both practical and highly noticeable. Even if we are very low on the engagement scale, say 15%, if we improve just 10% per year, it will take us around 5 years to get to 70%. On the one hand, 5 years sounds like a long time. But when, in the first year, you improve engagement by an absolute 10%, everyone from the newest floor worker to the CEO will be giddy with excitement as your engagement levels have relatively improved by 67%. It will not only be obvious to everyone, worker and visitor alike, and it will not only be well received – but extremely well received.

If we improve too fast, we do not give the culture an opportunity to integrate, accommodate and perpetuate the changes. With rapid and large improvements, it is too easy to think you "have arrived". And with that belief guiding your behavior, it is easy to lose your focus and slippage can easily occur.

Implement well …

As you institute corrective actions to improve your engagement levels, make sure you ask and critically answer the three guidance questions:

- What is my objective?
- How will I measure success?
- What am I prepared to do?

From there, use the Six Questions of Continuous Improvement to guide your efforts.

And finally, while implementing, follow the Process Improvement Mantra:

- Create the standard … make it visual
- Train the standard … make it visual
- Execute the standard … make it visual
- Reflect and improve

Continuously improve

By reviewing your engagement survey, the analysis of the five HLPs and digging deeper into your losses, you will be able to develop an imposing list of activities indeed. You will be off and running, and very likely you will see early gains. This is the easier part. The more difficult part is to keep the focus on this effort to improve employee engagement. However, the answer is really quite simple. Make employee engagement a key performance metric and include this as an element of your Hoshin Kanri (HK) policy deployment effort. In so doing, you equate engagement with the other key metrics, which probably include profits, cost reductions, quality, delivery and growth. Your HK plan will then create a programmed way to institute both engagement sustainment and engagement improvements.

Chapter Summary … To improve our engagement levels, we will need an improvement strategy. It begins by making sure we do not create an "initiative" or anything that sounds like an event. Improving engagement is not a new thing; it is a matter of doing the things we need to do, just doing them much better. We need to create a change in "just how we do things around here" rather than changing the "things" we do. This cultural change must start with changing the beliefs of the senior management to be in line with appropriate engagement paradigms. While educating the management team, we will use four basic teaching/learning techniques that are experiential, interactive and introspective in nature. They include interactive teaching/learning for the suggested starter list of 11 items. Next, we elaborated on how we execute this plan by hiring an external consultant, completing our first engagement survey, analyzing the survey and data, then creating action lists. Finally, to sustain and improve employee engagement, we recommend you make it part of your normal Hoshin Kanri planning process, with employee engagement as a key company metric.

What's next?? Chapter 19, the final chapter, is next. It contains, fittingly, some final thoughts.

Chapter 19

Final Thoughts

Aim of this Chapter ... to discuss some final thoughts on your journey into employee engagement. We will frankly discuss some serious obstacles you will encounter with the senior management and maybe a way to address the worst of them. We will end with a final word.

The power of employee engagement

Our firm, Quality Consultants, specializes in cultural evaluation, redesign and change. Very few companies look to simply modify their culture. Normally they adopt some type of improvement strategy. A number of fads have permeated the market such as the Zero Defects movement and the Six Sigma efforts. These were largely technical approaches to improving the bottom line, and although they professed them to be cultural changing efforts, they were not. There were also the Value Analysis and Value Engineering (VA/VE) efforts, Team-Based Efforts and a litany of others. Yet recently, the only one that really had a decent chance of being culture-changing was the lean movement. Yet it largely failed because lean done following the Toyota model required you to address two cultural pillars simultaneously: the creation of a culture of continuous improvement and a creation of a culture of respect for people. Well, for reasons too long to explain here, those professing to implement lean took the continuous improvement pillar to heart but gave the respect for people pillar only lip service, if that. The results were uniformly the same. Some large early gains with no sustaining effort, and normally within 3–5 years, things had returned to the pre-lean days.

Well, the concept of employee engagement is probably not exactly what Toyota meant when they described their respect for people concept. But quite frankly, upon careful scrutiny, you cannot slip a piece of paper between the two. The techniques to achieve them are the same and the end results are the same. To me, they are the same concept, just with a different name.

And I can tell you without hesitation that creating and improving employee engagement in a facility is the most powerful cultural change I have seen. Once accomplished, people are acutely aware of the difference and want more. That has been my experience – without exception.

It's a joy to see it evolve

As a consultant for nearly 30 years, I have been a part of many cultural transformations. And I can tell you with certainty, when we embark on an effort to improve employee engagement, whether it is a stand alone objective or part of a lean transformation, it is the most personally rewarding work experience I can recall. When I see employees whose initiative has been stifled and they break free and use their imagination and creativity, it creates a new level of energy in the plant that is noticeable and immediately felt by all. When I see people being able to express their entire being by not only working hard but also thinking deeply about how to do things better, and caring enough to make it happen, something lights up inside me that is immensely satisfying; I can say it no other way. It is pure joy and I am both proud and humbled to be a part of it. It is the type of work that is so easy and yet so enjoyable. Although I could have retired several years ago, these engagement efforts make work so enjoyable that I have decided to keep pressing forward.

It is never easy

Although the first parts of an engagement effort often progress quite smoothly, the path is fraught with dangers. The biggest problem, and there is no way around it, is that the very people who need to change the most are those that are used to changing the least ... the senior management. However, lack of practice is the least of your concerns. These are normally your bosses and you need to look them in the eye and tell them that they – themselves – need to change. They need to change first and they need to change the most. And that message is pretty hard to convey without the actual or tacit understanding which says, Mr. Manager, you are the problem, you are the one who needs to change. The early response is often an "OK". However, as you get deeper into the transformation, you likely will get more resistance to change. It is not that these changes are technically difficult; rather, they are emotionally difficult.

It takes a high level of management courage and trust

Having been involved in a number of culture-changing transformations, I can tell you with certainty that the degree of success is directly proportional to the level of courage of the management team and the level of trust they have in their plans and in the guidance they are given.

Courage is a key issue as you are asking the managers to throw away some of their most cherished paradigms and replace them with new ones, with which they are not practiced. It is easy enough to intellectually convince them of the needed changes; I call this "head change". It is yet another matter to get them to take the steps to actually make the changes, because the "heart change" is far more difficult. When we ask others to change and venture into the unknown, it takes a huge dose of courage when they must, "Trust more what you say than what has served me well for the last 20 years".

As we embark on this effort to improve employee engagement, this acceptance and willingness to change by the management team is the limiting factor to change and success. Your success in improving engagement levels will be limited by the degree to which they understand, accept and execute the changes that are needed. Short, sweet and simple.

And what if you are the advisor in this cultural change?

Now that is really tough, and it makes little difference if you are an internal or external consultant. You have the awesome task to convince the key people that they must change. That although they created an inferior system in the past (you probably don't want to beat this drum too loud), they are no longer the problem; rather, they are the holders of the solutions. Meanwhile, they hold your future in their hands, and if that message is delivered incorrectly, it may be your last day of work with that company.

Worse yet, the truth may not be your ally. If the management team is one that is not open to new ideas and not comfortable with introspection and self-analysis, the truth may short-cut your efforts and broaden your unemployment opportunities.

Advising others that they need to change is a tightrope that is difficult to walk under the best of circumstances. Proceed with caution. (You can go to my website, www.qc-ep.com, and read the two articles on being a change agent. If you are a change agent, you will find these interesting.)

Just how do you walk that tightrope??

I may not be the best person to answer this question for you, because I too struggle with it. But I have found a technique that makes it easier for me. Early on, I talk to the management team about my three friends embodied in three quotes. They are:

ON AWARENESS

"Men stumble over the truth from time to time, but most pick themselves up and hurry off as if nothing happened".

Sir Winston Churchill

ON INTROSPECTION

"In the choice between changing one's mind and proving there's no reason to do so, most people get busy on the proof".

John Kenneth Galbraith

ON INITIATIVE

"Opportunity is missed by most people because it is dressed in overalls and looks like hard work".

Thomas Edison

In addition, as part of my work agreement with my clients, I review with them a document about our firm, Quality Consultants, describing who we are. It is entitled, "What we do, What we believe and How we do it". One section discusses my minimum standards of performance, which I have used since my early days as a supervisor with Chevron. It is a universal set of standards, and to that end, I used these in my 32 years as a soccer coach as well. As part of the document, we go on to discuss "what we don't do" and it says:

"What we don't do

*There are some problems, presented by some people, which we do not try to problem solve our way around. These problems need to be surfaced, discussed, and if these people do not wish to change, they must be removed from the workplace. These issues will prevent these people from complying with the **minimum performance standards of: understanding, accepting and executing the changes needed to implement a lean initiative.** These problems are:*

- *Militant ignorance…these people won't **understand** what is required. They have chosen to not learn, they refuse to study and consciously fail to learn from experience.*
- *Blind narcissism…these people always think they have a better way and **will not accept** what is required*
- *Laziness…these people **are not willing to execute** what is required*

For the reasons stated above we ask that you adopt the following 3 minimum performance standards for ALL your employees. That is, to work in our enterprise they must:

- *Understand your objectives*
- *Accept your objectives and*
- *Execute your objectives*

And that these 3 minimum standards of performance be the basis of a contract to work".

We discuss this with them as we hope it is enlightening guidance to them as they deal with all those under their supervision and control. At the same time, we are broaching some topics we will likely have to discuss with them in the future. This is not a panacea, however, when we then must discuss their need to change or their resistance to change; it is not the first time we will have discussed that topic.

The role of management in summary format …

Over 45 years ago, I had a discussion with my mentor. He told me, "Take care of your people, and they will take care of everything else". He went on to say, "Your job as a supervisor is to create an environment where it is possible for our people to perform; their job is to perform". In my career I used those word frequently, and I find them even more important today.

That is the essence of achieving engagement. When the management team "creates an environment where everyone can perform", they will. They want to, and when they create that environment, the people predictably respond, and the result is a happier, healthier and more productive workplace. Everyone benefits. Not just the employees but the customers and stockholders benefit as well.

I have come to understand that employee engagement, as a business strategy, is the strategy with the largest long-term effect. Anyone can go out and source the best of materials and purchase the best of machines to make the products. However, not everyone "can create the environment where it is possible for your people to perform". The performance that is necessary is to "create the environment" where your people are "all in". They are engaged with their body, with their mind and with their heart. They are operating with "vigor, dedication and absorption". That is a fully engaged workforce, and it is maybe the most powerful weapon you can supply to your business in the battle to compete and survive.

A final word

You may be a new manager reading these materials and truly understanding engagement for the first time; or a seasoned veteran who has dabbled in creating employee engagement but just never had the best advice. Or possibly you are an external consultant like me and want to get involved in employee engagement. Whatever your position or whatever your motivation, I can guarantee you that if you wish to guide this change, creating and improving employee engagement is a truly worthwhile experience. Once successful, you get to see people literally light up on the job. Even more rewarding is the impact you will make on people's personal lives. To me, there is nothing more rewarding at work than having some worker come up to me and tell me not only how achieving engagement has made work much more enjoyable but how it has touched their personal lives as well.

Go to my website (www.qc-ep.com) and read about Jill, Bob or Jack and see how improving their life at work had a huge positive impact on their kids, their spouses and their extended families as well. If you are a consultant in this field, these are the experiences you truly cherish … you get to improve business, make customers happy and improve the lives of those who are working there. Hard to beat.

As you embark on this journey toward a fully engaged workforce, I pray you will get the same enjoyment and job satisfaction I have experienced … it is exhilarating.

Be well,

Lonnie
July 5, 2018

Appendix A: The Six Questions of Continuous Improvement

A six-step process of structured problem solving and decision making to guide thinking so that both PDCA and hypothesis testing are incorporated into the thought process.

The Six Questions of Continuous Improvement have an interesting history. I first learned about them when I took a course in practical problem solving that was patterned after a Toyota course of the same name. This was around 1975. The instructors taught us the Five Questions of Problem Solving, which consisted of the first four questions listed below, plus a fifth question, "When can we go see?"

Since they are used for both decision making and problem solving, I later renamed them the "Five Questions of Continuous Improvement". After that, I reworded and expanded question 5 to include the three aspects now listed so it would better address the concept of hypothesis testing, which is integral to operating a lean facility. Also, we always practiced the mantra "learn–do–reflect", and since this always followed the activities of the kaizen, I simply incorporated them into the final question, and now I teach the Six Questions of Continuous Improvement.

They constitute the first and the most important practice that must be incorporated in any lean transformation. This will be the first skill your champion of problem solving will teach among the Six Initial Skill Focus Areas.

Everyone will use the six questions, from those in the C-suite to the operators and mechanics in the field, and they will use them from this day forward. Recall that the questions are:

1. What is the present condition?
2. What is the desired future condition?

3. What is preventing us from reaching the desired condition?
4. What is something we can do, right now, to get closer to the desired condition?
5. When we do this, what should we expect?
   a. What will happen?
   b. How much of it will happen?
   c. When will it happen so we can "go see?"
6. What have we learned?

If you go to my website (www.qc-ep.com) and bring down the menu item "Lean Manufacturing", you will see a menu item "Problem Solving". Click on that and you will find a tab on A3 Problem Solving, which uses the six-question format, and you will see that the A3 is designed to guide you through this logic. All the materials on my website are available for your use; note that you now have a downloaded copy of the documents you reviewed.

Appendix B: Article on Engagement

Several years ago, I wrote an article on employee engagement for *IndustryWeek* magazine … it is reprinted below for your information

Find the missing pieces in your employee–engagement effort

by Lonnie Wilson, founder, Quality Consultants

March 20, 2012

You know what engaged employees look like?? They are active; they are trying to get the task done; they are clearly focused on the objectives at hand; when they reach roadblocks they do work-arounds or they seek help. They do not sit, they don't fret, they don't wait, they don't sit around waiting for instructions and **they don't make excuses … Engaged employees are actively getting the right work done in the right way to meet the right goals**.

When I teach engagement to a new management team, I teach that engagement has five measurable behavioral traits. An engaged worker, floor worker or manager alike:

1. Knows what to do to accomplish the task at hand. That is, they understand and can execute the major steps to their job.
2. Knows how to do the job. That is, they have the skills, techniques and talent to produce a quality product safely and efficiently.
3. Has the resources to do the job. They have not just the physical tools but the training, support and leadership as well. The resources also include such items as a plantwide support system of just-in-time (JIT) problem solving, JIT management support and JIT maintenance, to name a few.

4. Wants to do the job (more on this later).
5. Wants to do the job better (more on this later).

As management teams attempt to "make" employees engaged, they almost always give a lot of attention to the last two attributes. That is, they believe: If only we had enough "employee want to", then we would have engaged employees.

They could not be more wrong!!

The vast, vast majority of workers who enter your facility have tons of "want to", at least at day one. Most of the workers I have encountered – be they factory-floor workers, engineers hired right out of college, line supervisors hired from the outside or recently appointed or promoted managers – act the same. They want to do a good job, and, furthermore, they instantly have ideas about how to improve their new work.

At day one.

At day one they come motivated. At day one they come wanting to do a good job. At day one they come ready to make it better.

So what happens? In a sentence: We, managers and leaders, get in the way of their desires.

Continued engagement requires fuel

Not all efforts at work enrichment and employee empowerment are unsuccessful. Some people have found a formula that works. Here is what I have observed: If you as a manager fail to supply any of the five key elements I list here, you will, sooner or later, demotivate your employees and steal from them some measure of the power of employee engagement.

The five key elements are:

1. A sense of meaningfulness
2. A sense of control
3. A sense of accomplishment
4. A sense of growth
5. A sense of community

Think about each of these:

1. **A sense of meaningfulness:** Do your workers show greater interest in the work when they understand they are working for a meaningful task? When they are serving a higher purpose? Do they understand the company mission and vision to represent a company that seeks to be

competitive, thriving, growing, a company that not only makes money but gives back to the employees and is a good corporate citizen in the community? Or are your management actions solely focused on the goal of making money?

If management's actions are heavily focused or solely focused on "the bottom line at all costs", your employees' sole focus will, predictably, be, "What's in it for me?" They won't "want to" work for the company, only for themselves – and they won't "want to" improve the workplace. Can your employees "see" that their contributions are not only necessary but significant? That their ideas are considered? Or are they just another fungible piece of easily replaced hardware?

2. **A sense of control:** Do your workers have some way to get input into the things they can affect and the things they should affect? Do they have ways to control what and how they do things or are they just following the instructions some engineer wrote from his desk away from the production floor? If it is a "my way or the highway" management style, employees will find the highway as soon as something slightly better appears.

3. **A sense of accomplishment:** Do your workers have ways to determine whether they have done a good job? Can they answer the question, "How did I (we) do today?" Can they go home knowing they did well? Or is "not getting your ass chewed out" the definition of a "good day"? Can they tell each hour of each day if they are doing their job well? Are their visual indicators in place? Can they codify and quantify their contribution?

4. **A sense of growth:** Do your workers have a way to contribute and grow as individuals? Can they improve their skills via cross-training and advancement? Is there a conscious effort to create "future opportunities", or does your company supply no sense of hope for the future of the individual? Can your company reward your employees with opportunities to exercise their demonstrated skills, such as writing new procedures or training other employees to their level of competence?

5. **A sense of community:** Do your employees have a true sense of teamwork at work? Do your employees have reason to proudly wear the company logo on their shirts or do they only proudly wear their "Big 10 Killers" shirt from the bowling league? Or worse yet, is there a sense of community focused on the union and not the company? Humans are a social animal, and if their sense of community is not fed at work, they will seek it out elsewhere.

You can perform a reality test on these five key elements. Simply ask yourself, "How is it that volunteer organizations can function and persist year after year?" For the most part, volunteer organizations understand how to utilize these five elements to acquire and retain their workers. Consequently, for-profits can learn a lot by studying how not-for-profits retain a highly engaged workforce.

More pay does not equal more work

For-profits need to give up the belief that if they pay people more, employees will work harder. This thought might have worked to motivate workers in the United States 100 years ago and still might be true in some Third World countries, but it simply is no longer true for our North American culture.

Managers must learn that developing continued engagement – beyond day one – among their employees is largely an issue of recognizing and feeding the five key elements. Some call this "motivating the employees". Since I believe they come to work "motivated", I have another name for it, which I will share soon.

Once recognized, what can managers do to feed the five key elements? Four suggestions cover most of the ground needed. They are:

- **Create and live – and I mean live – your company mission and vision.** Many create them; far fewer live them. Give your mission and vision the "tombstone test". That is: Is this a mission and vision that I would want on my tombstone to represent me and the type of company I work for?
- **Create goals, and metrics for those goals, that properly reflect all of the vision and mission.** Make sure the goals are aligned and focused throughout the organization. Hoshin Kanri planning is one method to get aligned and focused, and its use of "catchball" is a simple tool to assist this effort.
- **Provide the support needed at each level** so everyone can contribute to the execution of the goals and, hence, the mission and the vision. This includes providing clear work instructions, training in those instructions and the other resources to accomplish the goals.
- **Make the goals and metrics "transparent"** at the floor level with the use of visual management tools. With such tools, everyone is clear

on what is required and "how we're doing right now". Support these visual tools with management feedback systems that include going to the "gemba" and finding someone doing something right and recognizing that accomplishment.

If you find the list of four suggestions above not very earthshaking … neither do I. This thing that many call motivation, I simply call **good management**.

Good management is what is required to satisfy the first three measurable behavior traits of worker engagement, which I outlined at the beginning of this article. Since your employees come to work with No. 4 and No. 5 – and if you as a manager supply No. 1, No. 2 and No. 3 –that covers all five. And "voila", you get engagement not just at day one but long-term engagement that works to the benefit of not only the company but the employees and stockholders as well.

Or, as I like to say, "It's all about the management. The rest is just details".

Lonnie Wilson has been teaching and implementing lean and other culture-changing techniques for more than 40 years. His book, "How To Implement Lean Manufacturing" was released in August 2009. Wilson is a frequent speaker at conferences and seminars. In addition to IndustryWeek, he has published articles in Quality Digest and is a frequent contributor to iSixSigma magazine. His manufacturing experience spans 20 years with Chevron, where he held a number of management positions. In 1990 he founded Quality Consultants, www.qc-ep.com, which teaches and applies lean and other culture-changing techniques to small entrepreneurs and Fortune 500 firms, principally in the United States, Mexico and Canada. In particular, he specializes in lean revitalizations, assisting firms that have failed or failing lean implementations and want to "do it right". In his not-so-spare time, Wilson is the men's varsity soccer coach at Cathedral High School in El Paso, Texas. You can e-mail him at law@qc-ep.com.

Appendix C: The Toyota Way, 2001: Toyota Motor Corporation, April 2001

INTERVIEW WITH MR. FUJIO CHO, PRESIDENT,
TOYOTA MOTOR CORPORATION, JULY 2003

QUESTION:

What is the relationship between the Toyota Way and Toyota's management?

ANSWER:

The Toyota Way, which has been passed down since the Company's founding, is a unique set of values and manufacturing ideals.

Clearly, our operations are going to become more and more globalized. With this in mind, we compiled a booklet, "The Toyota Way, 2001", in order to transcend the diverse languages and cultures of our employees and to communicate our philosophy to them.

Toyota Motor Corporation Annual Report, 2003, page 19

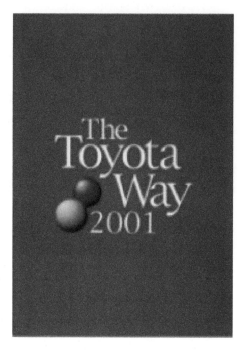

Illustration from Toyota Motor Corporation Environmental & Social Report 2004, page 75

Since Toyota's founding, we have adhered to the core principle of contributing to society through the practice of manufacturing high-quality products and services. Our business practices and activities based on this core principle created values, beliefs and business methods that over the years have become a source of competitive advantage. These are the managerial values and business methods that are known collectively as the Toyota Way.

Mr. Fujio Cho, President, Toyota Motor Corporation, from the Toyota Way, 2001 document

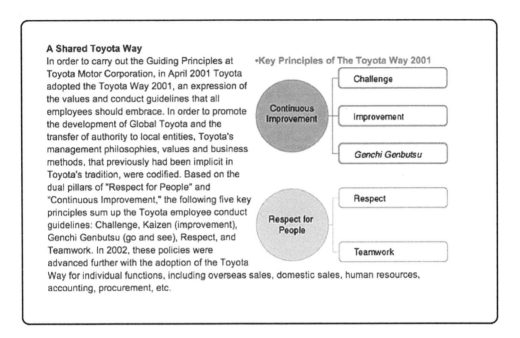

Toyota Motor Corporation, Environmental & Social Report 2003, page 80

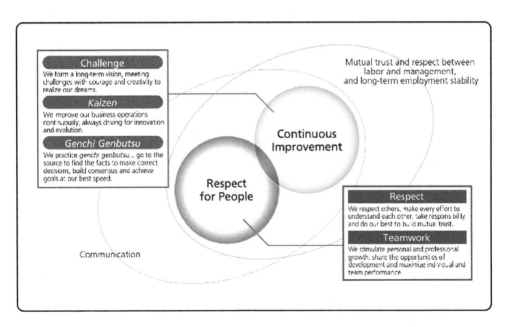

Toyota Motor Corporation Sustainability Report, 2009, page 54

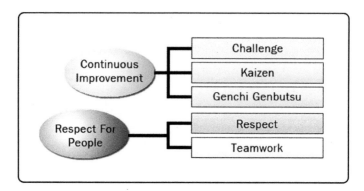

Toyota Motor Manufacturing Turkey Website (http://www.toyotatr.com/eng/t oyotaway.asp)

Appendix D: Key Paradigms Discussed

On Paradigms

A paradigm is a standard, a commonly held belief, a perspective or even a set of ideas. Paradigms are underlying assumptions that color and subtly dictate both our thinking and our subsequent actions. For example, if you hold the belief that people only come to work for a paycheck, you will treat them accordingly, and then your efforts to improve motivation will focus almost solely on pay, benefits and other perks.

There are two problems with paradigms: sometimes our paradigms are wrong; but worse yet, most paradigms are unconscious and we are not really aware of them. And since these paradigms are our underlying beliefs, and we are not aware of them – ***unwittingly*** – they will control our behavior.

In this book, I will give you a number of "paradigm shifts" businesses likely must undergo. These are important changes we must make by replacing the usual way of thinking about or doing something with a new and different way of both thinking and behaving.

That means three very basic things … as a minimum. First, we must openly, honestly and introspectively challenge our beliefs and underlying assumptions so we can make them conscious. Next, we must critically and dispassionately decide what paradigms we should keep and which paradigms we must change. Finally, we need to change our behaviors to be in harmony with our new found beliefs, values and assumptions.

This is not easy … all three steps are very challenging technically, but even more so they are emotionally challenging. Changing paradigms is an ego-challenging effort and hence requires great courage.

Below is a list of the paradigm shifts discussed in this book. I have restated them here, for your reference. They are roughly in their order of importance, not in chronological order, in the book. Well, paradigm shifts

1–4 are in order, with the management paradigms taking precedence. Beyond 4, the order is not quite so critical.

Paradigm Shift No. 1A

The system of engagement is owned and controlled by management. To create engagement takes a cooperative effort led by management. (Found in Chapter 7.)

Paradigm Shift No. 1B

Management must rid themselves of the mental model that engagement is "worker thing" only. Rather, to get workers to behave as if they owned the business the management team has a lot to do. The workers will only become engaged after the management team is engaged. (Found in Chapter 15)

Paradigm Shift No. 1C

The concept of distance management must be abolished and replaced with Genchi Genbutsu. (Found in Chapter 8.)

Paradigm Shift No. 2

Management must rid themselves of the mental model that engagement is synonymous with hard-working and has only a physical component. It is more than that. It involves a physical, emotional and intellectual commitment. Engaged workers behave as if they owned the business. (Found in Chapter 5.)

Paradigm Shift No. 3

Creating engagement is not a **new thing.** *Although there are some new techniques and skills, a full 95% of the work is just doing what you do now do,* **but doing it better.** *Your existing management system will need to change. (Found in Chapters 15 & 18.)*

Paradigm Shift No. 4

The "new normal" for EVERYONE in the business, worker and manager alike, is to: first execute their job as designed; and second, to work on kaizens

*for product, process and service improvements. Or in leanspeak, create a cul-
ture of continuous improvement. (Found in Chapters 15 & 18.)*

Paradigm Shift No. 5

*In your position as a plant manager, or any management position, you are
not able to "buy" creativity. If you manage and lead well, you are able to
"encourage" and even "cultivate" creativity, but since it is intrinsically motivated behavior, extrinsic motivators won't work; worse yet, they are destructive of creativity. This requires a revolution in management awareness.
(Found in Chapter 12.)*

Paradigm Shift No. 6

*The system optimum is not the sum of the local optima. To assure you will not
achieve a system optimum, work to achieve local optima. (Found in Chapter
13)*

Paradigm Shift No. 7

*Creating and sustaining engagement is not done in a simple linear process; it
is done in a complex dynamic system. (Found in Chapter 13.)*

Paradigm Shift No. 8

*Both "negativity" and "positivity" are powerful change forces. However,
neither can be created directly; both will "ensue". Almost exclusively they
will ensue from the actions of management. So, do not try to create positivity
directly or try to counteract negativity directly; you will be thwarted even with
the best of efforts. Rather, manage the system properly and you will indirectly
"inflate the balloon of positivity" and "deflate from the balloon of negativity".
(Found in Chapter 14.)*

Paradigm Shift No. 9

*The cultural network is a more powerful change mechanism than all the
meetings you can hold, all the memos you can write and all the webexes
you can produce … combined. Hence, to "arm" the cultural network, don't
send memos and hold meetings – create transparency. Furthermore, only*

the cultural network is effective enough to create cultural change. (Found in Chapter 14.)

Paradigm Shift No. 10

To learn effectively in a business environment, you must be able to not only comprehend the technical information, you must be able to apply it. Listening and regurgitating back information is not learning. (Found in Chapter 9.)

Paradigm Shift No. 11

We learn by doing ... and in no other way. (Found in Chapter 9.)

Appendix E: The Five Tests of Management Commitment

The Five Tests of Management Commitment are a generic list of questions that can apply to any field of management. They originally appeared in *How To Implement Lean Manufacturing* (Wilson, 2009) and were tailored as a tool to be used introspectively and personally by the management team to assess their individual commitment. This list has been adapted from that original list.

The Five Tests of Management Commitment to creating and sustaining a fully engaged workforce

1. Are you actively studying about and working at creating and sustaining a fully engaged workforce? (All must continue to learn and must be actively engaged; no spectators allowed!)
2. Are you willing to listen to critiques of your facility and then understand and change the areas, in your facility, in which you do not have full engagement? (We must be intellectually open.)
3. Do you honestly and accurately assess your levels of employee engagement among the rank and file and the leadership team as well? (We must be intellectually honest.)
4. Do your actions fully support that you are committed physically, intellectually and emotionally to achieving a fully engaged workforce? This includes your:
   □ Time
   □ Presence
   □ Management attention

    □ Support (including manpower, capital and emotional support)
    (We must be doing it; we must be on the floor, observing, talking to people and imagining how to do it better. Creating and sustaining engagement is not a management spectator sport)

5. Are you willing to ask, answer to and act on, "How can I improve our levels of employee engagement, at all levels? (We must be inquisitive, willing to listen to all, including peers, superiors and subordinates alike, no matter how painful it may be and then be willing and able to make the needed changes.)

'Yes' to all 5 questions means you have passed the Commitment Tests; any 'No' means there is an opportunity for Management Improvement.

Appendix F: HK planning simplified

Hoshin Kanri – Summarizing the 10-step model

PDCA	Step	Activity	Purpose
Plan	1	Develop the mission, vision, company values, company motto, etc.	To define "who we are," how we are unique – our niche
	2	Develop key strategies (steps 3–8)	To survive and prosper in your niche. Should review what is changing in the external environment including the competition, customer needs and regulatory changes; have key strategy "owners" to integrate laterally; use tools such as SWOT analysis
	3	Collect and analyze data	To evaluate how you compare with last year's results, with next year's demands; how you compare with competition; how you meet your customer's needs; and how you meet all external demands
	4	Plan targets and means	To determine the performance levels you need to reach and how you will measure them. Use the top-down method and "catchball" to integrate vertically and laterally. This integrates targets with the means. Catchball is also used in steps 5–8
	5	Set control items	To have specific measurables that will show progress or lack of progress

Do	6	Deploy the policy checks	To identify what is to be controlled and by whom, when to achieve results and what is to be inspected by whom when evaluating the means. The policy checks are made hourly, daily, weekly, monthly, quarterly, etc.
	7	Deploy the control items	To identify what is to be monitored and checked, who is doing the monitoring and checking and how frequently, essentially answering the planning question, "Who is to do what by when?" All control items need to have both normal results and abnormal results defined in quantitative terms
	8	Implement the policy	In addition to routine monitoring and evaluation, to develop projects, implement training, change existing practices, etc.
Check	9	Check results	To check annually, monthly, weekly, daily, hourly … all within the policy as it is deployed
Act	10	Evaluate status	To act on the "abnormal" results, to review the "normal" results for applicability and improvement opportunities, to determine what is the next step and to return to the plan step if needed

Bibliography

Ababneh, Omer and Macky, Keith, The meaning and measurement of employee engagement: A review of the literature, *The New Zealand Journal of Human Resource Management*, 15(1): 1–35, 2015.

Ackoff, Russell, *Ackoff's Best: His Classic Writings on Management*, Wiley and Sons, 1999.

Ackoff, Russell, *Differences that Make a Difference*, Triarchy Press, 2010.

Argyris, Chris, *Knowledge for Action: A Guide to Overcoming Barriers to Organizational Change*, Jossey-Bass, 1993.

Argyris, Chris, *Organizational Traps: Leadership, Culture, Organizational Design*, Oxford University Press, 2010.

Ariely, Dan, *The Upside of Irrationality*, Harper Collins, 2010.

Buckingham, Marcus and Coffman, Curt W., *First, Break All the Rules: What the World's Greatest Managers do Differently*, Gallup Press, 1999.

Covey, Stephen R., *The 7 Habits of Highly Effective People*, Rosetta Books, 1989.

Csikszentmihalyi, Mihaly, *Flow*, Harper Collins, 1990.

Deal, Clarence and Kennedy, Allen, *Corporate Cultures – The Rites and Rituals of Corporate Life*, Addison Wesley, 1982.

Deci, Edward, *Why We Do What We Do*, Penguin Books, 1995.

Deci, Edward and Ryan, Richard, *Handbook of Self-Determination Research*, University of Rochester Press, 2002.

Deci, Edward and Ryan, Richard, Self-determination theory and the facilitation of intrinsic motivation, social development, and well-being, *American Psychologist*, 55(1): 68–78, 2000.

Deming, W. Edwards, *Out of the Crisis*, MIT-CAES, 1982.

Deming, W. Edwards, *The New Economics: For Industry, Government, Education*, MIT Press, 1994.

Forrester, Jay, Counterintuitive behavior of social systems, *Technology Review*, 73(3): 52–68, 1975.

Forrester, Jay, *System Dynamics and the Lessons of 35 Years*, Forrester, 1991.

Fredrickson, Barbara, What good are positive emotions, *Review of General Psychology*, 2(3): 300–319, 1998.

Gallup, *State of the American Workplace*, Gallup, 2012.

Gallup, *State of the Global Workplace*, Gallup, 2013.

Gallup, *State of the American Workplace*, Gallup, 2017.

Grant, Adam, Motivating creativity at work: The necessity of others is the mother of invention, *American Psychological Association*, 2011. Retrieved from: http://www.apa.org/science/about/psa/2011/07/motivating-creativity.aspx.

Harter, Schmidt, *Killham and Asplund, Q12 Meta-Analysis*, Gallup, 2006.

Hayakawa, S.I., *Language in Thought and Action*, Harcourt Brace, 1963.

Hayes, Bob E., *Measuring Customer Satisfaction – Development and Use of Questionnaires*, ASQC Press, 1992.

Hersey, Paul, *The Situational Leader*, Center for Leadership Studies, 1984.

Herzberg, Frederick, One more time: How do you motivate employees? *Harvard Business Review*, 2003.

Herzberg, Frederick, Mausner, Bernard and Snyderman, Barbara B., *The Motivation to Work*, 2nd Edition, John Wiley and Sons, 1959.

Ishakawa, Kauro, *Guide to Quality Control*, Asian Productivity Organization, 1982.

Japanese Union of Scientists and Engineers, *QC Circle Koryo*, General Principles of the QC Circle, JUSE, 1980.

Kahn, William H., Psychological conditions of personal engagement and disengagement at work., *Academy of Management Journal*, 33(4): 692–724, 1990.

Kohn, Alfie, *Punished by Rewards*, Houghton Mifflin Co., 1993.

Kotter, John, *A Force for Change*, Free Press, 1990.

Locke, Robert R. and Spencer, J.C *Confronting Managerialism: How the Business Elite and Their Schools Threw Our Lives Out of Balance*, Zed Books, 2011.

Macey, William H. and Schneider, Benjamin, The meaning of employee engagement, *Industry and Organizational Psychology*, 1(1): 3–30, 2008.

Maslow, Abraham H., *Motivation and Personality*, Harper and Brothers, 1954.

Maslow, Abraham H., *Eupsychian Management*, Richard D. Irwin, Inc., 1965.

Maslow, Abraham H., *Maslow on Management*, John Wiley and Co., 1998.

McChesney, Chris, Covey, Sean and Huling, Jim., *The 4 Disciplines of Execution: Achieving Your Wildly Important Goals*, Free Press, 2012.

McGregor, Douglas, *The Human Side of Enterprize*, McGraw Hill, 1960.

Meadows, Donella., *Thinking in Systems: A Primer*, Sustainability Institute, 2008.

Newman, Daniel A. and Harrison, David A., Been there, Bottled that: Are State and Behavioral Work Engagement New and Useful Constructs "Wines", *Industry and Organizational Psychology*, 1(1): 31–35, 2008.

Ohno, Taiichi, *Toyota Production System: Beyond Large Scale Production*, Productivity Press, 1988.

Pascale, Richard T. and Athos, Anthony G. *The Art of Japanese Management*, Simon and Schuster, 1981.

Schaufeli, Wilmar B., Salanova, Marisa, Gonzalez-Roma, Vicente and Bakker, Arnold B., The measure of engagement and burnout: A two-sample confirmatory factor analytic approach, *Journal of Happiness Studies*, 3(1): 71–92, 2002.

Scherkenbach, William W., *The Deming Route to Quality and Productivity*, CEEP Press, 1988.

Shewhart, Walter A., *Statistical Method from the Viewpoint of Quality Control*, Dover Publications, 1939.

Snyder, C.R. and Lopez, Shane J. (Editors), Csikszentmihalyi, *The Oxford Handbook of Positive Psychology*, Oxford University Press, 2009.

Toyota Motor Corp., *The Toyota Way, 2001*, Toyota Institute, 2001.

Truss, Catherine, Delbridge, Rick, Alfes, Kerstin, Shantz, Amanda and Soane, Emma, *Employee Engagement in Theory and Practice*, Taylor and Francis, 2015.

Wilson, Lonnie, *How to Implement Lean Manufacturing*, 2nd Edition, McGraw Hill, 2015.

Wilson, Lonnie, *Lean Refining: How to Improve Performance in the Oil Industry*, Industrial Press, 2017.

Index